HTML

Illustrated Complete
Second Edition

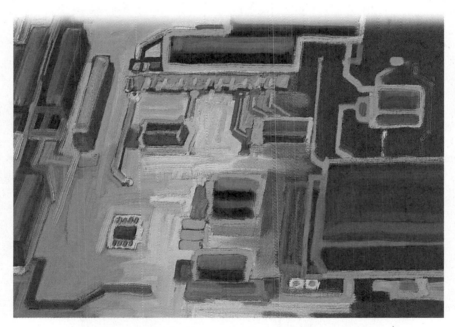

Elizabeth Eisner Reding ◆ Sasha Vodnik

**COURSE
TECHNOLOGY**

™

THOMSON LEARNING

Australia • Canada • Mexico • Singapore • Spain • United Kingdom • United States

COURSE TECHNOLOGY
™
THOMSON LEARNING

HTML – Illustrated Complete, Second Edition
Elizabeth Eisner Reding, Sasha Vodnik

Managing Editor:
Nicole Jones Pinard
Product Manager:
Emily Heberlein
Editorial Assistant:
Danielle Roy

Production Editors:
Megan Cap-Renzi, Anne Valsangiacomo
Associate Product Manager:
Emeline Elliott
Contributing Author:
Donald Barker
Composition House:
GEX, Inc.

QA Manuscript Reviewers:
Ashlee Welz, Andrew Sciarretta,
Jeff Schwartz
Text Designer:
Joseph Lee, Black Fish Design
Cover Designer:
Doug Goodman, Doug Goodman Designs

ISBN **0-619-01880-1**

Exciting New Products

Try out Illustrated's New Product Line: Multimedia Tools

Multimedia tools teach students how to create text, graphics, video, animations, and sound, all of which can be incorporated for use in printed materials, Web pages, CD-ROMs, and multimedia presentations.

New Titles

► Adobe Photoshop 5.5—Illustrated Introductory
(0-7600-6337-0)

► Adobe Illustrator 9.0—Illustrated Introductory
(0-619-01750-3)

► Macromedia Director 8 Shockwave Studio—
Illustrated Introductory
(0-619-01772-4)

► Macromedia Director 8 Shockwave Studio—
Illustrated Complete
(0-619-01779-1)

► Macromedia Concepts—Illustrated
Introductory
(0-619-01765-1)

Master Microsoft Office 2000

Master Microsoft Office 2000 applications with the Illustrated Series. With *Microsoft Office 2000—Illustrated Introductory*, students will learn the basics of Microsoft Office 2000 Professional Edition. *Microsoft Office 2000—Illustrated Second Course* focuses on the more advanced skills of Office 2000 applications, and it includes coverage of all of the software in the Premium Edition.

Illustrated also offers individual application books on Access, Excel, Word, PowerPoint, and FrontPage 2000. Each book covers basic to advanced skills for the application and meets Microsoft Office User Specialist (MOUS) certification. Other titles cover Outlook, PhotoDraw, and Publisher. Visit us at www.course.com/illustrated for a complete listing of our titles.

Check Out Computer Concepts and E-Commerce Concepts

Computer Concepts—Illustrated Brief or Introductory, Third Edition, is the quick and visual way to learn cutting-edge computer concepts. The third edition has been updated to include advances to the Internet and multimedia, changes to the industry, and an introduction to e-commerce and security.

E-Commerce Concepts—Illustrated Introductory teaches the basic concepts and language of e-commerce. Designed to teach students to explore and evaluate e-commerce technologies, sites, and issues, *E-Commerce Concepts* is the ideal introduction to the quickly developing world of e-commerce. The continually updated Student Online Companion allows students to explore relevant sites and articles, ensuring a complete and current learning experience.

Create Your Ideal Course Package with CourseKits™

If one book doesn't offer all the coverage you need, create a course package that does.
With Course Technology's CourseKits—our mix-and-match approach to selecting texts—you have the freedom to combine products from more than one series. When you choose any two or more Course Technology products for one course, we'll discount the price and package them together so your students can pick up one convenient bundle at the bookstore.

Preface

Welcome to *HTML—Illustrated Complete, Second Edition*. This highly visual book offers users a comprehensive hands-on introduction to HTML. In the Second Edition, the first seven units have been revised based on customer feedback.

► Organization and Coverage

This text contains fourteen units that cover basic HTML skills. In these units students learn to create HTML documents, format text, add graphics and multimedia to Web pages, and create online forms. Students also learn how to work with tables, control Web page layout, design Web pages, and scripting for HTML. Five units focus on working with cascading style sheets to create dynamic text and images, control positioning, and bind data to a Web page. The last unit of the book introduces students to the basics of XML. An appendix at the end of the book includes information about publishing to the Web, increasing Web traffic to your site, reference tables for HTML tags, color names, special characters, JavaScript, cascading style sheets, and more.

► About this Approach

What makes the Illustrated approach so effective? It's quite simple. Each concept is presented on two facing pages, with the concepts or step-by step instructions on the left page, and large screen illustrations on the right. Students can focus on a single concept without having to turn the page. This unique design makes information extremely accessible and easy to absorb, and provides a great reference for after the course is over. This hands-on approach also makes it ideal for either self-paced or instructor-led classes.

Each 2-page spread focuses on a single skill or concept.

Easy-to-follow introductions to every lesson focus on a single concept to help students get the point quickly.

Paintbrush icons introduce the real-world case study used throughout the book.

Creating Links to Other Web Pages

One defining feature of HTML documents is the ability to move from one Web page to another using links. A **link**, or **hyperlink**, is a specially formatted Web page object that the user can click to open a different Web page, known as the **target**. The target often is located in the same group of Web pages, or **Web site**, as the original document, and the links serve as an easy way for a user to find specific information among those pages. However, many Web pages also include links to pages on other Web sites. For example, when you submit a search to a search engine, the results page displays links to other sites that may contain the information you want. ⬤ Grace plans to create separate Web pages for Nomad's two divisions, as well as a page describing the company's history. She adds the links between these pages to the layout she is developing.

Steps

1. Click to the right of the **</H4> tag**, then press **[Enter]** twice
2. Type **<A HREF="construction.htm">sporting gear</A>**, then press **[Enter]**
   The HTML for Grace's link uses the <A>..</A> tag pair, which is short for "anchor." She also uses the HREF attribute. **Attributes** are extra settings available in most HTML tags, and allow you to add to or change a tag's default features. Grace uses the equal sign to set the value of the HREF attribute equal to the location of the file to open. Because Grace has not yet created the Web document that eventually will be the target for this link, she references a placeholder file called construction.htm. A **placeholder** is a simple document containing text explaining that the Web page is incomplete. Table A-4 explains a few of the possible targets for the HREF attribute.
3. Type **
, press **[Enter], type **<A HREF="construction.htm">adventure travel</A>**, then press **[Enter]**
4. Type **
, press **[Enter], then type **<A HREF="construction.htm">about Nomad Ltd</A>**
   Compare your document with Figure A-10.
5. Save your work, then click the **browser program button** on the taskbar
   The browser displays the last version of the document that you opened. It does not reflect your most recent changes.
6. Click the **Refresh** or **Reload button**
   The browser now displays the most recent version of your document, as shown in Figure A-11. The linked text is underlined and appears in blue.

Trouble?

If the construction page does not open in your browser, check to make sure nomad.htm and the construction.htm files are saved in the same location.

7. Click one of the links
   The construction page opens in the browser, informing you that the page is not yet completed.
8. Click the browser's **Back button**, then click the **text editor program button** on the taskbar

TABLE A-4: Selected values for the <A>..</A> tag pair HREF attribute

value	description
http://*filename*	opens a file located on a network, such as the Internet
filename	opens a file in the same location as the current file
mailto:*e-mail address*	creates a new outgoing message in the default e-mail program, using the given address

► HTML A-10 **CREATING AN HTML DOCUMENT**

Hints as well as troubleshooting advice, right where you need it – next to the step itself.

Tables provide quickly accessible summaries of key terms, toolbar buttons, or keyboard alternatives connected with the lesson material. Students can refer easily to this information when working on their own projects at a later time.

Clear step-by-step directions explain how to complete the specific task. What students will type is in red.

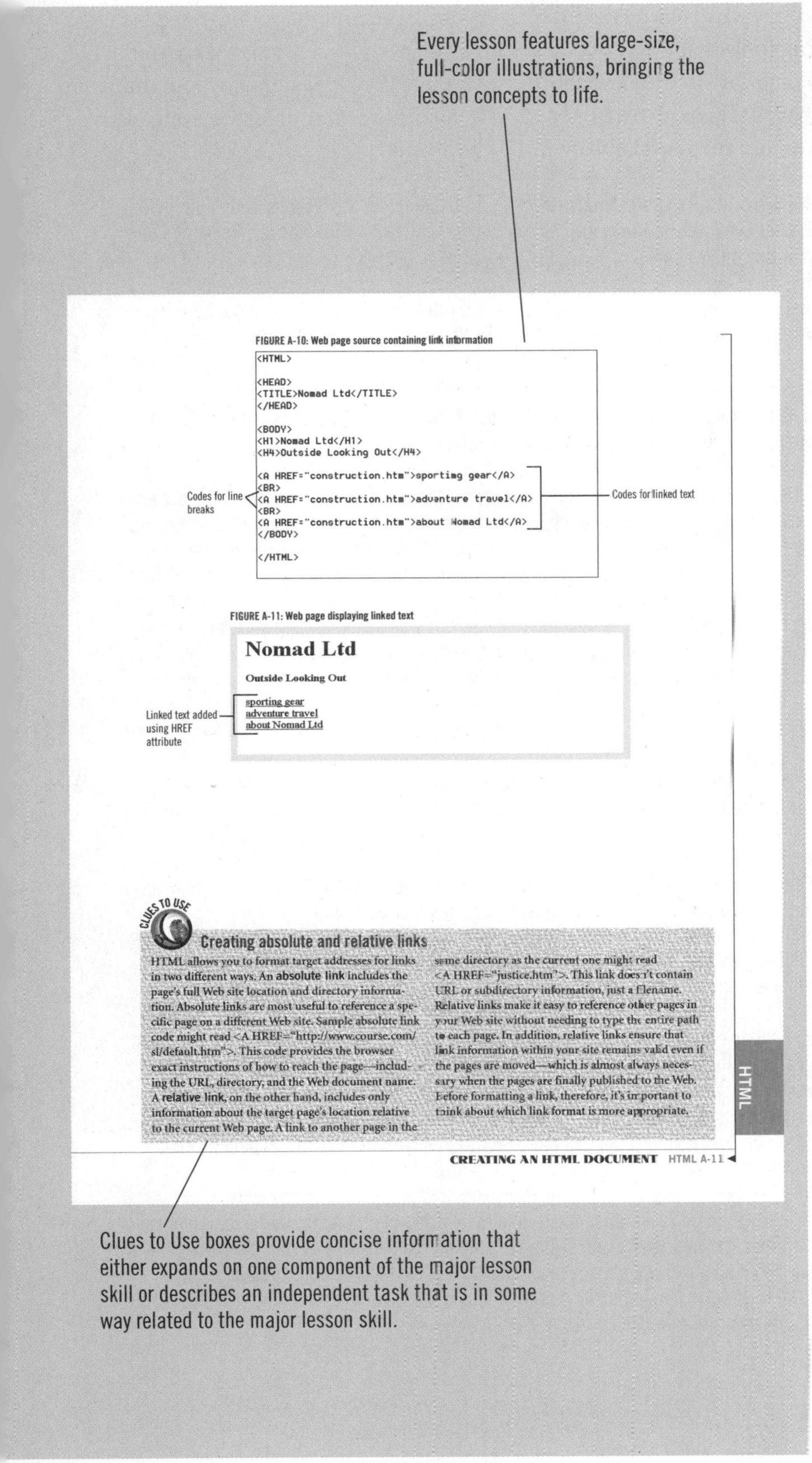

Every lesson features large-size, full-color illustrations, bringing the lesson concepts to life.

FIGURE A-10: Web page source containing link information

```
<HTML>

<HEAD>
<TITLE>Nomad Ltd</TITLE>
</HEAD>

<BODY>
<H1>Nomad Ltd</H1>
<H4>Outside Looking Out</H4>

<A HREF="construction.htm">sporting gear</A>
<BR>
<A HREF="construction.htm">adventure travel</A>
<BR>
<A HREF="construction.htm">about Nomad Ltd</A>
</BODY>

</HTML>
```

Codes for line breaks

Codes for linked text

FIGURE A-11: Web page displaying linked text

Nomad Ltd

Outside Looking Out

sporting gear
adventure travel
about Nomad Ltd

Linked text added using HREF attribute

CLUES TO USE

Creating absolute and relative links

HTML allows you to format target addresses for links in two different ways. An **absolute link** includes the page's full Web site location and directory information. Absolute links are most useful to reference a specific page on a different Web site. Sample absolute link code might read <A HREF="http://www.course.com/sl/default.htm">. This code provides the browser exact instructions of how to reach the page—including the URL, directory, and the Web document name. A **relative link**, on the other hand, includes only information about the target page's location relative to the current Web page. A link to another page in the

same directory as the current one might read <A HREF="justice.htm">. This link doesn't contain URL or subdirectory information, just a filename. Relative links make it easy to reference other pages in your Web site without needing to type the entire path to each page. In addition, relative links ensure that link information within your site remains valid even if the pages are moved—which is almost always necessary when the pages are finally published to the Web. Before formatting a link, therefore, it's important to think about which link format is more appropriate.

CREATING AN HTML DOCUMENT   HTML A-11

HTML

Clues to Use boxes provide concise information that either expands on one component of the major lesson skill or describes an independent task that is in some way related to the major lesson skill.

Other Features

The two-page lesson format featured in this book provides the student with a powerful learning experience. Additionally, this book contains the following features:

► **Real-World Case**
The skills used throughout the book are designed to be "real-world" in nature and representative of the kinds of activities that students encounter when working with HTML. With a real-world case, the process of solving problems will be more meaningful to students.

► **End-of-Unit Material**
Each unit concludes with a Concepts Review that tests students' understanding of what they learned in the unit. The Concepts Review is followed by a Skills Review, which provides students with additional hands-on practice of the skills they learned in the unit. The Skills Review is followed by Independent Challenges, which pose case problems for students to solve. At least one Independent Challenge in each unit asks students to use the World Wide Web to solve the problem as indicated by a Web Work icon. The Visual Workshops that follow the Independent Challenges help students develop critical thinking skills. Students are shown completed Web pages or screens, and are asked to find or evaluate them.

Instructor's Resource Kit and Online Resources

The Instructor's Resource Kit is Course Technology's way of putting the resources and information needed to teach and learn effectively into your hands. With an integrated array of teaching and learning tools that offers you and your students a broad range of technology-based instructional options, we believe this kit represents the highest quality and most cutting edge resources available to instructors today. Many of these resources are available at www.course.com. The resources available with this book are:

Project Files Project Files contain the files students will need to complete the lessons and end of unit material. The Project Files are available on the Instructor's Resource Kit CD-ROM, the Review Pack, and can also be downloaded from www.course.com.

Solution Files Solution Files contain every file students are asked to create or modify in the lessons and end-of-unit material. A Help file on the Instructor's Resource Kit includes information for using the Solution Files.

Figure Files Figure Files contain all the figures from the book in bitmap format. Use the figure files to create transparency masters or to enhance a PowerPoint presentation.

Instructor's Manual Available as HTML files, the Instructor's Manual is quality-assurance tested and includes unit overviews, detailed lecture topics for each unit with teaching tips, solutions to all lessons and end-of-unit material, and extra Independent Challenges. The Instructor's Manual is available on the Instructor's Resource Kit CD-ROM, or you can access it from www.course.com.

Course Test Manager Designed by Course Technology, this Windows-based testing software helps instructors design, administer, and print tests and pre-tests. A full-featured program, Course Test Manager also has an online testing component that allows students to take tests at the computer and have their exams automatically graded.

Course Faculty Online Companion
You can browse this textbook's password-protected site to obtain the Instructor's Manual, Project Files, Solution Files, and any updates to the text. Contact your Customer Service Representative for the site address and password.

MyCourse.com MyCourse.com is a quick and easy way to put your course online. MyCourse.com is an easily customizable online syllabus and course enhancement tool. This tool adds value to your class by offering brand new content designed to reinforce what you are already teaching. MyCourse.com even allows you to add your own content, hyperlinks, and assignments. For more information, visit our Web site at www.course.com/at/distancelearning/#mycourse.

WebCT WebCT is a tool used to create Web-based educational environments and also uses Web browsers as the interface for the course-building environment. The site is hosted on your school campus, allowing complete control over the course materials. WebCT has its own internal communication system, offering internal e-mail, a Bulletin Board, and a Chat room. Course Technology offers content for this book to help you create your WebCT class, such as a suggested Syllabus, Lecture Notes, Practice Test questions, and more. For more information, visit our Web site at www.course.com/at/distancelearning/#webct.

Blackboard Like WebCT, Blackboard is a management tool to help you plan, create, and administer your distance learning class, without knowing HTML. Classes are hosted on Blackboard's or your school's servers. Course Technology offers content for this book to help you create your Blackboard class, such as a suggested Syllabus, Lecture Notes, Practice Test questions, and more. For more information, visit our Web site at www.course.com/at/distancelearning/#blackboard.

Brief Contents

Contents

HTML

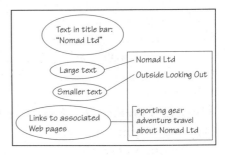

```
</UL>

<P><FONT COLOR="#238E68">Need Ideas?</FONT> Our most
popular U.S. destinations:
<OL>
   <LI>Olympic Peninsula, Washington
   <LI>Grand Teton mountains, Wyoming
   <LI>Appalachian Trail, East coast
</OL>

<P ALIGN="right"><FONT SIZE='-1'>The clearest way into
the Universe is through a forest wilderness.
<BR>
-John Muir</FONT>

</FONT>
</BODY>

</HTML>
```

Contents

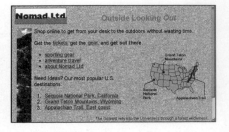

Controlling Page Layout   HTML F-1

Designing Web Pages   HTML G-1

Contents

window
- location
- frames
- history
- navigator
- event
- screen
- document
  - links
  - anchors
  - images
  - filters
  - forms
  - applets
  - embeds
  - plug-ins
  - frames
  - scripts
  - all
  - selection
  - stylesheets
  - body

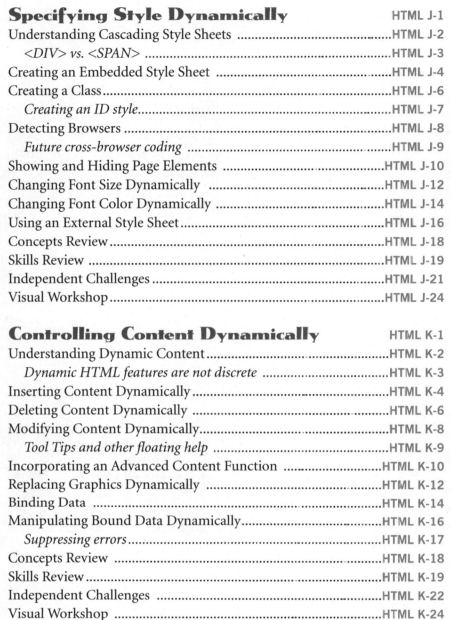

Contents

Structuring Data with XML

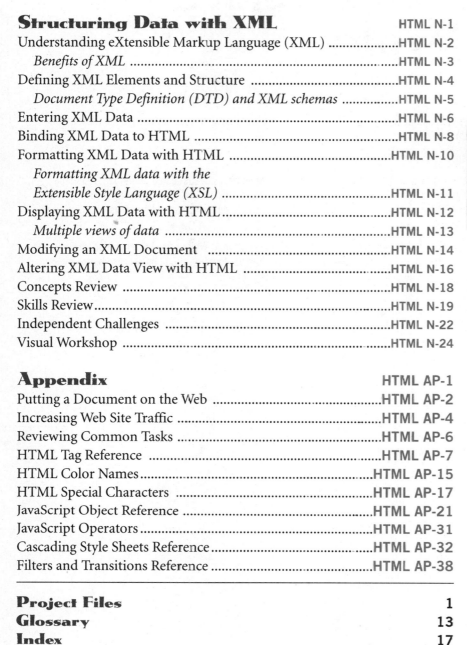

Appendix

Read This Before You Begin

In order to use this book, you will need:

- **Project Files**, which can be downloaded from the Web or available from your instructor. See the inside back cover for more information.

- **A text editor**, such as NotePad or WordPad.

- **A Web browser**. This book was written to be non-browser specific, and was tested using both Netscape Navigator and Microsoft Internet Explorer. While you only need one browser installed to use the book, a good practice to establish is to test Web pages in different browsers to insure your pages appear as you intend them to in different browsers.

The author of this book assumed the location of the Project Disk is Drive A. While this is the location shown in the illustrations and used in the steps, you can save your files to whatever location you choose or is chosen by your instructor. If you are using floppy disks, you should have one disk per unit.

Creating
an HTML document

Objectives

► **Understand HTML**
► **Plan an HTML document**
► **Write an HTML document**
► **Preview and edit a Web page**
► **Create links to other Web pages**
► **Print an HTML document**

Your ability to navigate the World Wide Web with a browser is a useful skill. By mastering just a few more basic concepts, you also can create and publish your own Web pages. You can add content to the Web by learning **Hypertext Markup Language (HTML)**, the language in which all pages on the Web are written. ✒ Grace Dekmejian works in the Information Systems department at Nomad Ltd, a travel and sporting goods company. One of her new projects is to create a Web site for the company.

Understanding HTML

HTML is the standard language used for all pages on the World Wide Web. It allows various computer systems to interpret the information on the Web in the same way. A Web page, also called an **HTML document** or an **HTML file**, is simply a text file made up of text and HTML instructions. Each of these instructions is commonly referred to as a **tag**. In general, HTML works by surrounding each page element—such as a heading, or the text for a table—with a pair of tags. The first tag indicates the beginning of a specific feature, such as boldface for text. The second tag marks the location in your document where the feature ends. Figure A-1 shows an example of the <H1>..</H1> tag pair in an HTML document. This tag pair formats text as a heading. HTML includes hundreds of different tags, which allow you to describe the way you want each of your Web page elements to appear in browsers. Figure A-2 shows the appearance in a browser of the H1 text from Figure A-1. Grace needs to design and create a Web site that is easy to use, so Nomad Ltd customers easily can find information on its products and services. HTML includes many design features for Grace to make her pages intuitive and engaging, such as:

Text formatting

HTML allows you to format text with some of the same features found in popular word processors. Those features include various type sizes and fonts, and enhancements such as bold and italics.

Hyperlinks

In your own experience using the Web, you've probably moved from one Web page to another using links. **Links**, or **hyperlinks**, are Web site addresses (called **uniform resource locators** or **URLs**) that are coded into an HTML document. Clicking a link opens its target Web page, allowing users an easy way to pursue the information they find most useful or interesting.

Tables and lists

A table often can be the most concise way to present information. HTML allows you to organize information in tables, and to format various table aspects, including borders and background color. You also can create simple bulleted or numbered lists with HTML.

Graphics, sound, and video support

Good Web pages make judicious use of graphics to balance text content. HTML allows you to easily add graphics, and it offers options to control a graphic's appearance in the browser window. You also can add code to Web pages that integrates sound and video with a page's text and graphics, creating **multimedia**. The availability of these features broadens the palette available to you when designing Web pages.

FIGURE A-1: <H1>..</H1> tag pair in HTML document

Marks end of heading text format

Marks beginning of heading text format

```
<HTML>

<HEAD>
<TITLE>Nomad Ltd</TITLE>
</HEAD>

<BODY>
<H1>Nomad Ltd</H1>
<H4>Outside Looking Out</H4>

<A HREF="construction.htm">sporting gear</A>
<BR>
<A HREF="construction.htm">adventure travel</A>
<BR>
<A HREF="construction.htm">about Nomad Ltd</A>
</BODY>

</HTML>
```

FIGURE A-2: Appearance of HTML document in a Web browser

Text formatted with <H1..</H1> tag pair

H1 format starts here

H1 format ends here

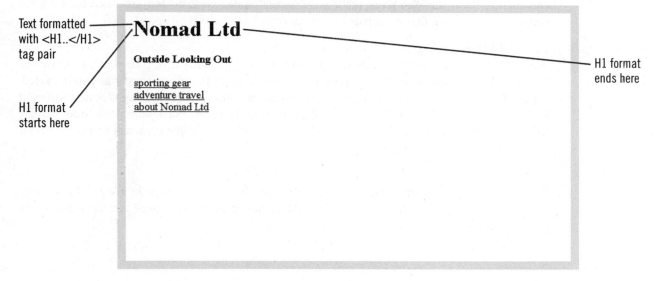

Nomad Ltd

Outside Looking Out

sporting gear
adventure travel
about Nomad Ltd

HTML

Planning an HTML Document

Before writing an HTML document, you should have a preliminary idea of how you want your final Web page to look. Although you'll inevitably modify your initial page format, a master plan helps keep you focused on the information you want to convey. ◀▬▬ Grace used the Web to research the HTML document-creation process. She found a list of suggested steps for planning and creating a Web page:

Details

Sketch your Web page
Create a rough sketch showing how you want your final Web page to look. The goal of this process—which is called **story boarding**—is to show the elements you want to include and how you want them arranged on the Web page. You then can make sure you know how to use or implement the necessary tags for each element, and you can research parts of your design that you haven't used before. Grace created a sketch of the first few elements she wants to add to her Nomad Ltd Web page. Her drawing is shown in Figure A-3.

Enter structuring tags for the file
Every Web page begins and ends with common tags that identify it as an HTML document and provide basic information about it to the browser. A Web page usually contains tags to divide it into a number of main sections.

Enter each Web page element, along with its formatting tags
The most common Web page elements are the text that is shown on the screen, and the references to files containing graphics. You can enter tags to add special formatting to text, to create tables, or to add links to other Web pages. It's generally best to add one new element at a time, and then preview the Web page; if the page doesn't appear as expected, you then have a good idea of which HTML tag or tag pair is likely to contain the error.

Preview the Web page
While creating your page, you should examine it often by using a Web browser, as shown in Figure A-4. These previews allow you to notice any elements that don't appear as you intended. Correcting errors often can be as simple as adding or editing an HTML tag. Because different Web browsers, such as Microsoft Internet Explorer or Netscape Navigator, sometimes display the same code differently, it's best to preview your work in multiple browsers to ensure that it appears as you planned for all users.

Test links
If your document contains links to other Web pages, preview your page in a Web browser and test each link by clicking it. If clicking a link does not open the Web page you intended as the target, you can edit the code.

FIGURE A-3: Grace's sketch for the Nomad Ltd Web page

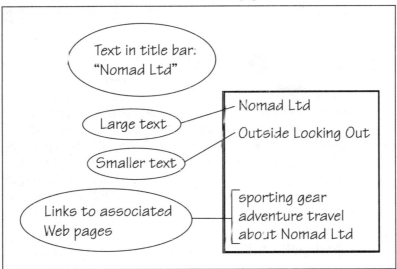

Text in title bar: "Nomad Ltd"

Large text ——— Nomad Ltd

Smaller text ——— Outside Looking Out

Links to associated Web pages ——— [sporting gear
adventure travel
about Nomad Ltd

FIGURE A-4: Web page previewed in a Web browser

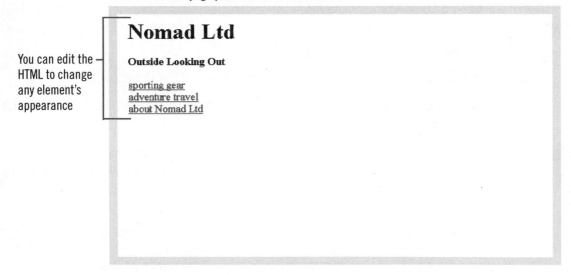

You can edit the HTML to change any element's appearance

Nomad Ltd

Outside Looking Out

sporting gear
adventure travel
about Nomad Ltd

CLUES TO USE

Using a text editor versus a word processor

Many word processors, such as Microsoft Word, offer a Save as HTML command in the File menu. This feature allows you to create and format a document using word-processing features with which you're familiar, then automatically create a Web page that contains the same information and layout. Such a feature makes Web-page authoring possible even for people who don't know anything about HTML. However, this automated method has its drawbacks. In some cases, page elements do not appear in a Web browser exactly as they did in the word processor. Also, making any change to the Web page requires regenerating the HTML code from the word processor. On the other hand, creating pages by entering the HTML tags yourself—known as **hand-coding**—gives you more precise control over the exact appearance of your Web pages. Additionally, you can fine-tune a page's appearance by making direct and specific changes to the HTML code. Because you are studying HTML, you should use a plain-text editor such as Notepad or WordPad to complete these lessons. If you choose to use a word processor instead, be sure to save each file in *text format*. Do not use the word processor's *native format* (.doc, .wpd) or its HTML document type.

HTML

HTML

Writing an HTML Document

Once you've planned how you want your document to look, you can start creating its structure and adding page elements. You can create an HTML document in any application that allows you to enter and save text. Notepad and WordPad, which are text editor programs installed along with Windows, are popular tools for hand-coding HTML. These applications include simple methods of saving a document in text format, without the additional formatting added by some word processors. ⟍⟍⟍ Grace decides to create her HTML document using Notepad. She begins the Nomad Ltd Web page by entering the structuring tags and adding some basic page elements.

Steps

QuickTip

Use a plain text editor, such as Notepad or WordPad, to ensure results like those found in these lessons.

1. Click **Start** on the taskbar, point to **Programs**, point to **Accessories**, click **Notepad**, then maximize the screen, if necessary

A blank Notepad document opens.

2. Insert your Project Disk in the appropriate drive

QuickTip

Be sure *not* to use the "Save as HTML" command if you are creating your HTML document in a word processor.

3. Click **File** on the menu bar, then click **Save**

The Save As dialog box opens. See Figure A-5.

4. Click the **Save in list arrow**, then select the location of the Project Disk

5. Select the text in the **File name text box**, then type **nomad-a.htm** to replace the default filename

Trouble?

Some text editors automatically add the .txt extension to your filename when you select it; double-check your filename to make sure it ends with .htm.

6. Make sure **Text Documents** appears in the Save as type list box, then click **Save**

The Save As dialog box closes, and the filename appears in the title bar at the top of the document.

7. Type **<HTML>** then press **[Enter]**

Every HTML document begins with the <HTML> tag, and ends with the </HTML> tag. This tag pair identifies the document's contents as HTML to the Web browser. Table A-1 illustrates this tag pair, along with the other common structural tags. A browser can interpret HTML tags that are in either uppercase or lowercase. However, to make your Web documents easy for yourself and others to edit, it's best to consistently use either all uppercase or all lowercase.

8. Type the remaining text shown in Figure A-6

You can use uppercase and lowercase letters, line spaces, tabs, and hard returns to make your HTML document easier to read without affecting its appearance as a Web page. Your Web document should match the one shown in Figure A-6.

FIGURE A-5: Save As dialog box

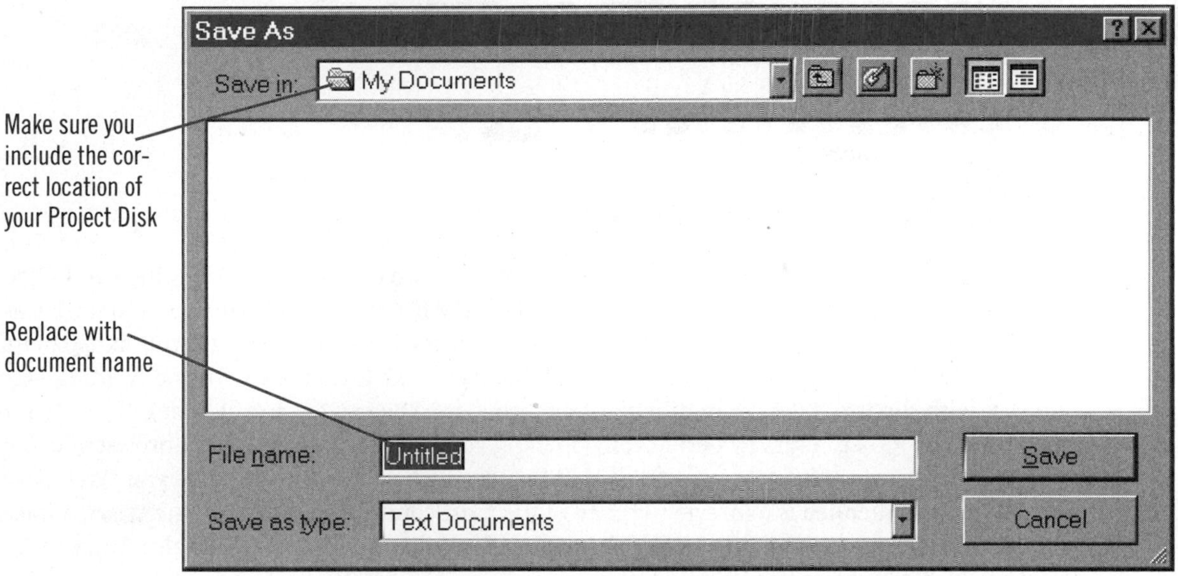

Make sure you include the correct location of your Project Disk

Replace with document name

```
Save As                                          ? X

Save in:  My Documents    ▾  ⬆  ⬚  ⬚  ⬚  ⬚

                                                    

File name:    Untitled                        Save

Save as type: Text Documents            ▾    Cancel
```

FIGURE A-6: Nomad Ltd Web page HTML code

```
<HTML>

<HEAD>
<TITLE>Nomad Ltd</TITLE>
</HEAD>

<BODY>
Nomad Ltd
Outside Looking Out
</BODY>

</HTML>
```

TABLE A-1: HTML structuring tag pairs

tag pair	purpose
`<HTML>..</HTML>`	Identifies the file as an HTML document to the program opening it.
`<HEAD>..</HEAD>`	Identifies the document's head area, where you can code information about your document, including its title.
`<TITLE>..</TITLE>`	Formats the document title, which appears in the browser's title bar.
`<BODY>..</BODY>`	Identifies the document's body area, which contains the Web page contents that appear in the browser window.

Previewing and Editing a Web Page

HTML includes many tags that allow you to format text. Two of the most basic, <BR> and <P>, allow you to control the space between lines of text and where those lines break on the screen, as explained in Table A-2. Some of the most efficient tags for formatting text are the six tag pairs designed for headings, and are described in Table A-3. Text formatted with the heading tags appears with slight differences in different Web browsers. You can get a rough idea of how your Web page will look to users by periodically opening your HTML document in a browser during the creation process. However, as with all HTML tags, the best way to make sure your Web page appears as you intended is to preview it in all of the most common Web browsers. Grace wants to format the company name with a heading that calls attention to it. She also wants to see how her Web page appears in a browser.

Steps

1. **Click to the left of the word Nomad at the top of the body section of the document, type <H1>, press [End] to move the insertion point to the end of the line, then type </H1>**
The H1 tag formats the company name using the largest size heading. The opening tag, <H1>, begins the H1 format just before the word Nomad starts, and the closing tag, </H1>, ends this format after the end of the company name.

2. **Click to the left of the word Outside, type <H3>, press [End] to move the insertion point to the end of the line, then type </H3>**
The H3 tags format the company slogan smaller than the company name. Compare your document with Figure A-7.

3. **Save your work**

4. **Start your browser, cancel any dial-up operations, then open the file nomad-a.htm**
A Web browser can open a Web document from any location to which it has access, including your local hard drive or floppy drive. Compare your page with Figure A-8. Notice that just like the <P> tag, the heading tags add a blank line before and after the current paragraph.

5. **Click the text editor program button on the taskbar**

6. **Change the <H3> tag to <H4>, then change the </H3> tag to </H4>**
Grace wants the size of the slogan decreased, so you will use a heading tag with a smaller size.

7. **Save your work, click the browser program button on the taskbar, then click the browser's Refresh or Reload button**
The browser opens the most recent version of the Web page saved to disk, as shown in Figure A-9.

8. **Click the text editor program button on the taskbar**

> **QuickTip**
>
> To open a Web page from your local disk on most browsers, click File on the Menu bar, click Open or Open Page, click Browse or Choose File, select the file, click Open, then click Open or OK.

TABLE A-2: Basic HTML text tags

tag	description	sample	result in browser
 	adds a line break; does not require a closing tag	paragraph 1 paragraph 2	paragraph 1 paragraph 2
<P>	adds a blank line before and after the current paragraph; does not require a closing tag	<P>paragraph 1 <P>paragraph 2	paragraph 1 paragraph 2

FIGURE A-7: Web page source containing heading tags

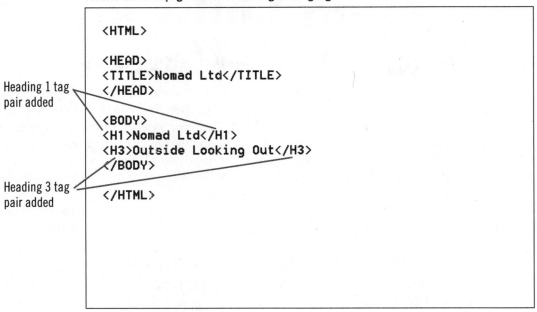

Heading 1 tag
pair added

Heading 3 tag
pair added

```
<HTML>

<HEAD>
<TITLE>Nomad Ltd</TITLE>
</HEAD>

<BODY>
<H1>Nomad Ltd</H1>
<H3>Outside Looking Out</H3>
</BODY>

</HTML>
```

FIGURE A-8: Web page formatted with heading tags

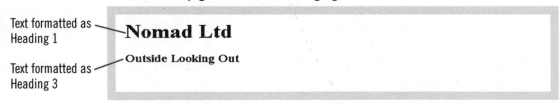

Text formatted as
Heading 1

Nomad Ltd

Text formatted as
Heading 3

Outside Looking Out

FIGURE A-9: Web page reflecting heading tag edits

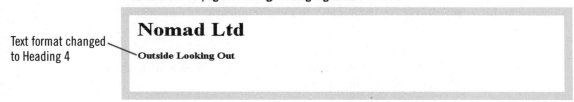

Text format changed
to Heading 4

Nomad Ltd

Outside Looking Out

TABLE A-3: HTML headings

tags	sample	result
<H1>..</H1>	<H1>Heading 1</H1>	Heading 1
<H2>..</H2>	<H2>Heading 2</H2>	Heading 2
<H3>..</H3>	<H3>Heading 3</H3>	Heading 3
<H4>..</H4>	<H4>Heading 4</H4>	Heading 4
<H5>..</H5>	<H5>Heading 5</H5>	Heading 5
<H6>..</H6>	<H6>Heading 6</H6>	Heading 6

Creating Links to Other Web Pages

HTML

One defining feature of HTML documents is the ability to move from one Web page to another using links. A **link**, or **hyperlink**, is a specially formatted Web page object that the user can click to open a different Web page, known as the **target**. The target often is located in the same group of Web pages, or **Web site**, as the original document, and the links serve as an easy way for a user to find specific information among those pages. However, many Web pages also include links to pages on other Web sites. For example, when you submit a search to a search engine, the results page displays links to other sites that may contain the information you want. ◄───── Grace plans to create separate Web pages for Nomad's two divisions, as well as a page describing the company's history. She adds the links between these pages to the layout she is developing.

1. **Click to the right of the </H4> tag, then press [Enter] twice**

2. **Type <A HREF="construction.htm">sporting gear</A>, then press [Enter]**
   The HTML for Grace's link uses the <A>..</A> tag pair, which is short for "anchor." She also uses the HREF attribute. **Attributes** are extra settings available in most HTML tags, and allow you to add to or change a tag's default features. Grace uses the equal sign to set the value of the HREF attribute equal to the location of the file to open. Because Grace has not yet created the Web document that eventually will be the target for this link, she references a placeholder file called construction.htm. A **placeholder** is a simple document containing text explaining that the Web page is incomplete. Table A-4 explains a few of the possible targets for the HREF attribute.

3. **Type <BR>, press [Enter], type <A HREF="construction.htm">adventure travel</A>, then press [Enter]**

4. **Type <BR>, press [Enter], then type <A HREF="construction.htm">about Nomad Ltd</A>**
   Compare your document with Figure A-10.

5. **Save your work, then click the browser program button on the taskbar**
   The browser displays the last version of the document that you opened. It does not reflect your most recent changes.

6. **Click the Refresh or Reload button**
   The browser now displays the most recent version of your document, as shown in Figure A-11. The linked text is underlined and appears in blue.

   Trouble?
   If the construction page does not open in your browser, check to make sure nomad-a.htm and the construction.htm files are saved in the same location.

7. **Click one of the links**
   The construction page opens in the browser, informing you that the page is not yet completed.

8. **Click the browser's Back button, then click the text editor program button on the taskbar**

TABLE A-4: Selected values for the <A>..</A> tag pair HREF attribute

value	description
http://*filename*	opens a file located on a network, such as the Internet
filename	opens a file in the same location as the current file
mailto:*e-mail address*	creates a new outgoing message in the default e-mail program, using the given address

FIGURE A-10: Web page source containing link information

```
<HTML>

<HEAD>
<TITLE>Nomad Ltd</TITLE>
</HEAD>

<BODY>
<H1>Nomad Ltd</H1>
<H4>Outside Looking Out</H4>

<A HREF="construction.htm">sporting gear</A>
<BR>
<A HREF="construction.htm">adventure travel</A>
<BR>
<A HREF="construction.htm">about Nomad Ltd</A>
</BODY>

</HTML>
```

Codes for line breaks

Codes for linked text

FIGURE A-11: Web page displaying linked text

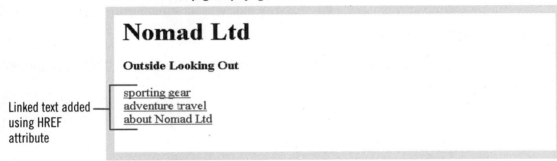

Nomad Ltd

Outside Looking Out

sporting gear
adventure travel
about Nomad Ltd

Linked text added using HREF attribute

Creating absolute and relative links

HTML allows you to format target addresses for links in two different ways. An **absolute** link includes the page's full Web site location and directory information. Absolute links are most useful to reference a specific page on a different Web site. Sample absolute link code might read <A HREF="http://www.course.com/sl/default.htm">. This code provides the browser exact instructions of how to reach the page—including the URL, directory, and the Web document name. A **relative link**, on the other hand, includes only information about the target page's location relative to the current Web page. A link to another page in the same directory as the current one might read <A HREF="justice.htm">. This link doesn't contain URL or subdirectory information, just a filename. Relative links make it easy to reference other pages in your Web site without needing to type the entire path to each page. In addition, relative links ensure that link information within your site remains valid even if the pages are moved—which is almost always necessary when the pages are finally published to the Web. Before formatting a link, therefore, it's important to think about which link format is more appropriate.

HTML

Printing an HTML Document

Even though HTML documents are designed to facilitate information exchange over the Internet, sometimes you need to print hard copies. You can print the HTML code, or **source**, of your pages using the same text editor you used to create them. Web browsers also allow you to print your Web pages as they appear in the browser window. ◀■■■■ Grace wants to bring her preliminary work on the Nomad Ltd Web page to her team meeting later today. She prints both the HTML source and the Web browser display.

Steps 1234

1. **In your text editor, click File, then click Print**
   The text editor prints a single copy of the source, as shown in Figure A-12.

2. **Click the browser program button on the taskbar**

3. **Click the Print button on the toolbar, then, if necessary, click OK**
   The page prints as it appears in the browser window, as shown in Figure A-13.

4. **Click the browser window Close button**

5. **If necessary, click the text editor program button on the taskbar, then click the text editor window Close button**

Changing browser headers and footers

When you print a Web page from a browser, the output includes information about the Web page, such as its location and the page title, as shown in Figure A-13. Both Netscape Navigator and Microsoft Internet Explorer Web browsers allow you to customize the information that prints, whether you created the Web page or not. In both browsers, you click File, then click Page Setup to change header and footer information. In Navigator, the Header and Footer sections include checkboxes that allow you to select or deselect header and footer items from a list. By default, all five items are selected. Instead of checkboxes, Internet Explorer uses codes consisting of an ampersand (&) and a letter. Although using codes takes a bit more work, Internet Explorer offers more choices of what you can show in the header and the footer, and also allows you to choose the order of the elements. To display an index of the Internet Explorer codes and their meanings, place the insertion point in the Header or Footer text box, then press F1.

FIGURE A-12: Printed source for Nomad Ltd Web page

```
                              nomad-a.htm




<HTML>

<HEAD>
<TITLE>Nomad Ltd</TITLE>
</HEAD>

<BODY>
<H1>Nomad Ltd</H1>
<H4>Outside Looking Out</H4>

<A HREF="construction.htm">sporting gear</A>
<BR>
<A HREF="construction.htm">adventure travel</A>
<BR>
<A HREF="construction.htm">about Nomad Ltd</A>
</BODY>

</HTML>
```

Page 1

FIGURE A-13: Printed browser display of Nomad Ltd web page

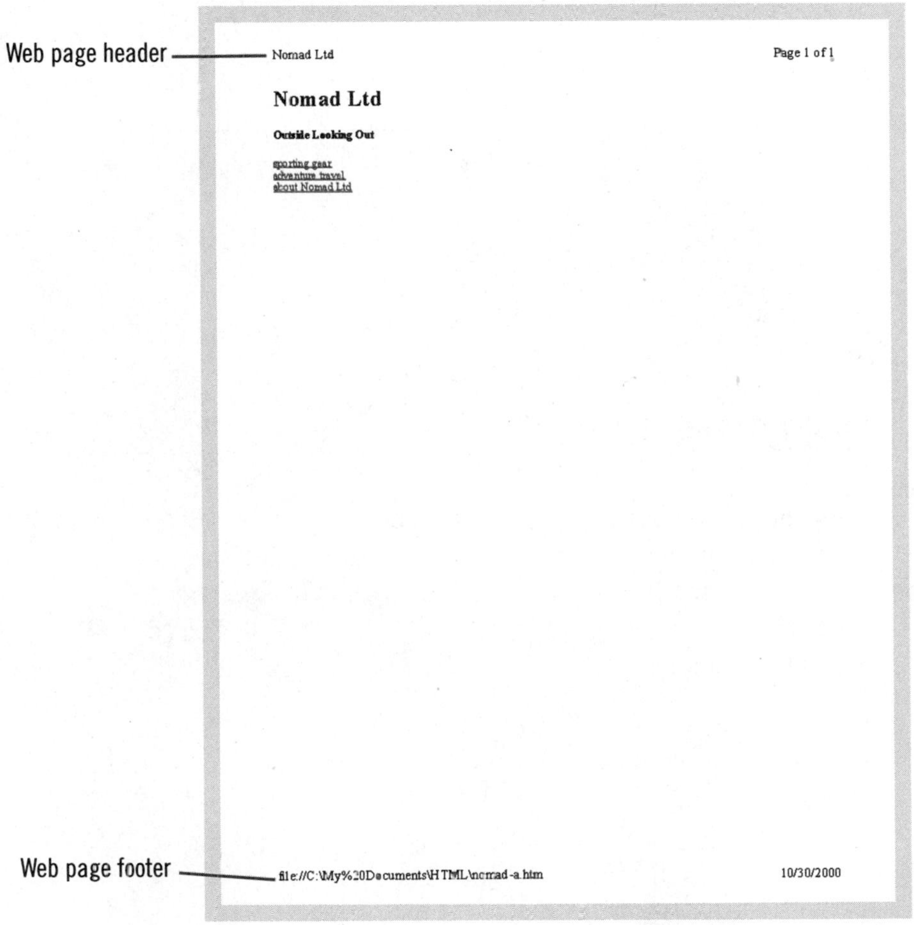

Web page header ———— Nomad Ltd   Page 1 of 1

Nomad Ltd

Outside Looking Out

sporting gear
adventure travel
about Nomad Ltd

Web page footer ———— file://C:\My%20Documents\HTML\nomad-a.htm   10/30/2000

Practice

▶ Concepts Review

Name the function of each marked element of the Notepad screen shown in Figure A-14.

FIGURE A-14

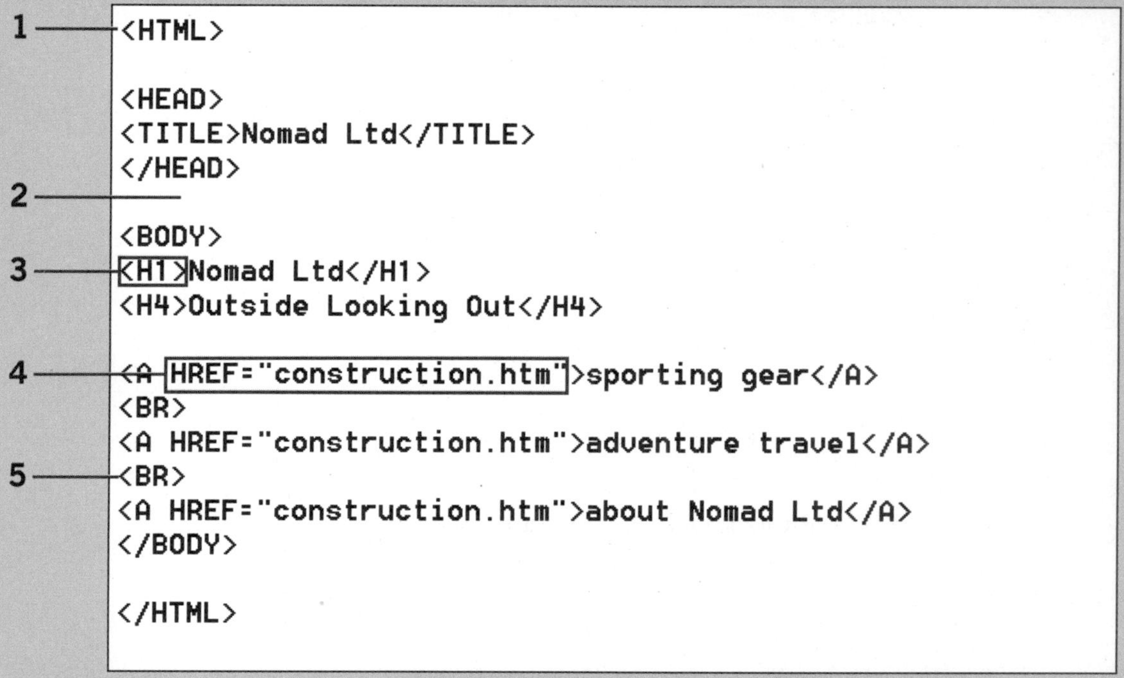

```
1 ──── <HTML>

        <HEAD>
        <TITLE>Nomad Ltd</TITLE>
        </HEAD>
2 ────
        <BODY>
3 ──── <H1>Nomad Ltd</H1>
        <H4>Outside Looking Out</H4>

4 ──── <A HREF="construction.htm">sporting gear</A>
        <BR>
        <A HREF="construction.htm">adventure travel</A>
5 ──── <BR>
        <A HREF="construction.htm">about Nomad Ltd</A>
        </BODY>

        </HTML>
```

Match each statement with the term that it describes.

6. An instruction in HTML
7. Tag pair surrounding Web page contents that appear in the browser window
8. Tag pair for text to appear in the browser's title bar
9. The Web page opened by a link
10. The HTML code used to create a Web page

a. <TITLE>..</TITLE>
b. <BODY>..</BODY>
c. Tag
d. Target
e. Source

Select the best answer from the list of choices.

11. **If you wanted to reduce the text size of a Heading 4, which tag pair would you use?**
    a. <HEAD>..</HEAD>
    b. <H3>..</H3>
    c. <H5>..</H5>
    d.
..</BR>

12. **When typing HTML tags, you should type the tags using**
    a. uppercase for the opening tag; lowercase for the closing tag.
    b. either uppercase or lowercase.
    c. uppercase only.
    d. lowercase only.

13. **Which menu is used to open a local file in a browser?**
    a. Format
    b. View
    c. Edit
    d. File

14. **HTML stands for**
    a. HyperText Markup Language.
    b. HyperText Modern Language.
    c. HyperTool Modern Linkage.
    d. HyperTool Markup Linkage.

15. **In what situation would you use a placeholder?**
    a. In place of a tag, when you're not sure which tag to use
    b. When you have no code to enter into the body section
    c. When you want to format a link, but haven't yet created the target page
    d. In place of your company name, when you want the page to remain anonymous

16. **Which tag pair marks the beginning and the end of an HTML document?**
    a. <BODY>..</BODY>
    b. <HTML>..</HTML>
    c. <TITLE>..</TITLE>
    d. <HEAD>..</HEAD>

17. **Which tag pair marks an element that you see in the browser's title bar?**
    a. <BODY>..</BODY>
    b. <HTML>..</HTML>
    c. <TITLE>..</TITLE>
    d. <HEAD>..</HEAD>

18. **Which of the following are not structuring tags?**
    a. <BODY>..</BODY>
    b. <HTML>..</HTML>
    c. <TITLE>..</TITLE>
    d. <HEAD>..</HEAD>

19. **Which HTML tag creates a new paragraph?**
    a. <NEW>
    b. <P>
    c. <PARA>
    d. <NP>

▶ Skills Review

1. **Write an HTML document.**
   a. Start your text editor with a blank document.
   b. Save your work as a text document called cco-a.htm.
   c. Enter the HTML code shown in Figure A-15.

2. **Preview and Edit an HTML document.**
   a. Format the text "Crystal Clear Opticals" in the body section as a level 1 heading.
   b. Format the text "Visionary Eyewear for 50 Years" in the body section as a level 2 heading.
   c. Save your work.
   d. Open your browser, then open the file cco-a.htm.
   e. Open the HTML document in your text editor, then change the level 2 heading to a level 3 heading.
   f. Save your work.
   g. Reload the page in your browser to see the effect of the heading size change.

FIGURE A-15

```
<HTML>
<HEAD>
<TITLE>Crystal Clear Opticals</TITLE>
</HEAD>

<BODY>
Crystal Clear Opticals
Visionary Eyewear for 50 Years
</BODY>
</HTML>
```

3. **Create links to other Web pages.**
   a. In your text editor, on the line below the text "Visionary Eyewear for 50 years", add the text "Basic Styles" and link it to the placeholder file construction.htm . (*Hint*: Use the <A>..</A> tag pair with the HREF attribute.)
   b. On the next line, add a line break, then add the text "Designer Lines" and link it to the construction.htm file.
   c. On the next line, add a line break, then add the text "Eye Health Tips" and link it to the construction.htm file.
   d. On the next line, add a line break, then add the text "About Us" and link it to the construction.htm file.

e. Save your work.

f. Reload the page in your browser to display the latest version of the document.

g. Click one of the links to view the construction page.

4. Print an HTML document.

a. In your text editor, print the HTML document.

b. In the browser program, print the Web page.

c. Close the browser window.

d. If necessary, close the text editor program.

► Independent Challenges

1. You have recently started a consulting business called Star Dot Star. It is a priority for you to provide a Web site so potential clients can research your available services and business history. Using the skills you learned in this unit, plan and create a Web page for your consulting firm. Use a text editor to write your HTML tags, then use your browser to view the finished page. Your page should include at least two headings, as well as links to other Web pages or sites.

To complete this independent challenge:

a. Create a sketch of your Web page, including a page title, at least two headings, and two or more links.

b. On your sketch, define which HTML tags you will use for each page element.

c. Start your text editor and enter the structuring tags for the page, along with the title and heading elements.

d. Save your work as sds-a.htm.

e. Preview your page in your Web browser, then edit the source, if necessary, to format the page as you want it to appear.

f. Edit your HTML document to include links, using construction.htm as the target, then save the file and preview it in your browser.

g. Print the document in your text editor and in your browser.

2. You have volunteered to help create a Web page for your employer, Metro Water, the local water department. The priority for your Web page development team is to create an information source of your community's water resources. Because you are familiar with the topic of water resources in your area and with HTML, you've volunteered to sketch the page and share your knowledge of HTML to structure the document and add basic elements.

To complete this independent challenge:

a. Create a sketch that includes the items you want to include on your Web page, along with the HTML tags you'll use to create each item.

b. Start your text editor and enter the structuring tags for the page, along with the title and the heading elements, then save your file as mw-a.htm.

c. Preview your page in your browser, then edit the source, if necessary, to format the page as you want it to appear.

d. Edit your HTML document to include links, using construction.htm as the target, then save the file and preview it in your browser.

e. Print the document in your text editor and in your browser.

f. Exit your text editor and browser.

3. In this unit you have practiced using basic HTML tags to create some of the fundamental elements of a Web page. As you learn more tags and their functions, you will be able to add different elements and formats to your Web pages. The Web itself can be one of the most useful tools for learning more about HTML. Try it out by seeing what you can find on the Web about a tag or a tag pair that you haven't used yet.

To complete this independent challenge:

a. Connect to the Internet, and use your browser to go to one of the following online HTML references:
www.w3.org
hotwired.lycos.com/webmonkey
www.webreference.com
If you have trouble locating these pages, go to *www.course.com*, navigate to the page for this book, click the link for the Student Online Companion, click the link for this unit, and use the links listed there as a starting point for your search.

b. Click the link for HTML if you see one, then use the site's search utility to find information about one of the following tag pairs:
<U>..</U>
<I>..</I>
<OL>..</OL>
<UL>..</UL>

c. Print at least two pages that discuss what the selected tag does, and how you use it in Web page code.

d. Write a paragraph about your selected tag. Include the following information:
  • Its name (what the letters in the tag stand for)
  • What feature(s) it adds to a Web page
  • An example of where in Web page design you think the selected tag would be useful

4. As you begin to use your HTML skills to create Web pages and learn more tags for adding and formatting page elements, the underlying design of your pages will become increasingly important. Organizing and designing your pages well is crucial to ensuring users can easily locate needed information. One of the most basic sources of design ideas is published Web pages. Use the Web to find examples of effective Web pages, then print those pages. Identify familiar HTML tags, and describe the advantages and drawbacks of each page's design.

To complete this independent challenge:

a. Connect to the Internet, and use your browser to open Web pages that interest you, or that you are familiar with. If you need help finding particular pages, try a search engine, such as:
  - Google (*www.google.com*)
  - Alta Vista (*www.altavista.com*)
  - Yahoo (*www.yahoo.com*).
  If you have trouble locating a search engine, go to *www.course.com*, navigate to the page for this book, click the link for Student Online Companion, click the link for this unit, and use the links listed there as a starting point for your search.

b. Print pages from at least three Web sites. Be sure to view the page source for each Web site.

c. On your printouts, indicate familiar elements (such as titles, headings, empty lines, and paragraphs of text) as well as the tag you think was used to create each element.

d. For each page you printed, list at least two design aspects that you think make the page functional (such as placement of elements, colors, and text phrasing). Be sure to refer to specific elements of each page.

e. For each page you printed, list at least one aspect that could be improved. Write a paragraph describing how you would improve the design of each Web page.

f. If necessary, disconnect from the Internet.

► Visual Workshop

You work at a small bookstore called Touchstone Booksellers. You want to convince the owner that she could reach a wider audience by conducting some of her business on the Web. You decide to use the HTML skills you have learned to create a basic Web page, to illustrate the benefits of Web commerce. Create the Web page shown in Figure A-16. Be sure to include HTML code in your document to display the business name in the browser's title bar. Save your HTML file as a text document called tsb-a.htm, then print the document in your text editor and in your browser.

FIGURE A-16

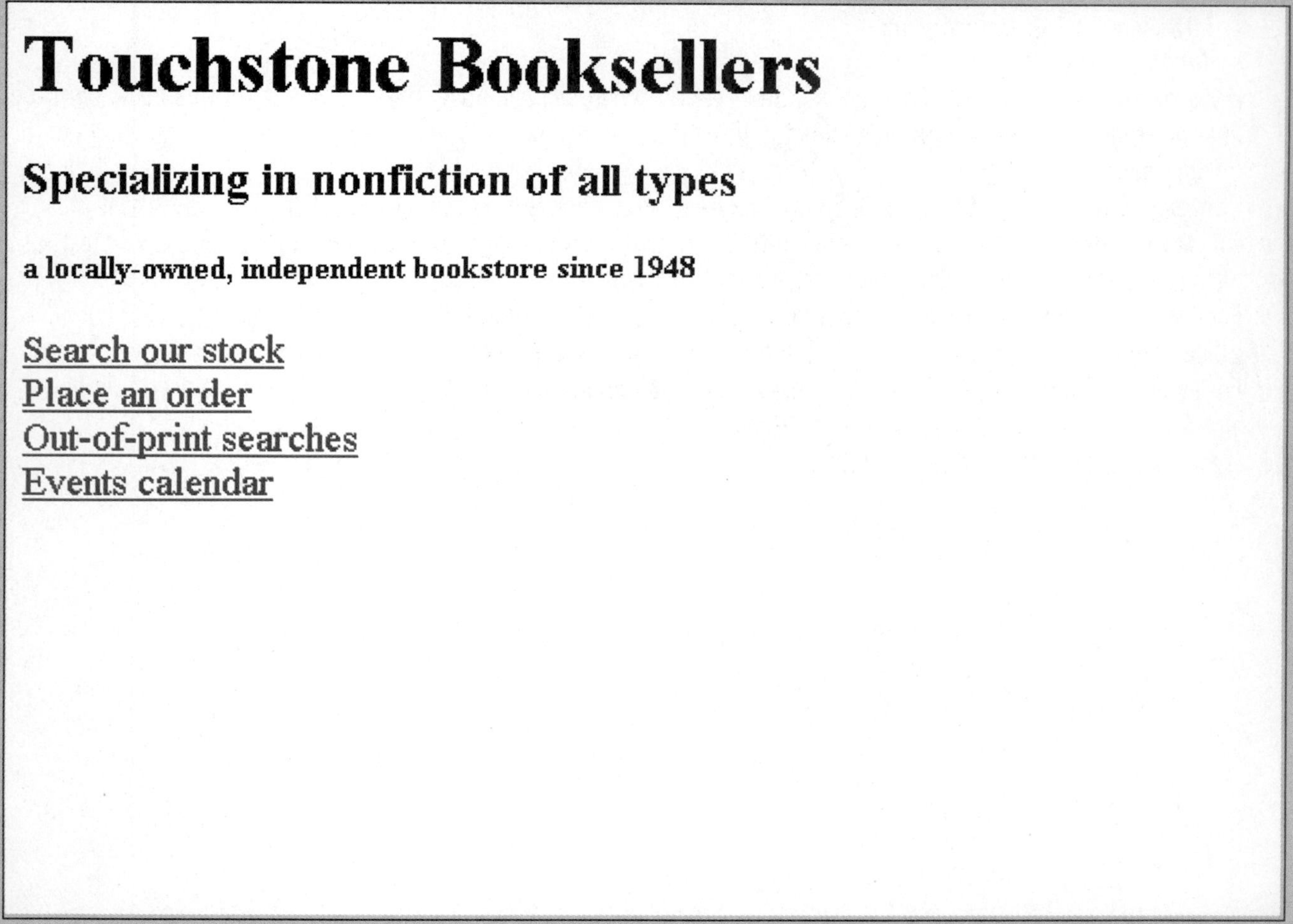

Touchstone Booksellers

Specializing in nonfiction of all types

a locally-owned, independent bookstore since 1948

Search our stock
Place an order
Out-of-print searches
Events calendar

Formatting
Text With HTML

Objectives

- ▶ **Plan text formatting**
- ▶ **Create an ordered list**
- ▶ **Create an unordered list**
- ▶ **Format characters**
- ▶ **Control font selection**
- ▶ **Customize fonts**
- ▶ **Align text**

Just as HTML allows you to include different kinds of text elements on your Web pages, it also enables you to determine the way text appears in the browser window. You can use tags to change text appearance by applying fonts and simple styles. Other tags modify the alignment of text in the browser window. Formatting the text in your Web pages can improve the organization of information and make it easier for users to find what interests them. ✒ Grace Dekmejian works in the Information Systems department at Nomad Ltd, a travel and sporting goods company. Along with her co-workers, Grace is creating a company Web site. She wants to enhance the work she's done so far by formatting the text of the Web pages.

Planning Text Formatting

Text formatting is a powerful tool for organizing the content on your Web pages and making it easier for users to navigate. Because HTML was not originally designed to format text in complex ways, you cannot easily add all the text features to a Web page that you might if you created the page in a word processor. However, HTML does include several tags and tag pairs that allow you to add basic and useful text formatting to your Web pages. Figure B-1 shows a sample page that uses several of these formats. Grace reviews the formats that she wants to use for the Nomad Ltd Web site:

Details

Lists

HTML includes tags to automatically format several types of lists. The most commonly used lists include ordered and unordered lists. By surrounding a set of list items with the appropriate tag pair, you can format an ordered list, in which the items automatically appear with sequential numbers. The same method allows you to create an unordered list, where a bullet character appears in place of the number next to each item. Grace thinks the list of links on the Web page would stand out more clearly by using one of the list formats.

Character Styles

The three standard character styles—bold, italic, and underline—have their own tag pairs in HTML. Both bold and italic are useful tools for setting apart words or areas of text. However, because the default format for links includes underlining, use of this tag set to format unlinked text generally causes confusion for users. Grace wants to use bold and italic to format several short phrases on her Web page.

Fonts

HTML includes a tag pair for changing the font style in blocks of text. This tag pair has some limitations, but when used appropriately offers another avenue for customizing the way your Web pages appear to users. Grace plans to experiment with font style to see how her page appears in fonts other than the default font of the browser; she also will change the font color and size in parts of her page.

Alignment

By default, Web page text is aligned along the left edge of the browser window. HTML's alternate alignment options for blocks of text offer you yet another utility in your Web page design toolbox. Grace thinks changing the alignment of certain text on the Nomad Ltd Web page will help separate the page into distinct, easily recognizable sections.

FIGURE B-1: Web page incorporating text formatting

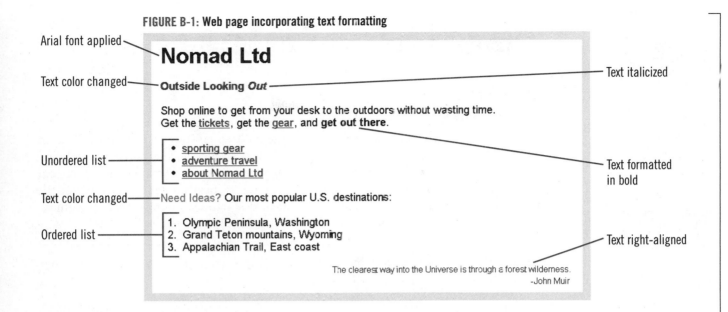

Arial font applied

Text color changed

Unordered list

Text color changed

Ordered list

Text italicized

Text formatted in bold

Text right-aligned

Guidelines for Web page formatting

Using text formats in moderation can make your Web pages easier to use. However, keep in mind that the overuse of text formatting can have an opposite effect, making a Web page more difficult to understand and navigate. When reading, we all use differences in fonts as clues that the blocks of text contain different types of information. Creating too many varieties of text on a single page requires more work from the reader to understand how different elements of information on the Web page are related. This difficulty and confusion may be enough of a discouragement to cause a potential user to close your Web page without reading it. Additionally, Web users tend to scan text rather than read it, so the presentation is even more important in this medium. By keeping blocks of text small, and choosing just two or three fonts and colors to use throughout each page, you can make your Web pages inviting and easy to use.

Creating Ordered Lists

HTML

One of the keys to an effective online layout is to divide text into small pieces that a user can easily digest. HTML's list formats provide an easy avenue for keeping your pages Web friendly. An ordered list, which uses the tags explained in Table B-1, is an ideal format for steps, rankings, and other sets of information for which order is important. ◄═══ The marketing department suggested some text to add to the Nomad Ltd Web page. Grace incorporated these ideas, and the document now includes a list of the most popular travel destinations among Nomad customers. Grace recognizes that she can easily format this list by using HTML's ordered list tags.

Steps

1. Start your text editor program, open the file **HTM B-1.htm**, then save it as a text document with the filename **nomad-b.htm**

2. Locate the line containing the text "Need Ideas?" in the second half of the document, select the **
 tag** on the next line, press **[Delete]**, then type **<OL>**
   The <OL> tag marks the start of an ordered list. Most HTML tags are abbreviations; OL is short for Ordered List.

QuickTip

While no closing tag is required for a list item, you may find it helpful to add the optional tag </LI> at the end of long entries; this can make your Web page code easier to understand.

3. Move the insertion point to the left of the word **Olympic** at the beginning of the following line, press **[Spacebar]** twice, then type **<LI>**
   The <LI> tag marks the text that follows it as a list item. Grace adds two spaces before the list item to indent it. This makes it stand out from the surrounding lines of code, and makes it clear to anyone reading the HTML that the list items are enclosed within another set of tags.

4. Select the **
 tag** in the line that follows, then press **[Delete]** twice

 tags aren't necessary in lists. Each list item automatically starts on a new line.

5. Make sure the insertion point is to the left of the word **Grand**, press **[Spacebar]** twice, then type **<LI>**

6. Repeat Steps 4 and 5 to remove the final **
 tag** in the list, and to mark the line beginning with **Appalachian** as a list item

7. Move the insertion point to the end of the last list item, to the right of the word **coast**, press **[Enter]**, then type **</OL>**
   Your document should resemble the one shown in Figure B-2.

8. Save your work, start your Web browser, cancel any dial-up activities, then open the file **nomad-b.htm**
   The three items appear numbered sequentially, as shown in Figure B-3.

9. Click the **text editor program button** on the taskbar

TABLE B-1: HTML tags for creating an ordered list

name	tags	location	example
Ordered List	<OL>..</OL>	Surround all the items that are part of an ordered list	<OL> <LI>Item 1 <LI>Item 2 <LI>Item 3 </OL>
List Item	<LI>	Marks the beginning of each item in an ordered list; no closing tag is required	<LI>Item 1 <LI>Item 2 <LI>Item 3

FIGURE B-2: HTML document containing code for ordered list

```
<BR>
<A HREF="construction.htm">adventure travel</A>
<BR>
<A HREF="construction.htm">about Nomad Ltd</A>

<P>Need Ideas? Our most popular U.S. destinations:
<OL>
    <LI>Olympic Peninsula, Washington
    <LI>Grand Teton mountains, Wyoming
    <LI>Appalachian Trail, East coast
</OL>

<P>The clearest way into the Universe is through a forest
wilderness.
<BR>
-John Muir

</BODY>
```

<LI> tags mark items within list

<OL>..</OL> tag pair marks start and end of ordered list format

FIGURE B-3: Web page containing ordered list

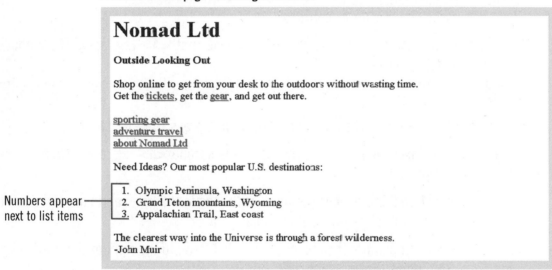

Nomad Ltd

Outside Looking Out

Shop online to get from your desk to the outdoors without wasting time.
Get the tickets, get the gear, and get out there.

sporting gear
adventure travel
about Nomad Ltd

Need Ideas? Our most popular U.S. destinations:

1. Olympic Peninsula, Washington
2. Grand Teton mountains, Wyoming
3. Appalachian Trail, East coast

The clearest way into the Universe is through a forest wilderness.
-John Muir

Numbers appear next to list items

Customizing list numbering

When you format an ordered list using the <OL>..</OL> tag pair and <LI> tags, a browser displays each item numbered sequentially beginning with 1. However, the <OL> tag can be modified by two attributes that customize the characters that appear. Instead of displaying numbers, you can set the TYPE attribute to "a" for lowercase letters, "A" for uppercase letters, "i" for lowercase Roman numerals, or "I" for uppercase Roman numerals. If you want the numbering or lettering to start with a value other than the first (such as 1 or A), set the START attribute equal to the numerical equivalent of the starting value. For example, to format a numbered list with lowercase letters starting with d (the fourth letter), the opening tag would read <OL TYPE="a" START="4">.

Creating Unordered Lists

Like an ordered list, an unordered list is a simple way to divide Web page text into smaller portions. While the items in an ordered list are numbered in order, an unordered list appears with a bullet icon next to each item. This format works well for listing sets of ideas when each item is equally important and order doesn't matter. Table B-2 explains the HTML tags used to create an unordered list. ✎ The Nomad Ltd Web page that Grace created already contains a list of three links. She thinks that formatting the links with the unordered list format will help users quickly recognize the links as a set of related information.

Steps

1. In your text editor, locate the line of text ending with "out there", select the **<P> tag** at the start of the line below it, then press **[Delete]**
   Formatting this section as a bulleted list makes the <P> tag unnecessary.

2. Type **<UL>** then press **[Enter]**
   <UL> is the opening tag for an unordered list.

3. Make sure the insertion point is to the left of the first **<A> tag**, press **[Spacebar]** twice, then type **<LI>**
   Just as in an ordered list, <LI> marks the text that follows as a list item, and does not require a closing tag.

4. Select the **
 tag** in the line that follows, then press **[Delete]** twice

5. Make sure the insertion point is to the left of the second **<A> tag**, press **[Spacebar]** twice, then type **<LI>**

6. Repeat Steps 4 and 5 to remove the final **
 tag** in the list, and to mark the third line beginning with the "**</A> tag**" as a list item

7. Move the insertion point to the end of the last list item, to the right of the third closing **</A> tag**, press **[Enter]**, then type **</UL>**
   Your document should resemble the one shown in Figure B-4.

8. Save your work, click the **browser program button** in the taskbar, then reload **nomad-b.htm**
   The three links are indented, and each is preceded by a circular bullet character, as shown in Figure B-5.

9. Click the **text editor program button** on the taskbar

TABLE B-2: HTML tags for creating an unordered list

tag(s)	description	example
<UL>..</UL>	Surround all the items that are part of an unordered list	<UL> <LI>*Item 1* <LI>*Item 2* <LI>*Item 3* </UL>
<LI>	Marks the beginning of each item in an unordered list; no closing tag is required	<LI>*Item 1* <LI>*Item 2* <LI>*Item 3*

FIGURE B-4: HTML document containing code for unordered list

```
</HEAD>

<BODY>
<H1>Nomad Ltd</H1>
<H4>Outside Looking Out</H4>

Shop online to get from your desk to the outdoors without
wasting time.
<BR>
Get the <A HREF="construction.htm">tickets</A>, get the
<A HREF="construction.htm">gear</A>, and get out there.

<UL>
<LI><A HREF="construction.htm">sporting gear</A>
<LI><A HREF="construction.htm">adventure travel</A>
<LI><A HREF="construction.htm">about Nomad Ltd</A>
</UL>

<P>Need Ideas? Our most popular U.S. destinations:
```

<LI> tags mark items within list

<UL>..</UL> tag pair marks start and end of unordered list format

FIGURE B-5: Links formatted as unordered list

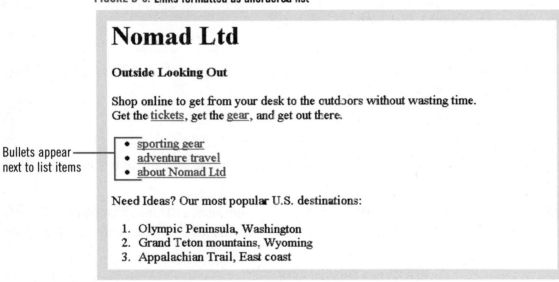

Nomad Ltd

Outside Looking Out

Shop online to get from your desk to the outdoors without wasting time.
Get the tickets, get the gear, and get out there.

Bullets appear next to list items

- sporting gear
- adventure travel
- about Nomad Ltd

Need Ideas? Our most popular U.S. destinations:

1. Olympic Peninsula, Washington
2. Grand Teton mountains, Wyoming
3. Appalachian Trail, East coast

Other list types

In addition to ordered and unordered lists, HTML includes code for formatting several other list types. In practice, however, only one other is commonly used: the definition list. You use the <DL>..</DL> tag pair to format items as a definition list, which does not add icons such as bullets or numbers to list items. Instead, each item is divided into two parts, a term—marked with <DT>—and a definition—marked with <DD>. The <DT> and <DD> tags, such as <LI>, do not require closing tags. As Figure B-6 shows, each definition appears indented below its associated term. This list format is useful for glossaries or any other list that matches items with corresponding values.

FIGURE B-6: Web page containing definition list

E-mail
(Electronic Mail) -- Messages, usually text, sent from one person to another via computer. E-mail can also be sent automatically to a large number of addresses (*Mailing List*).

See Also: Listserv® , Maillist

Ethernet
A very common method of networking computers in a *LAN*. Ethernet will handle about 10,000,000 bits-per-second and can be used with almost any kind of computer.

See Also: Bandwidth , LAN

HTML

Formatting Characters

Sometimes words or phrases on your Web pages need to stand out. In documents created in a word processor, this is most often accomplished using three standard formats: **bold**, *italic*, and underline. While you can easily add any of these formats to your Web page text, their use in HTML comes with some caveats. As you have learned, a link's default format in the browser includes underlining. Therefore, it's best not to underline unlinked text in a Web page, then you avoid confusing the users. Additionally, both bold and italic formatting can each be created by two different tag pairs. The most obvious choices—<B>..</B> for bold and <I>..</I> for italic—render these formats only visually on a browser. Because some Web users require different interfaces—for example, audio devices that read Web content to visually impaired people—using the alternate tags <STRONG> for bold and <EM> for italic is preferable. Table B-3 summarizes the tags available for character formatting. ✐ Grace is cautious about overusing different formats on her page, which might distract the user from the page's focus. However, she has identified two small sections where extra formatting would provide a needed contrast. She decides to apply bold and italic format using the alternate tags, to ensure that the Nomad Ltd page is accessible to the widest possible audience.

Steps

1. In your text editor, locate the line formatted with the "<H4>..</H4> tag pair", near the top of the page

2. Click to the left of the third word, **Out**, then type **<EM>**
   <EM> marks the beginning of a word Grace wants to italicize.

3. Move the insertion point to the right of the word **Out**, making sure it is to the left of the **</H4> tag**, then type **</EM>**

Trouble?

The end of this sentence may wrap to a second line.

4. Locate the line of text that starts with "Get the", move the insertion point to the left of the **g** in the phrase "get out there" at the end of the sentence, then type **<STRONG>**

5. Move the insertion point to the left of the **period** at the end of the sentence, then type **</STRONG>**
   The phrase "get out there" at the end of the sentence will appear in boldface in the browser. Your document should resemble the one shown in Figure B-7.

6. Save your work, click the **browser program button** on the taskbar, then reload **nomad-b.htm**
   As shown in Figure B-8, the word "Out" in the company's slogan appears italicized, and the phrase "get out there" appears in boldface.

7. Click the **text editor program button** on the taskbar

FIGURE B-7: HTML document containing bold and italic tags

```
</HEAD>

<BODY>
<H1>Nomad Ltd</H1>
<H4>Outside Looking <EM>Out</EM></H4>

Shop online to get from your desk to the outdoors without
wasting time.
<BR>
Get the <A HREF="construction.htm">tickets</A>, get the
<A HREF="construction.htm">gear</A>, and <STRONG>get out
there</STRONG>.

<UL>
  <LI><A HREF="construction.htm">sporting gear</A>
  <LI><A HREF="construction.htm">adventure travel</A>
  <LI><A HREF="construction.htm">about Nomad Ltd</A>
</UL>
```

Tag pair marks text as italic

Tag pair marks text as bold

FIGURE B-8: Web page displaying bold and italic formats

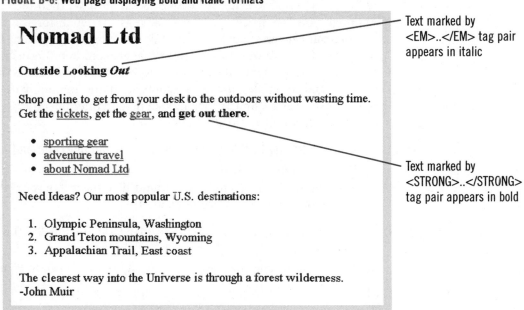

Nomad Ltd

Outside Looking *Out*

Shop online to get from your desk to the outdoors without wasting time.
Get the tickets, get the gear, and **get out there**.

- sporting gear
- adventure travel
- about Nomad Ltd

Need Ideas? Our most popular U.S. destinations:

1. Olympic Peninsula, Washington
2. Grand Teton mountains, Wyoming
3. Appalachian Trail, East coast

The clearest way into the Universe is through a forest wilderness.
-John Muir

Text marked by <EM>..</EM> tag pair appears in italic

Text marked by <STRONG>..</STRONG> tag pair appears in bold

TABLE B-3: HTML text-formatting tags

name	tag(s)	function	notes
Underlined text	<U>..</U>	adds underline format to text	avoid using; may be confused with linked text
Boldface text	<B>..</B>	adds bold format to text	applies to visual format only; use <STRONG>..</STRONG> instead to allow widest accessibility
Italicized text	<I>..</I>	adds italic format to text	applies to visual format only; use <EM>..</EM> instead to allow widest accessibility
Strong text	<STRONG>..</STRONG>	marks text as strong; interpreted by browsers as bold	interpretable by different Web interfaces; use instead of <B>..</B>
Emphasized text	<EM>..</EM>	marks text as emphasized; interpreted by browsers as italic	interpretable by different Web interfaces; use instead of <I>..</I>

HTML

Unit **B**
HTML

Controlling Font Selection

So far, you have used several text-formatting features to change the characteristics of small sections of text. HTML also allows you to alter text appearance more fundamentally, and on larger areas of the page. One tool for customizing the basic appearance of Web page text is the <FONT>..</FONT> tag pair. The opening tag can be modified with several different attributes including FACE, which changes the font in which text appears. Grace is used to working with different fonts in a word processor, and wants to see how the Nomad Ltd Web page would look in another font.

Steps

1. In your text editor, move the insertion point to the right of the **<BODY>** tag near the top of the document, then press **[Enter]**

2. Type **<FONT FACE="arial, helvetica, sans serif">**, then press **[Enter]**
   Although you can specify any font name as the FACE for the marked section, a user's browser can change the default font only if the replacement font is installed on the user's computer. Thus, it's wisest to use fonts that are commonly available. FACE also allows you to specify multiple fonts; the browser checks if the first one is available, and if not, checks the next, and so on. Because certain fonts are more commonly used in different operating systems, Grace lists a similar-looking font used in three operating systems: arial (Windows), helvetica (Macintosh), and sans serif (UNIX).

3. Click in the empty line above the **</BODY>** tag near the end of the document, press **[Enter]**, then type **</FONT>**
   The opening and closing font tags surround all of the text in your Web page. Your document should resemble the one shown in Figure B-9.

4. Save your work, click the **browser program button** on the taskbar, then reload **nomad-b.htm**
   All the text on the page now appears in Arial font, as shown in Figure B-10.

5. Click the **text editor program button** on the taskbar

CLUES TO USE

Serif and Sans Serif Fonts

While thousands of fonts exist, each falls into one of two categories: serif or sans serif. **Serif** fonts take their name from the decorative tails at the ends of the lines that make up each letter. The text you are reading is set in a serif font. **Sans serif** literally means "without serifs;" fonts in this group do not have decorative tails. The title of this Clues to Use section is in a sans serif font. In traditional print media, large blocks of text are easier to read in a serif font, while titles and smaller bits of text use sans serif fonts.

However, Web users read text on a brightly lit screen, instead of in print. Therefore, traditional font rules are not totally applicable to the Web. A consensus seems to be growing among Web designers that sans serif text is easier to read on a computer screen. As you accumulate more experience designing Web pages, you can make your own decisions about how to use fonts. Until then, a sans serif font such as Arial or Helvetica is generally an excellent choice for Web pages.

FIGURE B-9: HTML document containing font tags

Location of opening <FONT> tag

```
</HEAD>

<BODY>
<FONT FACE="arial, helvetica, sans serif">

<H1>Nomad Ltd</H1>
<H4>Outside Looking <EM>Out</EM></H4>

Shop online to get from your desk to the outdoors without
wasting time.
<BR>
Get the <A HREF="construction.htm">tickets</A>, get the
<A HREF="construction.htm">gear</A>, and <STRONG>get out
there</STRONG>.

<UL>
   <LI><A HREF="cor
   <LI><A HREF="cor
   <LI><A HREF="cor
```

```
      <LI><A HREF="construction.htm">about Nomad Ltd</A>
   </UL>

   <P>Need Ideas? Our most popular U.S. destinations:
   <OL>
      <LI>Olympic Peninsula, Washington
      <LI>Grand Teton mountains, Wyoming
      <LI>Appalachian Trail, East coast
   </OL>

   <P>The clearest way into the Universe is through a forest
   wilderness.
   <BR>
   -John Muir
```

Location of closing </FONT> tag

```
   </FONT>
   </BODY>

   </HTML>
```

FIGURE B-10: Nomad Ltd Web page in Arial font

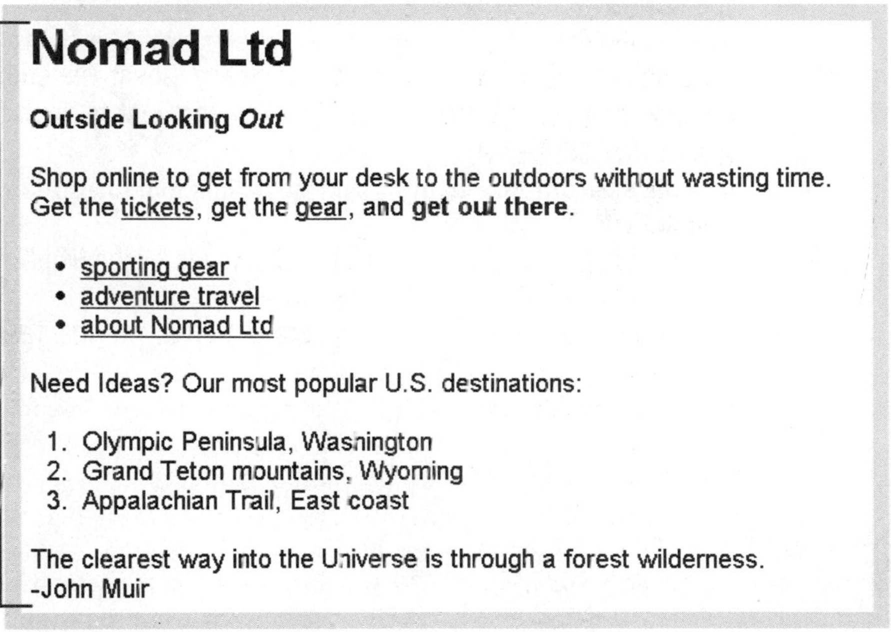

Nomad Ltd

Outside Looking *Out*

Shop online to get from your desk to the outdoors without wasting time.
Get the tickets, get the gear, and **get out there**.

Entire text of Web page changed to Arial font

- sporting gear
- adventure travel
- about Nomad Ltd

Need Ideas? Our most popular U.S. destinations:

1. Olympic Peninsula, Washington
2. Grand Teton mountains, Wyoming
3. Appalachian Trail, East coast

The clearest way into the Universe is through a forest wilderness.
-John Muir

Unit B

HTML

Customizing Fonts

The <FONT>..</FONT> tag pair allows you to change text format in several ways. In addition to changing the font itself with the FACE attribute, you can use the COLOR attribute to change text to a color other than black. You also can customize font appearance with the SIZE attribute, which changes the size of characters. Table B-4 summarizes the tags and attributes for working with fonts. Grace thinks that adding color to a few phrases on the Nomad Web page would make them stand out without being distracting.

Steps

1. In your text editor, move the insertion point to the right of the **<H4> tag** near the top of the document, just to the left of the text **Outside Looking**

2. Type **<FONT COLOR="#A52A2A">**
   Although you can use descriptive words for colors, such as "green" or "navy," to specify a color for the COLOR attribute, using the numerical equivalent is a good habit to develop. These six-digit numbers, known as **hexadecimal equivalents**, or **hexadecimals**, tell the browser mathematically how to create the color you want. Hexadecimal equivalents also are interpretable by a wider range of browsers than are color names. Additionally, while all browsers treat hexadecimals the same, browsers may vary in how they display named colors. Grace wants her page to display as predictably as possible for all users of the Nomad Ltd Web page, so she looked up the hexadecimal equivalent of a medium brown color on the Web.

3. Move the insertion point to the left of the **</H4> tag** at the end of the line, just to the right of the **</EM> tag**, then type **</FONT>**

QuickTip

Hexadecimals use the numbers 0-9 and the letters A-F; therefore the character "0" always means the number zero, since the letter O is not used in this system.

4. Move the insertion point to the left of the text **Need Ideas?** in the middle of the page, just to the right of the **<P> tag**, then type **<FONT COLOR="#238E68">**
   This is the hexadecimal equivalent of a medium green color, which Grace looked up in an online HTML reference on the Web. She chose two colors that work well together, and which enhance the outdoors theme of the page's content.

5. Move the insertion point to the right of the **question mark** after the text **Need Ideas?**, then type **</FONT>**
   Figure B-11 shows the Web page code, including these two color changes.

6. Locate the line that begins "<P>The clearest way", near the end of the document, move the insertion point to the right of the **<P> tag**, just to the left of the word **The**, then type **<FONT SIZE="-1">**
   Grace uses the SIZE attribute to format the quote in a font one size smaller than the Web page's default font.

7. Move the insertion point to the end of the line that reads "-John Muir", then type **</FONT>**
   Figure B-12 shows the source code for the font size change.

8. Save your work, click the **browser program button** on the taskbar, then reload **nomad-b.htm**
   As Figure B-13 shows, the text on Grace's Web page now includes two font colors, and a variation in font size.

9. Click the **text editor program button** on the taskbar

CLUES TO USE

Customizing linked text

While allowing you to customize standard Web page text, HTML also includes special attributes to customize a page's linked text. You can change the color of all the links in a Web page using the LINK, VLINK, and ALINK attributes of the opening <BODY> tag. LINK affects the color of links that have not been followed, which is blue by default. VLINK (short for "viewed link") specifies the color for links that were previously followed, which is purple by default. ALINK (short for "active link") sets the color of links when they are clicked; the default color for these links is red. While the default colors work best in most situations, changing one or more link colors is useful for certain Web page designs.

FIGURE B-11: HTML document with font COLOR attributes

<FONT> tags to change text color to brown

```
<H1>Nomad Ltd</H1>
<H4><FONT COLOR="#A52A2A">Outside Looking
<EM>Out</EM></FONT></H4>

Shop online to get from your desk to the outdoors without
wasting time.
<BR>
Get the <A HREF="construction.htm">tickets</A>, get the
<A HREF="construction.htm">gear</A>, and <STRONG>get out
there</STRONG>.

<UL>
  <LI><A HREF="construction.htm">sporting gear</A>
  <LI><A HREF="construction.htm">adventure travel</A>
  <LI><A HREF="construction.htm">about Nomad Ltd</A>
</UL>

<P><FONT COLOR="#238E68">Need Ideas?</FONT> Our most
popular U.S. destinations:
```

<FONT> tags to change text color to green

FIGURE B-12: HTML document with font SIZE argument

<FONT> tags to decrease to next smaller size

```
<P><FONT SIZE="-1">The clearest way into the Universe is
through a forest wilderness.
<BR>
-John Muir</FONT>
```

FIGURE B-13: Nomad Ltd Web page with font color and size changes

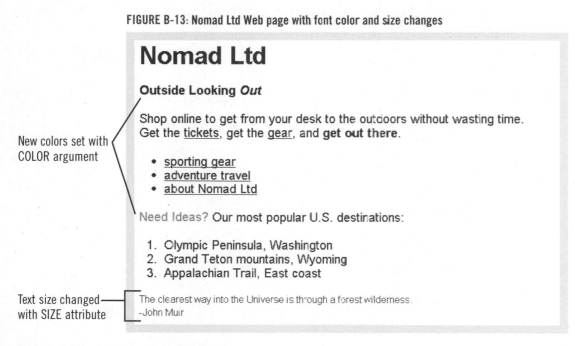

New colors set with COLOR argument

Text size changed with SIZE attribute

Nomad Ltd

Outside Looking *Out*

Shop online to get from your desk to the outdoors without wasting time.
Get the tickets, get the gear, and **get out there**.

- sporting gear
- adventure travel
- about Nomad Ltd

Need Ideas? Our most popular U.S. destinations:

1. Olympic Peninsula, Washington
2. Grand Teton mountains, Wyoming
3. Appalachian Trail, East coast

The clearest way into the Universe is through a forest wilderness.
-John Muir

TABLE B-4: HTML font formatting tags and attributes

tags	attribute	function	example
<FONT>..</FONT>	FACE	changes font; may list several alternate fonts in order of preference	<FONT FACE="arial, helvetica, sans serif">This text appears in a different font than the surrounding text.</FONT>
	COLOR	changes text color; color can be specified as a name or six-digit number	<FONT COLOR="23238E">This text appears in navy blue.</FONT>
	SIZE	changes text size; specify a number between 1 (smallest) and 7 (largest), or use + or - plus a number for incremental changes from the default	<FONT SIZE="7">This text appears in the largest size available.</FONT> <FONT SIZE="+1">This text appears one size larger than the default text.</FONT>

HTML

HTML

Aligning Text

In addition to the methods you've used to control what text looks like, HTML also provides some basic control over where text appears on the page. Common paragraph tags, including <P> and the heading tag pairs <H1>..</H1> through <H6>..</H6>, support the ALIGN attribute. The default value for ALIGN is "left," meaning that each line of text is flush with the left edge of the browser window. Other valid settings are "right," which sets each line of text even with the right edge of the window, and "center," which centers each line between the two edges of the window. Recent browsers also support a value of "justify," which stretches each line of text so it's flush with both the left and right edges of the browser window. Table B-5 summarizes the ALIGN attribute. Grace wants to separate the quote at the bottom of the page from the other page items. She thinks that right alignment would accomplish this.

1. In your text editor, locate the line beginning with "<P><FONT SIZE="-1">The clearest way"

2. Move the insertion point immediately to the right of the letter **P** in the <P> tag

3. Press **[Spacebar]**, then type **ALIGN="right"**
   Your page should resemble the one shown in Figure B-14.

4. Save your work, click the **browser program button** on the taskbar, then reload **nomad-b.htm**
   As Figure B-15 shows, the quote at the bottom of the Web page now lines up with the right edge of the browser window.

5. Close your browser and text editor

TABLE B-5: HTML ALIGN attribute

tags	attribute	examples	results
<P>, <H1>..</H1> through <H6>..</H6>	ALIGN	<P ALIGN= "left">	Jasper Barber started Nomad Ltd in 1987 as a single store in Boulder, Colorado.
		<P ALIGN= "right">	Jasper Barber started Nomad Ltd in 1987 as a single store in Boulder, Colorado.
		<P ALIGN= "center">	Jasper Barber started Nomad Ltd in 1987 as a single store in Boulder, Colorado.
		<P ALIGN= "justify">	Jasper Barber started Nomad Ltd in 1987 as a single store in Boulder, Colorado.

FIGURE B-14: HTML document containing ALIGN attribute

```
</UL>

<P><FONT COLOR="#238E68">Need Ideas?</FONT> Our most
popular U.S. destinations:
<OL>
  <LI>Olympic Peninsula, Washington
  <LI>Grand Teton mountains, Wyoming
  <LI>Appalachian Trail, East coast
</OL>

<P ALIGN="right"><FONT SIZE="-1">The clearest way into
the Universe is through a forest wilderness.
<BR>
-John Muir</FONT>

</FONT>
</BODY>

</HTML>
```

ALIGN attribute lines up paragraph with right edge of browser window

FIGURE B-15: Nomad Ltd Web page containing right-aligned text

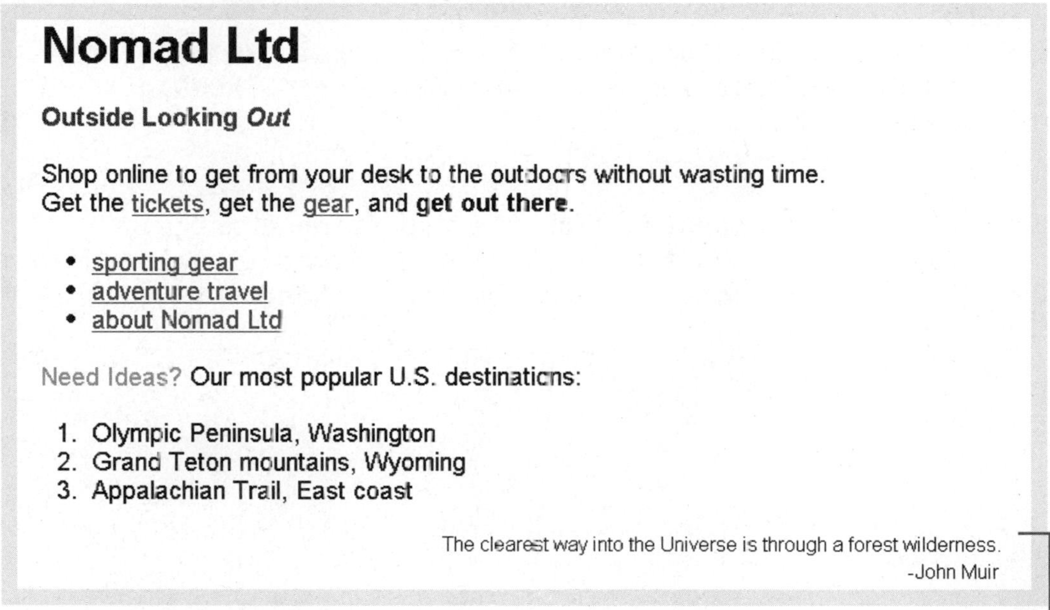
Nomad Ltd
Outside Looking Out
Shop online to get from your desk to the outdoors without wasting time.
Get the tickets, get the gear, and get out there.
sporting gear
adventure travel
about Nomad Ltd
Need Ideas? Our most popular U.S. destinations:
1. Olympic Peninsula, Washington
2. Grand Teton mountains, Wyoming
3. Appalachian Trail, East coast
The clearest way into the Universe is through a forest wilderness.
-John Muir

Text aligned with right edge of browser window

HTML

Practice

▶ Concepts Review

Identify the function of each item labeled in Figure B-16.

FIGURE B-16

```
<BODY>
<FONT FACE="arial, helvetica, sans serif">

<H1>Nomad Ltd</H1>
<H4><FONT COLOR="#A52A2A">Outside Looking
<EM>Out</EM></FONT></H4>

Shop online to get from your desk to the outdoors without
wasting time.
<BR>
Get the <A HREF="construction.htm">tickets</A>, get the
<A HREF="construction.htm">gear</A>, and <STRONG>get out
there</STRONG>.

<UL>
  <LI><A HREF="construction.htm">sporting gear</A>
  <LI><A HREF="construction.htm">adventure travel</A>
  <LI><A HREF="construction.htm">about Nomad Ltd</A>
</UL>
```

1
2
3
4
5

Match each attribute with the HTML tag it modifies (you may use each tag more than once).

6. COLOR
7. ALIGN
8. TYPE
9. START
10. FACE
11. SIZE

a. <FONT>
b. <OL>
c. <P>

Select the best answer from the list of choices.

12. Which one of the following HTML codes would you use to format text in an ordered list?
    a. <P ALIGN="center">
    b. <STRONG>..</STRONG>
    c. <OL>..</OL>
    d. <FONT COLOR="#A52A2A">..</FONT>

13. Which one of the following HTML codes would you use to change character style to bold?
    a. <P ALIGN="center">
    b. <STRONG>..</STRONG>
    c. <OL>..</OL>
    d. <FONT COLOR="#A52A2A">..</FONT>

14. Which one of the following HTML codes would you use to change font color?
    a. <P ALIGN="center">
    b. <STRONG>..</STRONG>
    c. <OL>..</OL>
    d. <FONT COLOR="#A52A2A">..</FONT>

15. Which one of the following HTML codes would you use to center-align a paragraph?
    a. <P ALIGN="center">
    b. <STRONG>..</STRONG>
    c. <OL>..</OL>
    d. <FONT COLOR="#A52A2A">..</FONT>

16. Which of the following tag pairs should you avoid using, so that users aren't confused?
    a. <U>..</U>
    b. <B>..</B>
    c. <EM>..</EM>
    d. <STRONG>..</STRONG>

17. Which of the following tag pairs adds a text format that can be interpreted by Web interfaces other than browsers?
    a. <B>..</B>
    b. <I>..</I>
    c. <U>..</U>
    d. <STRONG>..</STRONG>

18. Which of the following tag pairs is the best choice for a list of information where order is important?
    a. <FONT>..</FONT>
    b. <OL>..</OL>
    c. <UL>..</UL>
    d. <STRONG>..</STRONG>

Skills Review

1. Create an ordered list.

a. Start your text editor, open the file HTM B-2.htm, then save it as a text document with the filename cco-b.htm.

b. Locate the line beginning with "<P>Let our eyewear" in the second half of the document, click in the blank line below, press [Enter], then insert the <OL> tag with an attribute to mark each list item with a capital letter.

c. Replace the <P> tags at the beginning of the three list item lines with two spaces and the <LI> tag.

d. Delete the two <BR> tags between the three list items.

e. Move the insertion point to the blank line below the last list item, type "</OL>", then press [Enter].

f. Save your work.

g. Start your Web browser, view the file cco-b.htm, and verify that the ordered list appears correctly.

2. Create an unordered list.

a. In your text editor, locate the line beginning with "<H3>" near the top of the document, click in the blank line below, press [Enter], then insert the <UL> tag.

b. Insert two spaces and the <LI> tag to the left of each <A> tag for the four list items below the text "Visionary Eyewear for 50 Years".

c. Delete the three <BR> tags between the list items.

d. Move the insertion point to the end of the last list item, to the right of the fourth closing </A> tag, press [Enter], then type "</UL>".

e. Save your work.

f. Reload the page in your browser to verify that the unordered list appears correctly.

3. Format characters.

a. In your text editor, locate the line near the bottom of the page that begins "<P>Ask about", position the insertion point to the right of the <P> tag, just to the left of the word Ask, then type "<EM>".

b. Move the insertion point to the end of the line, to the right of the word eyewear, then type "</EM>".

c. Save your work.

d. Reload the page in your browser to verify that the last line of text appears in italics.

4. Control font selection.

a. In your text editor, move the insertion point to the right of the <BODY> tag near the top of the document, then press [Enter].

b. Type "<FONT FACE="arial, helvetica, sans serif">".

c. In the empty line above the </BODY> tag near the end of the document, press [Enter], then type "</FONT>".

d. Save your work.

e. Reload the page in your browser to verify that all the text on the page appears in Arial.

5. Customize fonts.

a. In your text editor, move the insertion point to the right of the <H1> tag near the top of the document, just to the left of the word Crystal.

b. Insert a <FONT> tag that includes a COLOR attribute set to "# 236B8E".

c. Move the insertion point to the left of the </H1> tag at the end of the line, just to the right of the word Opticals, then insert the </FONT> tag.

d. In the last list item in the ordered list near the bottom of the document, place the insertion point to the left of the word Crystal, then add a <FONT> tag that includes a COLOR attribute set to "# 236B8E".

e. Move the insertion point to the right of the word Opticals in the same line, then insert the </FONT> tag.

f. Save your work.

g. Reload the page in your browser to verify that the text color is changed in the two designated locations.

6. Align text.

a. In your text editor, locate the line near the end of the document that begins with "<P><EM>Ask about", then move the insertion point immediately to the right of the letter P in the <P> tag.

b. Press [Spacebar], then insert the ALIGN attribute with a value of "center".

c. Save your work.

d. Reload the page in your browser to verify that the last line of text is centered between the two edges of the window.

e. Close your browser and text editor.

► Independent Challenges

1. You want to use the new HTML formatting features you have learned to enhance the Web page for Star Dot Star, your consulting business.

To complete this independent challenge:

a. Start your text editor, open the file HTM B-3.htm, then save it as a text document with the filename sds-b.htm.

b. Use the <UL>..</UL> and <LI> tags to format the list of links as an unordered list.

c. Use the <EM>..</EM> tag pair to italicize the words "get the most" near the top of the document.

d. Use the <FONT>..</FONT> tag pair to change the font of the document to Arial.

e. Use the <FONT>..</FONT> tag pair to change the color of the heading, "Star Dot Star Consulting," at the top of the page, to color #8E2323.

f. Use the ALIGN attribute to center the last line of text "Upgrades are our specialty!".

g. Save your work.

h. Preview the Web page in your browser.

i. Print the Web page in your browser.

2. You have been developing a Web page for your employer, Metro Water, the local water department. You have added links to informational pages as you originally planned. Now you want to work with the development team to enhance the text format of the Web page.

To complete this independent challenge:

a. Start your text editor, open the file HTM B-4.htm, then save it as a text document with the filename mw-b.htm.

b. Format the list of links to related information as an unordered list.

c. Italicize the word "difference" near the end of the document.

d. Change the font of the entire document to Arial.

e. Change the color of the two headings at the top of the page to color #008B8B.

f. Center-align the two headings at the top of the page.

g. Save your work.

h. Preview the Web page in your browser.

i. Print the Web page in your browser.

3. You have recently opened your own video store, Film Clips, and plan to design an in-store information system that uses HTML and a browser. With this system, customers can learn more about the movies in the store.
To complete this independent challenge:

a. Sketch the opening Web page for this information system. Include the store name, a slogan, and a linked list of movie genres (comedy, drama, horror, foreign, etc.).

b. Create a new text document and save it with the filename fc-b.htm.

c. Enter structural tags and the text for your page, and format the links to target the file construction.htm.

d. Format the list of movie genres as an unordered list.

e. Change the font of the page to Arial.

f. Change at least two other text formats on your page, such as bold text, italic text, font color, font size, or text alignment.

g. Save your work.

h. Preview the Web page in your browser.

i. Print the Web page in your browser.

4. Adding color to a Web page is both easy to do and useful as a design tool. However, when you don't have an HTML reference book handy, figuring out the correct hexadecimal code for a color you want to use can be intimidating. Fortunately, many free and useful HTML resources are available on the Web. To complete this independent challenge:

a. Create a simple Web page named colors-b.htm containing one or two paragraphs of sample text.

b. Choose three font colors to apply to words or phrases.

c. Connect to the Internet and use your browser to go to one of the following online HTML references:
   www.w3.org
   hotwired.lycos.com/webmonkey
   www.webreference.com
   If you have trouble locating these pages, go to www.course.com, navigate to the page for this book, click the link for the Student Online Companion, click the link for this unit, and use the links listed there as a starting point for your search.

d. Look up the hexadecimal equivalents for the three colors you chose, then apply each color to a word or phrase in your sample Web page.

e. Save your work.

f. Preview the Web page in your browser.

g. Print the document in your browser.

h. Disconnect from the Internet.

i. Exit your text editor and browser.

Visual Workshop

At your job at Touchstone Booksellers, a small bookstore, you are working to convince the owner that she could reach a wider audience by doing business on the Web. She was intrigued by the sample Web page you showed her, so you decide to format the text to give the page a more sophisticated design. Open the file HTM B-5.htm, save it as a text document called tsb-b.htm, then edit the file to match the Web page shown in Figure B-17.

FIGURE B-17

Touchstone Booksellers

Specializing in *nonfiction* of all types

- Search our stock
- Place an order
- Out-of-print searches
- Events calendar

Ask about our **preferred reader** program for 10% off!

a locally-owned, independent bookstore since 1948

Adding
Graphics and Multimedia

Objectives

- ► Plan graphics use
- ► Insert graphics
- ► Specify graphic size
- ► Link graphics
- ► Insert an image map
- ► Add a background image
- ► Explore multimedia options

Text is often the most important part of a Web page, as it conveys the information that serves as the page's focus. Nevertheless, as in print media, graphics are also an important part of Web design. In addition to sometimes conveying information better than text, graphics can make a page easier to read, and play an integral part in giving a page a unique style and mood. Recent trends in graphics for the Web involve supplementing visuals with sound and animation. ◢ Grace Dekmejian works in the Information Systems department at Nomad Ltd, a travel and sporting goods company. Along with her co-workers, Grace is creating a company Web site. To strengthen the layout and tone of the Web site, Grace wants to add Nomad's logo and other graphic images to the pages she is developing. She's also interested in learning more about incorporating sound and animation into the Web pages.

Planning Graphics Use

The use of graphics is a popular and practical way to enrich Web pages, and an important part of virtually all pages on the Web today. As with other design tools, moderation is the key to effective graphics use. A Web page filled with text but devoid of graphics can be uninviting and difficult for users to read. On the other hand, a Web page with too much space devoted to graphics can overwhelm and distract users from the focus of the page. To implement graphics most effectively, first clarify the goal of your Web page or Web site. Then, plan and incorporate limited graphics that support your layout without overwhelming it. Figure C-1 shows a Web page that balances text with limited graphics.  Grace plans to incorporate the Nomad Ltd company logo into the Web site she is creating. She also wants to add two small graphics that contribute to the page's outdoor theme. While planning the use of graphics, it's important to keep a few guidelines in mind:

Details

QuickTip

You usually can tell the format of a file by checking the filename's three-character extension. For example, the name of a JPG file usually ends with .jpg.

Use supported file formats

Unlike Web page text, which is actually a part of the HTML document that creates a Web page, Web page graphics are separate files that are referenced in a page's HTML code. Many graphic file formats exist, but only three are widely supported by Web browsers: GIF, JPG, and PNG. Table C-1 gives more information about each of these three formats. As you create or acquire graphics for your Web site, make sure they are GIF, JPG, or PNG files. When Grace requests graphic files from Nomad Ltd's marketing and graphic design departments, she specifies that they need to be in one of the three Web-compatible formats.

Add alternate text

Images are a central part of the Web today, and are almost universally supported by browsers. Even so, users may be unable to view a Web page's images because of a faulty Web connection or a visual impairment. Or, they may choose not to view the images in order to speed up Web page download times. To accommodate these users, it's important that Web pages convey the same information with or without the images. The HTML tag for adding an image to a Web page also supports an attribute that allows you to specify alternate text, which appears when a graphic does not. While planning how she will incorporate graphics into her layout, Grace considers the alternate text that would be most appropriate for each.

Use graphics judiciously

If a few graphics can make a Web page more interesting, then can a lot of graphics make a Web page super-interesting? The answer is "usually not." Extra graphics actually are counterproductive, and make a Web page difficult to understand and use. The most reliable way to effectively incorporate graphics into your Web pages is to use limited graphics to support a page's structure and function, rather than add graphics for their own sake. Grace plans to add only three graphics to the Nomad Ltd home page. The logo will connect the page with the company's established identity, and the other two graphics will build on the Web page's outdoor theme.

TABLE C-1: Web-compatible graphic formats

format	best for	notes
GIF	line art and animations	proprietary format; use requires licensing fees in some cases
JPG (or JPEG)	photographs	variable compression allows tradeoff between better image quality and smaller file size
PNG	line art and photographs	recently developed format; browser support not as widespread

FIGURE C-1: Web page enhanced with graphics

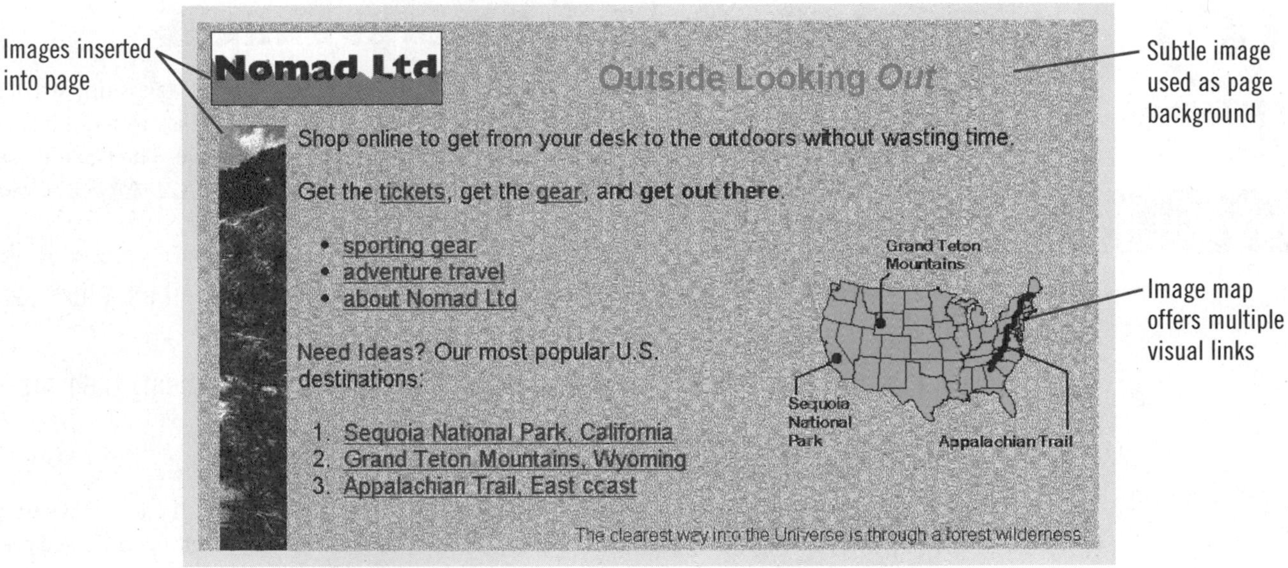

Images inserted into page

Subtle image used as page background

Image map offers multiple visual links

Nomad Ltd

Outside Looking *Out*

Shop online to get from your desk to the outdoors without wasting time.

Get the tickets, get the gear, and **get out there**.

- sporting gear
- adventure travel
- about Nomad Ltd

Need Ideas? Our most popular U.S. destinations:

1. Sequoia National Park, California
2. Grand Teton Mountains, Wyoming
3. Appalachian Trail, East ccast

Grand Teton Mountains

Sequoia National Park

Appalachian Trail

The clearest way into the Universe is through a forest wilderness.

CLUES TO USE

Minimizing Web page download times

A Web page's download time is an important usability factor in which the size of graphics plays a large role. **Download time** is the amount of time it takes for the page and its associated files to transfer from their location on the Web to a user's browser. HTML files alone are relatively small, and most download within a few seconds, even over the slowest Internet connection. Graphic files, however, tend to be much larger, and take much longer to download. Download time is another reason to minimize the number and size of graphics on your Web pages; more graphics mean that users must wait longer to see and use a page. New technologies—known as **broadband** technologies—that allow faster downloads are becoming more widespread. Universities and many large corporations also have Web connections that enable near-instantaneous downloads. However, remember that in many parts of the United States and the world, such technology is not available or prevalent; this means that on the Web as a whole, slower connections are the rule, not the exception. By adhering to sound graphics design principles, you can ensure that your Web pages are easily viewable over all types of Internet connections.

HTML

Inserting Graphics

HTML uses the <IMG> tag to incorporate images into a Web page. The <IMG> tag is unpaired; it requires no closing tag. However, like the opening tag for a link, the <IMG> tag always requires an attribute. This attribute, SRC, indicates the name and location of the graphic file. The <IMG> tag also supports many other attributes, several of which are explained in Table C-2. ➤ Grace wants to add the Nomad Ltd logo graphic to the company's Web page.

Steps

1. Start your text editor program, open the file **HTM C-1.htm**, then save it as a text document with the filename **nomad-c.htm**

2. Select the text **<H1>Nomad Ltd</H1>** near the top of the document, then press **[Delete]**

3. Type **<IMG SRC="images/nomad.gif" ALIGN="left">**
   Grace replaced the page heading code containing the company name with the <IMG> tag referencing the logo graphic. To keep the files for the Nomad Web site organized, Grace created a folder called "images" where she stores the site's graphic files. Therefore, she specified the folder "images" along with the graphic's filename, "nomad.gif," in the SRC attribute. Although images are aligned at the left margin by default, specifying "left" with the ALIGN attribute ensures that the text following the graphic runs alongside, rather than below it.

4. Move the insertion point to the end of the line that begins with "<H2>", press **[Enter]** twice, then type **<IMG SRC="images/tree.jpg" ALIGN="left">**
   The <IMG> tag adds an outdoor photo to the Web page.

Trouble?

Some versions of Internet Explorer do not correctly display bulleted and numbered lists adjacent to a graphic.

5. Save your work, start your Web browser, cancel any dial-up activities, then open the file **nomad-c.htm**
   The Nomad Ltd logo graphic appears in the upper-left corner of the browser window, and the graphic of the tree runs near or along the left edge. Grace wants to clean up the layout around the graphics.

6. Click the **text editor program button** on the taskbar, move the insertion point to the beginning of the line that starts with "<H2>", type **
, then press **[Enter]
   Adding a line break before the remaining heading creates more space above it.

7. Click between the **2** and the **>** in the **<H2> tag** below the **
** you just entered, press **[Spacebar]**, then type **ALIGN="center"**
   Figure C-2 shows the completed code for the <IMG> tags and surrounding text.

8. Save your work, click the **browser program button** on the taskbar, then reload **nomad-c.htm**
   The heading "Outside Looking *Out*" is now separated from the logo. See Figure C-3.

9. Click the **text editor program button** on the taskbar

CLUES TO USE

Text images

In addition to adding art and photos, the <IMG> tag also can be used to add text to Web pages. Because few fonts are common to the majority of computer systems, Web page designers are generally limited to a small number of fonts for page text. However, a designer can enter text into a graphics program, such as Adobe Illustrator, format the text with any font they choose, and create a graphic of the text. They then can insert the graphic in a Web page, where any user who can view graphics can see the text in the font selected by the designer. Such graphics, known as **text images**, are best for only small areas of text, such as headings, to keep the page's download time to a minimum. However, text images provide an additional tool for creating well-designed, interesting Web pages that can be viewed by nearly all Web users.

FIGURE C-2: Web page code containing <IMG> tag

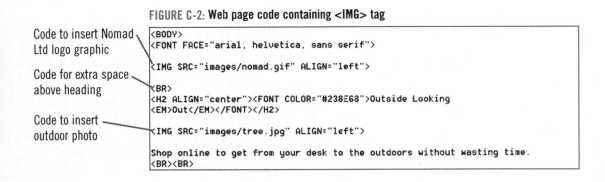

Code to insert Nomad Ltd logo graphic

Code for extra space above heading

Code to insert outdoor photo

```
<BODY>
<FONT FACE="arial, helvetica, sans serif">

<IMG SRC="images/nomad.gif" ALIGN="left">

<BR>
<H2 ALIGN="center"><FONT COLOR="#238E68">Outside Looking
<EM>Out</EM></FONT></H2>

<IMG SRC="images/tree.jpg" ALIGN="left">

Shop online to get from your desk to the outdoors without wasting time.
<BR><BR>
```

FIGURE C-3: Web page incorporating logo and photo

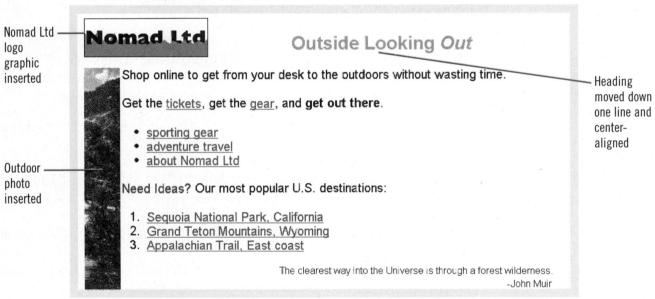

Nomad Ltd logo graphic inserted

Outdoor photo inserted

Heading moved down one line and center-aligned

TABLE C-2: Commonly used IMG attributes

attribute	specifies	possible values	example
ALIGN	graphic's alignment between the left and right margins, and with respect to adjacent text	"bottom", "left", "middle", "right", "top"	ALIGN="right"
ALT	alternate text for users who don't use graphics	any text is valid, including spaces	ALT= "2000-year-old trees in Sequoia National Park"
HEIGHT	the image's display height, in pixels	a number representing this dimension	HEIGHT="550"
SRC	the location and filename of the image file	the name of the file, with location information if necessary	SRC="/graphics/ sequoia.jpg"
WIDTH	the image's display width, in pixels	a number representing this dimension	WIDTH="275"

HTML

Specifying Graphic Size

The <IMG> tag supports the HEIGHT and WIDTH attributes, which specify a graphic's display dimensions. The units for these attributes are **pixels** (short for "picture elements"—abbreviated "px"), which are the points of light that make up the display on a computer screen. An important feature of the HEIGHT and WIDTH attributes is that they are used to reserve space on the page for a graphic, making it unnecessary to adjust the size of the graphic itself. By letting the browser know an image's dimensions before the file finishes downloading, these attributes allow the browser to correctly lay out the rest of the page before the graphics appear. You also can supplement these attributes with the ALT attribute, which allows you to specify text that will appear in place of the graphics while they are downloading. ✎ Grace wants to add the HEIGHT and WIDTH attributes to her page's images so that users see the intended layout from the moment the page opens. She has also created some alternate text to add to each graphic.

Steps

1. In your text editor, locate the <IMG> tag that references the graphic "nomad.gif," then click to the left of the closing >

QuickTip
You can look up graphic dimensions with Netscape Navigator. Click File, click Open, then open the graphic file. The dimensions, in pixels, appear in the title bar.

2. Press [Spacebar], then type **HEIGHT="63" WIDTH="201" ALT="Nomad Ltd"**
Grace used a graphics-editing program—like Paint, a free accessory included with Windows—to look up the exact height and width of the Nomad Ltd logo image.

3. Locate the <IMG> tag that references the graphic "tree.jpg," then click to the left of the closing >

QuickTip
While you can use the HEIGHT and WIDTH attributes to display a graphic smaller or larger than its actual size, image quality can be significantly reduced. Instead, you should use a graphics program to edit the file to the correct dimensions.

4. Press [Spacebar], then type **HEIGHT="468" WIDTH="58" ALT="View through an evergreen toward a mountainous skyline and blue sky"**

5. Save your work, click the **browser program button** in the taskbar, then reload **nomad-c.htm**
Although you may not notice the change in the graphic display, users who view your published page on the Web will see the correct page layout from the start.

6. Click the **text editor program button** on the taskbar, locate the <IMG> tag that references the graphic "tree.jpg," then click to the left of the closing >

7. Press [Spacebar], then type **HSPACE="10"**
The HSPACE attribute adds horizontal space between the image and the page elements to the left and right of the image. Figure C-4 shows the completed HTML document.

Trouble?
Because your images are already on your local disk, they download virtually instantaneously. Therefore, you may not see the alternate text before the graphics appear.

8. Save your work, click the **browser program button** in the taskbar, then reload **nomad-c.htm**
As shown in Figure C-5, the alternate text appears while the images are downloading, and the tree graphic is separated from the text to its right.

9. Click the **text editor program button** on the taskbar

FIGURE C-4: Web page code for sized images

Code for —
Nomad logo
with sizing
and alternate
text attributes

Code for —
outdoor photo
with sizing,
alternate text
and horizontal
space
attributes

```
<BODY>
<FONT FACE="arial, helvetica, sans serif">

<IMG SRC="images/nomad.gif" ALIGN="left" HEIGHT="63" WIDTH="201" ALT="Nomad
Ltd">

<BR>
<H2 ALIGN="center"><FONT COLOR="#238E68">Outside Looking
<EM>Out</EM></FONT></H2>

<IMG SRC="images/tree.jpg" ALIGN="left" HEIGHT="468" WIDTH="58" ALT="View
through an evergreen toward a mountainous skyline and blue sky" HSPACE="10">

Shop online to get from your desk to the outdoors without wasting time.
<BR><BR>
```

FIGURE C-5: Web page containing sized images and alternate text

ALT text —
appears in
graphic
placeholder
boxes

Placeholder —
boxes appear
while
graphics are
loading

Other uses of the ALT attribute

You've seen that text specified with the ALT attribute appears while its associated image is downloading. However, this text continues to play a role in your Web pages even after the image appears. When a user moves the pointer over an image, the alternate text is visible for a few seconds in a small box. This HTML feature lets you include additional information on your Web pages. Implementation of the ALT text attribute also plays an important part in Web use by visually impaired people, who can access the Web using an interface that speaks the contents of a page. Upon encountering a graphic, these interfaces speak the graphic's associated alternate text, if available. To maximize the availability of graphical content to these users, the alternate text should be both brief and descriptive, like the text Grace used with her outdoor photo.

HTML

Linking Graphics

Just as you can format sections of text as links, you also can add link formatting to graphics on a Web page. You simply surround the <IMG> tag with the <A>..</A> tag pair, and add the HREF attribute. You can use linked images to simplify navigation around your Web site by placing an identical linked image at the same location on each page. A user can click this image on any page to open the home page. ▶ Grace has created another page for the Nomad Ltd Web site describing the tours Nomad offers. Grace has placed the Nomad logo in the upper-left corner and wants to link the logo graphic to the home page. When the Web site is completed, a user will be able to click the Nomad logo on any page to return to the home page.

1. In your text editor, open the file **HTM C-2.htm**, then save it as a text document with the filename **tours-c.htm**
   The source for Grace's Web page about Nomad tours appears in the text editor.

2. Locate the <IMG> tag that references the graphic "nomad.gif," click at the beginning of the line, type **<A HREF="nomad-c.htm">**, then press **[Enter]**

3. Click in the blank line below the "<IMG>" tag, type **</A>**, then press **[Enter]**
   Figure C-6 shows the completed source code for this file. The <IMG> tag for the Nomad logo graphic uses extra attributes, which are explained in Table C-3.

4. Save your work, click the **browser program button** on the taskbar, open the file **tours-c.htm** in your browser, then move the pointer over the **Nomad logo** graphic
   The pointer changes to a pointing hand when it is moved over the logo graphic, as shown in Figure C-7. This lets users know that a graphic is linked.

5. Click the **Nomad logo** in the upper-left corner
   The Nomad home page opens.

6. Click the **text editor program button** on the taskbar, then open the file **nomad-c.htm**

7. Locate the line beginning with "Get the", select the filename **construction.htm** in the first <A> tag (before the word "tickets"), press **[Delete]**, then type **tours-c.htm**

8. Repeat Step 7 for the filename **construction.htm** in the second list item ("adventure travel") in the bulleted list (under the <UL> tag)
   Figure C-8 shows the completed Web document.

9. Save your work, click the **browser program button** in the taskbar, reload the **nomad-c.htm** page, click the second link in the bulleted list, **adventure travel**, then click the **Nomad logo**
   The first link opens the Nomad Tours page, and the linked logo graphic reopens the home page.

TABLE C-3: Additional <IMG> attributes

attribute	specifies	possible values	example
BORDER	the width of an optional border placed around the image; by default, a blue border appears around a linked graphic	a number representing this width, in pixels; to remove default border, set value to 0	BORDER="0"
VSPACE	the size of the space between the top and bottom of the graphic, and the surrounding page elements; short for "vertical space"	a number representing this space, in pixels	VSPACE="5"
HSPACE	the size of the space between the left and right edges of the graphic, and the surrounding page elements; short for "horizontal space"	a number representing this space, in pixels	HSPACE="5"

FIGURE C-6: Web page code for linked graphic

```
<BODY>
<A HREF="nomad-c.htm">
<IMG SRC="images/nomad.gif" ALIGN="left" VSPACE="20" HSPACE="20" BORDER="0"
ALT="Nomad Ltd">
</A>

<H2>A guide to</H2>
<H1>Nomad Ltd Tours</H1>
```

Tag pair formats graphic as a link

FIGURE C-7: Web page containing linked graphic

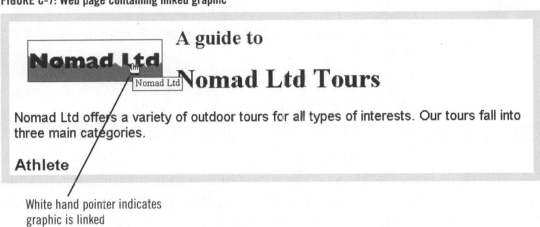

A guide to
Nomad Ltd Tours

Nomad Ltd offers a variety of outdoor tours for all types of interests. Our tours fall into three main categories.

Athlete

White hand pointer indicates graphic is linked

FIGURE C-8: Web page code containing links to the second page of the Web site

```
Shop online to get from your desk to the outdoors without wasting time.
<BR><BR>
Get the <A HREF="tours-c.htm">tickets</A>, get the <A
HREF="construction.htm">gear</A>, and <B> get out there</B>.
<BR><BR>

<UL>
  <LI><A HREF="construction.htm">sporting gear</A>
  <LI><A HREF="tours-c.htm">adventure travel</A>
  <LI><A HREF="construction.htm">about Nomad Ltd</A>
</UL>
```

Target changed for first link

Target changed in bulleted list

Inserting an Image Map

While the ability to link a graphical image to a Web page is a useful tool in Web page design, sometimes a single graphic conveys information that's appropriate for more than one link. You can take advantage of such an image by making it into an **image map**, a graphic that has different areas which are linked to different Web pages. Each of these areas, known as **hot spots**, is defined with a coordinate system that uses the <MAP> and <AREA> tags. The image map information associated with a graphic can be located anywhere in a Web document; you specify a name for each map, and use the USEMAP attribute to reference the map name in the <IMG> tag that uses it. Because it's a challenging task to specify the exact pixel coordinates of areas within a graphic, most Web designers use software that simplifies image map creation by allowing you to draw the hot spots over the graphic.
Grace has designed a graphic that shows the locations of popular travel destinations in the United States. She also has created an image map for the graphic; the image map splits the image into three hot spots. She wants to insert the image map code into the home page she's creating.

Steps

1. Click the **text editor program button** on the taskbar, open the file **HTM C-3.txt**, then examine the code in the file
   This file contains the image map information that Grace created. Along with inserting the correct values in the <MAP> and <AREA> tags, the software Grace used also generated the <IMG> tag for the associated graphic.

QuickTip

To ensure that you select all the text in the file, you can click Edit, then click Select All.

2. Select **all the text in the file**, press [Ctrl][C] to copy it to the Clipboard, then close the file, if necessary

3. Open the file **nomad-c.htm** in the text editor, place the insertion point in the blank line above the **<UL> tag**, press [Enter], press [Ctrl][V] to paste the image map code from the Clipboard, then press [Enter]
   Figure C-9 shows the completed code for the Web page containing the image map.

4. Save your work, click the **browser program button** on the taskbar, then reload the **nomad-c.htm** page
   The image map indicating the locations of popular destinations appears as shown in Figure C-10.

Trouble?

Some versions of Netscape Navigator display ALT text for only the first hot spot over which the pointer moves.

5. Move the pointer over the **graphic showing travel destinations**
   The text Grace specified for each <AREA> tag's ALT attribute appears in a box when the pointer is over the matching hot spot. In addition to the pointing hand icon, the appearance of this text is another cue for the user that this image contains links.

6. Click the **Sequoia National Park hot spot** on the image map
   A Sequoia National Park Web page that Grace has begun to create opens.

7. Click the **Nomad logo** in the upper-left corner of the browser window
   The logo's placement and link are consistent with Grace's site navigation plan, and the Nomad home page reopens.

8. Click the **Grand Teton Mountains hot spot** to open its link, click the **Nomad logo** to return to the home page, click the **Appalachian Trail hot spot**, then click the **Nomad logo** to return to the home page
   All three hot spots work as Grace intended.

FIGURE C-9: Completed code for Web page containing image map

```
<BR><BR>
Get the <A HREF="tours-c.htm">tickets</A>, get the <A
HREF="construction.htm">gear</A>, and <B> get out there</B>.
<BR><BR>

<MAP NAME="parks">
<AREA HREF="apptrail.htm" SHAPE="poly" COORDS="270, 0, 270, 205, 95, 205, 213,
0" ALT="Appalachian Trail">
<AREA HREF="sequoia.htm" SHAPE="poly" COORDS="94, 205, 0, 205, 0, 42, 132,
137" ALT="Sequoia National Park">
<AREA HREF="teton.htm" SHAPE="poly" COORDS="2 2, 0, 132, 136, 42, 71, 42, 0"
ALT="Grand Teton Mountains">
</MAP>

<IMG SRC="images/ideas.gif" WIDTH="270" HEIGHT="205" ALIGN="right" BORDER="0"
ALT="U.S. map showing locations of popular destinations" USEMAP="#parks" >

<UL>
```

Code for Appalachian Trail hot spot

Code for Sequoia National Park hot spot

Code for Grand Teton Mountains hot spot

HTML code for hot spot coordinates

Preformatted <IMG> tag

FIGURE C-10: Web page containing image map

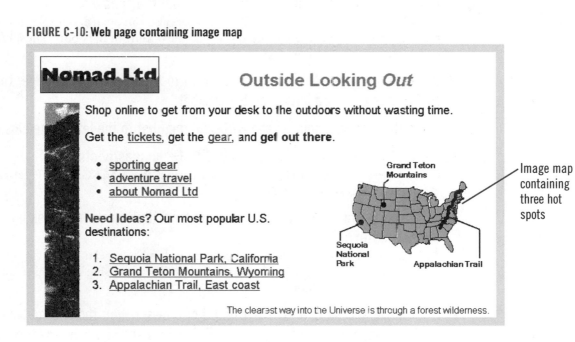

Image map containing three hot spots

TABLE C-4: Image map tags

tag or tag pair	function	attribute	specifies	example
<MAP>.. </MAP>	marks a section of HTML code as a named image map	NAME	name of image map (for reference by <IMG> tag)	<MAP NAME="parks">
<AREA>	describes shape and function of a hot spot	HREF	target link address	<AREA HREF="sequoia.htm"
		SHAPE	geometric shape of area; can be "circle," "rect" (rectangle), or "poly" (polygon)	SHAPE="poly"
		COORDS	pixel coordinates that describe the boundaries of the hot spot	COORDS="94, 205, 0, 205, 0, 42, 132, 137"
		ALT	alternate text to display or speak	ALT="Sequoia National Park">

Adding a Background Image

By default, Web pages appear with the background color set by the user's computer; that color is usually white. HTML allows you to replace the default background with an image, giving you access to another design tool. An image that you select for a Web page background needs to contrast well with the page's text and other elements. Because most Web pages format text in dark colors, such as the default of black, it's best for a background image to be a light color so the page remains legible. Additionally, the best background images have uniform color, so that users then can read text that appears over any part of the image. ✈ One of Grace's co-workers in the graphic design department gave her a graphic of a pair of hiking boots, which is suitable for use as a background image. She decides to add it to the Nomad home page to accent the page's outdoor theme.

Steps 1 2 3 4

Trouble?

If you don't see the file bootbg.jpg listed in the images folder, make sure the Files of type list box in the Open window displays either "All Files" Or "JPEG Files."

1. In your browser, open the file **bootbg.jpg** from the "images" folder

In addition to HTML documents, Web browsers also can open and display graphic files. The boots graphic is light colored, and shows just the outline of the boots. Thus, Web page users still will be able to read the text.

2. Click the browser's **Back** button to return to the Nomad home page, then click the **text editor program button** on the taskbar

3. Place the insertion point in the **<BODY> tag**, just to the left of the closing **>**

4. Press **[Spacebar]**, then type **BACKGROUND="images/bootbg.jpg"**

Grace references the background image using the BACKGROUND attribute of the <BODY> tag, as shown in Figure C-11.

5. Save your work, click the **browser program button** on the taskbar, then reload **nomad-c.htm**

As Figure C-12 shows, Grace's small background image repeats, so that it covers the entire page. This effect is called **tiling** because of its similarity to using identical small tiles to cover a large area such as a floor.

6. If you have access to a different brand of browser than the one you've used to view your Web page in this lesson, start that Web browser, and open the file **nomad-c.htm** in the second browser

Because different browsers interpret some HTML code differently, Grace makes sure she has access to the two most popular browsers—Netscape Navigator and Microsoft Internet Explorer—and she previews her page in both browsers to ensure that the page appears as she intended.

7. Close your browser(s) and text editor

FIGURE C-11: Web page to include the background image

```
<HTML>

<HEAD>
<TITLE>Nomad Ltd</TITLE>
</HEAD>

<BODY BACKGROUND="images/bootbg.jpg">
<FONT FACE="arial, helvetica, sans serif">

<IMG SRC="images/nomad.gif" ALIGN="left" HEIGHT="63" WIDTH="201" ALT="Nomad
Ltd">
```

BACKGROUND attribute references background image

FIGURE C-12: Web page containing tiled background image

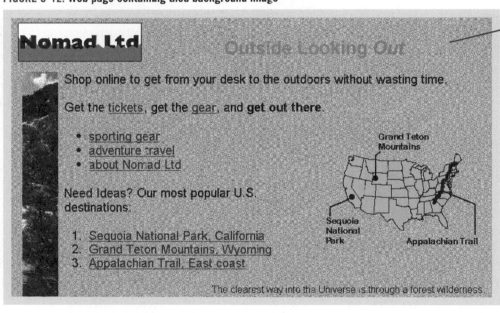

Background image is tiled to cover entire page

Applying a background color

In addition to using an image, you also can specify a color for your Web page's background. You indicate a color in the <BODY> tag by setting the BGCOLOR attribute equal to the color's hexadecimal equivalent. As with a background image, it's important to select a background color that contrasts well with a page's text.

Exploring Multimedia Options

Advances in Web page design have always concentrated on increasing interactivity and making more information user-accessible, without increasing a page's clutter. In addition to adding features to HTML, today's cutting-edge advances toward these goals focus on integrating sound and video with a page's basic text and graphics. The product of this integration is known as **multimedia**. One obstacle to multimedia Web sites has been **bandwidth**, which is the data transfer capacity of a Web user's Internet connection. Because video and audio files have been much larger than HTML and image files, the download time for a Web page that included video or audio blocked its smooth integration into Web pages. Recently, multimedia has become a reality on the Web as the result of two trends: high-bandwidth Internet connections (such as DSL and cable modems), and improved compression that shrinks the size of video and audio files. Today you can be certain when you publish a multimedia Web page that many users will experience all of the page's aspects. Table C-5 summarizes the requirements for creating and playing back the main multimedia technologies. Grace has not yet planned for any multimedia in her Web site design, and wants to keep her site simple for now. However, she decides to learn more about Web multimedia so she'll understand her options as she plans for the future of the Nomad Ltd site. Multimedia implementations on the Web include:

 ### Animated GIF

The GIF file format for images allows you to combine two or more images into a single file, and to include instructions on how the images are presented. Creating such a file, known as an **animated GIF**, was for years the only widely viewable multimedia effect on the Web. Low-cost or free software is readily available for creating such effects; one program is shown in Figure C-13. The animated GIF is most prevalent in Web page banner advertisements, as it allows advertisers to display one or two images to attract a reader's interest before displaying the company logo or other target information.

 ### Macromedia Flash animation

Flash animation is a recently developed multimedia technology, owned by Macromedia Inc. Such an animation can be created only with Macromedia's Flash software, which allows designers to create complex and highly compressed multimedia animations. Flash animations use an image format of higher quality than any of the common Web graphics formats. To experience a Flash animation, users must install a small program that works with the browser. Users can download this software, called an **add-on**, from the Web for free.

 ### Traditional audio and video

Recent higher-bandwidth connections and more compressed formats have facilitated the wider incorporation of traditional audio and video media into Web sites. Many news organizations, such as printed newspapers and television stations, include relevant video clips alongside articles on their Web sites; musicians and record companies also use the Web to promote music and videos. As shown in Figure C-14, a clip often is embedded as a link, which a user can click to view or hear the associated file. Many radio and television stations have added **Webcasting** to their Web sites, meaning that they make their stations' normal programming available live on their Web sites. This technology also has allowed people and organizations to disseminate video and audio media programming without the financial costs of using traditional media channels.

FIGURE C-13: Animated GIF frames in a creation tool

Tools for creating and editing animation

Individual frames of bird in flight

Tools for changing properties of selected frame

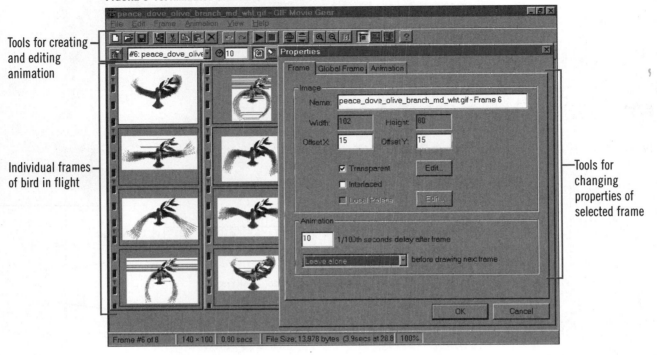

FIGURE C-14: Web site for musical artist with video and audio links

Link to online audio

Link to online video

TABLE C-5: Comparison of multimedia options

technology	creation tool(s)	playback tool
animated GIF	software commonly available, free or at low cost	Web browser
Flash animation	Macromedia Flash software	Web browser with Flash add-on
traditional audio and video	audio and/or video computer translation hardware, with associated software	Web browser

Practice

▶ Concepts Review

Name the function of each section of code indicated in Figure C-15.

FIGURE C-15

```
1 ── <BODY BACKGROUND="images/bootbg.jpg">
     <FONT FACE="arial, helvetica, sans serif">

2 ── <IMG SRC="images/nomad.gif" ALIGN="left" HEIGHT="63" WIDTH="201" ALT="Nomad
     Ltd">

     <BR>                                                                    ─── 5
     <H2 ALIGN="center"><FONT COLOR="#238E68">Outside Looking
     <EM>Out</EM></FONT></H2>
                                                                             ─── 6
     <IMG SRC="images/tree.jpg" ALIGN="left" HEIGHT="468" WIDTH="58" ALT="View
     through an evergreen toward a mountainous skyline and blue sky" HSPACE="10">

     Shop online to get from your desk to the outdoors without wasting time.
     <BR><BR>
     Get the <A HREF="tours-c.htm">tickets</A>, get the <A
     HREF="construction.htm">gear</A>, and <B> get out there</B>.
     <BR><BR>

3 ── <MAP NAME="parks">
     <AREA HREF="apptrail.htm" SHAPE="poly" COORDS="270, 0, 270, 205, 95, 205, 213,
     0" ALT="Appalachian Trail">
4 ── <AREA HREF="sequoia.htm" SHAPE="poly" COORDS="94, 205, 0, 205, 0, 42, 132,
     137" ALT="Sequoia National Park">
     <AREA HREF="teton.htm" SHAPE="poly" COORDS="212, 0, 132, 136, 42, 71, 42, 0"
     ALT="Grand Teton Mountains">
     </MAP>
```

Match each statement with the term it describes.

7. A graphic in which different areas are linked to different Web pages
8. Each linked area in an image map
9. A graphic that allows any user to see text in a font selected by the designer
10. A group of technologies that allows faster downloads
11. One of the points of light that makes up the display on a computer screen

a. Broadband
b. Hot spot
c. Pixel
d. Image map
e. Text image

Select the best answer from the list of choices.

12. Which one of the following is a graphics file format commonly used on the Internet?
    a. MP3
    b. JPG
    c. TIFF
    d. BMP

13. Which one of the following attributes for the <IMG> tag adds space to the left and right of the image?
    a. ALIGN
    b. VSPACE
    c. SRC
    d. HSPACE

14. Which one of the following attributes for the <IMG> tag specifies the name of the image file to display?
    a. ALT
    b. VSPACE
    c. SRC
    d. HSPACE

15. Which one of the following attributes for the <IMG> tag is sometimes used to specify alternate text to replace the image?
    a. ALT
    b. VSPACE
    c. SRC
    d. HSPACE

16. To specify a background image for a Web page, you add an attribute to which tag?
    a. <HTML>
    b. <HEAD>
    c. <BODY>
    d. <IMG>

17. Which <IMG> attribute(s) do you use to specify a graphic's display dimensions?
    a. COORDS
    b. SHAPE
    c. HSPACE and VSPACE
    d. HEIGHT and WIDTH

18. The default measurement unit for image size is
    a. Pixels.
    b. Inches.
    c. Centimeters.
    d. Millimeters.

HTML

19. Which has long been the only widely viewable multimedia effect on the Web?
    a. JPG graphics
    b. Animated GIFs
    c. Macromedia Flash
    d. Traditional audio and video

 # Skills Review

1. Insert graphics.
    a. Start your text editor, open the file HTM C-4.htm, then save it as a text document with the filename cco-c.htm.
    b. Position the insertion point on the blank line just above the line that starts with "<UL>", press [Enter], type "<IMG SRC="images/glasses.jpg" ALIGN="left">", then press [Enter].
    c. Save your work, start your Web browser, then open the file cco-c.htm in your browser.
    d. In your text editor, move the insertion point to the end of the line containing the "<IMG> tag" you inserted, press [Enter], type "

", then press [Enter].
    e. Move the insertion point to the blank line below the "</UL> tag", press [Enter], type "

", then press [Enter].
    f. Save your work.
    g. Reload the page in your browser to verify the graphics.

2. Specify graphic size.
    a. In your text editor, locate the "<IMG>" tag that references the graphic "glasses.jpg", then move the insertion point near the end of the line, just to the left of the closing ">".
    b. Press [Spacebar], then type "HEIGHT="186" WIDTH="250" ALT="Top-quality eyewear"".
    c. Save your work, then reload the page in your browser.
    d. In your text editor, locate the "<IMG>" tag that references the graphic "glasses.jpg," then move the insertion point near the end of the line, just to the left of the closing ">".
    e. Press [Spacebar], then type "HSPACE="5"".
    f. Save your work.
    g. Reload the page in your browser.

3. Link graphics.
    a. In your text editor, open the file HTM C-5.htm, then save it as a text file with the name styles-c.htm.
    b. Locate the "<IMG>" tag that references the graphic "cco.gif", move the insertion point to the beginning of the line, type "<A HREF="cco-c.htm">", then press [Enter].
    c. Click the blank line after the "<IMG> tag", type "</A>", then press [Enter].
    d. Save your work, then view the file styles-c.htm in your browser.
    e. Click the Crystal Clear Optics logo in the upper-left corner.
    f. In your text editor open the file cco-c.htm.
    g. Locate the first list item, Basic Styles in the bulleted list, select the filename "construction.htm" in the first <A> tag, press [Delete], then type "styles-c.htm".
    h. Save your work, reload the file cco-c.htm in your browser, click the first link in the bulleted list, Basic Styles, then click the Crystal Clear Optics logo in the page that opens.

4. Insert an image map.

a. In your text editor, open the file HTM C-6.txt, then examine the code in this file.

b. Select all the text in the file, press [Ctrl][C] to copy it to the Clipboard, then close the file if necessary.

c. In your text editor, open the file cco-c.htm, place the insertion point in the blank line above the "<IMG> tag", press [Enter], press [Ctrl][V] to paste the image map code from the Clipboard, then press [Enter].

d. Move the insertion point near the end of the "<IMG> tag", just to the left of the closing ">", press [Spacebar], then type "BORDER="0" USEMAP="#glasses"".

e. Save your work, then reload the file cco-c.htm in your browser.

f. Move the pointer over the graphic showing a pair of glasses.

g. Click one of the "lenses" hot spots on the image map.

h. Click the Crystal Clear Opticals logo in the upper-left corner of the browser window to return to the home page.

i. Click anywhere on the "frames" hot spot to open its link, then click the Crystal Clear Opticals logo to return to the home page.

5. Add a background image.

a. In your browser, open the file eggshell.jpg from the "images" folder.

b. Click the browser's Back button to return to the CCO home page, then open the text editor.

c. Place the insertion point in the "<BODY>" tag, just to the left of the closing ">".

d. Press [Spacebar] then type "BACKGROUND="images/eggshell.jpg"".

e. Save your work.

f. Reload the page in your browser.

g. If you have access to another Web browser besides the one you've been using (Netscape Navigator, Microsoft Internet Explorer, or others), start that Web browser, and open your Web page in the second browser to verify that the elements appear as you intended.

6. Explore multimedia options.

a. Review the different types of multimedia described in this unit, then consider how you might incorporate one multimedia format into the Crystal Clear Opticals Web page.

b. Print the Crystal Clear Opticals Web page as it appears in the browser.

c. Sketch the multimedia object's placement in your printout

d. Write a description of the multimedia object you sketched. Include a detailed description of the graphics and/or sound it plays, its benefits to the Web page's design, and its potential drawbacks for the page's users.

e. Close and exit your browser(s) and text editor.

▶ Independent Challenges

1. You have been working on a Web page for your consulting business, Star Dot Star. A friend who is studying graphic arts has created a logo for you, and gave you a copy in a Web-ready file format. Now you want to add the logo to your Web page, along with a background image.

To complete this independent challenge:

a. Start your text editor, open the file HTM C-7.htm, then save it as a text document with the filename sds-c.htm.

b. Insert the file sds.jpg from the images folder above the <H1> text; be sure to specify height (155), width (214), alignment, and alternate text (*.*).

c. Save your work.

d. Start your Web browser, and preview the Web page in your browser.

e. In your text editor, add 10 pixels of horizontal space around the logo graphic.

f. Use <BR> tags to insert space before and after the headings, so that only the heading text appears to the right of the logo graphic in the browser.

g. If you have access to another Web browser besides the one you've been using (Netscape Navigator, Microsoft Internet Explorer, or others), start that Web browser, and open your Web page in the second browser to verify that the elements appear as you intended.

2. In your job with the local water department, Metro Water, you have created a basic Web site that eventually will provide information on water resources in your area. Your co-workers in the public relations department have given you a copy of the department logo, in GIF format. You also have located an appropriate background image for the page; you want to enhance the page's layout and appearance by adding these graphics.

To complete this independent challenge:

a. In your text editor, open the file HTM C-8.htm and save it as mw-c.htm.

b. Insert the graphic mw.gif from the images folder so it appears in the upper-left corner of the Web page. Be sure to include alternate text (water spout), and image dimensions (147 x 147).

c. Adjust the page layout by adding horizontal space around the image, and inserting line breaks before and after the text. The heading text should appear to the right of the graphic, and the rest of the page's text should appear below the graphic.

d. Add the graphic waterbg.jpg from the images folder as the page's background.

WEB WORK

3. You have begun work on an HTML-based in-store information system at your video store, Film Clips. You want to enhance the home page layout by adding graphics. Instead of using text links on the home page, you also have created a text image from which you want to create an image map.

To complete this independent challenge:

a. Create a basic Web page for the store. The page should contain the store name and introductory information on how to use the Web browser. Save your file as fc-c.htm. Use at least two different text formats.

b. Connect to the Internet, start your Web browser, and use your browser to go to a search engine, such as one of the following:

www.google.com

www.altavista.com

www.yahoo.com

If you have trouble locating a search engine, go to *www.course.com*, navigate to the page for this book, click the link for the Student Online Companion, click the link for this unit, and use the links listed there as a starting point for your search.

c. Use the search engine to find pages containing free film- or video-related clip art, then download an appropriate image for your Web page. (*Hint*: You might use search terms such as "film", "clip art", and/or "video".)

d. Add the image to your Web page, then adjust the page layout if necessary to make the image fit appropriately. If possible, be sure to preview the page in different browsers.

e. If you have access to software that allows you to create image maps, use it to map each rectangle on the image file "genres.jpg" to the placeholder file "construction.jpg". Be sure to add appropriate alternate text for each hot spot. (*Hint:* If you have trouble using the software, most programs provide access to a Help system when you press [F1] or click Help on the menu bar.)

f. If you created an image map, add it to your Web page, along with the appropriate <IMG> tag for the associated graphic file, "genres.jpg". Test each hot spot on the image map to be sure the link works, and that the alternate text appears when the pointer is over the hot spot. If possible, repeat the test in a different browser.

WEB WORK

4. Learning how to create and integrate multimedia into your Web pages is beyond the scope of this unit. However, it's a good practice to become familiar with the features of each technology, and with the different ways that Web designers are using those features.

To complete this independent challenge:

a. Connect to the Internet, start your Web browser, and use your browser to open one of the following pages:

macromedia.com/showcase (Flash animations)

www.animfactory.com (animated GIFs)

www.oneparadigm.com/newspaper.html (traditional audio/video)

If you have trouble opening these sites, go to *www.course.com*, navigate to the page for this book, click the link for the Student Online Companion, click the link for this unit, and use the links listed there as a starting point for your search.

b. Choose one of the three multimedia formats, and open and examine at least three examples of how it is used.

If you chose Flash animations or traditional audio/video, complete the following:

c. For each page you examine, write a paragraph analyzing the multimedia content. Include a description of how it was used, how it enhanced the page, how it detracted from the page (if applicable), and how you would change or add to the multimedia on each of the pages you find.

If you chose animated GIF, complete the following:

d. Write a paragraph analyzing each animation you examine. Include a description of the idea the animation conveyed or its purpose, the context in which it would be useful, how it would enhance a Web page, how it might detract from a page, and how you would change or add to the animation for specific applications.

HTML

▶ Visual Workshop

At your job at Touchstone Booksellers, a small bookstore, you have been talking with the owner about the potential benefits of doing business on the Web. You were excited to recently learn that she has assigned you the task of developing the store's Web site. You have been working on a basic Web page for the store, and want to polish the appearance of the page by adding graphics. In your text editor, open the file HTM C-9.htm, save it as a text document called tsb-c.htm, then edit the file to match the Web page shown in Figure C-16. Use the file eggshell.jpg for the background, and book.gif (148 X 148) for the open book image. Be sure to include alternate text for the book image as shown in the figure.

FIGURE C-16

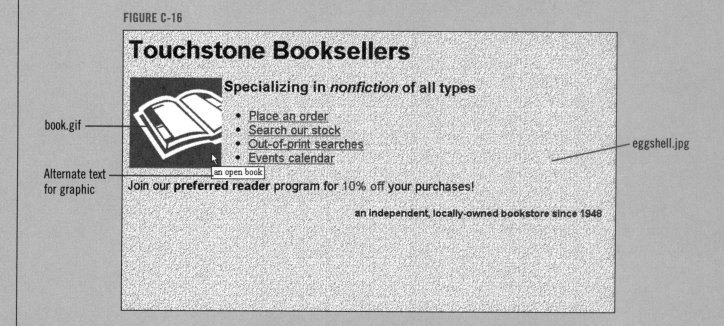

Using
Forms to Control Input

Objectives

► Plan a form
► Create a text entry field
► Add radio buttons
► Add checkboxes
► Create a pull-down menu
► Add a push button
► Connect a form's back end

While the Web is an effective means to make information available, HTML also includes interactive aspects. On many Web sites, in addition to reading information, users can submit information as well. The main HTML element that facilitates interactivity is called a form. A **form** is the set of Web page elements with which you interact to submit a query to a search engine or provide credit card and shipping information when you make purchases on the Web. ◢◣ Grace Dekmejian works in the Information Systems department at Nomad Ltd, a travel and sporting goods company. Nomad is forming a corporate division to handle online sales. Along with her co-workers, Grace is creating a company Web site. The next task for Grace and her Web development team is to create a Web page form that allows potential customers to provide the necessary information to complete their orders.

Planning a Form

Including a form on your Web site is a simple and straightforward way to allow your site's users to send you feedback or other information. If you are using the Web to sell products or services, forms are vital. As shown in Figure D-1, a Web form can allow users to enter information, but it also can provide predefined choices from which users can select. Most forms include several **fields**, which are the form elements, such as text boxes or pull-down menus, that allow user input. Each field or group of fields is usually associated with a **label**, which is the text that explains what information is required by the adjacent field. Grace has met with her co-workers who are designing the Nomad online store, to determine the information users need to provide when making an online purchase. Grace reviews the different types of form fields available in HTML, and selects the most appropriate field for each type of information. Figure D-2 shows the sketch of Grace's planned form, she plans to create, which includes the following types of fields:

Details

 Single-line text box

A single-line text box is ideal for requesting limited user input, such as first or last name, or street address. HTML allows you to specify the size of a single-line text box, as well as the maximum character length of user input allowed.

 Checkboxes and radio buttons

Checkboxes and radio buttons simplify Web forms by allowing users to select from a list of options. Users can select multiple checkboxes, which are ideal for a set of options from which a user might choose either none, one, or several—for example, pizza toppings. On the other hand, within a set of radio buttons, a user can select only one. Radio buttons are the best choice for a mutually exclusive set of choices, such as t-shirt size (S, M, L, or XL).

 Pull-down menus and scroll boxes

Pull-down menus and scroll boxes both serve a similar function to radio buttons: they allow users to make one selection from among multiple items. When your list of choices is lengthy, pull-down menus and scroll boxes conserve Web page space. A pull-down menu shows one choice by default, and displays the remaining choices after a user clicks the down arrow. By contrast, a scroll box always shows the same number of choices, which is customizable. Users view the hidden options by clicking an arrow and scrolling through the list.

 Multi-line text areas

Multi-line text areas are designed to allow less-structured input by the user. Such an area is often used to allow additional comments or questions at the end of a form. You can specify the dimensions of this area on the page.

 Push buttons

HTML includes code to create two kinds of predefined buttons that users can click to execute common form-related tasks. You can configure one of these buttons to submit the information entered by users to the appropriate processing system. The other button allows users to clear information they have entered and start over.

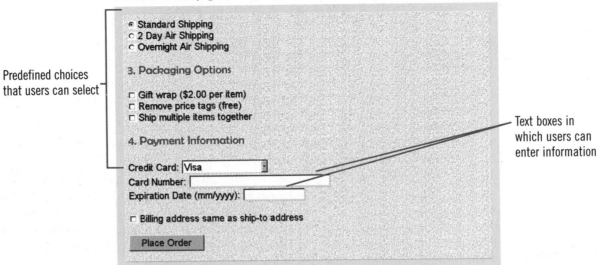

Predefined choices
that users can select

Text boxes in
which users can
enter information

FIGURE D-2: Grace's sketch of the Nomad Ltd checkout form

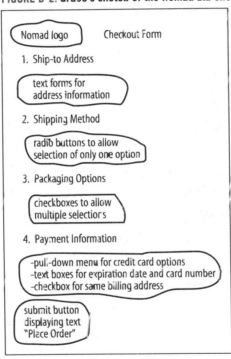

Web users and privacy

Surveys consistently show that most Web users are concerned that their personal information is not adequately secure when they interact on the Web. The topic of security is important when considering whether your Web site will include forms which are often designed to collect information that people want to keep as private as possible. A Web designer is not often in a position to decide a company's policy on use of personal information collected from Web users. You can, however, make users of your site feel more secure by clearly communicating your organization's policy regarding use of the information you request. Nearly all Web sites that request information allow users to select options within the form that keep their information off e-mail and printed material mailing lists. Finally, sometimes organizations want to collect additional information if users are willing to provide it. Be sure your Web page makes it clear that such fields are optional; then you avoid losing the business of potential customers who refuse to answer such questions.

HTML

Creating a Text Entry Field

In HTML, the text and fields that compose a form are always surrounded by the <FORM>..</FORM> tag pair. Within a form, you add most common fields with the <INPUT> tag, and use the TYPE attribute to specify the kind of field you want to create. To create a text entry field, you set the TYPE attribute value to "text". Table D-1 explains the syntax and commonly-used attributes for the <FORM>..</FORM> and <INPUT> tags. Text entry fields are useful for collecting basic information in most forms, which usually include the user's name and address. ▰▰▰ Grace has already created the HTML document structure for the form, and has inserted headings for the various sections of the form. She also added comments indicating where each form element should be placed. She begins coding the form by adding the <FORM>..</FORM> tag pair to her document. She uses, the <INPUT> tag to create the text fields and labels for shipping and billing information.

Steps

1. Start your text editor program, then open the file **HTM D-1.htm**, and save it as a text document with the filename **nomad-d.htm**

2. Select the text **<!-- BEGIN FORM -->** near the top of the document, press **[Delete]**, then type **<FORM NAME="checkout">**
Although Grace doesn't expect to immediately make use of the NAME values, she plans to include the NAME attribute with each of her form elements to facilitate future enhancements to the form.

3. Move the insertion point near the bottom of the document, select the text **<!-- END FORM -->**, press **[Delete]**, then type **</FORM>**
Grace will enter code for all her form fields between these beginning and ending tags.

4. Move the insertion point near the top of the document, select the text **<!-- SHIPPING ADDRESS - TEXT ENTRY FIELDS -->**, then press **[Delete]**

5. Type **First Name: <INPUT TYPE="text" SIZE="20" NAME="shipfirstname">**, press **[Enter]**, press **[Spacebar] four times**, type **
, then press **[Enter]
This step creates the label and associated field where the user will enter the first name of the order's recipient. The SIZE attribute specifies the width of the text box. Just like the NAME attribute associated with the <FORM> tag in Step 2, including NAME for each form element makes it easier to add advanced features to your form in the future.

6. Enter the remaining code for the shipping information section, as shown in Figure D-3
This portion of your completed HTML document should look like the one shown in Figure D-3, although your lines may wrap differently.

7. Save your work, start your Web browser, then open the file **nomad-d.htm** in your browser
The text entry boxes and labels appear beneath the heading "1. Ship-to Address," as shown in Figure D-4.

8. Click in the **First Name text box**, type your first name, press **[Tab]**, type your last name in the **Last Name text box**, then continue to press **[Tab]** to complete the remaining fields using your own (or fictitious) information
Grace tests her fields to be sure that they allow input as expected, and that the length of each field is appropriate.

FIGURE D-3: Web page code containing form and text box tags

Opening <FORM> tag

Form field labels

<INPUT> tags for text entry boxes

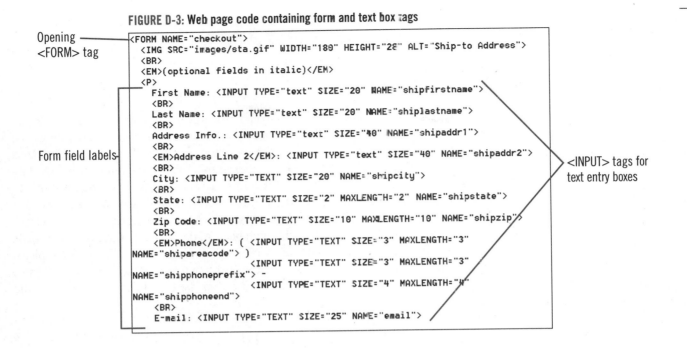

```
<FORM NAME="checkout">
 <IMG SRC="images/sta.gif" WIDTH="189" HEIGHT="28" ALT="Ship-to Address">
 <BR>
 <EM>(optional fields in italic)</EM>
 <P>
  First Name: <INPUT TYPE="text" SIZE="20" NAME="shipfirstname">
  <BR>
  Last Name: <INPUT TYPE="text" SIZE="20" NAME="shiplastname">
  <BR>
  Address Info.: <INPUT TYPE="text" SIZE="40" NAME="shipaddr1">
  <BR>
  <EM>Address Line 2</EM>: <INPUT TYPE="text" SIZE="40" NAME="shipaddr2">
  <BR>
  City: <INPUT TYPE="TEXT" SIZE="20" NAME="shipcity">
  <BR>
  State: <INPUT TYPE="TEXT" SIZE="2" MAXLENGTH="2" NAME="shipstate">
  <BR>
  Zip Code: <INPUT TYPE="TEXT" SIZE="10" MAXLENGTH="10" NAME="shipzip">
  <BR>
  <EM>Phone</EM>: ( <INPUT TYPE="TEXT" SIZE="3" MAXLENGTH="3"
NAME="shipareacode"> )
                   <INPUT TYPE="TEXT" SIZE="3" MAXLENGTH="3"
NAME="shipphoneprefix"> -
                   <INPUT TYPE="TEXT" SIZE="4" MAXLENGTH="4"
NAME="shipphoneend">
  <BR>
  E-mail: <INPUT TYPE="TEXT" SIZE="25" NAME="email">
```

FIGURE D-4: Web page displaying labeled text boxes

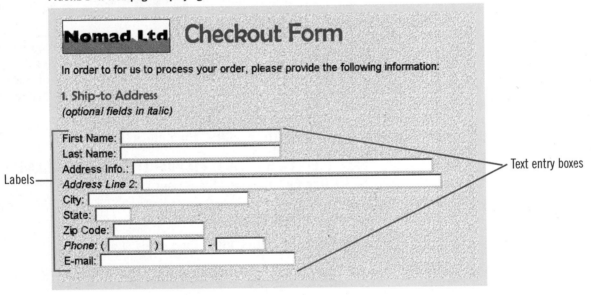

Labels

Text entry boxes

TABLE D-1: Common form field tags

tag(s)	attribute	description	example
<FORM>..</FORM>	NAME	creates a form name; used to easily reference a form when adding advanced features	<FORM NAME= "checkout">..</FORM>
<INPUT>	TYPE	specifies the type of form field to create	<INPUT TYPE="text">
	SIZE	specifies the display length of the form field	<INPUT SIZE="20">
	MAXLENGTH	sets the largest number of characters allowed in the current form field; extra typing is ignored after this number is reached	<INPUT MAXLENGTH="40">

Adding Radio Buttons

Text boxes are ideal tools for allowing form users to enter the information unique to each person. But, in many other situations, you can reduce the potential for user input error by providing a list of choices from which the user can select. This eliminates the possibility that a user will enter a selection that the order-processing system doesn't understand. HTML includes several list formats for forms; each format is appropriate for different situations and types of information. To create a set of options that a user can see all at once, and from which a user can make only one selection, you create radio buttons. **Radio buttons** are small white circles, each appearing next to explanatory text. When a user clicks a circle, it fills with black to designate it as selected. You create radio buttons using the <INPUT> tag, with the TYPE attribute set to "radio." Table D-2 explains the <INPUT> attributes commonly used when creating radio buttons. Nomad offers its customers a choice between three shipping speeds. Grace adds these to the form as a set of radio buttons.

Steps

1. In your text editor, select the text **<!-- SHIPPING METHOD - RADIO BUTTONS -->** near the middle of the document

2. Press **[Delete]**, then type **<INPUT TYPE="radio" NAME="shipvia" VALUE="standard" CHECKED>Standard Shipping**, then press **[Enter]**
   Unlike most form elements, to work properly, a set of radio buttons requires the NAME attribute. HTML uses this attribute to identify the radio buttons that you group together. The NAME attribute defines the set from which users can make only one selection. The CHECKED attribute signifies that the radio button should appear as selected when the page opens in the browser.

3. Press **[Spacebar] four times**, type **
, then press **[Enter]

4. Press **[Spacebar] four times**, type **<INPUT TYPE="radio" NAME="shipvia" VALUE="priority">2 Day Air Shipping**, then press **[Enter]**
   Each remaining item in the radio button list uses the same TYPE and NAME settings as the first item, but has a different VALUE and label text.

5. Press **[Spacebar] four times**, type **
, then press **[Enter]

6. Press **[Spacebar] four times**, then type **<INPUT TYPE="radio" NAME="shipvia" VALUE="overnight"> Overnight Air Shipping**
   Your HTML document should look like the one shown in Figure D-5.

7. Save your work, click the **browser program button** on the taskbar, reload the form in the browser window, then scroll down if necessary to view the radio buttons
   The three labeled radio buttons appear as a group, as shown in Figure D-6.

8. If necessary, click the **Standard Shipping radio button**, click the **2 Day Air Shipping radio button**, then click the **Overnight Air Shipping radio button**
   When you click a radio button, a black dot appears in the center, indicating that it is selected. When a radio button is selected and you click another radio button, only the most recently clicked button is marked as selected.

FIGURE D-5: Web page code containing tags for radio button list

```
<BR><BR>

<IMG SRC="images/sm.gif" WIDTH="200" HEIGHT="28" ALT="Shipping Method">
<P>
   <INPUT TYPE="radio" NAME="shipvia" VALUE="standard" CHECKED>Standard
Shipping
   <BR>
   <INPUT TYPE="radio" NAME="shipvia" VALUE="priority">2 Day Air Shipping
   <BR>
   <INPUT TYPE="radio" NAME="shipvia" VALUE="overnight">Overnight Air
Shipping

<BR><BR>
```

<INPUT>
tags for
radio
buttons

Radio button labels

FIGURE D-6: Web page displaying radio button list

E-mail: [   ]

2. Shipping Method

Radio
button list

⊙ Standard Shipping
○ 2 Day Air Shipping
○ Overnight Air Shipping

3. Packaging Options

TABLE D-2: Radio button <INPUT> tag attributes

attribute	function	example
TYPE	setting a value to "radio" identifies the form element as a radio button	<INPUT TYPE="radio">
NAME	assigns a name to the associated radio buttons, identifying them as a group	<INPUT TYPE="radio" NAME="shipvia">
VALUE	Specifies the text to be submitted to the order- processing system if the current radio button is selected	<INPUT TYPE="radio" VALUE="priority">
CHECKED	marks the current radio button to appear in the browser as selected when page opens; only one radio button per set may include this attribute	<INPUT TYPE="radio" CHECKED>

CLUES TO USE

More about the CHECKED attribute

By default, all the fields in a set of radio buttons appear empty. This means that none of the buttons is selected unless the user clicks one of them. You can include the CHECKED attribute in the <INPUT> tag for one of the radio buttons in a set, causing it to appear as selected when the Web page opens. The CHECKED attribute can simplify the form for your users by saving them a click. It's most useful for the least expensive or most commonly selected items in a list. In general, you use the CHECKED attribute in a list that requires a selection by the user; you avoid using it in a list which doesn't require that a user make a selection.

HTML

Adding Checkboxes

While radio boxes allow users to make a single choice from a set of options, sometimes you want to allow users to make multiple selections from a list. For situations like this, HTML offers **checkboxes**, which display an array of choices that are all visible at once, and from which users may select any, all, or none. A checkbox appears as a small white box next to its label. When a user clicks an empty checkbox, a check mark appears in the box; clicking a checked box removes the check mark. You create checkboxes using the <INPUT> tag, with the TYPE attribute set to "checkbox." Unlike radio buttons, each checkbox should have a unique NAME value. Additionally, code for checkboxes does not require a VALUE attribute, and multiple checkboxes may use the CHECKED attribute to display a check mark by default.   Nomad Ltd offers customers several choices regarding how their purchases are packaged. Because these choices are not exclusive of each other, Grace adds them to the form as checkbox fields.

Steps

1. In your text editor, select the text <!--PACKAGING OPTIONS - CHECKBOXES -->, then press [Delete]

2. Type <INPUT TYPE="checkbox" NAME="wrap">Gift wrap ($2.00 per item), then press [Enter]

   This code creates a checkbox field with the name "wrap," and adds a descriptive label next to it. Because all the items in her checkbox list are optional, Grace decides not to use the CHECKED attribute.

3. Press [Spacebar] four times, type <BR>, then press [Enter]

4. Press [Spacebar] four times, type <INPUT TYPE="checkbox" NAME="tags">Remove price tags (free), then press [Enter]

5. Press [Spacebar] four times, type <BR>, then press [Enter]

6. Press [Spacebar] four times, then type <INPUT TYPE="checkbox" NAME="together">Ship multiple items together

   Your HTML document should look like the one shown in Figure D-7.

7. Save your work, click the browser program button on the taskbar, reload the form in the browser window, then scroll down if necessary to view the checkbox list

   As Figure D-8 shows, the three labeled checkboxes are grouped under the heading "Packaging Options."

8. Click each checkbox to check it, then click each checkbox again to remove the check marks

   Clicking an empty checkbox adds a check mark, while clicking a checked checkbox removes the check mark. This is known as a **toggle**.

```
<BR><BR>

<IMG SRC="images/po.gif" WIDTH="221" HEIGHT="28" ALT="Packaging Options">
<P>
  <INPUT TYPE="checkbox" NAME="wrap">Gift wrap ($2.00 per item)
  <BR>
  <INPUT TYPE="checkbox" NAME="tags">Remove price tags (free)
  <BR>
  <INPUT TYPE="checkbox" NAME="together">Ship multiple items together

<BR><BR>

<IMG SRC="images/pi.gif" WIDTH="249" HEIGHT="28" ALT="Payment Information">
```

<INPUT> tags for
checkboxes

Checkbox labels

FIGURE D-8: Web page displaying checkbox list

○ 2 Day Air Shipping
○ Overnight Air Shipping

3. Packaging Options

☐ Gift wrap ($2.00 per item)
☐ Remove price tags (free)
☐ Ship multiple items together

4. Payment Information

Checkbox list

Labeling radio buttons and checkboxes

The text that you enter as a label next to a radio button or a checkbox is just like plain text elsewhere on your Web page. Even though form fields would be meaningless to users without labels, HTML has no rules about how to label the fields. Therefore, you're free to put a label to the left or right of a field, or even above or below it. The most important guideline is to make sure it's obvious to a user which label and field go together. From a design standpoint, it's also important to make the fields easy for a user to find. This is why most Web designers align the fields on Web page forms, rather than aligning the field labels.

HTML

Creating a Pull-Down Menu

Radio buttons and checkboxes lay out a group of related options so that they all are visible on the Web page. Sometimes, however, you may want to save space on your Web page, or you may have such an extensive set of choices that it would be impractical to include all of them in the Web page's layout. For this type of situation, HTML allows you to format your options with a more efficient form field called a pull-down menu. A **pull-down menu**—or **drop-down list**—appears on the page like a single-line text field, but also contains a button marked with an arrow. When a user clicks the button, a menu of choices opens. When the user clicks a choice, the list closes, and the user's selection appears in the field. The pull-down menu is popular on Web page forms because it uses space efficiently, and because most users are already familiar with it from common operating systems and software. To create a pull-down menu, you use the <SELECT>..</SELECT> tag pair to surround the list of choices. Each choice is marked with the <OPTION> tag. Table D-3 explains the common attributes used with these tags. The last section in Grace's planned form allows customers to enter credit card information. Because Nomad Ltd accepts six different types of credit cards, Grace wants to list them in a pull-down menu to save space.

Steps

1. In your text editor, select the text **<!-- CREDIT CARD - PULL-DOWN MENU -->**, press **[Delete]**, type **Credit Card:**, then press **[Enter]**

2. Press **[Spacebar] six times**, type **<SELECT NAME="card">**, then press **[Enter]**
   The <SELECT> tag marks the start of the pull-down menu.

3. Press **[Spacebar] eight times**, type **<OPTION VALUE="v">Visa**, then press **[Enter]**

4. Repeat Step 3 to enter the remaining five options for the credit card pull-down menu, shown in Figure D-9

5. Press **[Spacebar] six times**, type **</SELECT>**, then press **[Enter]**
   The </SELECT> tag marks the end of the pull-down menu list.

QuickTip

Many Web pages also use pull-down menus to allow users to select the month and year of a credit card expiration date, rather than typing it.

6. Replace the comment **<!-- CARD INFO - TEXT ENTRY FIELDS + CHECKBOX -->** with the code shown in Figure D-9
   Your Web document should match the one shown in Figure D-9.

7. Save your work, click the **browser program button** on the taskbar, reload the form in the browser window, then scroll down to view the pull-down menu
   As shown in Figure D-10, the Web page displays a pull-down menu field in the "Payment Information" section.

8. Click the **Credit Card pull-down arrow**, then click one of the options on the menu that opens
   The option you clicked now appears in the pull-down menu box.

FIGURE D-9: Web page code containing tags for pull-down menu

Pull-down menu code

Code to replace CARD INFO comment

```
<BR><BR>

<IMG SRC="images/pi.gif" WIDTH="249" HEIGHT="28" ALT="Payment Information">
<P>
   Credit Card:
     <SELECT NAME="card">
       <OPTION VALUE="v">Visa
       <OPTION VALUE="m">MasterCard
       <OPTION VALUE="a">American Express
       <OPTION VALUE="i">Diners Club
       <OPTION VALUE="d">Discover
       <OPTION VALUE="j">JCB
     </SELECT>
   <BR>
   Card Number:
   <INPUT TYPE="text" SIZE="20" MAXLENGTH="20" NAME="cardno">
   <BR>
   Expiration Date (mm/yyyy):
   <INPUT TYPE="text" SIZE="7" MAXLENGTH="7" NAME="cardexp">
   <BR><BR>
   <INPUT TYPE="checkbox" NAME="sameaddr">Billing address same as ship-to
address

   <BR><BR>
```

FIGURE D-10: Web page displaying pull-down menu

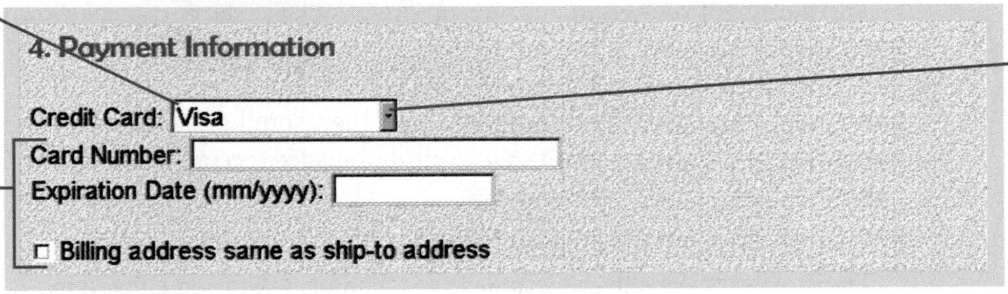

Pull-down menu displaying default menu choice

Additional Payment Information fields

Click to display menu

4. Payment Information

Credit Card: Visa
Card Number:
Expiration Date (mm/yyyy):

☐ Billing address same as ship-to address

TABLE D-3: Pull-down menu tags and attributes

tag(s)	function	attribute	description
<SELECT>.. </SELECT>	creates a list field, in which some choices are hidden; start and end tags surround list options, which are marked with <OPTION>	NAME	creates a field name; used to easily reference a field when adding advanced features
		SIZE	sets the number of items which appear by default; if omitted, choices appear as a pull-down menu; if set to 2 or more, list appears as a scroll box
		MULTIPLE	sets the number of options user may select from the list, and automatically formats list as a scroll box; if omitted, user may select only one list item
<OPTION>	precedes each item in a list field; must occur between <SELECT> and </SELECT> tags	VALUE	specifies the text to be submitted to order-processing system if the current option is selected; optional
		SELECTED	specifies the current option to appear in the field text box by default when the Web page opens in the browser

HTML

Adding a Push Button

Occasionally, while completing Web page forms, users need the browser to perform an action on the form. Most users commonly need to indicate that they are finished with the form, and they need to submit their information to your organization for processing. To allow users to execute tasks, HTML forms include **push buttons**, which are labeled objects that a user can click to perform a task. You create a push button using the <INPUT> tag, and you specify its functions with different attributes. HTML includes two predefined functions, reset and submit, that you can assign to buttons by using the TYPE attribute. A **reset button** clears all the input in a form, allowing a user to start over. Reset buttons are no longer common on the Web, since forms today are generally easy to edit. The **submit button** performs one of the most common form activities: submitting information for processing. Table D-4 explains basic <INPUT> attributes for creating a submit button. According to her sketch, Grace needs to add just one more element to her form: a submit button.

1. In your text editor, select the text **<!-- SUBMIT BUTTON -->** near the bottom of the Web document, then press **[Delete]**

2. Type **<INPUT TYPE="submit" VALUE="Place Order" NAME="order">**
   This portion of your HTML document should look like the document shown in Figure D-11.

3. Save your work, then click the **browser program button** on the taskbar

4. Reload the form in the browser window, then scroll down to view the submit button
   Grace added a submit button code to create a shaded rectangular button with the text "Place Order," as shown in Figure D-12.

5. Click the **Place Order button**
   The browser reloads the page and clears the information you entered in the form. Once the Nomad Ltd online ordering system is functional, it will respond to the submission by opening a different Web page, confirming that the user's order was received.

TABLE D-4: Basic <INPUT> attributes for push buttons

attribute	description
TYPE	**submit** creates a button for sending entered data to the organization for processing **reset** clears all the fields in the current form **button** creates a generic button that you can customize using advanced Web authoring skills **image** uses a graphic (specified by the SRC attribute) as the button
NAME	creates a field name; used to easily reference a field when adding advanced features
VALUE	defines the text that appears on the button, as well as the value submitted to the order-processing system when the current button is pushed

FIGURE D-11: Web page code containing tag for push button

<INPUT>
tag for
submit
push button

```
<BR><BR>

<INPUT TYPE="submit" VALUE="Place Order" NAME="order">
</FORM>

</BODY>
```

FIGURE D-12: Web page displaying push button

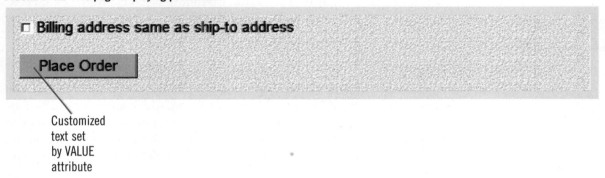

☐ **Billing address same as ship-to address**

Place Order

Customized
text set
by VALUE
attribute

Using a graphic as a push button

The VALUE attribute allows you to customize the text on a push button to fit its specific function on your Web pages. You can further customize a button to fit your page's overall theme by specifying a graphic to use as a button. To use a graphic as a push button, set the <INPUT> tag TYPE attribute to "image," and specify the path and name of the graphic file with the SRC attribute. Like other images in your Web pages, you should specify alternate text for a graphical button by using the ALT attribute.

FIGURE D-13: Web page using a graphic as push button

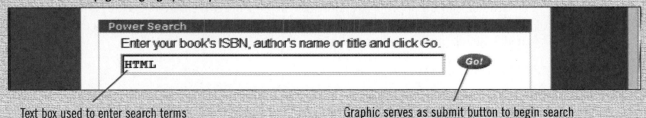

Power Search

Enter your book's ISBN, author's name or title and click Go.

HTML   Go!

Text box used to enter search terms   Graphic serves as submit button to begin search

HTML

Connecting a Form's Back End

Like tags to format other Web page elements such as text and graphics, the HTML tags for creating a form simply generate the Web page that users see in their browsers; that page is known as the **front end**. Once a user clicks the submit button, however, the information entered requires processing that is not performed by the page's HTML code. When a submit button is correctly programmed, it instructs the browser to send the entered data to your Web server for processing. The programs that reside on an organization's computer system and are responsible for processing the submitted data make up the **back end**. Figure D-14 shows the different parts of the front end and the back end, and how data moves between them. Generally, Web page designers are responsible for creating the front end, while other people in an organization, such as the Web site administrator, handle the back end tasks. However, it's important that the front-end designer work with the people responsible for the back end to ensure that the parts of the Web site that both of you create will work together as expected.   Grace is meeting with Cleveland Mack, the Nomad Ltd Web site administrator, to begin coordinating their work on the checkout process for the online store. Cleveland explains the process of submitting information entered in a form:

Browser packaging

When a user clicks the submit button, the browser refers to the <FORM> tag attributes for details on how to submit the information. These attributes, which are described in Table D-5, allow you to specify where the information entered in a form is sent, how the browser sends it, and in what format. Cleveland has not yet finalized the submission requirements, but will provide Grace with these settings in time to test the system before the checkout page goes into use.

CGI

The border between a Web site's front end and back end is the communication between the Web server—where the HTML document is stored—and the programs that process the information collected in a form. This communication takes place using a standardized protocol known as **CGI (Common Gateway Interface)**. The target on the Web server for the form contents is a file containing a short set of instructions, known as a script, which uses CGI to specify how the data is sent to the back end. Once you know how to create a Web page in HTML, learning to create the script for a form is generally an elementary task. However, since Grace is creating her first Web site, Cleveland offers to take responsibility for the script.

Order processing and confirmation

The final step in submitting form contents is the processing by the appropriate software. Because forms have many uses, they require different types of processing—for example, searching for information in a database, adding information to a database, or transforming in some way the data that was submitted. In any case, form submission and processing always requires an acknowledgement to the user, which confirms that the information was submitted, and which may also contain the results of the submission. For the Nomad Ltd checkout system, Cleveland's department is using **e-commerce software**, which can bill the user's credit card for the amount of the order, and send instructions to the company warehouse to ship the purchased items to the appropriate address. When the order is entered into the Nomad Ltd system, the software will instruct the Web server to display the confirmation Web page that Grace created, which is shown in Figure D-15.

FIGURE D-14: Web page front end and back end

Processing
Programs
Back End
CGI
Front End
Web
Server
Nomad
Ltd
Internet
Web Page

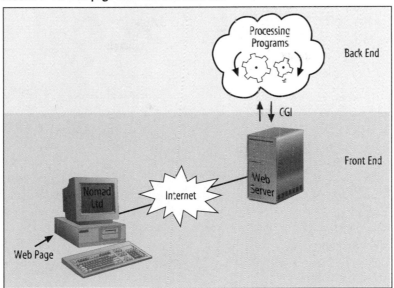

FIGURE D-15: Nomad Ltd order confirmation Web page

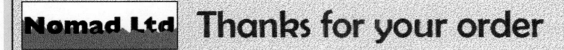

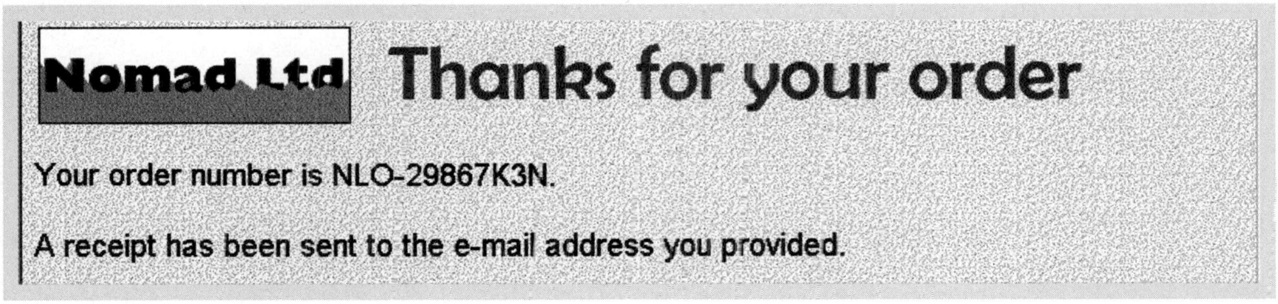

Nomad Ltd
Thanks for your order
Your order number is NLO-29867K3N.
A receipt has been sent to the e-mail address you provided.

TABLE D-5: <FORM> tag attributes for submitting information

attribute	description	example
METHOD	indicates how the data entered by the user will be submitted to the server; value may be "get" or "post"	METHOD="get"
ENCTYPE	specifies how the browser connects the user responses on the form before submitting them to the server	ENCTYPE="application/x-www-form-urlencoded"
ACTION	indicates the path and name of the processing program that the server must run when the form is submitted	ACTION= "/cgi-bin/ExecMacro/input"

HTML

Practice

► Concepts Review

Label each element of the browser screen shown in Figure D-16

FIGURE D-16

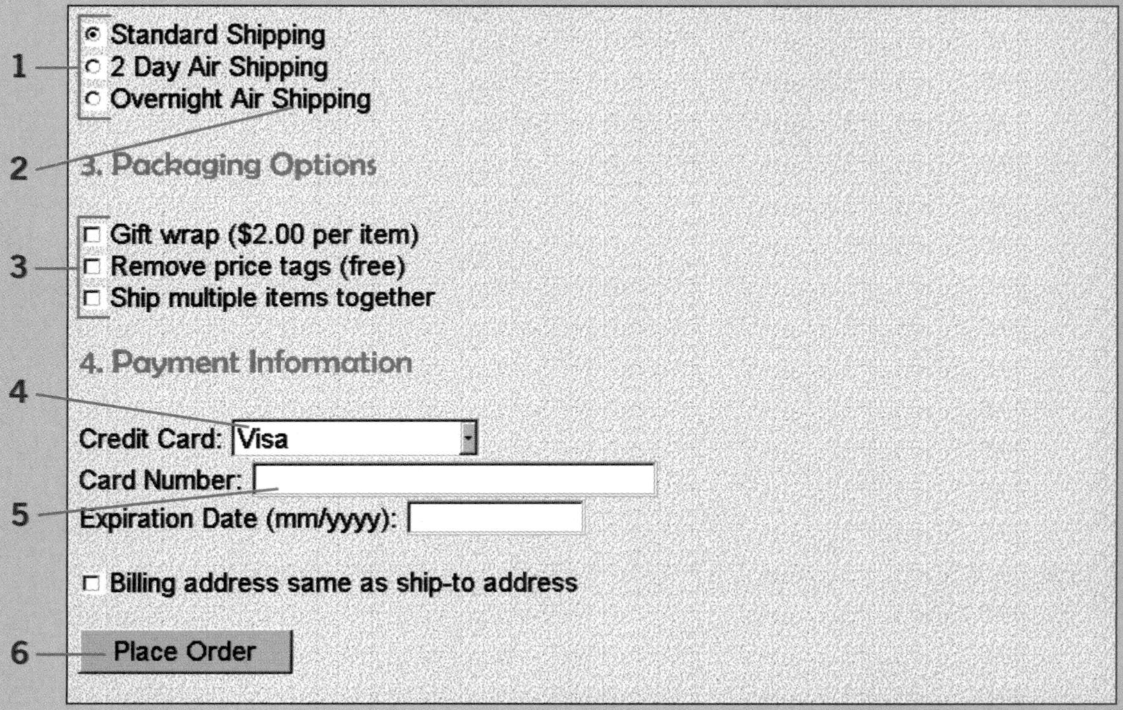

```
        ⊙ Standard Shipping
1 ───   ○ 2 Day Air Shipping
        ○ Overnight Air Shipping

2 ───   3. Packaging Options

        ☐ Gift wrap ($2.00 per item)
3 ───   ☐ Remove price tags (free)
        ☐ Ship multiple items together

        4. Payment Information
4 ───
        Credit Card: │Visa          ▼│
        Card Number: │                    │
5 ───   Expiration Date (mm/yyyy): │          │

        ☐ Billing address same as ship-to address

6 ───   │  Place Order  │
```

Match each statement with the HTML INPUT attribute it describes

7. Descriptive text that accompanies a field
8. The programs that reside on an organization's computer system, and which are responsible for processing the submitted data
9. A form element that allows user input
10. A group of HTML elements that facilitates interactivity
11. The protocol for exchanging information between a Web server and processing software

a. Form
b. Field
c. Label
d. CGI
e. Back end

Select the best answer from the list of choices.

12. Which tag(s) do you use to create a form?
 a. <FORM>..</FORM>
 b. <INPUT>
 c. <SELECT>..</SELECT>
 d. <OPTION>

13. Which attribute can you use to preselect an item in a radio button list?
 a. TYPE
 b. CHECKED
 c. LENGTH
 d. ORDER

14. Which of the following form fields requires the VALUE attribute?
 a. Text box
 b. Radio button
 c. Checkbox
 d. Pull-down menu

15. Which tag(s) mark a menu item in a pull-down menu?
 a. <FORM>..</FORM>
 b. <INPUT>
 c. <SELECT>..</SELECT>
 d. <OPTION>

16. **Which attribute allows you to customize the text on a push button?**
    a. TEXT
    b. TYPE
    c. NAME
    d. VALUE

17. **The Web page that users see in their browsers is called the Web site's**
    a. Form.
    b. Front end.
    c. Back end.
    d. Script.

18. **E-commerce software is part of which step in form submission?**
    a. Browser packaging
    b. CGI
    c. Scripting
    d. Order processing and confirmation

 # Skills Review

1. **Create a text entry field.**
    a. Start your text editor, then open the file HTM D-2.htm, and save it as a text document with the filename search-d.htm.
    b. Replace the text "<!-- BEGIN FORM -->" with "<FORM NAME="search">".
    c. Replace the text "<!-- END FORM -->" with "</FORM>".
    d. Replace the text "<!-- SEARCH TERMS - TEXT ENTRY FIELD -->" with "<INPUT TYPE="text" SIZE="50" NAME="searchterms">".
    e. Save your work, start your Web browser, then open the file search-d.htm.
    f. Click in the text box, then type a few words.

2. **Add radio buttons.**
    a. In your text editor, replace the text "<!-- RESULTS PER PAGE - RADIO BUTTONS -->" with "<INPUT TYPE="radio" NAME="results" VALUE="10" CHECKED>10", then press [Enter].
    b. Insert four spaces, type "<BR>", then press [Enter].
    c. Insert four spaces, then type "<INPUT TYPE="radio" NAME="results" VALUE="20">20".
    d. Save your work, click the browser button on the taskbar, reload the form in the browser window, then scroll down if necessary to view the radio buttons.
    e. Click the "20" radio button, then click the "10" radio button.

3. Add checkboxes.

a. In your text editor, replace the text "<!-- INCLUDE - CHECKBOXES -->" with "<INPUT TYPE="checkbox" NAME="gear" CHECKED>outdoor store", then press [Enter].

b. Insert four spaces, type "<BR>", then press [Enter].

c. Insert four spaces, type "<INPUT TYPE="checkbox" NAME="corp">corporate information", then press [Enter].

d. Insert four spaces, type "<BR>", then press [Enter].

e. Insert four spaces, then type "<INPUT TYPE="checkbox" NAME="basement">bargain basement".

f. Save your work, click the browser button on the taskbar, reload the form in the browser window, then scroll down if necessary to view the checkbox list.

g. Click each unchecked checkbox to check it, then click each checkbox again to remove the check marks.

4. Create a pull-down menu.

a. In your text editor, replace the text "<!-- LANGUAGE - PULL-DOWN MENU -->" with "<SELECT NAME="language">", then press [Enter].

b. Insert six spaces, type "<OPTION VALUE="e">English", then press [Enter].

c. Repeat Step b to enter each of the remaining four options for the language pull-down menu:
<OPTION VALUE="s">Spanish
<OPTION VALUE="f">French
<OPTION VALUE="j">Japanese
<OPTION VALUE="g">German

d. Insert four spaces, type "</SELECT>", then press [Enter].

e. Save your work, click the browser button on the taskbar, reload the form in the browser window, then scroll down to view the pull-down menu.

f. Click the Language pull-down arrow, then click one of the options on the menu that opens.

5. Add a push button.

a. In your text editor, replace the text "<!-- SUBMIT BUTTON -->" with "<INPUT TYPE="submit" VALUE="Search" NAME="search">".

b. Save your work, then click the browser button in the taskbar.

c. Reload the form in the browser window, then scroll down to view the submit button.

d. Click the Search button.

▶ Independent Challenges

1. You are maintaining a Web site for your computer consulting business, Star Dot Star. In addition to giving basic information to prospective clients, you want to add services to your Web site for your current clients as well. As a first step, you decide to add Web search capabilities to your home page.

To complete this independent challenge:

a. Start your text editor, open the file HTM D-3.htm, and save it as a text document with the filename sds-d.htm.

b. Insert the opening and closing <FORM> tags, along with any necessary attributes.

c. Add a text box for search terms, along with a label.

d. Create a checkbox for selecting the format of search results, and label it "show headers only."

e. Create a pull-down menu listing options for number of results per page; include at least five options, and appropriately label the field.

f. Include a submit button with a label of your choice.

g. Save your work, open the file in your browser, then test the Web page.

2. In your job at the local water department, you have created a Web site that includes information on the local watershed. You want the site to have a feedback form that allows users to submit questions.

To complete this independent challenge:

a. Start your text editor, open the file HTM D-4.htm, and save it as a text document with the filename mw-d.htm.

b. Insert the opening and closing <FORM> tags, along with any necessary attributes.

c. Create a pull-down menu with the label "Topic" that lists the following possible topics: Local watershed, Metro Water rates, Water conservation, Other topic.

d. Add a checkbox that allows users to indicate whether or not they wish to be contacted by Metro Water; be sure to include an appropriate label.

e. Add an appropriately sized text box with the label "E-mail address."

f. Add a large text box with the label "Your question or comment:".

g. Create a submit button labeled "Submit."

h. Save your work, open the file in your browser, then test the Web page.

3. You're expanding an in-store information system for your video store, Film Clips. You created the information system with HTML documents. You want to include a form in the system so customers to can tell you about their film preferences and suggest videos they'd like to rent, then you can take their desires into account when you order new stock.

To complete this independent challenge:

a. Start your text editor, create a new document, and save it as a text document with the filename fc-d.htm.

b. Create a pull-down menu along with an appropriate label that lets a customer select the genre of movie they view the most often (such as drama, action, documentary, or comedy).

c. Create a series of labeled checkboxes that ask about video technologies the user has at home (for example, VCR, DVD, HDTV, and Other).

d. Add a labeled text box that allows users to specify additional technologies if they checked "Other."

e. Add a large labeled text box for users to list movies they'd like to rent from Film Clips.

f. Save your work, open the file in your browser, then test the Web page.

4. One of the popular uses of forms on the Web is search engines. Although many popular search engines exist, each uses a different technology to perform the search. Thus, each search engine's front end is slightly different, depending on the type of information the search engine needs to collect from users. Examining the code for different search engine Web pages can suggest different uses of the form fields with which you're familiar.

To complete this independent challenge:

a. Connect to the Internet and use your browser to go to a search engine, such as one of the following:
www.google.com
www.altavista.com
www.yahoo.com
If you have trouble locating a search engine, go to www.course.com, navigate to the page for this book, click the link for the Student Online Companion, click the link for this unit, and use the links listed there as a starting point for your search.

b. Instead of performing a search, click View, then click Source (or Page Source) in your browser to view the HTML code for the Web page.

c. Locate the opening <FORM> tag, then study the form's field tags. Note any interesting, unusual, or useful implementations of the tags that you've learned; write down tags or attributes within the form code that are unfamiliar to you.

d. Repeat steps a-c two more times, for a total of three browsers.

e. Use a search engine to research one of the unfamiliar tags or attributes you noted.

f. Write a paragraph for each browser, summarizing its new, interesting, or unfamiliar code elements. Write an additional paragraph that gives an overview of the new tag or attribute you researched.

Visual Workshop

As part of your job at Touchstone Books, you've been working to create a Web presence for the store. The store's owner has been researching e-commerce software, and wants you to create a front end form that would allow Web users to order books online. Open the file HTM D-5.htm in your text editor, save it as a text document called tsb-d.htm, then add a form to the Web page so it matches the page shown in Figure D-17.

FIGURE D-17

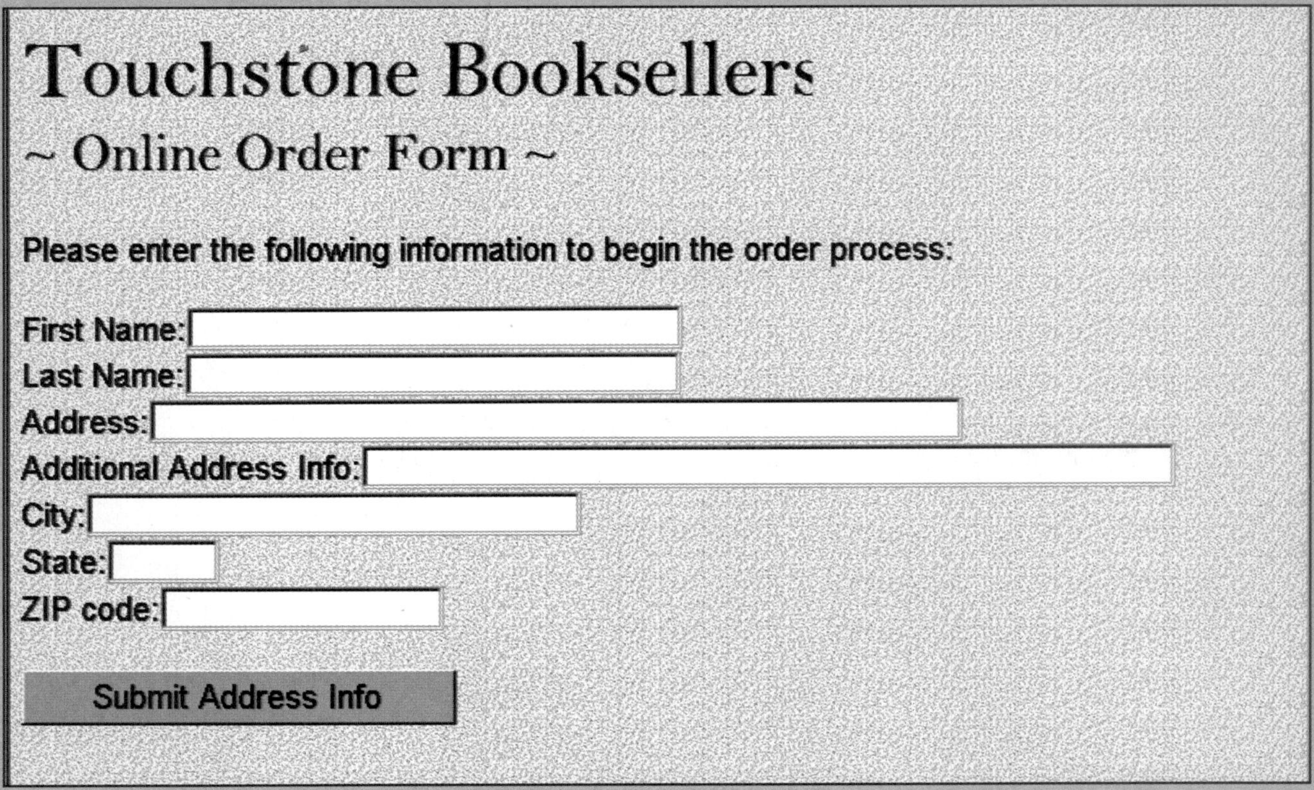

Touchstone Booksellers
~ Online Order Form ~

Please enter the following information to begin the order process:

First Name: [   ]
Last Name: [   ]
Address: [   ]
Additional Address Info: [   ]
City: [   ]
State: [   ]
ZIP code: [   ]

[Submit Address Info]

Working
with Tables

▶ **Plan a table**
▶ **Create a simple table**
▶ **Span rows**
▶ **Format borders**
▶ **Modify table backgrounds**
▶ **Change table dimensions**
▶ **Align table contents**
▶ **Position page elements**

Although paragraphs are a useful way to present most information on a
Web page, certain contents require other formats. HTML includes
extensive support for one of the most common alternate layouts: the
table, which allows you to present information in a grid. A table is useful for creating a compact list of the traits or attributes of all the items in
a set. ✐ Jaime Chavez works in the Information Systems department at Nomad Ltd, a travel and sporting goods company. His current
project is to add information to the company Web site about each of the
tours that Nomad Ltd offers. Tour information formatted with a table
allows Web page users to easily compare different aspects of each tour.

HTML

Planning a Table

A table is a useful way to summarize many types of data, including results from a database search or the differences among a fixed set of choices. As shown in Figure E-1, table data is organized into rows and columns; a **row** is a single horizontal line of data, while a **column** is a single vertical line of data. The intersection of a row and a column is a single unit of table data, called a **cell**. While all Web page tables use a standard layout, many other aspects of tables are customizable. You can tailor tables to fit the data they contain, as well as tailor the designs of the Web pages where the tables are located. As he prepares to create the table for the Nomad Ltd tours Web page, Jaime plans his table layout. HTML allows you to control many aspects of a table's appearance. Those characteristics are shown in Figure E-2, and include:

Details

Structure and border
You can customize a table to include exactly the number of columns and rows that your data requires. You also can modify a table's structure so that one or more cells are part of multiple rows or columns. By default, each cell is slightly separated from the cells that surround it. To make the boundaries between cells clearer, you can add cell borders to a table. HTML allows you to customize border color and thickness.

Alignment
Just as with standard Web page elements or paragraphs of text, you can align cell contents along the cell's right or left edges, or centered between the two edges. Additionally, you can set the vertical alignment flush with the top border or the bottom border, or centered between the two borders.

Background
By default, a Web page table is transparent, showing the same background image or color as the Web page. However, tables can accommodate a custom background color, which you can apply to the entire table, specific rows, or individual cells.

Dimensions
In addition to customizing the number of rows and columns in the table structure, you can specify the sizes of table elements, as well as different aspects of the spacing between them. You can set the entire table to a fixed width or height, or you can specify that the browser automatically resize it to a specific percentage of the window size. You also can set the amount of blank space around the contents of each cell, as well as the distance between each cell.

Positioning
Because tables are so flexible and customizable, Web designers have found many uses for them. One of the most common uses of tables is to position page elements in specific locations on the page. You cannot create this type of layout solely with HTML tags such as <P> and <IMG>.

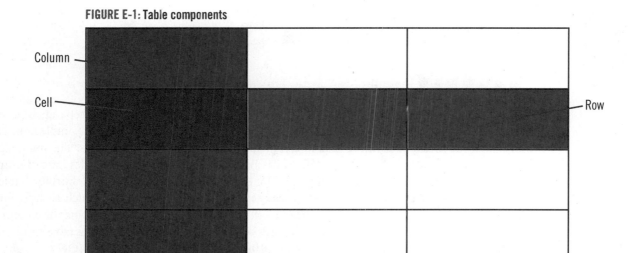

Column

Cell

Row

Positioned
page elements

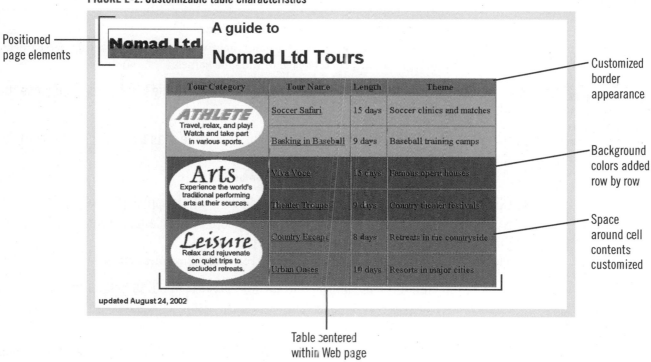

A guide to

Nomad Ltd

Nomad Ltd Tours

Tour Category	Tour Name	Length	Theme
ATHLETE Travel, relax, and play! Watch and take part in various sports.	Soccer Safari	15 days	Soccer clinics and matches
	Basking in Baseball	9 days	Baseball training camps
Arts Experience the world's traditional performing arts at their sources.	Viva Voce	15 days	Famous opera houses
	Theater Troupe	9 days	Country theater festivals
Leisure Relax and rejuvenate on quiet trips to secluded retreats.	Country Escape	8 days	Retreats in the countryside
	Urban Oases	10 days	Resorts in major cities

updated August 24, 2002

Customized
border
appearance

Background
colors added
row by row

Space
around cell
contents
customized

Table centered
within Web page

CLUES TO USE

Formatting cell contents

Although you can manipulate many aspects of a table's appearance, formatting table contents can be tricky. A browser treats the contents of each table cell as a separate window. As a result, table cells do not inherit any properties that you set for the page outside the table. For example, even if you change your page's font using a <FONT> tag at the start of the body section, text in the table is still formatted in the browser's default font. Though tedious, the only solution to implementing the HTML style changes for table data is to add code—such as <FONT>..</FONT> tags—to the contents of each cell that you want to change. Although this restriction seems significant, Web page designers generally find that the power and versatility of Web page tables more than makes up for their limitations.

HTML

Creating a Simple Table

While a table is a compact way to show relationships between information, each separate unit of information requires a separate HTML code. As a result, the code to create even a simple table is longer that most other basic HTML, and can include several nested layers of tags. The main tag pair for creating a table is <TABLE>..</TABLE>. Between these tags, you add codes for each row using <TR>, which is short for "table row," and for each cell using <TD>, which is short for "table data." The cells in the first row of most tables use an additional tag: <TH>, which is short for "table header." <TH> formats the contents of a cell as centered and boldface, making the column headings stand out from the contents of the cells below them. You also can add a table caption, which is centered above the table by default, using the <CAPTION>..</CAPTION> tag pair. However, when a table is the only element on a Web page, a large heading is usually a better choice for labeling the table contents. Table E-1 summarizes the HTML tags used to create a table. Jaime has created a Web page for Nomad Ltd tours information, and has received a text file from the marketing department. The file contains the contents of a table that describes the tours. He copies the table text into his Web page and formats it with the HTML table tags.

1. Start your text editor, then open the file **HTM E-1.txt**
   This file contains the tours table text that Jaime received from the marketing department, along with link tags that he added to each of the tour names.

QuickTip
To ensure that you select all the text in the file, you can click Edit, then click Select All.

2. Select **all the text in the file**, press **[Ctrl][C]** to copy it to the Clipboard, then close the file, if necessary

3. Open the file **HTM E-2.htm** in your text editor, then save it as a text document with the filename **nomad-e.htm**
   This document contains headings and the Nomad Ltd logo.

4. Click the blank line below the text formatted with <H1>, press **[Enter]**, type **<TABLE BORDER>**, press **[Enter]**, press **[Ctrl][V]** to paste the table text from the Clipboard, press **[Enter]**, type **</TABLE>**, then press **[Enter]**
   The BORDER attribute in the <TABLE> tag creates dividing lines between the cells.

5. Click at the end of the opening <TABLE> tag, press **[Enter]**, press **[Spacebar]** twice, then type **<TR>**
   <TR> marks the start of a row.

6. Click to the left of the text **Tour Name**, press **[Spacebar]** four times, type **<TH>**, then repeat this step for the two lines of text that follow
   <TH> marks the text that follows it as the contents of a cell, and applies the header format.

7. Click the blank line below the last <TH> tag you added, press **[Spacebar]** twice, type **</TR>**, then press **[Enter]** twice

8. Add a **<TR>** tag indented two spaces, indent the three items that follow with four spaces and add the **<TD>** tag before each one, add the closing **</TR>** tag indented two spaces, then repeat this step for the remaining groups of cells
   Your Web document should resemble the one shown in Figure E-3.

9. Save your work, start your Web browser, cancel any dial-up activities, then open the file **nomad-e.htm**
   The data appears in a table of three columns and seven rows, as shown in Figure E-4.

FIGURE E-3: Web document containing basic table tags

```
HSPACE="20" ALT="Nomad Ltd">
<H2>A guide to</H2>
<H1>Nomad Ltd Tours</H1>

<TABLE BORDER>
  <TR>
    <TH>Tour Name
    <TH>Length
    <TH>Theme
  </TR>

  <TR>
    <TD><A HREF="construction.htm">Soccer Safari</A>
    <TD>15 days
    <TD>Soccer clinics and matches
  </TR>

  <TR>
    <TD><A HREF="construction.htm">Basking in Baseball</A>
    <TD>9 days
    <TD>Baseball training camps
  </TR>

  <TR>
    <TD><A HREF="construction.htm">Viva Voce</A>
    <TD>15 days
    <TD>Famous operahouses
```

```
    <TD>Famous operahouses
  </TR>

  <TR>
    <TD><A HREF="construction.htm">Theater Troupe</A>
    <TD>9 days
    <TD>Country theater festivals
  </TR>

  <TR>
    <TD><A HREF="construction.htm">Country Escape</A>
    <TD>8 days
    <TD>Retreats in the countryside
  </TR>

  <TR>
    <TD><A HREF="construction.htm">Urban Oases</A>
    <TD>10 days
    <TD>Resorts in major cities
  </TR>
</TABLE>

<H5>updated August 24, 2002</H5>

</FONT>
</BODY>
</HTML>
```

Opening and closing <TABLE> tags

FIGURE E-4: Web page containing table

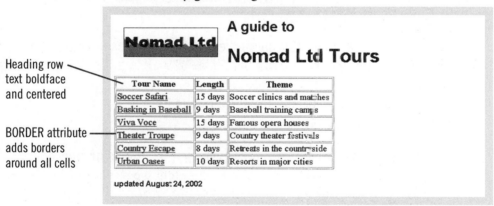

Heading row text boldface and centered

BORDER attribute adds borders around all cells

A guide to
Nomad Ltd Tours

Tour Name	Length	Theme
Soccer Safari	15 days	Soccer clinics and matches
Basking in Baseball	9 days	Baseball training camps
Viva Voce	15 days	Famous opera houses
Theater Troupe	9 days	Country theater festivals
Country Escape	8 days	Retreats in the countryside
Urban Oases	10 days	Resorts in major cities

updated August 24, 2002

TABLE E-1: HTML table tags

tag(s)	function
<TABLE>..</TABLE>	define start and end of table contents
<TR>..</TR>	mark contents of each table row
<TH>	marks contents that follow as a table cell, and applies header format
<TD>	marks contents that follow as a standard table cell
<CAPTION>..</CAPTION>	formats text to appear as a caption, centered above the table; can appear anywhere within the <TABLE>..</TABLE> tag pair

Spanning Rows

A basic table contains cells of data arranged in columns and rows. However, sometimes the contents of a cell apply to more than one row or column. You can mark a single cell to be part of multiple rows or columns—known as **spanning**—by using attributes in the <TH> or <TD> tags. Table E-2 explains these attributes, ROWSPAN and COLSPAN. ◢ Nomad Ltd tours are divided into three categories: athlete, arts, and leisure. Jaime wants to add a table column that shows the category of each tour. Since two of the tours belong to each category, each category cell will span two rows.

Steps

1. In your text editor, click to the right of the <TR> tag for the column heading section, press [Enter], press [Spacebar] four times, then type **<TH>Tour Category**
   This code adds the header cell for the new column.

2. Click to the right of the <TR> tag above the text Soccer Safari, press [Enter], press [Spacebar] four times, then type **<TD ROWSPAN="2"><IMG SRC="images/athlete.gif" WIDTH="203" HEIGHT="116" ALT="athlete">**
   This code adds the tour category cell that aligns with the first two rows of data. Instead of text, Jaime uses an <IMG> tag as the cell contents. The tag references a logo graphic for the athlete tours. Jaime received the graphic from the marketing department.

3. Click to the right of the <TR> tag above the text **Viva Voce**, press [Enter], press [Spacebar] four times, then type **<TD ROWSPAN="2"><IMG SRC="images/arts.gif" WIDTH="202" HEIGHT="121" ALT="Arts">**

4. Click to the right of the <TR> tag above the text Country Escape, press [Enter], press [Spacebar] four times, then type **<TD ROWSPAN="2"><IMG SRC="images/leisure.gif" WIDTH="197" HEIGHT="124" ALT="Leisure">**
   Your Web document should resemble the one shown in Figure E-6.

5. Save your file **nomad-e.htm** as a text document

6. Click the **browser program button** on the taskbar, then reload **nomad-e.htm**
   As shown in Figure E-7, each graphic logo for the three tour types appears in a cell in the new column on the left edge of the table. Each cell spans two rows.

CLUES TO USE

Spanning Columns

The process of spanning table columns is very similar to spanning rows. Instead of using the ROWSPAN attribute in a <TH> or <TD> tag, you use COLSPAN. One of the most popular uses of spanned columns is to display a two-level column head, as shown in Figure E-5.

FIGURE E-5: Web page table containing spanned columns

City	January		July	
	Minimum (°F)	Maximum (°F)	Minimum (°F)	Maximum (°F)
Accra, Ghana	87	73	81	73
Amsterdam, Netherlands	40	34	69	59
Athens, Greece	54	42	90	72
Auckland, New Zealand	73	60	56	46
Baghdad, Iraq	60	39	110	76

Average Temperatures for Selected World Cities

FIGURE E-6: Web document containing code for cells spanning rows

```
<H1>Nomad Ltd Tours</H1>

<TABLE BORDER>
  <TR>
    <TH>Tour Category
    <TH>Tour Name
    <TH>Length
    <TH>Theme
  </TR>

  <TR>
    <TD ROWSPAN="2"><IMG SRC="images/athlete.gif" WIDTH="203" HEIGHT="116"
ALT="athlete">
    <TD><A HREF="construction.htm">Soccer Safari</A>
    <TD>15 days
    <TD>Soccer clinics and matches
  </TR>

  <TR>
    <TD><A HREF="construction.htm">Basking in Baseball</A>
    <TD>9 days
    <TD>Baseball training camps
  </TR>

  <TR>
    <TD ROWSPAN="2"><IMG SRC="images/arts.gif" WIDTH=
ALT="Arts">
```

Code for header cell for new column

Tags for cells in new column use ROWSPAN attribute

```
ALT="Arts">
    <TD><A HREF="construction.htm">Viva Voce</A>
    <TD>15 days
    <TD>Famous operahouses
  </TR>

  <TR>
    <TD><A HREF="construction.htm">Theater Troupe</A>
    <TD>9 days
    <TD>Country theater festivals
  </TR>

  <TR>
    <TD ROWSPAN="2"><IMG SRC="images/leisure.gif" WIDTH="197" HEIGHT="124"
ALT="Leisure">
    <TD><A HREF="construction.htm">Country Escape</A>
    <TD>8 days
    <TD>Retreats in the countryside
  </TR>

  <TR>
    <TD><A HREF="construction.htm">Urban Oases</A>
    <TD>10 days
    <TD>Resorts in major cities
  </TR>
</TABLE>
```

FIGURE E-7: Web page table containing spanned rows

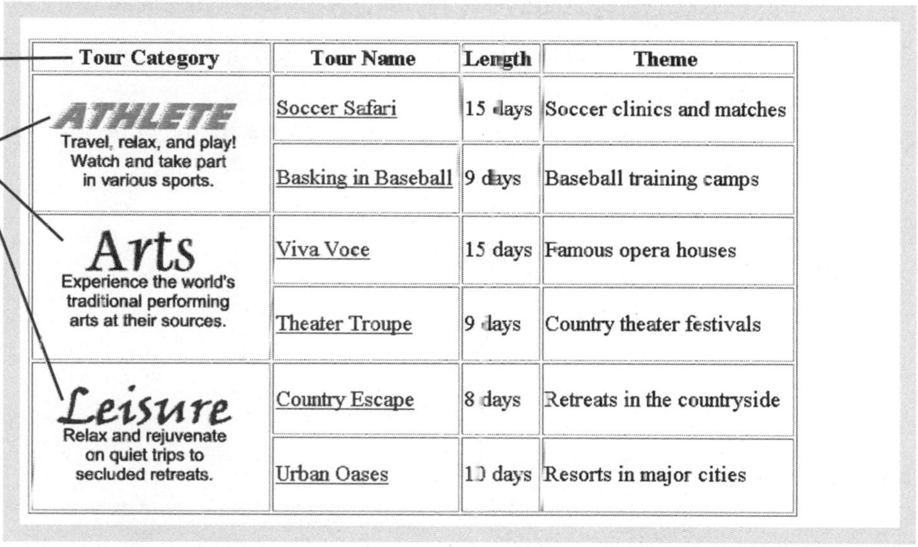

New column added

Each new cell spans two rows

Tour Category	Tour Name	Length	Theme
ATHLETE Travel, relax, and play! Watch and take part in various sports.	Soccer Safari	15 days	Soccer clinics and matches
	Basking in Baseball	9 days	Baseball training camps
Arts Experience the world's traditional performing arts at their sources.	Viva Voce	15 days	Famous opera houses
	Theater Troupe	9 days	Country theater festivals
Leisure Relax and rejuvenate on quiet trips to secluded retreats.	Country Escape	8 days	Retreats in the countryside
	Urban Oases	10 days	Resorts in major cities

TABLE E-2: Spanning attributes

tag	attribute	description	example
<TH> or <TD>	ROWSPAN	indicates number of rows the current cell should span	<TD ROWSPAN="2">
	COLSPAN	indicates number of columns the current cell should span	<TD COLSPAN="2">

HTML

Formatting Borders

Just as you can control the arrangement of cells in a table, you also can alter the properties of the borders between cells. By assigning a value in pixels to the BORDER attribute in the <TABLE> tag, you can change the thickness of the table's outside border. This attribute also gives you minimal control over the border around each cell. When the BORDER attribute is present in the <TABLE> tag, cell borders appear as lines one pixel wide. However, if BORDER is set equal to zero, or if the attribute is not present, cells will not display any borders. Another way to affect the relationship between cells is the CELLSPACING attribute, which sets the distance in pixels between cell borders. By default, this distance is two pixels; setting it to zero gives the appearance of a single-line gridwork dividing cells, while higher number settings increase the blank area on all sides of cells. Table E-3 summarizes border attributes. Jaime wants to customize the look of his table to fit its contents. He starts by formatting the table and cell borders.

Steps

1. **In your text editor, click to the right of BORDER in the <TABLE> tag, then type ="5"**
   Jaime originally entered the BORDER attribute without a value, which turned on the display of cell borders and added a table border with the default value of one pixel. Setting the BORDER attribute to a larger value allows you to see how the table looks with a thicker border.

2. **Save your work**

3. **Click the browser program button on the taskbar, then reload nomad-e.htm**
   The table's outside border appears thicker, as shown in Figure E-8. This thickness makes the border's three-dimensional effect more noticeable.

QuickTip

Be sure not to delete the BORDER attribute, so the table still will display the table and cell borders.

4. **Click the text editor program button on the taskbar, select ="5" in the <TABLE> tag, then press [Delete]**
   Jaime prefers the small default table border size.

5. **Click to the right of BORDER in the <TABLE> tag, press [Spacebar], then type CELLSPACING="0"**
   Figure E-9 shows the completed code for the table and cell borders. Setting the CELLSPACING attribute equal to zero removes the blank space between the cell borders.

6. **Save your work, click the browser program button on the taskbar, then reload nomad-e.htm**
   As shown in Figure E-10, the cell and table borders are the same width, and appear as a grid of single lines.

TABLE E-3: Table and cell border attributes

tag	attribute	description	default value	example
<TABLE>	BORDER	adds borders around the table and each cell; optional value determines thickness of table border	1 px (if attribute is specified without a value)	<TABLE BORDER="5">
	CELLSPACING	determines gap between borders of adjacent cells	2 px (if attribute is not specified)	<TABLE CELLSPACING="0">

FIGURE E-8: Web page table with 5-pixel border

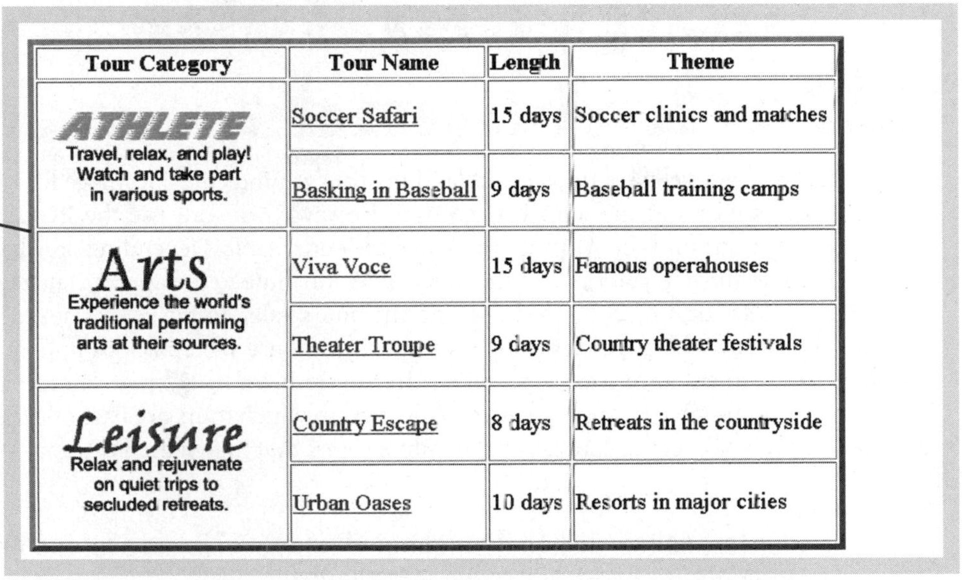

Tour Category	Tour Name	Length	Theme
ATHLETE Travel, relax, and play! Watch and take part in various sports.	Soccer Safari	15 days	Soccer clinics and matches
	Basking in Baseball	9 days	Baseball training camps
Arts Experience the world's traditional performing arts at their sources.	Viva Voce	15 days	Famous operahouses
	Theater Troupe	9 days	Country theater festivals
Leisure Relax and rejuvenate on quiet trips to secluded retreats.	Country Escape	8 days	Retreats in the countryside
	Urban Oases	10 days	Resorts in major cities

Outer table border thickened by BORDER value

FIGURE E-9: Web document containing border formatting

```
<H1>Nomad Ltd Tours</H1>

<TABLE BORDER CELLSPACING="0">
  <TR>
    <TH>Tour Category
    <TH>Tour Name
```

Valueless BORDER attribute defaults to 1-pixel table border

CELLSPACING setting removes empty space between adjacent cells

FIGURE E-10: Web page table with cellspacing removed

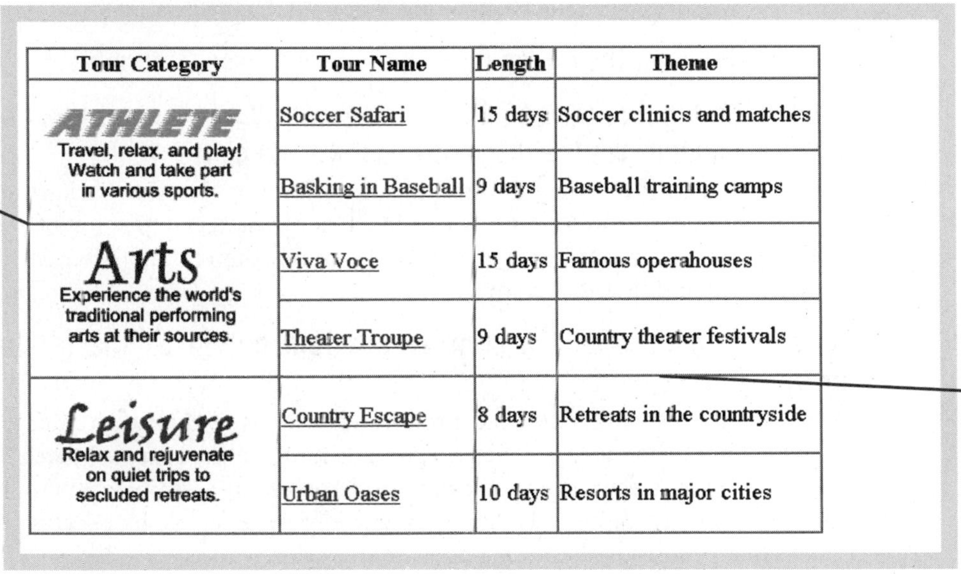

Tour Category	Tour Name	Length	Theme
ATHLETE Travel, relax, and play! Watch and take part in various sports.	Soccer Safari	15 days	Soccer clinics and matches
	Basking in Baseball	9 days	Baseball training camps
Arts Experience the world's traditional performing arts at their sources.	Viva Voce	15 days	Famous operahouses
	Theater Troupe	9 days	Country theater festivals
Leisure Relax and rejuvenate on quiet trips to secluded retreats.	Country Escape	8 days	Retreats in the countryside
	Urban Oases	10 days	Resorts in major cities

Table border displays at default thickness

Space removed between cell borders

Modifying Table Backgrounds

By default, table cells are transparent, and the background color or image for the rest of the Web page also appears as the table background. However, you can use the BGCOLOR attribute to assign a background color to a cell, a row, or the entire table. Depending on what part of the table you want to format, you can add the BGCOLOR attribute to the appropriate tag or tags—<TH>, <TD>, <TR>, or <TABLE>—and set the attribute's value to the color's hexadecimal equivalent. As with other Web page elements, it's important to use table background color sparingly and judiciously to enhance your page, rather than overwhelm it. ➤ Jaime wants to color-code the rows in his table to make it easier to distinguish which tours are part of each category. He has looked up hexadecimal equivalents for subtle colors that match each category's logo.

Steps

1. **In your text editor, click to the right of TR in the <TR> tag for the header row, press [Spacebar], then type BGCOLOR="#CC8800"**
   Including the BGCOLOR attribute in a <TR> tag sets the background color for all cells in that row. For the header row, Jaime selected the same color used in the Nomad Ltd logo at the top of the Web page.

2. **Click to the right of TR in the <TR> tag for the row containing the Soccer Safari information, press [Spacebar], then type BGCOLOR="#93DB50"**
   For this row, Jaime selected a green color that matches the Athlete tour category logo.

3. **Repeat Step 2 for the row containing the Basking in Baseball information**

4. **Click to the right of TR in the <TR> tag for the row containing the Viva Voce information, press [Spacebar], then type BGCOLOR="#DB7093"**
   The background color for this row is a shade of red that matches the associated category logo.

5. **Repeat Step 4 for the row containing the Theater Troupe information**

6. **Click to the right of TR in the <TR> tag for the row containing the Country Escape information, press [Spacebar], then type BGCOLOR="#8F8FBD"**
   This row will display a blue background that matches the Leisure tour category logo.

7. **Repeat Step 6 for the row containing the Urban Oases information**

8. **Click to the right of the text BODY in the <BODY> tag, press [Spacebar], then type LINK="#000000" VLINK="#2F4F4F" ALINK="#2F4F4F"**
   Jaime wants to make sure the link text is visible on the new background colors, so he changes the default link text color to black, and changes the color of previously viewed and active links to dark gray. Figure E-11 shows the completed code for the table row background and link text colors.

Trouble?
If you previously clicked any of the links in the table, the link text appears as dark gray rather than black.

9. **Save your work, click the browser program button on the taskbar, then reload nomad-e.htm**
   As shown in Figure E-12, the header row background is a light brown color that Jaime selected to match the corporate logo. The backgrounds for the other six rows match the colors in their associated tour category logos, allowing readers to easily identify which tours belong to each category. Jaime made sure the table text would remain legible by selecting light background shades that contrast with the default black font color.

```
<BODY LINK="#000000" VLINK="#2F4F4F" ALINK="#2F4F4F">
<FONT FACE="arial, helvetica, sans serif">

<IMG SRC="images/nomad.gif" HEIGHT="63" WIDTH="201" ALIGN="left" VSPACE="20"
HSPACE="20" ALT="Nomad Ltd">
<H2>A guide to</H2>
<H1>Nomad Ltd Tours</H1>

<TABLE BORDER CELLSPACING="0">
  <TR BGCOLOR="#CC8800">
    <TH>Tour Category
    <TH>Tour Name
    <TH>Length
    <TH>Theme
  </TR>

  <TR BGCOLOR="#93DB50">
    <TD ROWSPAN="2"><IMG SRC="images/athlete.gif" WIDTH="203" HEIGHT="116"
ALT="athlete">
    <TD><A HREF="construction.htm">Soccer Safari</A>
    <TD>15 days
    <TD>Soccer clinics and matches
  </TR>

  <TR BGCOLOR="#93DB50">
    <TD><A HREF="construction.htm">Basking in Baseball</A>
    <TD>9 days
```

Link color attributes added to <BODY> tag

BGCOLOR attribute added to each <TR> tag

```
    <TD>9 days
    <TD>Baseball training camps
  </TR>

<TR BGCOLOR="#DB7093">
    <TD ROWSPAN="2"><IMG SRC="images/arts.gif" WIDTH="202" HEIGHT="121"
ALT="Arts">
    <TD><A HREF="construction.htm">Viva Voce</A>
    <TD>15 days
    <TD>Famous operahouses
  </TR>

<TR BGCOLOR="#DB7093">
    <TD><A HREF="construction.htm">Theater Troupe</A>
    <TD>9 days
    <TD>Country theater festivals
  </TR>

<TR BGCOLOR="#8F8FED">
    <TD ROWSPAN="2"><IMG SRC="images/leisure.gif" WIDTH="197" HEIGHT="124"
ALT="Leisure">
    <TD><A HREF="construction.htm">Country Escape</A>
    <TD>8 days
    <TD>Retreats in the countryside
  </TR>

<TR BGCOLOR="#8F8FBD">
```

FIGURE E-12: Web page containing background colors

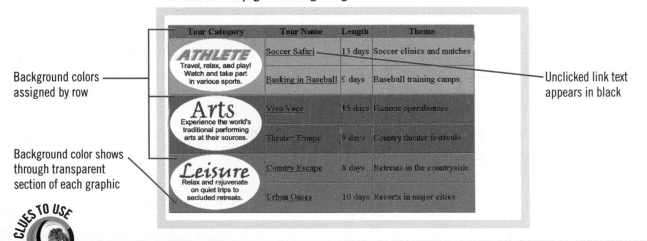

Background colors assigned by row

Background color shows through transparent section of each graphic

Unclicked link text appears in black

CLUES TO USE

Adding a background image to a table

In addition to the BGCOLOR attribute, Internet Explorer and the most recent versions of Navigator support the BACKGROUND attribute for the <TABLE>, <TH>, and <TD> tags. The BACKGROUND attribute allows you to specify a background image for the table or for specific table cells, as shown in Figure E-13. The <TR> tag does not support this attribute, so you can't apply background images row-by-row. The BACKGROUND attribute is not supported for any table tags in most versions of Navigator. Therefore, you should implement this attribute only if you are certain that everyone using your page will view it with Internet Explorer or one of the most recent Navigator versions, or if the page's layout and readability will not be compromised when the background image does not appear.

FIGURE E-13: Web page table using a background graphic

Bush	Type	Height	Fruit maturity	Yield per bush	Berry size	Berries per cup
Blue Ray	high	4-6 ft.	mid/late July	10-20 lb	large	60
Blue Jay	high	5-7 ft.	late July	7-10 lb	small/ medium	110
Jersey	high	5-7 ft.	late July	7-10 lb	small/ medium	110
Elliott	high	5-7 ft.	late Aug/early Sept.	10-20 lb	small/ medium	75
Northland	medium	3-4 ft.	early July	15-20	small	135

Changing Table Dimensions

As with other Web page elements, you can customize the dimensions of a table and of table cells using the HEIGHT and WIDTH attributes. The <TABLE>, <TH>, and <TD> tags support these attributes for setting minimum dimensions in pixels. In addition, these attributes allow measurements in percentages. For the <TABLE> tag, the browser calculates these dimensions as a percentage of the browser window size. For example, <TABLE WIDTH="90%"> widens the table, if necessary, to occupy 90% of the width of the user's browser window. The browser bases percentage dimensions for the <TH> and <TD> tags on the size of the table; the code <TD HEIGHT="10%"> causes the browser to make the cell taller, if necessary, so it takes up 10% of the overall height of the table. Because all the cells in a row will display at the same height, and all the cells in a column will display at the same width, you need to specify height or width for only one cell in order to change the dimension for the entire row or column. The <TABLE> tag supports one other attribute that affects table and cell dimensions: CELLPADDING. This attribute sets a cushion of blank space around the contents of every cell; that space is one pixel wide by default. Adding CELLPADDING usually increases the height and width of cells because they have to accommodate the blank padding space, in addition to the existing cell contents. Table E-4 summarizes the attributes for changing table dimensions. ▟▄▄▄▄ Jaime wants to test the effect of setting the table's width to a percentage of screen size. He also wants to make the table contents easier to read by adding cellpadding.

Steps

1. **In your text editor, click to the right of the text TABLE in the <TABLE> tag, press [Spacebar], then type WIDTH="100%"**
   Jaime wants to see how the page layout looks if the table always occupies the entire width of the window.

2. **Save your work, click the browser program button on the taskbar, then reload nomad-e.htm**
   Figure E-14 shows the table, including the WIDTH attribute. Figure E-15 shows the page on a large, high-resolution monitor, where the table is noticeably widened to take up more horizontal distance. The table cells include more empty space to make up the extra width.

QuickTip

Because of differences in users' monitors, it's best to regularly view your page at different sizes and resolutions as you develop it, in order to catch any potential problems.

3. **In your text editor, select the text WIDTH="100%" in the <TABLE> tag, press [Delete], then, if necessary, press [Delete] again to remove the extra space**
   Although he liked the effect of the WIDTH setting on the computer monitor at his desk, Jaime views the table with the new WIDTH setting at different screen sizes and resolutions and finds that the setting can detract from the page layout on large, high-resolution screens. Jaime decides that the Web page layout would look best to the widest possible audience if he positions the table at the default left-aligned position in the window.

4. **Click to the right of the text TABLE in the <TABLE> tag, press [Spacebar], then type CELLPADDING="5"**

5. **Save your work, click the browser program button on the taskbar, then reload nomad-e.htm**
   As shown in Figure E-16, the cell contents are surrounded by five pixels of space on all four sides. Jaime thinks this change makes the table contents easier to read.

FIGURE E-14: Web page table with WIDTH attribute

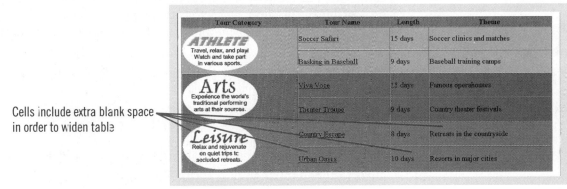

Table extends to right border, occupying full width of browser window

FIGURE E-15: Web page table with WIDTH attribute on large, high-resolution display

Cells include extra blank space in order to widen table

FIGURE E-16: Web page table including CELLPADDING attribute

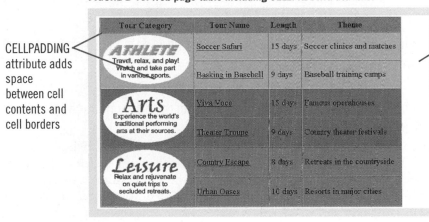

CELLPADDING attribute adds space between cell contents and cell borders

Removal of WIDTH attribute restores empty margin

TABLE E-4: Table dimension attributes

tag(s)	attribute	valid options	function
<TABLE>	WIDTH	value in pixels percentage	specifies fixed width of table specifies width of table as a percentage of browser window width
	HEIGHT	value in pixels percentage	specifies fixed height of table specifies height of table as a percentage of browser window height
	CELLPADDING	value in pixels	specifies thickness of empty zone surrounding contents of each cell
<TH> and <TD>	WIDTH	value in pixels percentage	specifies fixed width of cell, and applies to entire column specifies width of cell as a percentage of table width
	HEIGHT	value in pixels percentage	specifies fixed height of cell, and applies to entire row specifies height of cell as a percentage of table height

HTML

Aligning Table Contents

As when setting table backgrounds and dimensions, customizing the horizontal alignment of a table and its contents uses an attribute common to many Web page elements—the ALIGN attribute. While the ALIGN value in the <TR>, <TH>, and <TD> tags determines the alignment of row or cell contents within the cell borders, the ALIGN setting in the <TABLE> tag affects the horizontal alignment of the table as a whole within the Web page. The row and cell tags also support a second alignment attribute: VALIGN. This attribute determines the position of cell contents relative to the top and bottom borders. You can align cell contents flush with the top or bottom border, or center the contents between the two borders. Table E-5 explains the two alignment attributes for tables, and includes their permitted values. ✐ By default, all table contents are vertically centered and, except for header cells, aligned with the left edge of the cell. These defaults work well for all of the data in Jaime's table except the graphics, which would look better if centered horizontally. He also wants to experiment with the table's alignment within the page.

Steps

QuickTip

You can add the ALIGN and VALIGN attributes to a <TR> tag to set the alignment for an entire row.

1. In your text editor, click to the right of the word TABLE in the <TABLE> tag, press **[Spacebar]**, then type **ALIGN="center"**
   The ALIGN attribute in the <TABLE> tag sets the table's horizontal alignment within the browser window.

2. Locate the <TD> tag for the cell containing the graphic athlete.gif, click to the right of TD, press **[Spacebar]**, then type **ALIGN="center"**

3. Locate the <TD> tag for the cell containing the graphic arts.gif, click to the right of TD, press **[Spacebar]**, then type **ALIGN="center"**

4. Locate the <TD> tag for the cell containing the graphic leisure.gif, click to the right of TD, press **[Spacebar]**, then type **ALIGN="center"**
   Your Web document should resemble the one shown in Figure E-17.

5. Save your work, click the **browser program button** on the taskbar, then reload **nomad-e.htm**
   As Figure E-18 shows, the table is centered between the left and right edges of the browser window. Each of the logo graphics also is centered between its left and right cell borders. Because each graphic fits its cell almost exactly, the effect is almost unnoticeable except for the Leisure logo. Depending on the size and resolution of your screen, the centered table may appear in a different part of the screen relative to the other page elements.

6. In your text editor, select the text **ALIGN="center"** in the <TABLE> tag, press **[Delete]**, then if necessary, press **[Delete]** again to remove the extra space
   After viewing the centered table at different screen sizes and resolutions, Jaime decides that the layout would look best with the table at the default left-aligned position in the window, to match the standardized left alignment of the heading section.

7. Save your work, click the **browser program button** on the taskbar, then reload **nomad-e.htm**

```
<H1>Nomad Ltd Tours</H1>

<TABLE ALIGN="center" CELLPADDING="5" BORDER CELLSPACING="0">
  <TR BGCOLOR="#CCC800">
    <TH>Tour Category
    <TH>Tour Name
    <TH>Length
    <TH>Theme
  </TR>

  <TR BGCOLOR="#93DB50">
    <TD ALIGN="center" ROWSPAN="2"><IMG SRC="images/athlete.gif" WIDTH="203"
HEIGHT="116" ALT="athlete">
    <TD><A HREF="construction.htm">Soccer Safari</A>
    <TD>5 days
    <TD>Soccer clinics and matches
  </TR>

  <TR BGCOLOR="#93DB50">
    <TD><A HREF="construction.htm">Basking in Bas
    <TD>9 days
    <TD>Baseball training camps
  </TR>

  <TR BGCOLOR="#DB7093">
    <TD ALIGN="center" ROWSPAN="2"><IMG SRC="imag
HEIGHT="121" ALT="Arts">
```

ALIGN attribute in <TABLE> tag sets table position in Web page

```
HEIGHT="121" ALT="Arts">
    <TD><A HREF="construction.htm">Viva Voce</A>
    <TD>15 days
    <TD>Famous operahouses
  </TR>

  <TR BGCOLOR="#DB7093">
    <TD><A HREF="construction.htm">Theater Troupe</A>
    <TD>9 days
    <TD>Country theater festivals
  </TR>

  <TR BGCOLOR="#8F8FBD">
    <TD ALIGN="center" ROWSPAN="2"><IMG SRC="images/leisure.gif" WIDTH="197"
HEIGHT="124" ALT="Leisure">
    <TD><A HREF="construction.htm">Country Escape</A>
    <TD>8 days
    <TD>Retreats in the countryside
```

ALIGN attributes in <TD> tags set position of cell contents

FIGURE E-18: Web page table centered in browser window and containing centered contents

Blank space to left and right of table is equal

Logo graphics centered horizontally within cells

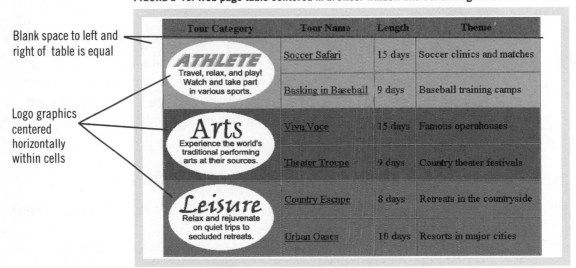

TABLE E-5: Table alignment attributes

tag	attribute	function	valid options (default value)
<TABLE>	ALIGN	sets horizontal position of table within browser window	(left), center, right
<TR> and <TD>	ALIGN	sets horizontal position of cell contents between left and right borders	(left), center, right
	VALIGN	sets vertical position of cell contents between top and bottom borders	top, (center), bottom
<TH>	ALIGN	sets horizontal position of cell contents between left and right borders	left, (center), right
	VALIGN	sets vertical position of cell contents between top and bottom borders	top, (center), bottom

Positioning Page Elements

Although tables were originally developed to display data in a grid, designers have found other innovative uses for them. One of the most popular uses of tables is to create layouts that HTML does not otherwise support. For example, basic HTML codes do not allow you to position elements in specific locations in the window. However, by placing elements in a table that does not display any borders, and adding blank cells of fixed widths, you can position the table contents anywhere on the page. ◆━━━ Jaime wants to more precisely position the elements in the Web page's heading section. He decides to redo the section's layout using a borderless table.

Steps 1 2 3 4

QuickTip

Although most recent versions of popular browsers support new protocols for placing elements, most Web page designers still prefer to use tables because virtually all browsers can display them.

1. In your text editor, click in the blank line above the <IMG> tag for the graphic nomad.gif, press [Enter], type **<TABLE>**, press [Enter], press [Spacebar] twice, then type **<TR>**
   When the BORDER attribute is absent from the <TABLE> tag, the table appears without table or cell borders.

2. Click to the left of the <IMG> tag for the graphic nomad.gif, press [Spacebar] four times, type **<TD>**, click to the right of the > at the end of the <IMG> tag, then press [Enter]

3. Press [Spacebar] four times, then type **<TD><FONT FACE="arial, helvetica, sans serif">**
   Jaime adds a <FONT> tag because a Web page's font settings do not affect the contents of a table.

QuickTip

Because font attributes are not inherited between cells, or between the browser window and the table, the <FONT> tag does not require </FONT> to close it.

4. Click to the left of the <H2> tag, press [Spacebar] six times, click to the left of the <H1> tag, then press [Spacebar] six times, click in the blank line below the <H1> heading, press [Spacebar] twice, type **</TR>**, press [Enter], type **</TABLE>**, then press [Enter]
   Figure E-19 shows the Web document containing the code for the borderless table.

5. Save your work, click the **browser program button** on the taskbar, then reload **nomad-e.htm**
   The logo and headings appear almost exactly as they did without the table in place.

QuickTip

No rules exist for calculating dimensions when sizing a table; the most reliable method is trial and error, until elements are positioned as you want them.

6. In your text editor, click to the right of TD in the first <TD> tag for the new table, press [Spacebar], then type **VALIGN="top" WIDTH="240"**
   This code positions the cell contents—the logo graphic—flush with the top of the cell. It also makes the cell wider than the graphic, which adds space between the logo and the text.

7. Locate the <IMG> tag for the graphic nomad.gif, select the text **VSPACE="20" HSPACE="20"**, press [Delete], then, if necessary, press [Delete] again to remove the extra space
   Jaime wants the logo in the upper-left corner of the browser window.

8. Click to the right of TD in the <TD> tag for the headings, press [Spacebar], then type **VALIGN="bottom" HEIGHT="140" ALIGN="center"**
   This code aligns the cell contents flush with the bottom of the cell, and increases the cell height so it's larger than the two headings. Jaime planned these settings so the top heading aligns with the middle of the logo.

9. Save your work, click the **browser program button** on the taskbar, then reload **nomad-e.htm**
   As shown in Figure E-20, the logo graphic is in the upper-left corner of the window, and the headings are center-aligned with each other, but positioned to the right of the logo.

FIGURE E-19: Web document containing code for borderless table

Table code added to page heading elements

```
<BODY LINK="#000000" VLINK="#2F4F4F" ALINK="#2F4F4F">
<FONT FACE="arial, helvetica, sans serif">

<TABLE>
  <TR>
    <TD><IMG SRC="images/nomad.gif" HEIGHT="63" WIDTH="201" ALIGN="left"
VSPACE="20" HSPACE="20" ALT="Nomad Ltd">
    <TD><FONT FACE="arial, helvetica, sans serif">
      <H2>A guide to</H2>
      <H1>Nomad Ltd Tours</H1>
  </TR>
</TABLE>

<TABLE CELLPADDING="5" BORDER CELLSPACING="0">
  <TR BGCOLOR="#CC8800">
```

FIGURE E-20: Web page including borderless table

Logo near upper-left edges of window

A guide to — Heading text centered within table cell, not within browser window

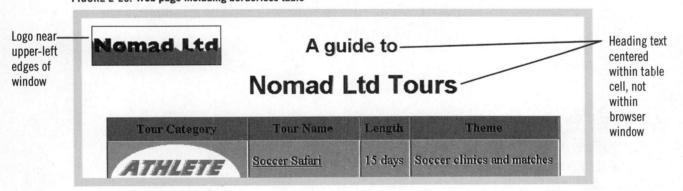

Practice

► Concepts Review

Name the function of each tag and attribute marked in Figure E-21.

FIGURE E-21

```
                                        1                    2
<TABLE ALIGN="center" CELLPADDING="5" BORDER CELLSPACING="0">
3 ─── <TR BGCOLOR="#CC8800">
        <TH>Tour Category
        <TH>Tour Name
4 ───── <TH>Length
        <TH>Theme
      </TR>

      <TR BGCOLOR="#93DB50">
5 ───── <TD ALIGN="center" ROWSPAN="2"><IMG SRC="images/athlete.gif" WIDTH="203"
HEIGHT="116" ALT="athlete">
        <TD><A HREF="construction.htm">Soccer Safari</A>
        <TD>15 days
        <TD>Soccer clinics and matches
      </TR>

      <TR BGCOLOR="#93DB50">
        <TD><A HREF="construction.htm">Basking in Baseball</A>
        <TD>9 days
        <TD>Baseball training camps
6 ─── </TR>

      <TR BGCOLOR="#DB7093">
        <TD ALIGN="center" ROWSPAN="2"><IMG SRC="images/arts.gif" WIDTH="202"
HEIGHT="121" ALT="Arts">
```

Match each Web page feature with the tag or attribute you use to create it.

7. Cell that spans multiple rows   a. CELLPADDING
8. Empty area around cell contents   b. BGCOLOR
9. Table header cell   c. <TH>
10. Background color   d. <TR>..</TR>
11. Table row   e. <TD>
12. Standard table data cell   f. ROWSPAN

Select the best answer from the list of choices.

13. Which one of the following attributes controls the gap between the borders of adjacent cells?
    a. ROWSPAN
    b. CELLPADDING
    c. VALIGN
    d. CELLSPACING

14. Which one of the following attributes controls the vertical alignment of the cell contents?
    a. ROWSPAN
    b. CELLPADDING
    c. VALIGN
    d. CELLSPACING

15. Which one of the following attributes creates a cell that spans multiple rows?
    a. ROWSPAN
    b. WIDTH
    c. VALIGN
    d. CELLSPACING

16. A single horizontal line of data is called a
    a. Table.
    b. Row.
    c. Column.
    d. Cell.

17. A single vertical line of data is called a
    a. Table.
    b. Row.
    c. Column.
    d. Cell.

18. Which one of the following tags supports the CELLPADDING attribute?
    a. <TABLE>
    b. <TR>
    c. <TH>
    d. <TD>

19. **Which one of the following tags marks the contents of a header cell?**
    a. <TABLE>
    b. <TR>
    c. <TH>
    d. <TD>

20. **A percentage value for the WIDTH attribute in the <TABLE> tag specifies the width of the table as a percentage of the**
    a. Overall table width.
    b. Browser window width.
    c. Width of the widest column.
    d. Width of the left-most column.

21. **A percentage value for the WIDTH attribute in a <TH> or <TD> tag specifies the width of the column as a percentage of the**
    a. Overall table width.
    b. Browser window width.
    c. Width of the widest column.
    d. Width of the left-most column.

► Skills Review

1. **Create a simple table.**
    a. In your text editor, open the file HTM E-3.htm, then save it as a text document with the filename travel-e.htm.
    b. Replace the tag <!-- with "<TABLE BORDER>", then replace the //--> tag with "</TABLE>".
    c. Insert a blank line above the text "Destination", then insert two spaces and the <TR> tag on this line.
    d. Before the text "Destination" insert four spaces and the <TH> tag, then repeat for the text "Location".
    e. Insert a blank line below the text "Location", then insert two spaces and the closing </TR> tag on this line.
    f. Insert a blank line above the first line beginning with <A HREF...>, then insert two spaces and the <TR> tag on this line.
    g. In the next line, insert four spaces and the <TD> tag before the <A> tag, then in the next line, insert four spaces and the <TD> tag before the text "California".
    h. Insert a blank line below the text "California", then insert two spaces and the </TR> tag.
    i. Repeat steps f through h for the remaining six sets of table row data.
    j. Save your work, start your Web browser, cancel any dial-up activities, then open the file travel-e.htm.

2. **Span rows.**
    a. In your text editor, insert a line above the closing </TR> tag for the column heading section, then insert four spaces and type "<TH>Activity" on this line.
    b. Insert a blank line below the text "California" in the first data row, then insert four spaces and type "<TD ROWSPAN="3">Hiking" on this line.

   c. Insert a blank line below the text "California" in the fourth data row, then insert four spaces and type "<TD ROWSPAN="2">Swimming/Boating" on this line.

   d. Insert a blank line below the text "Utah" in the sixth data row, then insert four spaces and type "<TD ROWSPAN="2">Mountain biking" on this line.

   e. Save your file travel-e.htm as a text document, then reload travel-e.htm in your browser.

3. Format borders.

   a. In your text editor, add the CELLSPACING attribute with a value of "0" to the <TABLE> tag.

   b. Save your work, then reload travel-e.htm in your browser.

4. Modify table background.

   a. In your text editor, add the BGCOLOR attribute with a value of "#F5F5DC" to the <TABLE> tag.

   b. Add the BGCOLOR attribute with a value of "#8F8FBD" to the <TR> tag of the header row.

   c. Save your work, then reload travel-e.htm in your browser.

5. Change table dimensions.

   a. In your text editor, add the CELLPADDING attribute with a value of "5" to the <TABLE> tag.

   b. Save your work, then reload travel-e.htm in your browser.

6. Align table contents.

   a. In your text editor, add the ALIGN attribute with a value of "center" to the <TD> for the text "Hiking" in the first data row.

   b. Repeat step a for the cells containing the text "Swimming/Boating" in the fourth row, and the text "Mountain biking" in the sixth row.

   c. Save your work, then reload travel-e.htm in your browser.

7. Position page elements.

   a. In your text editor, insert a blank line above the <IMG> tag for the graphic nomad.gif, then enter the <TABLE> tag on this line.

   b. Insert a blank line below the <TABLE> tag, then insert two spaces and the <TR> tag on this line.

   c. At the beginning of the line containing the <IMG> tag, insert four spaces followed by the <TD> tag, including the attributes VALIGN with a value of "top", and WIDTH with a value of "220".

   d. At the beginning of the line starting with the <H2> tag, insert four spaces followed by the <TD> tag, including the attributes VALIGN with a value of "center", and HEIGHT with a value of "90".

   e. In the <FONT> tag to the right of the <H2> tag, add the FACE attribute with a value of "arial, helvetica, sans serif".

   f. Insert a blank line after the closing </H2> tag, insert two spaces and the closing </TR> tag, insert another blank line below it, then insert the </TABLE> tag.

   g. Save your work, then reload travel-e.htm in your browser.

► Independent Challenges

1. You have created a Web site for your computer consulting business, Star Dot Star. The site has already attracted new customers, and you want to expand the site to include information that would be of interest to potential customers, as well as to your existing clients. You have created a list of troubleshooting suggestions for common computer problems, and decide to add a table containing this information to your Web site.

To complete this independent challenge:

a. Open the file HTM E-4.htm in your text editor, then save it as a text document with the filename sds-e.htm.

b. Replace the <!-- and //--> tags with the opening and closing tags for a table, then format the enclosed contents as a simple table with the column headings "Problem" and "Possible solutions".

c. If there are "Possible solutions" that apply to more than one "Problem", span rows, if necessary.

d. Start your Web browser, preview the table, and fix any errors, if necessary.

e. Select one or more appropriate background colors, look up the hexadecimal codes in an HTML reference, and add the colors to the table.

f. Make any other changes to the table layout that you feel are appropriate; at minimum, use two of the following: CELLPADDING, CELLSPACING, WIDTH, HEIGHT, or BORDER="*value*".

g. If you have access to other computers with different monitor sizes and/or resolutions, use them to preview your Web page, then make layout changes, if necessary, so the table is attractive and usable when viewed on each monitor.

2. You have been setting up the Web site for Metro Water, the local water department. Now that you know how to position page elements using borderless tables, you want to create an HTML document containing only the logo and main headings. The document will serve as a template for adding new pages to the Web site.

To complete this independent challenge:

a. Open the file HTM E-5.htm in your text editor and save it as mw-e.htm.

b. Create a table with one row and two columns, containing the graphic in the first column and the two headings in the second column.

c. Remove the spacing and alignment attributes from the image tag.

d. Format the cell containing the headings so the text is centered over a wide area.

e. Format the heading fonts to match the setting for the rest of the page.

f. Start your Web browser, and preview the template, then make changes if necessary.

3. At your video store, Film Clips, you maintain an HTML-based information system for customer use. You want to add a link on the opening page that opens a table of popular rentals and new releases.

To complete this independent challenge:

a. Sketch a table incorporating at least three columns with information about 10 recent video releases; use information on movies that you are familiar with, or create fictitious information.

b. Start your text editor and create a basic Web page including the logo (fclogo.gif) and any headings and hyperlinks you think are appropriate, then save your file as fc-e.htm.

c. Create the table of films based on your sketch.

d. Save your work, start your Web browser program to preview the page, then make corrections to the code, if necessary.

e. Customize the table layout using, at minimum, three of the following attributes: BGCOLOR, CELLPADDING, CELLSPACING, WIDTH, HEIGHT, or BORDER="*value*".

f. Save and preview the page, then make final corrections if necessary.

4. Nearly all Web sites today include tables. Although certain Web pages display information in tables with gridlines, this is a relatively uncommon use of tables in Web pages. Instead, Web designers have found various uses of tables for layout, and use them frequently. Explore the HTML code of several documents on the Web to learn how tables are used in Web pages today.
To complete this independent challenge:

a. Connect to the Internet and use your browser to open the home pages for three major, well-designed Web sites. These might include technology companies, search engines, media outlets, government sites, or colleges or universities, such as the following:
hotwired.lycos.com/webmonkey/
www.sfsu.edu
www.course.com
If you have trouble locating three appropriate pages, go to www.course.com, navigate to the page for this book, click the link for the Student Online Companion, click the link for this unit, and use the links listed there as a starting point for your search.

b. After each Web page opens, click View, then click Source (or Page Source) in your browser to view the HTML code for the Web page.

c. Locate any borderless tables in the page. If the code is long, search for the tags by pressing [Ctrl][F] (Navigator) or selecting Search>Find (Internet Explorer), entering "<TABLE>", and pressing [Enter].

d. Compare the code and the Web page displayed in the browser to determine the function of the page's table(s).

e. Create a Web page with the name table-e.htm and implement a borderless table for one of the uses you identified.

► Visual Workshop

As part of your job at Touchstone Books, you've been setting up the store's Web site. Your latest plans include adding a table that shows the top-selling books sorted by category. Open the file HTM E-6.htm and save it as tsb-e.htm. Use your text editor to modify the document so it matches Figure E-22 when viewed in your browser. Use a structuring table for the image and headings, then add a second table to display the book information.

FIGURE E-22

Touchstone Booksellers

Top-selling books for October, 2002

Category	Author	Title
Children's	Oppenheim	*I Wuv OO, Too!*
Fiction	Al-sayed	*The Only One You'll Ever Have*
Historical	Munoz	*The 44th President*
How-to	Jordan	*Classical Guitar in 5 Minutes a Day*
Non-fiction	Conrad	*How to be Your Child's Favorite Teacher*
Self-help	Wallach	*Kick It!*
Technical	Reding and Vodnik	*HTML - Illustrated*

Controlling

Page Layout

HTML was originally designed for identifying the content of each element on a Web page, rather than specifying how an element should appear in a browser. In early versions of the language, this underlying intent meant that Web designers couldn't implement the layout and readability features routinely found in print media. However, in the course of updates and extensions to HTML, the language added two features that opened the door to high-quality page layout on the Web: frames and tables. **Frames** allow you to divide the browser window into parts, each of which appears as a separate HTML document. Tables, in addition to displaying related data within a grid, also can create a page layout much like those created with frames. However, pages using tables can be easier to navigate than pages with frames, and are accessible to more users. ✐ Jaime Chavez works in the Information Systems department at Nomad Ltd, a travel and sporting goods company. He is responsible for converting Nomad's Web site to a new design, and for making the pages easier for users to navigate.

Understanding Layout Tools

An important feature of any visual layout designed to convey information is the layout's division into discrete sections. While you can divide a page using HTML elements such as headings and line breaks, such a format is **linear**, meaning it limits you to stacking page elements above and below each other, and provides few options for horizontal placement. Frames and tables both facilitate more effective layouts in HTML by allowing you to place elements anywhere on the screen, and by providing additional means of indicating divisions between them. In a frames page, such as the one shown in Figure F-1, each section of the page appears as a separate HTML document. A page organized with a table, as shown in Figure F-2, includes the entire page contents in one HTML file. Using either layout tool, you have the choice of displaying or hiding borders, and each option is appropriate for creating different effects. As Jaime prepares to enhance the layout of the Nomad Ltd Web pages, he reviews the principal advantages of laying out a Web site using frames and tables.

Details

Grids

Layouts in print media tend to use a **grid**, which is a set of columns and rows that positions and groups a page's elements. You can easily add a grid to a Web page by creating columns and rows with the HTML table tags. Implementing frames also provides this underlying structure, as each frame can serve as a separate column or row. The ability to create a layout grid is the underlying feature of tables and frames that makes them both especially valuable for page layout.

Unified appearance

As you incorporate more pages into a Web site, it becomes important to ensure that users can easily navigate the site. After following a trail of links away from the home page, a user may wish to explore another area of the site. Rather than requiring users to return to the main page, well-designed sites usually include a **navigation bar**—a set of links to the home page and main sections of the site—which appears on every page. In the most user-friendly sites, the navigation bar, as well as other page elements, appear in the same location on each page, giving all the site's pages a unified appearance. This predictable layout reassures users that they won't get lost, and encourages them to explore the site. You can easily implement a unified appearance on your site by creating a template document that codes only for the site's page structure, and by using this document as the basis for each Web page.

FIGURE F-1: Web page layout using frames

Each frame scrolls independently

FIGURE F-2: Web page layout using structuring table

Cascading Style Sheets

Although frames and tables both are powerful Web page layout tools, they were created for simpler tasks, and neither offers an exhaustive set of design options. However, HTML has been updated to include **Cascading Style Sheets (CSS)**, an HTML extension specifically designed for Web page formatting and layout. CSS allows you to specify settings for many properties of page elements, including horizontal and vertical positions. CSS is easy to use because it allows you to indicate values for an element as tag attributes, rather than requiring separate tags. CSS also is more intuitive and easier to implement than any earlier page design schemes. CSS is not consistently implemented in different brands of browsers, however, meaning that most Web users cannot yet reliably view Web pages that use CSS. Frames and tables therefore will remain the dominant tools for effective Web page layout until browsers more universally support CSS.

Creating a Navigation Bar

Although you can add a simple navigation bar to any page layout, creating a grid layout provides more choices for the bar's formatting and its location on the page. You can position the bar's paragraphs or graphics at the bottom of the screen in a linear layout, but positioning the bar in the same place on each page could require adding imprecise spacing elements, such as line breaks. By contrast, when using a frame or a table you can specify the exact dimensions of each component part, allowing you to easily use a consistent page location. Additionally, in a grid layout you can create a vertical navigation bar, running along the left or right edge of the browser window, and include other page elements alongside it. ▶ Jaime begins his redesign by creating a navigation bar which he can then incorporate into the page layout for the Nomad Web site.

Steps

1. **Start your text editor, open the file HTM F-1.htm, then save it as navbar.htm**
   Jaime created an HTML document containing the link text for a vertical toolbar, the codes for the Nomad Ltd logo, and a site search form.

2. **Locate the <IMG> tag that references the graphic gear.gif, click to the left of the opening <, then type <A HREF="construction.htm">**
   Jaime links the navigation bar elements to a placeholder file until he creates the remaining Web pages for the site.

3. **Click to the right of the closing > for the gear.gif <IMG> tag, then type </A>**

4. **Repeat Steps 2 and 3 for the <IMG> tags for the files travel.gif and about.gif**
   The graphics serve as headings that divide the links in the navigation bar by the site's three main sections.

5. **Locate the <LI> tag for the text Hiking/Camping, click to the right of the closing >, type <A HREF="construction.htm">, click at the end of the same line, then type </A>**

6. **Repeat Step 5 for the remaining list items in the navigation bar's three unordered lists**
   Figure F-3 shows the completed code for the links in the navigation bar. Jaime created most of the links with text, rather than graphics, so the Web page's download time is kept to a minimum.

7. **Save your work, start your Web browser, cancel any dial-up operations, then open the file navbar.htm**
   As shown in Figure F-4, the list of links appears on the left edge of the screen, along with the logo and the search form. Jaime can incorporate this navigation bar into the layout for each page in his new site design.

FIGURE F-3: Web page code for navigation bar

```
<A HREF="construction.htm"><IMG SRC="images/gear.gif" WIDTH="158" HEIGHT="25"
BORDER="0" ALIGN="center" ALT="Gear"></A>

<UL>
  <LI><A HREF="construction.htm">Hiking/Camping</A>
  <LI><A HREF="construction.htm">Biking</A>
  <LI><A HREF="construction.htm">Clothing</A>
  <LI><A HREF="construction.htm'>Climbing</A>
  <LI><A HREF="construction.htm'>Swimming</A>
  <LI><A HREF="construction.htm'>Boating</A>
  <LI><A HREF="construction.htm">Skiing</A>
</UL>

<A HREF="construction.htm"><IMG SRC="images/travel.gif" WIDTH="158"
HEIGHT="25" BORDER="0" ALIGN="center" ALT="Travel"></A>

<UL>
  <LI><A HREF="construction.htm">Leisure tours</A>
  <LI><A HREF="construction.htm">Athlete tours</A>
  <LI><A HREF="construction.htm">Arts tours</A>
  <LI><A HREF="construction.htm">Travel planning</A>
</UL>

<A HREF="construction.htm"><IMG SRC="images/about.
BORDER="0" ALIGN="center" ALT="About Us"></A>

<UL>
```

```
<A HREF="construction.htm"><IMG SRC="images/about.gif" WIDTH="158" HEIGHT="25"
BORDER="0" ALIGN="center" ALT="About Us"></A>

<UL>
  <LI><A HREF='construction.htm">Stores</A>
  <LI><A HREF="construction.htm">History</A>
  <LI><A HREF= 'construction.htm">Corporate Info</A>
  <LI><A HREF="construction.htm">Contact</A>
</UL>

<H5>updated August 24, 2002</H5>
```

Text and graphics
formatted as links

FIGURE F-4: Navigation bar

Contents appear in
narrow vertical strip

Text and graphics
are linked for easy
access to rest of
Web site

Creating a horizontal navigation bar

Just as with a vertical navigation bar, you can lay out a navigation bar horizontally using common Web page tags and elements. A vertical configuration often uses a list format, such as ordered or unordered lists, or a series of heading tags. To create a horizontal navigation bar, you can usually insert a unique dividing character between each adjacent set of link text. A character commonly used for this purpose is the **pipe** character (|), which you can type using the button above the Enter key on most keyboards. Figure F-5 shows a text-based horizontal navigation bar that uses pipes to separate adjacent links.

FIGURE F-5: Horizontal navigation bar

2-lines of text links
appear horizontally

Feedback | Help | About Us | Contribute | Jobs Advertise
Editorial Policy | Privacy Statement | Terms and Conditions

Text of adjacent links
separated by a pipe

Unit F

HTML

Creating a Frameset

In a Web page laid out with frames, each frame displays the contents of a separate HTML document. These component documents are created with the same tags used for standard Web pages. To specify the organization of these files within the browser window—known as a **frameset**— you create a separate HTML document that includes only the page's structural information. Figure F-6 shows the relationship between HTML files in a frames page. The organizing document requires three HTML tags and tag pairs to describe the frame layout. The tags and tag pairs are described in Table F-1, along with their attributes. ◢ Jaime has divided the contents of his new design into two separate HTML documents, similar to the sketch in Figure F-6. Each document will appear in a frame on the Nomad Ltd home page. Jaime lays out the page by creating a frameset.

Steps

1. **In your browser, open the file main.htm**
   This is the Nomad Ltd home page that will appear in the right frame of the frameset when users first opens the Nomad Web site. For the content of the left frame, Jaime will use the navigation bar he created.

2. **In your text editor, start a new document, if necessary, and save it as nomad-f1.htm**

3. **Type <HTML>, press [Enter] twice, type <HEAD>, press [Enter], type <TITLE>Nomad Ltd online</TITLE>, press [Enter], type </HEAD>, then press [Enter] twice**

> **QuickTip**
>
> To create a frameset composed of rows instead of columns, use the ROWS attribute in place of COLS.

4. **Type <FRAMESET COLS="235,*" FRAMEBORDER="0">, then press [Enter]**
   <FRAMESET> is the opening tag that marks the contents of a frameset. In a frameset document, this tag replaces the standard HTML <BODY> tag. You use the COLS attribute to indicate the width of each column, in pixels. Jaime specifies the width of the first column— the navigation bar—as 235 pixels, and uses an asterisk (*) for the width of the second column, indicating that it should occupy the remaining width of the browser window. He sets the FRAMEBORDER attribute equal to zero to remove the default border that appears between frames.

> **QuickTip**
>
> To divide a frame, you can enter a <FRAMESET> tag pair in place of a <FRAME> tag, and use <FRAME> tags within this pair to specify the sources of the pair's frame documents.

5. **Press [Spacebar] twice, type <FRAME SRC="navbar.htm" NAME="nav">, press [Enter], press [Spacebar] twice, type <FRAME SRC="main.htm" NAME="main">, press [Enter], type </FRAMESET>, then press [Enter] twice**
   Each frame requires a <FRAME> tag that specifies the name and location of its source file using the SRC attribute. It also is important to name each frame using the NAME attribute, so that each frame's hyperlinks work properly.

6. **Type <NOFRAMES>, press [Enter], type This page was designed to be viewed with frames. You can open individual pages using the <A HREF="navbar.htm">navigation bar</A>., press [Enter], type </NOFRAMES>, press [Enter] twice, then type </HTML>**
   Figure F-7 shows the completed code for the frameset Web page. The text enclosed in the <NOFRAMES>..<NOFRAMES> tag pair appears in the window of a browser that does not support frames. Jaime's alternate text provides a link to the navigation bar, and ensures that users of older browsers still can access the entire site.

7. **Save your work, click the browser program button on the taskbar, then open the file nomad-f1.htm**
   The browser displays both frames, as shown in Figure F-8. Notice that each frame includes a toolbar, allowing you to scroll one side of the screen without moving the other side's contents.

FIGURE F-6: HTML files composing a frames page

Separate HTML document contains contents of left frame

Separate HTML document contains contents of right frame

Frameset document specifies structure only

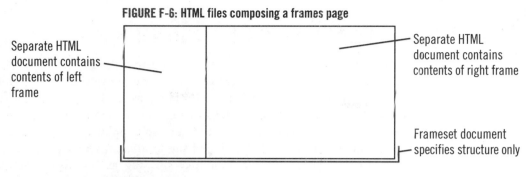

FIGURE F-7: Code for frameset file

Mark frameset contents

Format alternate content for incompatible browsers

Specify frame source files and names

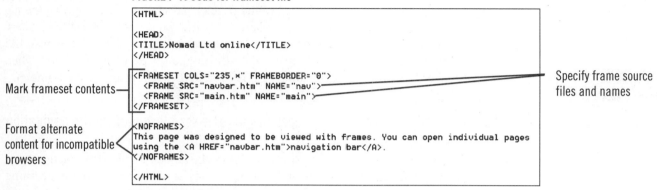

```
<HTML>

<HEAD>
<TITLE>Nomad Ltd online</TITLE>
</HEAD>

<FRAMESET COLS="235,*" FRAMEBORDER="0">
  <FRAME SRC="navbar.htm" NAME="nav">
  <FRAME SRC="main.htm" NAME="main">
</FRAMESET>

<NOFRAMES>
This page was designed to be viewed with frames. You can open individual pages
using the <A HREF="navbar.htm">navigation bar</A>.
</NOFRAMES>

</HTML>
```

FIGURE F-8: Frames page in browser

Page layout specified by nomad-f1.htm

Left frame displays navbar.htm

Right frame displays main.htm

Each frame scrolls independently

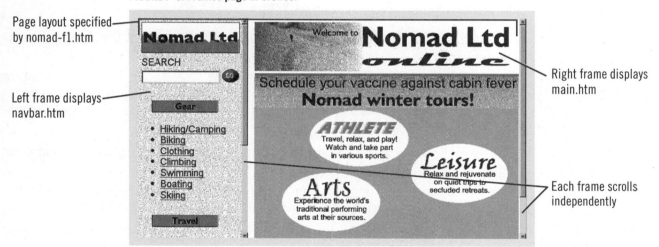

TABLE F-1: Frame tags and attributes

tag(s)	description	attributes	function
\<FRAMESET\>.. **\</FRAMESET\>**	mark frameset contents and describe their layout	ROWS	defines number and sizes of horizontal frames to create
		COLS	defines number and sizes of vertical frames to create
		FRAMEBORDER	turns border between frames on or off; set to "0" or "no" to turn borders off
\<FRAME\>	specifies a frame's source file and name	SRC	defines location and filename for frame contents
		NAME	defines frame name for reference by hyperlinks
\<NOFRAMES\>.. **\<NOFRAMES\>**	define alternate page content for browsers that don't support frames; require no attributes		

HTML

Targeting Links

When you click a link in a standard Web page, your browser usually displays the linked page in place of the current one. In a page structured with frames, however, you can choose in which frame the linked page will open. This feature of frames has facilitated a popular frameset layout that fixes a page of links in one frame, and displays content in another frame. When users click a link, the content of the other frame changes, but the display of links is preserved for further navigation. HTML offers two methods for setting the location where a linked page opens. One option is to add the TARGET attribute to a link's <A> tag, and set this attribute equal to the name of the frame in which the linked page should open. You also can create a global setting for all of a page's links by adding the <BASE> tag to the page's head section, and assigning the tag the appropriate TARGET setting. Table F-2 explains TARGET values with special behaviors. Jaime wants the navigation bar to remain visible to users as they explore the Nomad Ltd Web site. He adds the <BASE> tag with the TARGET attribute to the page's head section. Then when navigation bar links are clicked, the target pages open in the right frame of the frameset.

Steps

1. **Make sure the file nomad-f1.htm is open in your browser, click a link in the navigation bar, then click the Back button**
   When you click a link, the navigation bar is replaced by the link target file, construction.htm, and is no longer available in the frameset. By default, a linked page opens in the same frame as the link that opened it.

2. **In your text editor, open the file navbar.htm**

3. **Locate the </TITLE> tag in the head section, click to the right of the closing >, press [Enter], then type <BASE TARGET="main">**
   Figure F-9 shows the Web page code containing the <BASE> tag. When he created the frameset file, Jaime assigned the name "main" to the frame on the right side of the screen. By setting the TARGET attribute in the <BASE> tag, Jaime allows users to click any link in the left frame—the navigation bar—to change the contents of the right frame.

4. **Save your work, click the browser program button on the taskbar, then hold down [Shift] while you click your browser's Reload or Refresh button**
   In a frameset, refreshing the page simply reloads the current pages in each frame. Holding down [Shift] while refreshing reloads the default pages specified in the frameset file.

5. **Click a link from one of the unordered lists in the navigation bar**
   As shown in Figure F-10, a linked page opens in the right frame, and indicates that the site is still under construction. The navigation bar remains in the left frame, allowing you to continue moving around the site.

6. **Click your browser's Back button, then click one of the linked graphics in the right frame**
   The "under construction" page opens in the right frame. Because Jaime's opening page for the right frame doesn't specify a TARGET value for the links, the linked pages open by default in the same frame, as Jaime intended.

```
<HTML>

<HEAD>
<TITLE>Nomad Ltd navigation bar</TITLE>
<BASE TARGET="main">
</HEAD>

<BODY BACKGROUND="images/eggshell.jpg">
```

TARGET sets target
for all links in
HTML document

FIGURE F-10: Linked file opened in different frame

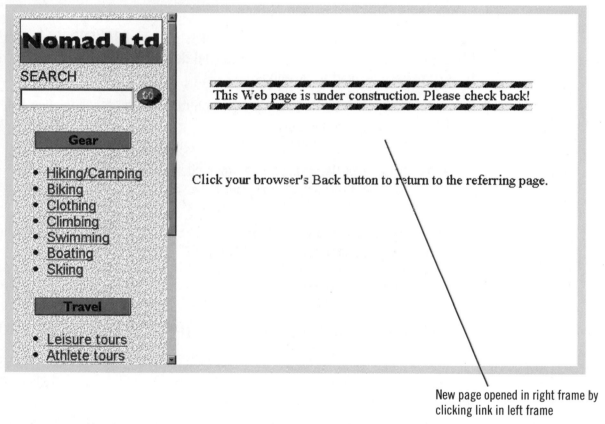

New page opened in right frame by
clicking link in left frame

TABLE F-2: Special values for the TARGET attribute

value	link behavior
_blank	opens in new browser window
_self	opens in current frame; this is the default setting
_parent	replaces current frameset; always include for links to pages outside your frameset
_top	replaces contents of current browser window

HTML

HTML

Formatting Frame Borders

Like most other Web page elements, frames support the attributes that change the frames' appearance in a browser. Several of these attributes are similar to those used to format tables. Although no borders appear between frames by default, you can use the FRAMEBORDER attribute in the <FRAMESET> tag to add them. Once a frameset includes borders, you can use other attributes to control border thickness and color, as well as the width of the margin between a frame's border and its contents. By default, Web page users can move the borders between frames to change the amount of the browser window that each frame occupies. If you want to make sure your layout remains fixed, you can add the NORESIZE attribute to <FRAME> tags to ensure that the frames remain the width or height you specified in the <FRAMESET> tag. Table F-3 describes several attributes available for formatting frames. ◆ Jaime wants to experiment with borders and border formats in his layout.

Steps

1. In your text editor, open **nomad-f1.htm**

2. Locate the opening <FRAMESET> tag, select the text **FRAMEBORDER="0"**, press **[Delete]**, then, if necessary, again press **[Delete]** or press **[Backspace]** to remove the extra space before the closing >

3. Save your work, click the **browser program button** on the taskbar, then hold down **[Shift]** while you reload **nomad-f1.htm**
   A vertical line marks the border between the two frames.

4. Move the pointer over the frame border, then click and drag to the right
   The pointer changes to a double arrow, indicating you can resize the frames. Dragging the border to the right resizes each frame.

5. In your text editor, locate the opening <FRAMESET> tag, click to the left of the closing >, press **[Spacebar]**, then type **BORDER="2" FRAMESPACING="2"**
   The BORDER and FRAMESPACING attributes change the thickness of borders between frames. Because each attribute is appropriate for different browsers, Jaime uses both with the same setting to ensure his frames appear similarly to all users.

6. Click to the left of the closing > in the first <FRAME> tag, press **[Spacebar]**, then type **NORESIZE**
   Figure F-11 shows the completed code for the frameset document. Adding the NORESIZE attribute to a <FRAME> tag prevents users from resizing that frame, as well as adjoining frames, in the browser window.

7. Save your work, click the **browser program button**, then hold down **[Shift]** while you reload **nomad-f1.htm**
   As shown in Figure F-12, the border between the two frames appears narrower.

8. Move the pointer over the frame border, then click and drag to the right
   Because you added the NORESIZE attribute to the left frame, the pointer does not change to a double arrow, and the frame border remains in its original location to maintain the frame sizes.

FIGURE F-11: Web page code for formatting frame borders

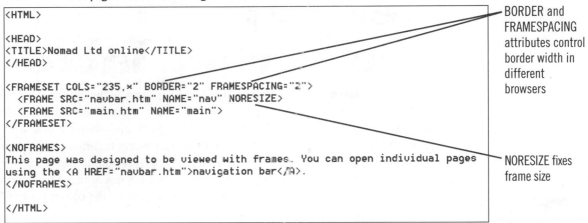

```
<HTML>

<HEAD>
<TITLE>Nomad Ltd online</TITLE>
</HEAD>

<FRAMESET COLS="235,*" BORDER="2" FRAMESPACING="2">
  <FRAME SRC="navbar.htm" NAME="nav" NORESIZE>
  <FRAME SRC="main.htm" NAME="main">
</FRAMESET>

<NOFRAMES>
This page was designed to be viewed with frames. You can open individual pages
using the <A HREF="navbar.htm">navigation bar</A>.
</NOFRAMES>

</HTML>
```

BORDER and FRAMESPACING attributes control border width in different browsers

NORESIZE fixes frame size

FIGURE F-12: Web page displaying border between frames

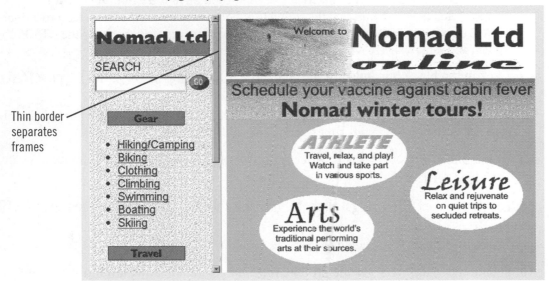

Thin border separates frames

TABLE F-3: Frame formatting attributes

tag	attribute	function	allowable values
<FRAMESET>	FRAMEBORDER	determines whether or not borders appear	"0" or "no" turns off borders; "1" or "yes" enables borders (the default setting)
	BORDER	specifies the space between frames in more recent browsers	a size in pixels
	FRAMESPACING	specifies the space between frames in older browsers	a size in pixels
	BORDERCOLOR	customizes color of lines separating frames	hexadecimal color value or corresponding color name
<FRAME>	MARGINHEIGHT	specifies space between frame contents and top and bottom borders	a size in pixels
	MARGINWIDTH	specifies space between frame contents and left and right borders	a size in pixels
	NORESIZE	prevents users from changing a frame's dimensions	requires no value; the presence of NORESIZE enables this option
	SCROLLING	controls the appearance of the frame's scrollbars	"yes" always includes scrollbars; "no" prevents scrollbars from appearing; when attribute is absent, scrollbars appear only as needed

HTML

Creating a Structuring Table

Besides using frames, you also can lay out a Web page in a grid by using a structuring table. This method reverses the way you are used to working with tables. Rather than including a table as one of a Web page's elements, you include all the page elements within one large table. A structuring table offers positioning benefits similar to frames, yet it simplifies for your users some of the practical aspects of working with the Web page. ◀ Jaime decides to try his layout in a structuring table, to compare its appearance with frames. Some areas of his Web page are already positioned using their own tables. These tables will in turn be the contents of individual cells in the structuring table, making them **nested tables**.

QuickTip

A few cells in the nested tables use the closing </TD> tag; while this tag is normally unnecessary, without it the contents of nested tables can unpredictably appear in some browsers.

1. In your text editor, open the file **HTM F-2.htm**, then save it as **nomad-f2.htm**
Jaime created this file by pasting the contents of both frames from the frameset into a single HTML document. He also indented each line six extra spaces—two each for the <TABLE>, <TR>, and <TD> tags in which each element will be nested.

2. Click in the blank line beneath the opening <BODY> tag, press [**Enter**], type **<TABLE BORDER CELLSPACING="0">**, then press [**Enter**]
Although a borderless structuring table is usually the most effective for layout, Jaime temporarily turns on the borders to facilitate the creation and editing process.

3. In the blank line below the <TABLE> tag you just entered, press [**Spacebar**] twice, then type **<TR>**

4. Locate the <FONT> tag, click to the left of the opening <, then type **<TD WIDTH="235">**
Figure F-13 shows the opening code for the structuring table.

5. Locate the <IMG> tag for the graphic welcome.jpg, click to the left of the opening <, then type **<TD VALIGN="top">**
Because Jaime does not specify a WIDTH value for the second column, it will occupy the remaining width of the browser window.

QuickTip

Just as in a table with other contents, you can include multiple rows in a structuring table.

6. Click the blank line above the closing </BODY> tag, press [**Enter**], press [**Spacebar**] twice, type **</TR>**, press [**Enter**], type **</TABLE>**, then press [**Enter**]
Figure F-14 shows the code for the right column, and the closing code for the structuring table.

7. Save your work, click the **browser program button** on the taskbar, then open the file **nomad-f2.htm**
The layout is nearly identical to the one Jaime created with frames.

8. In your text editor, scroll to the <TD> tag for the left cell in the structuring table near the top of the document, select the number **235**, press [**Delete**], then type **220**
Because the cell containing the navigation bar doesn't need to be as wide as the frame that contained it in the frameset, Jaime tries a lower WIDTH setting.

9. Save your work, click the **browser program button** on the taskbar, then open the file **nomad-f2.htm**
As shown in Figure F-15, the structuring table re-creates the layout of the frameset.

FIGURE F-13: Opening Web page code for structuring table

```
</HEAD>

<BODY>

<TABLE BORDER CELLSPACING="0">
  <TR>
    <TD WIDTH="235"><FONT FACE="arial, helvetica, sans serif">
      <TABLE>
        <FORM NAME="sitesearch">
```

Opening table and row tags, and tag for first cell

FIGURE F-14: Additional Web page code for structuring table

```
     <H5>updated August 24, 2002</H5>

  <TD VALIGN="top"><IMG SRC="images/welcome.jpg" ALT="Welcome to Nomad Ltd
online" WIDTH="540" HEIGHT="100">

     <TABLE CELLSPACING="0" CELLPADDING="0" BORDER="0" BGCOLOR="#B0E0E6"
```

Tag for second table cell

```
            <A HREF="construction.htm"><IMG SRC="images/skibar.jpg" WIDTH="500"
HEIGHT="63" BORDER="0" ALT="Ski off into the sunset - Fall into Winter sale,
October 3-8"></A>
```

```
         </TR>
      </TABLE>
```

Closing row and table tags

```
      </BODY>
```

FIGURE F-15: Web page laid out with structuring table

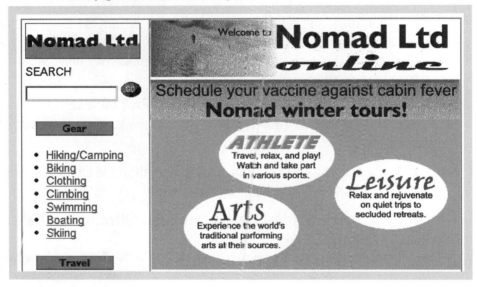

Frames vs. Tables

Frames and tables both have strengths and weaknesses for Web page layout. Frames offer several features that tables can't match—independently scrolling window areas and decreased bandwidth demands. Most professional Web designers, however, find that the practical advantages of tables outweigh the benefits of frames. Because all the page contents of a table layout are contained in one HTML file, table layouts are easier for users to print, and they provide more accurate data for search engine indexes. Additionally, while a browser's address bar always displays the name and location of the frameset file (regardless of which content pages are open in the frames), the URL for a page structured with a table always describes the exact location of the current content. This characteristic is especially important to accurately bookmark pages for later use. While frames are a valuable tool in your HTML toolbox and are appropriate for certain applications, tables are often the best choice for creating Web page layouts.

Adding a Two-Toned Background

When you create a page with frames, it's easy to distinguish the contents of separate frames by formatting each frame's background with a different graphic or color. The process for differentiating cell contents in a structuring table, however, is more restricted. While the <FRAME> tag supports settings for background images or color, not all browsers can display a background image for a table cell. Different colored cell backgrounds are a fine choice for many layouts. However, tables are always separated from the window edges by a margin of space, so Web designers have invented other solutions to create a frames-like layout. One of the most popular solutions is to use a customized graphic as the background for the entire page. By matching the measurements of the structuring table cells, the graphic can display a background image—usually in a vertical strip—behind the appropriate part of the Web page.   Jaime wants to include a background behind the navigation bar (as he did in the frames version of the page), in order to set it clearly apart from the rest of the page.

Steps

1. In your text editor, locate the <TD> tag for the first table cell, click to the left of the closing >, press [Spacebar], then type **BGCOLOR="#DAC79E"**
   Jaime experiments first with adding a background color to the navigation bar cell.

2. Save your work, click the **browser program button** on the taskbar, then reload **nomad-f2.htm**
   As Figure F-16 shows, the table displays the background color only within the borders of the navigation bar cell.

3. In your text editor, select the text **BGCOLOR="#DAC79E"** that you typed, press [**Delete**], again press [**Delete**], or press [**Backspace**] if necessary, to remove the extra space

4. Locate the opening <BODY> tag, click to the left of the closing >, press [**Spacebar**], then type **BACKGROUND="images/tablebg.jpg"**

5. Save your work, click the **browser program button** on the taskbar, then reload **nomad-f2.htm**
   The background image appears behind the contents of the left column only. Because browsers normally tile images to cover the entire Web page background, the Nomad Web design team set up the dimensions of this image to be wider than a normal browser window. The background pattern appears in the left edge of the image. The rest of the image is blank, ensuring that the background pattern appears behind only one column.

6. In your text editor, locate the opening <TABLE> tag for the structuring table, click to the right of the word BORDER, then type **="0"**
   Figure F-17 shows the completed code for the Web page. Because he has finished setting up the page, Jaime turns off borders on the structuring table to view the page's final appearance.

7. Save your work, click the **browser program button** on the taskbar, then reload **nomad-f2.htm**
   Figure F-18 shows the final appearance of Jaime's Web page.

FIGURE F-16: Navigation bar formatted with table cell background color

Color appears only within cell borders

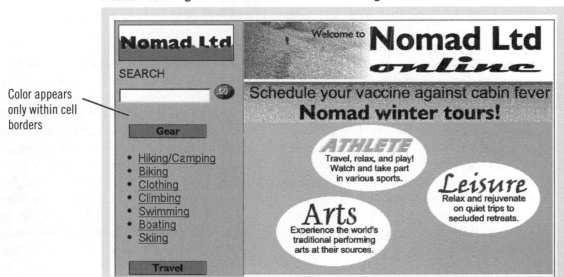

FIGURE F-17: Web page code containing final changes for background and border

Adds background image behind navigation bar only

Removes borders from structuring table

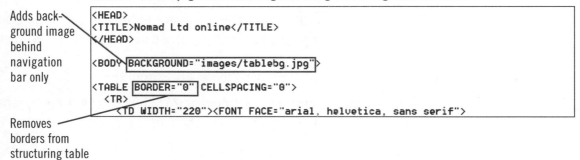

```
<HEAD>
<TITLE>Nomad Ltd online</TITLE>
</HEAD>

<BODY BACKGROUND="images/tablebg.jpg">

<TABLE BORDER="0" CELLSPACING="0">
  <TR>
    <TD WIDTH="220"><FONT FACE="arial, helvetica, sans serif">
```

FIGURE F-18: Final Web page layout with structuring table

Background image displays texture only behind navigation bar

HTML

Creating a Template

Once you finalize your site layout with a structuring table, it's important to uniformly implement the layout on all your Web site's pages. Rather than reentering the code for common elements for every page in your site, however, you can facilitate the application of your design by creating a template. A **template** contains the Web page code for the page's structure, along with any text or other elements that appear on every page. You can create a template by removing the page-specific items from your original layout. It also is good practice to add comments to the code, so that anyone using the template clearly understands where to insert their own page-specific elements. You then can use the template as a starting point to create each additional page for the Web site. ✐ After he presented his samples of both options and explained the advantages and drawbacks of each, Jaime's Web design team decided to use his structuring table design for the entire Nomad Web site. Jaime wants to create a template from his Web page to make the team's work on the site more efficient, and to ensure that each team member implements the same layout.

Steps

1. In your text editor, save a copy of **nomad-f2.htm** as **nltemp-f.htm**

2. Locate the <BODY> tag, click the blank line below the tag, press [Enter], type <!-- **Web page structuring table, one row by two columns** -->, then press [Enter]

3. Locate the <TR> tag for the structuring table, click to the right of the closing >, press [Enter] twice, type <!-- **first column - site-standard navigation bar** -->, then press [Enter]
   Figure F-19 shows the Web page code containing the first two comments.

4. Click the blank line below the text updated August 24, 2002, press [Enter], type <!--**second column - page-specific content** -->, then press [Enter]

5. Click and drag to select the text shown in Figure F-20, beginning with the <IMG> tag for the graphic welcome.jpg and ending with the </A> tag for the graphic skibar.jpg, then press [Delete]
   Figure F-21 shows the end section of the template with page-specific content removed. Jaime deleted the contents of the right column in the structuring table, leaving just the <TD> tag for the cell.

6. Save your work, then close your text editor and browser

FIGURE F-19: Opening comments in Web page template code

Comments describing page layout components

```
<BODY BACKGROUND="images/tablebg.jpg">

<!-- Web page structuring table, one row by two columns -->

<TABLE BORDER="0" CELLSPACING="0">
  <TR>

<!-- first column - site-standard navigation bar -->

    <TD WIDTH="220"><FONT FACE="arial, helvetica, sans serif">
```

FIGURE F-20: Template code showing content to delete

Comments marking page-specific cell tag

Page-specific content to delete

```
      <H5>updated August 24, 2002</H5>

<!--second column - page-specific content -->

    <TD VALIGN="top"><IMG SRC="images/welcome jpg" ALT="Welcome to Nomad Ltd
online" WIDTH="540" HEIGHT="100">

      <TABLE CELLSPACING="0" CELLPADDING="0" BORDER="0" BGCOLOR="#B0E0E6"
WIDTH="541">
        <TR>
          <TD COLSPAN="2"><A HREF="construction.htm"><IMG
SRC="images/gradient.jpg" WIDTH="540" HEIGHT="70" BORDER="0" ALT="Schedule
your vaccine against cabin fever - Nomad  winter tours!"></A>
        </TR>

        <TR>
          <TD AL
SRC="images/athl
BORDER="0"></A><
          <TD RO
HREF="constructi
ALT="Leisure" BO
        </TR>

        <TR>
          <TD HE
SRC="images/arts
```

```
          <TD ALIGN="right" WIDTH="300"><A HREF="construction.htm"><IMG
SRC="images/athlete.gif" WIDTH="203" HEIGHT="116" ALT="Athlete"
BORDER="0"></A></TD>
          <TD ROWSPAN="2" ALIGN="left" VALIGN="center"><A
HREF="construction"><IMG SRC="images/leisure.gif" WIDTH="197" HEIGHT="124"
ALT="Leisure" BORDER="0"></A>
        </TR>

        <TR>
          <TD HEIGHT="145" ALIGN="center"><A HREF="construction.htm"><IMG
SRC="images/arts.gif" WIDTH="202" HEIGHT="121" ALT="Arts" BORDER="0"></A>
        </TR>
      </TABLE>

      <BR>

      <A HREF="construction.htm"><IMG SRC="images/skibar.jpg" WIDTH="500"
HEIGHT="63" BORDER="0" ALT="Ski off into the sunset - Fall into Winter sale,
October 3-8"></A>

  </TR>
</TABLE>
```

FIGURE F-21: Template code with page-specific content deleted

```
      <H5>updated August 24, 2002</H5>

<!--second column - page-specific content -->

    <TD VALIGN="top">

  </TR>
</TABLE>
```

HTML

Practice

► Concepts Review

Describe the function of each tag and attribute marked in Figure F-22.

FIGURE F-22

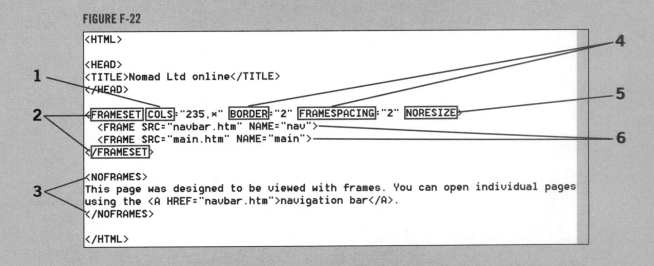

```
<HTML>

<HEAD>
<TITLE>Nomad Ltd online</TITLE>
</HEAD>
<FRAMESET COLS="235,*" BORDER="2" FRAMESPACING="2" NORESIZE>
  <FRAME SRC="navbar.htm" NAME="nav">
  <FRAME SRC="main.htm" NAME="main">
</FRAMESET>

<NOFRAMES>
This page was designed to be viewed with frames. You can open individual pages
using the <A HREF="navbar.htm">navigation bar</A>.
</NOFRAMES>

</HTML>
```

1
2
3
4
5
6

Match each term with its description.

7. Template
8. Frameset
9. Frame
10. Grid
11. Navigation bar

a. A file specifying the organization of frame files within the browser window
b. A set of links to the home page and main sections of a Web site, and which appears on every page
c. A tool containing the Web page code for the structural and content elements that appear on all the pages in a Web site
d. A window within a frameset, which displays a separate HTML document
e. A set of columns and rows that positions and groups a page's elements

Select the best answer from the list of choices.

12. In a Web page laid out with frames, each frame displays
    a. The contents of a separate Web document.
    b. The contents of a table cell.
    c. A hyperlinked page.
    d. The same Web document.

13. Which tag would you use to set all of a frame's links to open in a different frame?
    a. <BODY>
    b. <HEAD>
    c. <BASE>
    d. <!--

14. Which attribute do you use to name a frame?
    a. ID
    b. NAME
    c. TITLE
    d. TARGET

15. What is the function of the FRAMEBORDER attribute?
    a. Determines whether or not borders appear
    b. Specifies the space between frames
    c. Specifies space between frame contents and top and bottom borders
    d. Specifies space between frame contents and left and right borders

16. What is the function of the BORDER and FRAMESPACING attributes?
    a. Determine whether or not borders appear
    b. Specify the space between frames
    c. Specify space between frame contents and top and bottom borders
    d. Specify space between frame contents and left and right borders

17. To add a background image to a section of the screen, rather than to a table cell, when you use a structuring table, you reference a special graphic file in which tag?
    a. <TABLE>
    b. <TR>
    c. <TD>
    d. <BODY>

18. How many HTML files would you need in order to create a frameset that displays three frames?
    a. One
    b. Two
    c. Three
    d. Four

19. Which tag defines an individual frame?
    a. <TABLE>
    b. <FRAME>
    c. <FRAMESET>
    d. <NOFRAMES>

 # Skills Review

1. **Create a navigation bar.**
    a. Start your text editor, open the file HTM F-3.htm, then save it as cco-nav.htm.
    b. Use <A>..</A> tags with the HREF attribute to format the graphic cco.gif, and the text "Home" in the first list item in the unordered list, as links to the file cco-main.htm.
    c. Format the text for the remaining list items as links to the file construction.htm.
    d. Save your work, start your Web browser, cancel any dial-up operations, then open the file cco-nav.htm.

2. **Create a frameset.**
    a. In your browser, open the file cco-main.htm.
    b. In your text editor, open a new document, and save it as cco-f1.htm.
    c. Enter the opening tags for the document, head, and body, including the page title "Crystal Clear Opticals".
    d. In the page's body section, enter the opening tag for a frameset with two frames and no border; the width of the first frame should be 240 pixels, and the second frame should occupy the remaining space.
    e. Below the frameset tag, add a tag for each of the frames on an indented line. The source of the first frame is the file cco-nav.htm, and it should be named nav; the source of the second frame is the file cco-main.htm, and it should be named main.
    f. Add the following text to the page, formatted to appear only to users whose browsers do not support frames: "This page was designed to be viewed with frames. You can open individual pages using the <A HREF="cco-nav.htm">navigation bar</A>."
    g. Save your work, click the browser program button on the taskbar, then open the file cco-f1.htm.

3. **Target links.**
    a. Make sure the file cco-f1.htm is open in your browser, click a link in the navigation bar, then click the Back button.
    b. In your text editor, open the file cco-nav.htm.
    c. Add HTML code to the page's head section. The code should target all links in the navigation bar to open in the frame named main.
    d. Save your work, click the browser program button on the taskbar, then hold down [Shift] while you click your browser's Reload or Refresh button.
    e. Click a link in the navigation bar.

4. Format frame borders.

   a. In your text editor, open the file cco-f1.htm.

   b. In the opening tag for the frameset, remove the attribute that suppresses frame borders.

   c. Add HTML code to the document to display a two-pixel border between frames in all compatible browsers.

   d. Add HTML code to the document to prevent users from changing frame sizes.

   e. Save your work, click the browser program button on the taskbar, then hold down [Shift] while you reload cco-f1.htm.

5. Create a structuring table.

   a. In your text editor, open the file HTM F-4.htm, then save it as cco-f2.htm.

   b. At the beginning of the page's body section, add an opening table tag that includes the HTML code to display table borders and which sets the space between cells to zero.

   c. In the line below the opening table tag you just entered, indent two spaces and enter an opening row tag. On the next line indent four spaces and enter an opening table cell tag.

   d. Scroll down to the blank line above the opening table tag for the borderless table below the navigation bar section, indent four spaces, then add a table cell tag.

   e. In the blank line above the closing tag for the page's body section, insert two spaces, enter a closing row tag, then insert a new line and enter the closing table tag.

   f. Save your work, click the browser program button on the taskbar, then open the file cco-f2.htm.

6. Add a two-tone background.

   a. In your text editor, edit the table tag for the first cell in the structuring table to include the background color #A8A8A5.

   b. Save your work, click the browser program button on the taskbar, then reload the file cco-f2.htm.

   c. In your text editor, remove the code for the background color that you inserted, then add code to the opening body tag to use the graphic graybg.jpg (located in the images folder) as the page background.

   d. Save your work, click the browser program button on the taskbar, then reload the file cco-f2.htm.

   e. In your text editor, edit the opening table tag for the structuring table and make the borders invisible.

   f. Save your work, click the browser program button on the taskbar, then reload cco-f2.htm.

7. Create a template.

   a. In your text editor, save a copy of cco-f2.htm as ccotmp-f.htm.

   b. Add a comment below the opening tag for the body section, stating that the following section is the page's structuring table.

   c. Add a comment before the tag for the first cell in the structuring table that describes the column and contents that follow.

   d. Add a comment before the tag for the second cell in the structuring table that describes the column and its contents.

   e. Delete the text that appears after the tag for the second cell in the structuring table and before its closing row tag (the text to delete begins with "<TABLE WIDTH="520">", and ends with "</TABLE>").

   f. Save your work, click the browser program button on the taskbar, open the file ccotmp-f.htm, then close your text editor and browser.

▶ Independent Challenges

1. You maintain a Web site for your computer consulting business, Star Dot Star. To advertise your Web design expertise, you decide to redesign your site by using a structuring table and incorporating a navigation bar.
   To complete this independent challenge:

a. Use a borderless table to create a navigation bar based on the bulleted list in the file HTM F-5.htm. Include the logo graphic in the file sds.jpg in your layout, and save your work with the filename sds-f.htm.
b. Lay out your Web page using a structuring table with one row and two columns; the navigation bar should appear in the left column, and the contents of the file HTM F-6.htm should appear in the right column. Use the graphic file sdsbg.jpg as the page's background image.
c. Create a template from your file for the site's remaining pages, and save it with the name sdstmp-f.htm. Be sure to include comments for other designers who might use the template.

2. You are part of the Web site maintenance team in your job at Metro Water, the local water supplier. As you continue to add more pages to the Web site, you decide to redesign the page to include a navigation bar and a consistent layout between pages by using a structuring table.
   To complete this independent challenge:

a. Use a borderless table to create a navigation bar based on the bulleted list in the file HTM F-7.htm; include the logo graphic in the file mw.gif in your layout, and save your work with the filename mw-f.htm.
b. Lay out your Web page using a structuring table with one row and two columns; the navigation bar should appear in the left column, and the contents of the file HTM F-8.htm should appear in the right column. Use the graphic file waterbg.jpg as the page's background image.
c. Create a template from your file for the site's remaining pages, and save it with the name mwtemp-f.htm. Be sure to include comments for other designers who might use the template.

3. You have created and implemented an HTML-based in-store information system for your video store, Film Clips. To make the site easier for customers to use, you decide to standardize the layout of all pages and add a navigation bar. Because the system is used only in your store, and bookmarking and printing are not issues, you decide to implement your design with frames.
   To complete this independent challenge:

a. Create a Web page to serve as the navigation bar, saving it with the name fc-nav.htm. Include the Film Clips logo, which is provided in the graphic file fclogo.gif in the images directory. Divide the links into three sections—Videos, Games, and About Film Clips. Each section should include links to at least four subcategories (for example, Videos can include sublinks to different film genres).
b. Create a home page to appear in the right frame of your frameset, and save it with the name fc-main.htm. Include at least one topical clipart image; make up text you might expect to find on such a page.
c. Create a frameset file for the site, saving it with the name fc-f.htm. Size the frames as is appropriate, and turn on and format borders if you wish.
d. Preview the file fc-f.htm in your browser, then make changes to the component files as necessary. Be sure to format at least one of the frame files with a background color or image.

WEB WORK

4. Although frames have advantages over structuring tables in some circumstances, their use in well-designed Web pages is rare. Ever since their introduction in an HTML revision, frames have generated heated debate among Web designers and users; some people still have strong feelings on the issue, both pro and con.
To complete this independent challenge:

a. Connect to the Internet and use a search engine to find and view Web pages that argue for and against using frames in Web page design. Use your favorite search engine, or one of the following:
www.google.com
www.lycos.com
www.hotbot.com
If you have trouble locating a search engine, go to www.course.com, navigate to the page for this book, click the link for the Student Online Companion, click the link for this unit, and use the links listed there as a starting point for your search.

b. Read at least four pages that argue one side or the other of this issue, then write a paragraph summarizing each viewpoint; for each page include the URL, information about the author, whether they argue for or against frames, and the points they make to support their argument.

c. Write an additional paragraph or two giving your opinion of designing Web pages with frames in light of what you've read; reference specific Web pages, this text, or your own experience to support your points.

d. Disconnect from the Internet.

▶ Visual Workshop

You are updating the layout for the Web site you created in your job at Touchstone Booksellers. Create the layout shown in Figure F-23, using your choice of either frames or a structuring table. The navigation bar graphic, book.gif, and the graphic in the main page section, bookfair.gif, are located in the images folder. For a structured table, use the file tsbbg.jpg as the background; for frames, use color #8F8FBD. In either layout, the khaki color behind the text in the main page is #9F9F39. Save the table or frameset file with the name tsb-f.htm. If you create a frameset, save the navigation bar frame with the filename tsb-nav.htm. Save the main frame with the filename tsb-main.htm.

FIGURE F-23

HTML

Unit G

Designing
Web Pages

- ► **Understand design principles**
- ► **Examine Web-specific design issues**
- ► **Explore cross-platform issues**
- ► **Integrate fonts and color**
- ► **Incorporate images effectively**
- ► **Locate Web design resources**
- ► **Design an accessible Web page**
- ► **Explore Web writing guidelines**
- ► **Study usability factors**

Understanding how to create a well-designed Web page is the key to attracting users and making a functional Web site. It is not a requirement that Web designers be graphic design professionals, but creating effective Web pages requires some understanding of universal design guidelines and the unique design advantages and challenges that the Web poses. ✐ Jaime Chavez works in the Information Systems department at Nomad Ltd, a travel and sporting goods company. He has worked with the IS team to create a company Web site. They consult with the company's graphic design department, as well as Web page-specific design resources on the Web, to critique their original design and to get tips on increasing the site's usability.

Understanding Design Principles

When planning a graphic design, what you leave out is often just as important as what you include. While you can use graphics as well as font face and color variations to make a layout more interesting than a page of plain text, moderation is essential. Using too many layout elements makes the page overwhelming and leaves users unclear about its point. Finding a judicious balance between plainness and overuse of formatting elements is key to the effectiveness of any Web page design. Jaime's colleagues from the graphic design department share their basic design guidelines. Figure G-1 shows an effective layout that incorporates the following tips:

Use active white space

The term **white space** refers to any empty part of a page. While you want to avoid leaving large areas of unused space that don't serve a purpose for your design—known as **passive white space**—it also is important not to entirely eliminate white space. An empty zone deliberately placed between page elements—known as **active white space**—reinforces their separateness, and helps the user mentally group the page into sections.

Choose complementary colors and fonts, and limit their number

You can control color in several types of Web page elements: page background, table background, text, and graphics. Colored text can highlight main ideas or important points, or make text easier to read. As with white space, you also can use different colors and fonts to indicate separate ideas or sections in your layout. It's best to limit colors and fonts to two or three per page, and to be sure that those you select complement each other. In order for differences in colors and fonts to have maximal impact, you should use them sparingly so that each occurrence isn't cancelled out by others surrounding it.

Ensure content legibility

Regardless of the design you choose, it's important that users can read a page's contents. Legibility is a factor in the selection of each page component—choose font sizes that aren't illegibly small; avoid colors that are difficult to focus on (such as fuschia); and use images that aren't too bright or too dark. Legibility also is a factor in combining page elements. When you deviate from the default black text on a white page, it's important to select font and background colors that produce legible text. If you choose to use an image as the page background, you need to ensure that the image provides an appropriate contrast for all page contents.

Use a style that fits the message

In addition to testing the design merits of each page element, you need to ensure that all components of your layout reinforce the page's message. For example, the appropriate font face, page colors, and graphics for a business presentation would be quite different from those describing a Mardi Gras festival.

FIGURE G-1: Web page implementing basic design elements

Contrast and element colors make contents easily legible

Active white space separates adjacent elements

Background pattern reinforces casual, outdoors style

Page uses two main fonts

Examining Web-Specific Design Issues

In addition to design guidelines that apply to traditional media, Web page designers need to consider issues that are particular to the Web medium. Although Web pages can resemble traditional media, there are two significant differences. Unlike a magazine page, for example, a Web browser window is wider than it is tall. This requires a different layout. Additionally, Web users interact with Web pages, rather than just look at them; as a result, Web pages require additional planning. Whatever constraints it imposes on design, however, the Web's flexibility also offers designers significant advantages. In their research on the subject, members of the Nomad Web-design team find three main features of Web design that have unique advantages and requirements. Figure G-2 shows a Web page with contents that are not optimized for the Web. However, the Web page in Figure G-3 conforms to many aspects of the three features, which are:

Details

Web users

Studies have found that Web users generally know what they're looking for, and have little patience for sites that don't immediately look useful. While this finding suggests that users subject your Web site to a snap judgment, you can use this information to design your site so that it makes the cut. While keeping the page uncluttered, **make the site's contents obvious and easily accessible from every page**; one or two well-planned navigation bars efficiently accomplishes this. You should **limit the length of a Web site's home page** to what fits in most browser windows (800 x 600 pixels), so that users can locate the information they want without scrolling. Most readers are used to reading text in newspaper or magazine layouts. For this reason, it also is important to **limit paragraph length**, as users generally scan, rather than read entire Web pages.

Web browsers

Although some of the principles are similar, a Web browser presents a layout medium that is quite different from traditional print media. Unlike magazines and newspapers, **a Web page appears wider than it is tall**. Therefore, your layout should use the width of the page, rather than its length. For text content such as news stories and editorials, however, print media legibility rules apply. Therefore, **paragraphs of text should appear in narrow columns.** Because the Web is a dynamic medium, **each user's browser affects the appearance of your layout**, so it is vital to test your Web pages on different browser brands, browser versions, operating systems, and screen resolutions.

Web medium

The Web itself as a medium presents design advantages and challenges. Because users access Web pages over various types of Internet connections, it's important to **keep the size of your HTML and associated files as small as possible**, to minimize user wait time. Also, Web pages are not static documents published once, like magazines and newspapers. Rather, Web pages always give readers the impression that they are always viewing new documents. **You must schedule and budget regular updates to your Web site** in order for it to maintain its level of integrity. Finally, because Web pages are dynamic, and interpretation varies across interfaces, users with disabilities can access Web pages using specialized interfaces. To ensure such accessibility, you need to **use HTML code that is as widely interpretable as possible**—for example, use <EM>..</EM> instead of <I>..</I>.

FIGURE G-2: Web page lacking Web design aspects

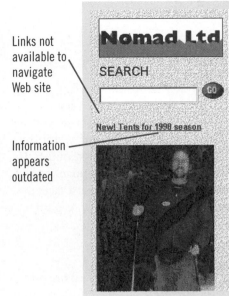

Links not available to navigate Web site

Information appears outdated

Nomad Ltd: Achieving our mission

Nomad Ltd has been in business for over ten years. During that time, we have offered tours all over the world and sold sporting equipment for bicycling, hiking, and other activities. Like most companies, our main goal is to make a profit. At the same time, we realize that as a business, we are also community members. Nomad Ltd is committed to contributing to community efforts and making each town where we do business a better place to live. We do that by hiring from the community, offering educational and financial benefits to our employees, and taking part in local community efforts.

Nomad history: Where we came from

Jasper Barber started Nomad Ltd in 1987 as a single store in Boulder, Colorado, a popular area for many types of outdoor recreation. Jasper set out to create a store offering

Long and wide paragraphs

FIGURE G-3: Web page design optimized for the Web

Toolbar provides connection to Web site structure

Nomad history: Where we came from

Jasper Barber started Nomad Ltd in 1987 as a single store in Boulder, Colorado, a popular area for many types of outdoor recreation. Jasper set out to create a store offering affordable, high-quality outdoor supplies. After opening two more stores in Colorado, Jasper began to

Text appears in narrow column

Exploring Cross-Platform Issues

Regardless of how carefully you design a Web page, certain computer setups can render the same HTML differently. Source interpretation varies among browser brand, browser version, and operating system. Additionally, a computer's screen resolution can affect what each user sees on the screen, and how each element is aligned on the page. Therefore, it is important to test your Web pages using as many variations as possible of all of these factors—characteristics that are collectively known as a user's **platform**. To give the Nomad Web development team a flavor of the differences among user platforms and screen resolutions, Jaime opens a page that was not designed for cross-platform compatibility in different browsers and screen resolutions. He also outlines the specific appearance issues across platforms and displays:

Browser interpretation

Although industry standards for each version of HTML are issued by an independent organization, the W3C (World Wide Web Consortium), in practice it's rare for browsers to fully comply with these standards. As a result, each browser brand supports different subsets of each version of HTML, and may interpret the features differently, as shown in Figure G-4. As long as different browsers and operating systems are available among Web users, Web page design will continue to require care, experimentation, and extensive testing in order for pages to appear similarly across platforms. Up-to-date information on the most widely used browsers—and the deficiencies of each—is important knowledge for Web design.

QuickTip

If it is likely that your Web page audience will be using older equipment, you may want to design pages compatible with the lowest possible resolution of 640 x 480. However, few Web users use such monitors.

Screen resolution

You can safely bet that a Web page does not appear on your screen exactly as all other readers see it. The reason is that monitor **resolution**—the screen's display dimensions (width by height, in pixels)—varies, depending on a user's monitor and computer hardware. Common resolutions include 800 x 600, 1024 x 768, and 1280 x 1024, with some platforms capable of displaying even larger areas. Figure G-5 shows the same Web page at these three resolutions. Notice that as the resolution increases, more of the page is visible in the browser window. Extremely large screen areas add blank space around the layout. Designers usually create Web pages that consistently appear at different resolutions by using a centered layout table no wider than the lowest common resolution—800 pixels.

Image display

Almost all Web users use one of two main types of computers: the Apple Macintosh, or the IBM-compatible PC. The two are virtually indistinguishable to Web page designers, except in one area: images. Among the many properties of a digitized image file are **gamma settings**, which specify the degree of contrast between midlevel gray values. The Mac and the PC have different standard gamma settings for their displays; this can cause the same image to appear noticeably different on the two platforms. An image with heavy contrast on a Macintosh may look very dark on a PC, whereas high-contrast Windows images may look flat and washed out on a Macintosh. Web designers generally split the difference, using images with a setting mid-range between the Mac and PC.

FIGURE G-4 : Web page as it appears in three different browser versions

Graphic positioned differently

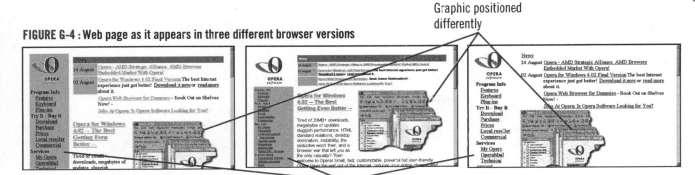

Background color interpreted differently

FIGURE G-5: Web page as it appears at three different screen resolutions

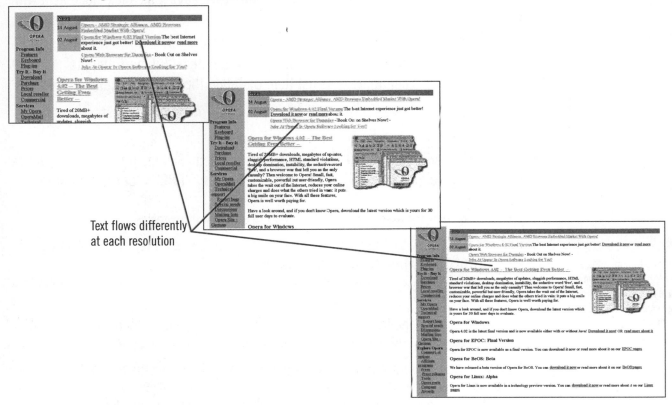

Text flows differently at each resolution

CLUES TO USE

Designing Web pages for handheld device users

In addition to considering different computer platforms when designing a Web page, you can further broaden a page's audience by making the page viewable on other sorts of devices. WebTV is one such platform, but this system—which integrates Internet functions into a television—is not widely used. Another audience that is growing quickly, however, is users of handheld devices such as cell phones and **personal digital assistants (PDAs)**. Browsers for such devices generally can render a subset of standard HTML codes. Because of their small screen sizes (usually from 160 x 160 to 240 x 320) and the prevalence of monochrome displays, page layout and content must be optimized for these devices.

Unit G HTML

Integrating Fonts and Color

Formatting text with different font faces and colors is one of the simplest design aspects to implement. For this reason it's especially important to be cautious and thoughtful when adding these features to a Web page. You should limit each page's text to two or three fonts and two or three colors. Additionally, most of the text should use one standard font and color—others should be used for small, specific applications that help users identify related page elements. ✎ The Web design team recently added three new categories to the Nomad Ltd Web site plan. Jaime adds them to the navigation bar in the development template and uses a special font and color to draw attention to them.

Steps

1. Start your text editor, open the file **HTM G-1.htm**, then save it as a text document with the filename **nomad-g.htm**
   This Web document is the template for adding Web pages to the Nomad Web site.

2. Scroll down to the unordered list beginning with the item "Hiking/Camping", click at the end of the line containing the list item Clothing, then press **[Enter]**

3. Press **[Spacebar]** eight times, then type **<LI><A HREF="construction.htm"> Fitness</A>**

4. Click at the end of the line containing the list item Skiing, press **[Enter]**, press **[Spacebar]** eight times, then type **<LI><A HREF="construction.htm"> Guidebooks</A>**
   Jaime added new list items for the Fitness and Guidebooks categories.

QuickTip

The code   adds a space; HTML inserts only one space between letters or page elements unless you use this code to specify extra spaces.

5. Click at the end of the line containing the list item Fitness, then type **   <FONT COLOR="#008080"><EM>NEW</EM></FONT>**
   Jaime adds two spaces after the linked text, then inserts the word NEW in an emphasized (italic) font and blue-green font color.

6. Repeat Step 5 for the line containing the Guidebooks list item, then save your work
   Your Web page code should resemble the document shown in Figure G-6.

7. Start your Web browser, cancel any dial-up operations, then open the file **nomad-g.htm**
   As shown in Figure G-7, the two new choices appear in the navigation bar, along with the colored and italicized text NEW. This text highlights the new options for users who may already be familiar with the site.

FIGURE G-6: Web page code selectively implements text color

```
        </TABLE>

        <BR>

        <A HREF="construction.htm"><IMG SRC="images/gear.gif" WIDTH="158"
HEIGHT="25" BORDER="0" ALIGN="center" ALT="Gear"></A>

        <UL>
          <LI><A HREF="construction.htm">Hiking/Camping</A>
          <LI><A HREF="construction.htm">Biking</A>
          <LI><A HREF="construction.htm">Clothing</A>
          <LI><A HREF="construction.htm">Fitness</A>  <FONT
COLOR="#008080"><EM>NEW</EM></FONT>
          <LI><A HREF="construction.htm">Climbing</A>
          <LI><A HREF="construction.htm">Swimming</A>
          <LI><A HREF="construction.htm">Boating</A>
          <LI><A HREF="construction.htm">Skiing</A>
          <LI><A HREF="construction.htm">Guidebooks</A>  <FONT
COLOR="#008080"><EM>NEW</EM></FONT>
        </UL>

        <A HREF="construction.htm"><IMG SRC="images/travel.gif" WIDTH="158"
HEIGHT="25" BORDER="0" ALIGN="center" ALT="Travel"></A>

        <UL>
          <LI><A HREF="construction.htm">Leisure tours</A>
          <LI><A HREF="construction.htm">Athlete tours</A>
```

New list items with NEW text

FIGURE G-7: Web page template incorporating text color

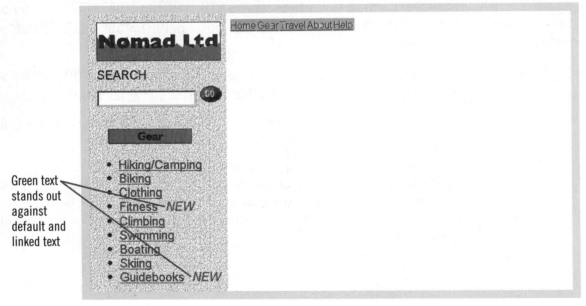

Green text stands out against default and linked text

Formatting text with style sheets

The HTML specification includes a simpler alternate method for formatting text and other page elements; the method is called **Cascading Style Sheets** (or **style sheets** or **CSS** for short). Style sheets allow you to specify settings as attributes for more than 50 properties of any page element, rather than requiring separate tags. Additionally, you can specify a named group of settings in a document's header section, and then apply the specified settings by referencing that name in any page element's opening tag. Style sheets facilitate tight formatting control of page elements with a minimum of extra code, and can help to ensure an exact match of the settings for different page elements. Style sheets are not yet widely used for Web page creation because the most popular browsers do not uniformly support them. However, as browser support becomes consistent and widespread, style sheets will replace tags such as <FONT> and <EM>, and attributes such as ALIGN, for Web page formatting.

Incorporating Images Effectively

Just as effective Web designs benefit from limited use of text color and font variation, you can strengthen your Web pages by keeping the use of graphics thoughtful and sparing. Graphics draw readers' attention and contribute to a page's mood—strong benefits of including graphics in a layout. However, using too many graphics on a page, especially unrelated ones, overwhelms users and prevents them from focusing on the most important part of the page. Also, because many Web users rely on relatively slow Internet connections via modems, minimizing the number of graphics in a Web page is vital to ensure relatively quick downloads. ✒ The Nomad Web design team is considering making the product category list in the navigation bars context-specific, so that the list only contains options relevant to the contents of the page on which it appears. To set up a model of this idea for evaluation, Jaime creates a second horizontal navigation bar that will appear at the top of the screen. This new bar contains options users will need, regardless of which page in the site they open.

Steps

1. In your text editor, scroll down to the second column in the page's structuring table, select the text **<!-- HORIZONTAL TOOLBAR ICONS -->**, then press **[Delete]**

2. Press **[Spacebar]** ten times, then type **<TD WIDTH="108" HEIGHT="55"> <IMG SRC="images/homeic.gif" WIDTH="50" HEIGHT="50" ALT="Home"> </TD>**

   > **QuickTip**
   >
   > Although the closing </TD> tag is not officially required, it can be useful in preventing browser errors when creating nested tables.

3. Press **[Enter]**, press **[Spacebar]** ten times, then type **<TD WIDTH="108"> <IMG SRC="images/gearic.gif" WIDTH="50" HEIGHT="50" ALT="Gear"></TD>**

4. Repeat Step 3 three times to enter the remaining three lines of code shown in Figure G-8
   Figure G-8 shows the completed code that adds the icons to the horizontal toolbar.

5. Save your work, open your browser, then reload the file **nomad-g.htm**
   As shown in Figure G-9, the horizontal toolbar appears along the top of the Web page. Each icon is small, minimizing the page's download time. The icons are similar in shape and appearance, which suggests their relatedness without distracting users from other parts of the Web page.

FIGURE G-8: Web page code implementing small, related graphics

```
<!-- second column -->

<!-- horizontal navigation bar -->

    <TD VALIGN="top" HEIGHT="275" WIDTH="550"><FONT FACE="arial, helvetica,
sans serif">
      <TABLE BGCOLOR="#C0D9D9" CELLSPACING="0" BORDER="0">
        <TR ALIGN="center" VALIGN="bottom">
          <TD WIDTH="108" HEIGHT="55"><IMG SRC="images/homeic.gif" WIDTH="50"
HEIGHT="50" ALT="Home"></TD>
          <TD WIDTH="108"><IMG SRC="images/gearic.gif" WIDTH="50" HEIGHT="50"
ALT="Gear"></TD>
          <TD WIDTH="108"><IMG SRC="images/travelic.gif" WIDTH="50"
HEIGHT="50" ALT="Travel"></TD>
          <TD WIDTH="108"><IMG SRC="images/aboutic.gif" WIDTH="50" HEIGHT="50"
ALT="About"></TD>
          <TD WIDTH="108"><IMG SRC="images/helpic.gif" WIDTH="50" HEIGHT="50"
ALT="Help"></TD>
        </TR>

        <TR ALIGN="center">
          <TD><FONT FACE="arial, helvetica, sans serif" SIZE="-1"><A
HREF="construction.htm">Home</A></TD>
          <TD><FONT FACE="arial, helvetica, sans serif" SIZE="-1"><A
HREF="construction.htm">Gear</A></TD>
          <TD><FONT FACE="arial, helvetica, sans serif" SIZE="-1"><A
HREF="construction.htm">Travel</A></TD>
```

Code for Horizontal
navigation bar icons

FIGURE G-9: Web page template selectively incorporates graphics

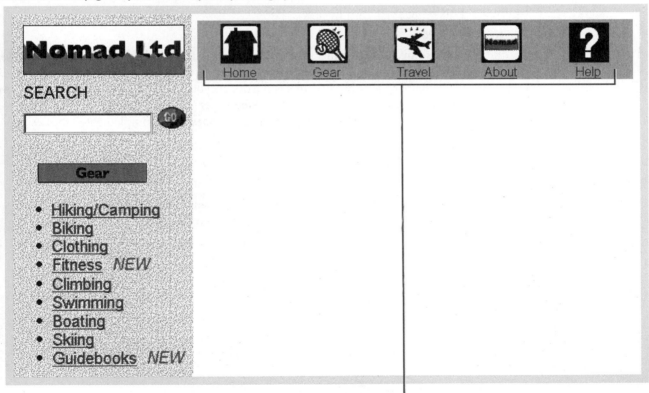

Graphics add
functionality
without distracting

HTML

Locating Web Design Resources

While you're familiar with the general design guidelines required by all Web pages, many other suggestions are useful or important depending on a page's contents, audience, or goal. Additionally, as Web technologies and languages evolve, it's important to stay current with the consensus on how to effectively use them. Fortunately, design guidelines are abundant on the Web itself. You can use a search engine to research relevant design pointers for your Web pages. Jaime reviews a few main categories of design resources with the Nomad Web design team, and describes their uses.

Details

Web design articles
The Web contains many sites that focus on HTML and related technologies and regularly add new articles and news. These sites, such as the one shown in Figure G-10, are a great way to keep current on design trends. They also provide advice from experienced designers, and can quickly bring you up to speed on industry conventions.

Style guides
Many large organizations—such as corporations and universities—include their Web design guidelines on their Web sites. While these guides, such as the one shown in Figure G-11, generally contain rules that members of the particular organization must follow when creating Web pages, they can shed light on the reasons some organizations use or avoid specific formatting or elements in their designs. By examining several such guides you also can get a sense of which style rules are in common use on the Web, and which are specific to an organization's image or its internal practices.

Existing Web sites
Another valuable source of design ideas is the sites you visit as a Web user. As you read the news, shop, research information, or check e-mail messages on the Web, pay attention to the design of each page that opens. When you find an interesting design, you can check the page code to see how it was created. You also should try to find other Web pages that use the same design; if you are unable to find any, there may be a good reason why other sites haven't implemented the design.

FIGURE G-10: Web design resource featuring regular articles

FIGURE G-11: Web style guide

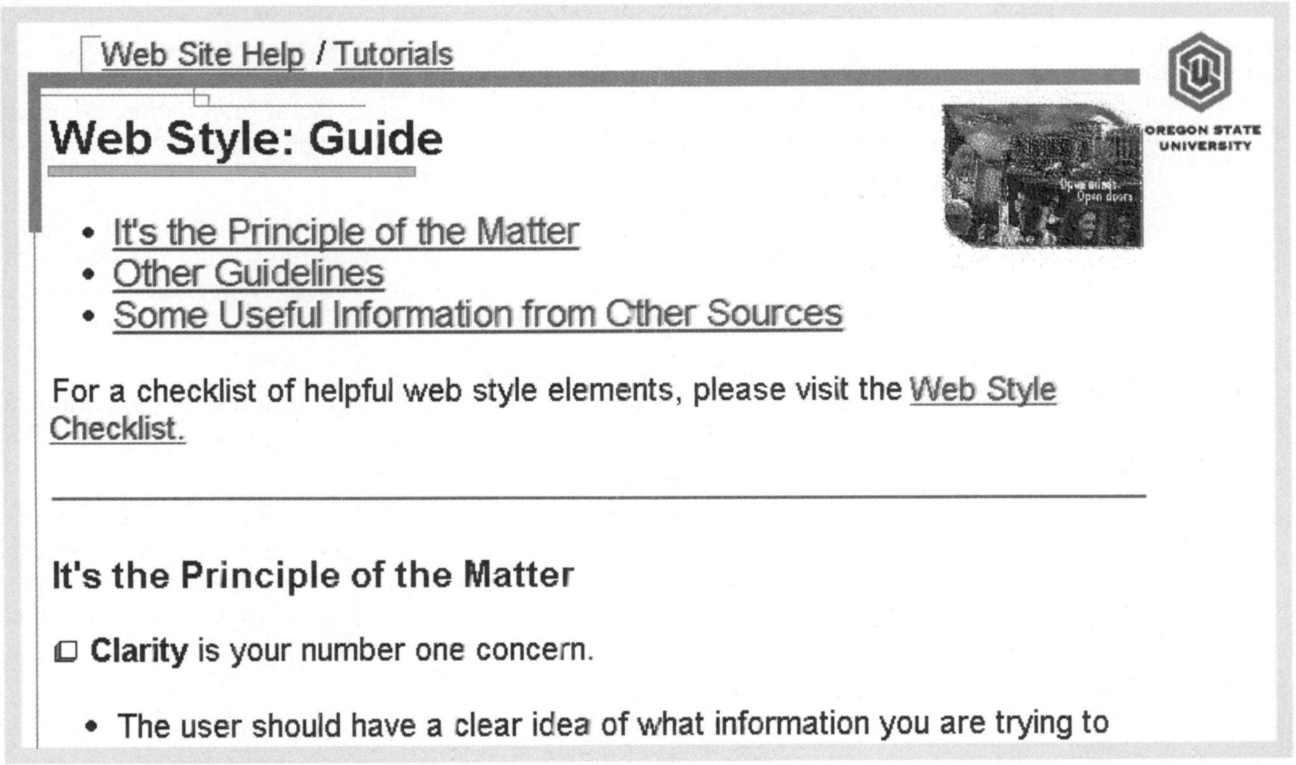

Web Site Help / Tutorials

Web Style: Guide

- It's the Principle of the Matter
- Other Guidelines
- Some Useful Information from Other Sources

For a checklist of helpful web style elements, please visit the Web Style Checklist.

It's the Principle of the Matter

☐ **Clarity** is your number one concern.

- The user should have a clear idea of what information you are trying to

Designing an Accessible Web Page

Careful planning and implementation of your Web page design can benefit the page's usability in several ways, such as producing a clearer and more focused visual layout. Additionally, close attention while designing your pages can help ensure that your pages are accessible for Web users with disabilities, including blindness, color blindness, and cognitive or learning disabilities. Although lists of specific areas to check are widely available on the Web, accessibility guidelines stem from three main requirements: the appearance or perception of color should not be necessary for interpreting information; all page elements should make sense when vocalized by a machine, rather than viewed on a screen; and the content should be clear and logically organized. Verifying that your pages meet these tests helps ensure their availability not only to people with disabilities, but also to Web users with older displays or browsers. Jaime reviews the Nomad site template shown in Figure G-12 against a list of the main accessibility guidelines to make sure he hasn't overlooked anything. He verifies that:

Images and multimedia include alternate text

Specifying alternate text using the ALT attribute for graphics and multimedia provides a key means of translating visual or aural information into a format that many devices can interpret. Alternate text can provide a description of a sound file, or explanatory text that is vocalized by a Web interface device for blind users. Jaime included a description of each icon in the template, using the ALT attribute.

Color differentiation is not required for viewing any part of the page

A popular visual design strategy applies color to selected layout elements to indicate a common meaning or similarity. For example, the text NEW in Jaime's vertical navigation bar appears in green, to differentiate it from neighboring text. Because some readers are unable to perceive differences in color—or may be using a monochrome display—you should not rely on color differences as the only formatting distinction between different types of information. Because it also is italicized, Jaime's NEW text remains distinguishable when viewed without color.

Headers in data tables are correctly formatted

When read aloud by a Web interface for the visually impaired, tables should still be able to convey the information expressed in their visual formats. It's important to format cells in the header row with the <TH> tag—and equally important not to use this tag for other cells in the table, even if their contents should be formatted as boldface and centered.

Table contents make sense if read row by row

Some older browsers and other Web interfaces have difficulty organizing text that wraps to multiple lines within a table cell. Ideally, cell contents in a data table should cover only a single line.

Link text doesn't rely on its context to indicate its function

A widely discouraged element of Web page design, and which is slowly disappearing from the Web, is the use of the text "click here" to create a link. Instead, linked text should always describe the contents of the target page. This style guideline is especially important to visually impaired users who might scan a page using the [Tab] key to move from link to link. Each of the text links in both of Jaime's navigation bars describes the contents of the Web page it opens.

Page content is logically organized

Ensuring that your pages contain simple, logical information makes them more accessible to people with cognitive disabilities, as well as to anyone who has difficulty reading. Use headings and ordered and unordered lists to clarify the relationships between page elements. Implementing site-wide navigation tools, such as navigation bars, explicitly denotes the relationship between different Web pages. The two navigation bars that Jaime incorporated into the Nomad template provide a structural context for all pages in the site.

FIGURE G-12: Nomad Web page template

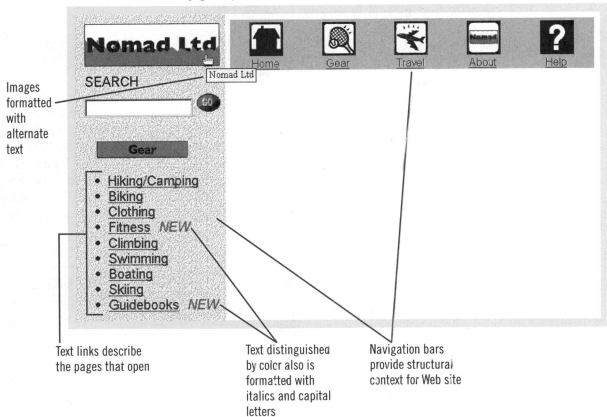

Images formatted with alternate text

Text links describe the pages that open

Text distinguished by color also is formatted with italics and capital letters

Navigation bars provide structural context for Web site

CLUES TO USE

Physical formatting vs. logical formatting

HTML offers more than one tag or tag pair for implementing several types of Web page formats. For example, bold and italic formats each can be coded using two different tag pairs: <B>..</B> or <STRONG>..</STRONG> for boldface, and <I>..</I> or <EM>..</EM> for italic. Although the functions of these tags appear to overlap, they simply illustrate the distinction between the two types of HTML formatting: physical and logical. A tag pair creates **physical formatting** when its sole function is to tell the Web browser to apply a specific visual format. For example, <B>..</B> tells the browser only that the marked text should appear in boldface.

Logical formatting, on the other hand, results from tags that mark a page element as fitting a certain function or role. Tags that specify logical format give the browser information on how an element relates to other parts of the Web page, and leave the interpretation and format choice to the user's interface device. <STRONG>..</STRONG> is an example of a logical tag pair; it marks text as requiring special attention, but leaves the ultimate format decision to the interface. Logical formatting is an important tool in building accessible Web pages, as it assists different devices in choosing the most appropriate way to convey page contents to the readers.

Exploring Web Writing Guidelines

At first glance, writing text for a Web page seems like a snap: as long as you take the layout differences into consideration, text for the Web should be similar to any other visual medium, right? In reality, several unique aspects of the Web require a markedly different writing style and organization. Because text on a screen is more difficult to read than printed text, users are less comfortable and more impatient reading Web pages. Fortunately, just as there are style guidelines available for printed media, many resources on the Web outline and explain effective writing for an online audience. Jaime and the other members of the Nomad Web design team researched the topic of writing for the Web, and use the guidelines implemented on the Web page in Figure G-13. These guidelines include:

 Keep your writing concise

Because a computer display is a less comfortable medium from which to read, compared to a printed page, it's best to minimize the amount of reading required to convey information. People read more slowly from a screen than from paper. When comparing printed with online text, a rule of thumb is to reduce the number of words by 50% for the online audience.

 Avoid long sections of text

One result of the reduced comfort and speed of reading from a computer monitor is that Web users skim most of the text they encounter. As a result, your pages are more useful if they help users find information that's relevant for them. Rather than forcing users to skim—or skip—a long section of text, break it up into several shorter sections, and add a meaningful heading to each. This allows users to quickly identify the main points of the page, and then give a closer reading to any section(s) that seem to match their interests.

 Divide text into page-size stand-alone units

Even if you divide information into sections below descriptive headings, you must give attention to the length of text on a single Web page. To allow users to scan and digest the contents of a page, limit the text length to nearly the length of the page. Instead of continuing a single article on additional Web pages, break it up into sections that can stand on their own, and place each on its own page.

 Link text that describes its target

In addition to accessibility factors for Web users with disabilities, ensuring that linked text is active is important in making Web text readable. Because linked text stands out from its surroundings on a page, users are more likely to notice it while scanning. Thus, this text should clearly state a specific point, and not be a useless phrase such as "click here." Eliminating such writing is an excellent way to start reducing the amount of text on your pages, and to ensure that all your text is used as efficiently as possible.

FIGURE G-13: Web page containing writing appropriate for the Web

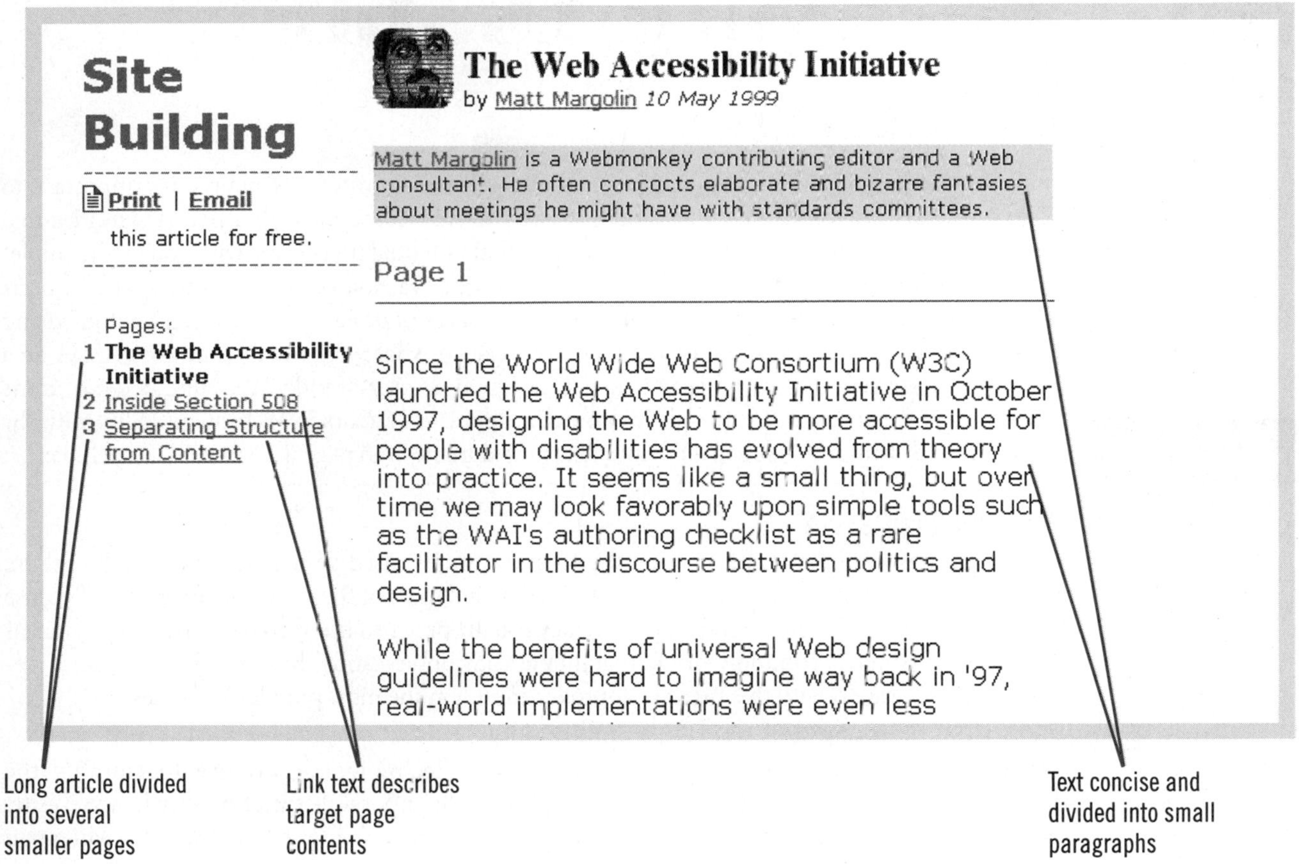

Site Building

📄 **Print** | **Email**

this article for free.

Pages:
1 **The Web Accessibility Initiative**
2 Inside Section 508
3 Separating Structure from Content

The Web Accessibility Initiative
by Matt Margolin *10 May 1999*

Matt Margolin is a Webmonkey contributing editor and a Web consultant. He often concocts elaborate and bizarre fantasies about meetings he might have with standards committees.

Page 1

Since the World Wide Web Consortium (W3C) launched the Web Accessibility Initiative in October 1997, designing the Web to be more accessible for people with disabilities has evolved from theory into practice. It seems like a small thing, but over time we may look favorably upon simple tools such as the WAI's authoring checklist as a rare facilitator in the discourse between politics and design.

While the benefits of universal Web design guidelines were hard to imagine way back in '97, real-world implementations were even less

Long article divided into several smaller pages

Link text describes target page contents

Text concise and divided into small paragraphs

Studying Usability Factors

In addition to creating Web pages that are laid out well and convey information, it's important to make sure that your pages are easily usable. While you may come up with a new design idea that seems more user-friendly, you should always ensure that potential users agree with you before implementing it. Like other aspects of design, many resources are available on the Web that analyze aspects of Web page usability. Additionally, usability is a unique area of design because it can be studied and measured. Thus, reviewing some of the available data on what works and what doesn't can be a rewarding investment of time, and can help you design more user-friendly Web sites. Jaime has studied some research, and shares his notes on important factors in Web site usability with the Nomad Web design team. Jaime's guidelines, illustrated in the Web page in Figure G-14, include:

Use a familiar layout

Web design has begun to standardize on the most commonly used design elements. Jakob Nielsen, a Web design usability expert, points out that, "users spend most of their time on *other* sites." Because Web users tend to value speed and efficiency, they usually prefer to use Web page elements—such as toolbars—laid out in a common format that they already understand. Thus, you should balance creativity in your designs with the interface approach found on the most popular Web sites.

Don't rush to implement the latest technology

Often, new developments in HTML or other Web technologies promise to simplify the designer's or the user's experience, or to allow previously impossible functionality in a Web site. However, implementing new technology can be tricky; if it generates errors for users when you first incorporate it into your site, you risk your reputation as a reliable, usable site—and users may not return. You should take the time to familiarize yourself with the technology and its potential drawbacks before using it, and give yourself time to test your implementation before making it available to users. New technology usually comes with compatibility problems, for disabled users as well as for anyone using an older Web browser. Usually, the best response to a new technology is to wait until the Web design community has established its limits and its most appropriate uses.

Minimize download times

Given most Web users' emphasis on speed, impatience is common when waiting for a Web page to download. Large Web pages that contain many screens of text, large graphics, or other technologies that require downloading can result in delays. At best, you annoy your audience; at worst, they give up on your page before it finishes loading, and go somewhere else. One of the keys to minimizing download time is to avoid animations and large graphics on your Web pages, and especially on a site's home page.

Keep information up to date

In order to attract users to regularly return to your Web site, you need to give them reason to trust the site and its contents. A crucial element to building this trust, which is specific to the Web, is to regularly update the site's contents and to include text that specifies the date of your last site update. For example, if you located a Web site containing information on a subject of interest, but then discovered that the site was last updated in 1997, you would probably assume that more recent information might be available, and that you'd do best to continue your search elsewhere.

Test your design

One of the best ways of maximizing the usability of your design is also one of the most obvious: test it. While a well-planned test with different types of people can help you exhaustively analyze your Web site, feedback from even a handful of people can identify major stumbling blocks or an aspect that could markedly improve from some fine-tuning. Remember, however, to test your pages with members of the target audience. Such users are usually not other designers, but rather are people who are less technically adept. Positive reviews from such testers are a good indication that your design is indeed easy to use.

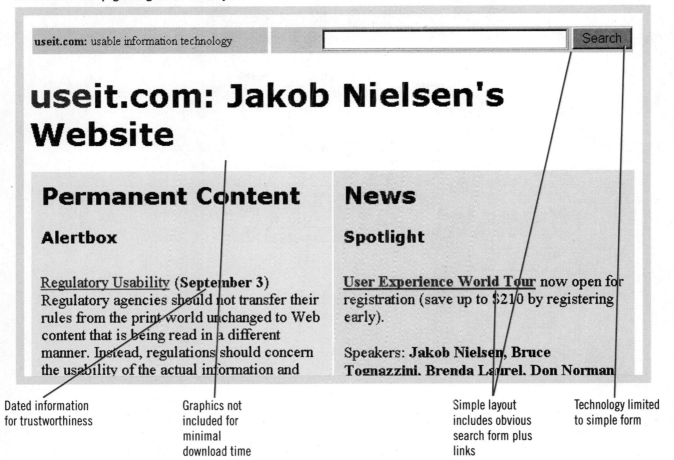

Dated information for trustworthiness

Graphics not included for minimal download time

Simple layout includes obvious search form plus links

Technology limited to simple form

Practice

►Concepts Review

Describe the accessibility value of each page element indicated in Figure G-15.

FIGURE G-15

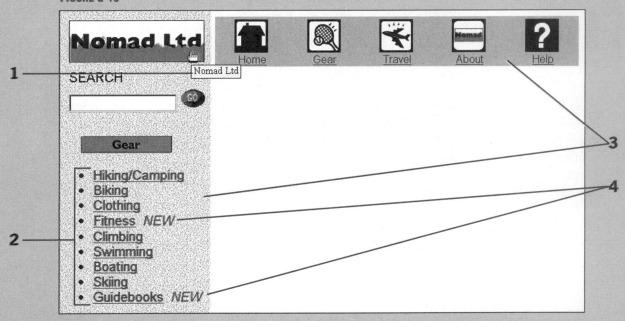

Match each recommendation with the design principle it describes.

5. Reinforce page's message by creating a common theme
6. Ensure these are complementary, and limited in number
7. Use this empty zone to deliberately separate page elements
8. Ensure users can read your page elements by choosing appropriate colors, font sizes, and text/background combinations

a. Active white space
b. Colors and fonts
c. Legibility
d. Style

Select the best answer from the list of choices.

9. Because of the unique dimensions of a computer monitor, paragraphs of Web page text should appear
   - a. Across the entire width of the screen.
   - b. In narrow columns.
   - c. Only at the bottom of a Web page.
   - d. In long paragraphs.

10. You can make a Web site's contents obvious and easily accessible from every page by implementing
    - a. A navigation bar.
    - b. White space.
    - c. Forms.
    - d. Frames.

11. You should limit the length of a site's home page to what fits in most users' browser windows because
    - a. Users can't view content that doesn't fit in a single screen.
    - b. Audio interfaces for disabled users can't read long Web pages.
    - c. Page content must match the length of the navigation bar.
    - d. You should provide users with a quick way of finding what they're looking for.

12. Which one of the following guidelines helps keep the size of your HTML and associated files as small as possible?
    - a. Limit the size and number of graphics.
    - b. Break up long sections of text into shorter paragraphs.
    - c. Ensure the text and background colors are compatible.
    - d. Add links to the text that describes the target page's content.

13. You must schedule and budget regular updates to your Web site in order to
    - a. Prevent pages from growing too long.
    - b. Minimize the time users wait for pages to download.
    - c. Maintain users' trust in the site's information.
    - d. Make the site accessible for disabled users.

14. In order to give users with disabilities access to your Web pages, you should
    - a. Limit use of linked text.
    - b. Avoid formatting page elements with color.
    - c. Remove graphics from your pages.
    - d. Use HTML code that is as widely interpretable as possible.

15. What is the width of the lowest common screen resolution?
    - a. 640 pixels
    - b. 800 pixels
    - c. 1024 pixels
    - d. 1280 pixels

16. The Apple Macintosh and the IBM-compatible PC are virtually indistinguishable to Web page designers, except in which area?
    - a. Images
    - b. Link format
    - c. Navigation bars
    - d. Text readability

17. What is a prudent upper limit on the number of text colors and fonts on a Web page?
    - a. One
    - b. One or two
    - c. Two or three
    - d. Three or four

18. Which one of the following design strategies is acceptable in an accessible Web page?

a. Distinguishing page elements from each other based only on color.

b. Including text whose meaning is clear only visually.

c. Including a navigation bar for navigation within the Web site.

d. Positioning page elements haphazardly to create a frenzied style.

19. Which one of the following features should text written for the Web include?

a. Organization into screen-size pages

b. The phrase "click here" for links

c. Long sections of text

d. Lengthy explanations

20. A usable Web page design should reflect prevalent designs currently in use because

a. New technologies rarely add new functionality to a Web page.

b. Users prefer Web page elements in a format that they already understand.

c. Testing a new design is rarely effective at identifying its weak points.

d. They don't need to be reviewed for accessibility compliance.

► Independent Challenges

1. You are evaluating the text content of the Web site you created for your computer consulting business, Star Dot Star. On one page you notice several details that you want to correct.

To complete this independent challenge:

a. Start your Web browser program, open the file HTM G-2.htm, then consider guidelines for writing for the Web as you explore the page.

b. Start your text editor, open the file HTM G-2.htm, then save it as a text document with the filename sds-g1.htm.

c. Remove the text "click here" from the navigation bar, then apply the link format instead to the descriptive text for each item.

d. Save your work, then save a copy of the page as a text document with the filename sds-g2.htm.

e. Delete the introductory text for the first list, describing creating Web pages; also delete the contents of the first list.

f. Change the page heading to "Creating Web sites," then format this text as centered.

g. In the introductory paragraph for the remaining list, format the text "creating Web pages" as a link to the Web page "sds-g1.htm."

h. Below the list, add the text "See also: Creating Web pages"; format the text "Creating Web pages" as a link to the Web page "sds-g1.htm."

i. Save your work, then open the text document sds-g1.htm.

j. Change the page heading to "Creating Web pages," then format this text as centered.

k. Delete the introductory text for the second list, describing creating Web sites, along with the contents of the second list.

l. Below the list, add the text "See also: Creating Web sites"; format the text "Creating Web sites" as a link to the Web page "sds-g2.htm."

m. Save your work, open the file sds-g1.htm in your browser, then click the link at the bottom of the list to open the file sds-g2.htm.

2. You are making accessibility and usability adjustments to the Web site for Crystal Clear Opticals.
To complete this independent challenge:

a. Start your Web browser, then open the file HTM G-3.htm.

b. Start your text editor, open the file HTM G-3.htm, then save it as a text document with the filename cco-g.htm.

c. Add the appropriate alternate text to each of the page's graphics.

d. In the navigation bar, use the BGCOLOR attribute to add a light-colored background to the cell containing the linked text.

e. In the page's main frame, format the text "Eclectic line" at the bottom of the page with a format of your choice, other than text color.

f. Save your work, then open the file cco-g.htm in your browser.

3. Researchers have conducted many Web site usability studies in order to pinpoint the factors that positively or negatively affect usability. This information, as well as commentary on it, is widely available on the Web. To better understand the factors that affect a user's interaction with your Web pages, research recent data about the topic of usability that has been published online.
To complete this independent challenge:

a. Connect to the Internet and open a Web site that discusses Web page usability, such as one of the following:
www.useit.com
www.usableweb.com
world.std.com/~uieweb
If you have trouble locating these sites, go to www.course.com, navigate to the page for this book, click the link for the Student Online Companion, click the link for this unit, then click one of the links listed there.

b. Read the results of research that interests you on one or more sites, then print three results that you find significant.

c. For each of the three results you printed, write a paragraph summarizing the finding and its implications, then write a second paragraph or create a sketch showing how you would implement the finding in a Web page design.

4. One of the best ways of learning to design effective Web pages is to critically evaluate other Web pages with less-than-optimal designs. Like all other aspects of Web design, several popular Web sites focus on this topic. To complete this independent challenge:

a. Connect to the Internet and open a Web site that spotlights or discusses poorly designed Web pages, such as one of the following:
www.webpagesthatsuck.com
www.usableweb.com
www.spinfrenzy.com/muddies/
If you have trouble locating these sites, go to www.course.com, navigate to the page for this book, click the link for the Student Online Companion, click the link for this unit, then click one of the links listed there.

b. View at least five Web sites. As you examine the pages, look for and write down at least three highlighted design errors that you've noticed elsewhere on the Web on other occasions. (Because such scrutiny often prompts a quick redesign of Web sites featured, you may be able to view only an image of the site's previous design, rather than actually use the poorly designed site.)

c. For one of the three design errors you noted, note the URL of another site that incorporates the error; print out the other site, then write a paragraph or note on the printout how you would correct the error.

▶ Visual Workshop

As the Web site designer for Touchstone Booksellers, you are reviewing the site to ensure that it is accessible for disabled Web users. Edit the file HTM G-4.htm so it appears as shown in Figure G-16 to colorblind users and users with monochrome monitors. Save your work with the filename tsb-g.htm.

FIGURE G-16

Touchstone Booksellers

Specializing in *nonfiction* of all types

- Place an order
- Search our stock
- Out-of-print search
- Events calendar

Updated June 9, 2002

Join us at the

County Bookfair

July 13-14
County Fair Building

Touchstone Booksellers: an *independent*, locally-owned bookstore since 1948.

Scripting
for HTML

Objectives

- ► **Understand scripting for HTML**
- ► **Create a script**
- ► **Debug a script**
- ► **Understand objects**
- ► **Use JavaScript event handlers**
- ► **Create a function**
- ► **Assign a variable**
- ► **Create a conditional**

HTML allows you to create basic Web pages easily. Using many of the newest features available in Web page design, however, requires the incorporation of **scripts**, which are programs in a Web page that run on the viewer's browser. Using scripts can expand the number of features you can add to your Web pages and can simplify some HTML commands. Lydia Burgos works in the information systems division of Nomad Ltd. Her supervisor heard about the advantages of scripts at a recent seminar and has asked Lydia to create a report on ways that scripts could enhance the company's current Web publication. Lydia begins by researching the fundamentals of **scripting**, which is the process of writing scripts.

Understanding Scripting for HTML

A **script** is a small program contained within an HTML document that can be executed by a Web browser. In the early days of the Web, scripts were separate files stored and run on a remote Web server. Today, Web page designers can place scripts within a page's standard HTML, and the scripts can run on each user's computer. This change is made possible by new techniques for data transfer on the Web as well as a new generation of more powerful home computers. Other forms of Web page programming (such as CGI files that process data from Web page forms) may also be referred to as scripts. However, scripts that run on a user's browser represent the most powerful and innovative form of scripting on the Web today. This is the definition we will use in this book. Figure H-1 shows the source code for a Web page containing a script, as well as the Web page generated by that code. In researching scripting fundamentals, Lydia Burgos has learned that using scripting in Web page development offers several advantages over using HTML alone. These advantages include the following:

 Flexibility

Scripting allows you to modify your Web pages in ways that are not yet part of standard HTML. Additionally, you can combine scripting codes in many different ways, which opens the door to more variety and creativity in your pages than with HTML alone. For example, you can have a message that runs automatically when the Web page is opened and that is updated automatically, such as a current list of top headlines for a news Web site.

 Simplification

You can script some tasks that you usually would code using HTML. In many cases, scripting is more efficient and allows you to create a more organized publication. One of the first areas in which scripting is replacing HTML is in assigning styles to text. Instead of adding attributes to the tags for each block of text in your publication, you can insert a small script that automatically assigns specific attributes, such as boldface type or text color, to specific blocks of text throughout an entire Web page or set of pages.

 Immediate response

Traditionally, to access many features available on a Web page, your browser contacts the Web site where the page resides and requests a linked Web page or new information based on your input. Embedded scripts eliminate the lag time involved in contacting the remote server, waiting for a response, and downloading new information. This is because the scripts run on your local computer and can change what your browser displays without downloading new information from the server.

Improved interactivity

The quick response time that local scripting provides allows you to incorporate an impressive amount of user interactivity into your Web pages. Since script processing occurs locally, your script can react almost instantaneously to any user action. For example, your script could display a short summary of a link when the user simply moves the pointer over the link without clicking it.

 Reduced server load

Local execution of scripts is an advantage not just for users, but for Web site administrators as well. The reduced demand on the server when some of the processing is shifted to local computers results in more free system resources. This may result in a decrease in download time for people viewing your site's pages and faster processing when a Web page does need to submit a request to the server.

FIGURE H-1: Web page script source code and browser document

Script embedded in HTML code

```
<HTML>

<HEAD>
<TITLE>Nomad Ltd online</TITLE>

<SCRIPT LANGUAGE="javascript">
<!--
var name=prompt("For personal service, please type your first name and click OK.","")

function submitted() {
      alert("Information submitted!")
}

function clearUp() {
      document.info.elements[0].value=""
      document.info.elements[1].value=""
      document.info.elements[2].value=""
      document.info.elements[3].value=""
      document.info.elements[4].value=""
      document.info.elements[5].value=""

}

//-->
</SCRIPT>
```

User name generated by script

Welcome to the Nomad Ltd home page, Lydia!

Nomad Ltd

Learn About Our Company's Philosophy

Nomad Ltd is a national sporting goods retailer dedicated to delivering high-quality sporting gear and adventure travel.
Nomad Ltd has been in business for over ten years. During that time, we have offered tours all over the world and sold sporting equipment for bicycling, hiking, and other activities. Like most companies, our main goal is to make a profit. At the same time, we realize that as a business, we are also community members. Nomad Ltd is committed to contributing to community efforts and making each town where we do business a better place to live. We do that by hiring from the community,

CLUES TO USE

Choosing a scripting language

Several languages are available when writing scripts for an HTML document. These include **JavaScript** and **JScript**, which are both adaptations of Sun Microsystems' Java programming language, as well as **VBScript**, which is Microsoft's adaptation of its Visual Basic programming language for Web use. Both Internet Explorer 4 and Netscape Navigator 4 are largely compatible with JavaScript. On the other hand, JScript and VBScript are not universally compatible, meaning that users of certain browsers might be unable to view the scripted elements of your page if you used one of these languages. This text uses JavaScript to create pages viewable by both Internet Explorer and Netscape Navigator users.

HTML

HTML

Creating a Script

You can add a script to a Web page just as you would add to or edit the Web page's HTML code. To do this, you can use a text editor such as WordPad or Notepad or a Web page editor such as FrontPage Express or Composer. In order for a browser to recognize a script, the script must be contained within <SCRIPT> HTML tags. It is also good practice to surround each script with a set of HTML tags to make it invisible to browsers incompatible with scripts. This second set of HTML tags tells incompatible browsers to bypass the script. ◀━━ While researching scripting fundamentals, Lydia found a sample script that validates a form before submitting it to a server by checking the form to be sure information has been entered in each field. If information has not been entered in each field and the user tries to send the form, then this form validation script displays a warning box which reminds the user to complete each field. Lydia decides to try adding this script to the Nomad Ltd home page in order to better understand how to insert scripts into HTML code.

QuickTip

When saving a file as HTML, be sure to select Text (.txt) as the file type to be saved and include the extension .htm in the filename.

1. **Start your text editor program, open the file HTML H-1.htm, then save it as a text document with the filename Scripted page.htm**
   If you use WordPad or Notepad, which are text editors built into Windows 95, the source code for the Web page appears as text in the text editor. If you use an HTML editing tool, such as Microsoft FrontPage or Netscape Composer, you will see the graphical representation of the file code. You must select the option Page Source or HTML from the View menu to see the HTML code for the page.

2. **Select the text [replace with opening script tags] below the TITLE tag, then press [Delete]**

3. **Type <SCRIPT LANGUAGE="javascript"> and press [Enter]**
   Now the beginning of the script is marked with the <SCRIPT> HTML tag and an attribute specifying the scripting language you're using, which is JavaScript.

QuickTip

All browsers ignore the remainder of the line after the <!-- tag; thus, some script writers add a normal language comment here, such as "HIDE," to make the script code easier for programmers to look at and understand.

4. **Type <!-- and press [Enter] twice**
   The tag <!-- tells an incompatible browser (one that can't process your script) to ignore the code that follows. A compatible browser (one that can interpret your script) will go ahead and process the script that follows.

5. **Select the text [replace with closing script tags], then press [Delete]**

6. **Type //--> and press [Enter], then type </SCRIPT> and press [Enter]**
   These tags mark the end of the script. Figure H-2 shows the Web page source code containing the opening and closing script tags and the dialog box generated by the script.

7. **Check the lines you added for errors, make changes as necessary, then save Scripted page.htm as a text document**

Trouble?

If the Web page does not display correctly, or if a dialog box opens describing an error in your script, click OK if necessary, read the next lesson to learn about debugging scripts, then return to look for errors in your Web page code.

8. **Start your Web browser program, cancel any dial-up activities, open the page Scripted page.htm, scroll down to the text fields near the bottom of the page, fill in sample information, then click the Send now! button**
   The script runs and displays the dialog box shown in Figure H-2.

9. **Click the OK button**
   The browser simulates form submission to a server. This script will save time for people using the Nomad Ltd Web page, since they do not have to wait for the form to be submitted to the server and then wait for an error message to be transmitted back to their computer.

FIGURE H-2: Source code for Web page dialog box

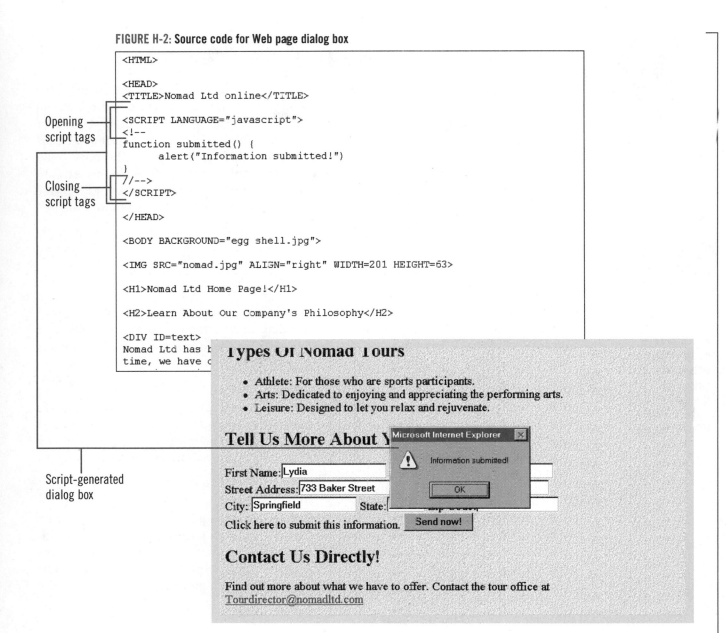

Opening script tags

Closing script tags

Script-generated dialog box

```
<HTML>

<HEAD>
<TITLE>Nomad Ltd online</TITLE>

<SCRIPT LANGUAGE="javascript">
<!--
function submitted() {
        alert("Information submitted!")
}
//-->
</SCRIPT>

</HEAD>

<BODY BACKGROUND="egg shell.jpg">

<IMG SRC="nomad.jpg" ALIGN="right" WIDTH=201 HEIGHT=63>

<H1>Nomad Ltd Home Page!</H1>

<H2>Learn About Our Company's Philosophy</H2>

<DIV ID=text>
Nomad Ltd has b
time, we have c
```

Types Of Nomad Tours

- Athlete: For those who are sports participants.
- Arts: Dedicated to enjoying and appreciating the performing arts.
- Leisure: Designed to let you relax and rejuvenate.

Tell Us More About Y

Microsoft Internet Explorer

⚠ Information submitted!

OK

First Name: Lydia
Street Address: 733 Baker Street
City: Springfield   State:
Click here to submit this information.   Send now!

Contact Us Directly!

Find out more about what we have to offer. Contact the tour office at
Tourdirector@nomadltd.com

Linking to an external script

In addition to typing script code directly into a Web page, you can add scripts to your pages by using an HTML code that references a separate file containing script code. A script located in an external file that you can link to a Web page is known as a **scriptlet**. Scriptlets make it easier to share code and to reuse scripts on multiple pages by allowing you to use a script without needing to paste its code into each Web page.

HTML

Debugging a Script

No matter how carefully scripting code is entered, a script often contains errors, or **bugs**, the first time your browser processes it. In general, a bug causes the script to return unexpected and undesired results. These may include improper text formatting, the display of HTML or JavaScript code in the browser window, or, in the worst case, requiring you to exit and restart the browser. It's doubtful that simple errors you make entering the scripts in this book could hang your browser. However, when your results are different than those shown in this text, you can use a process called **debugging** to systematically identify and fix your script's bugs. Lydia reads up on debugging scripts and learns about several main culprits that cause undesired results. These are illustrated in Figure H-3.

Details

QuickTip

You can type HTML tags and property names in either capital or lowercase without affecting the browser's interpretation. Only scripting languages—not HTML—are case-sensitive.

Capitalization

JavaScript is a **case-sensitive** language, meaning that it treats capital and lowercase versions of the same letter as different characters. Thus, depending on the script being entered, capitalizing or not capitalizing letters can result in errors. Always check that you have used capital letters where called for and that all the capital letters in your script are correct.

Spacing

When entering script code from a printed source, it is easy to add extra spaces or to leave spaces out. Some parts of JavaScript syntax allow for extra spaces, which makes code easier to view and understand. However, as in HTML, incorrect spacing in certain parts of a script can render otherwise-perfect code incomprehensible to the browser. The best way to avoid spacing errors is to pay careful attention to spacing while you enter code.

Parentheses ( ), brackets [ ], braces { }, and quotes " "

JavaScript often uses these four types of symbols to enclose arguments, values, or numbers upon which certain commands are executed. In more complex scripts, you may end up with several sets enclosing other sets, which makes it easy to forget to type one or more closing symbols. In lines or blocks of script where these symbols are concentrated, it can be difficult to check for accuracy. However, to ensure that your script will run properly, you must make sure that each one is paired with its counterpart.

Typographical errors (0 vs. O, 1 vs. l)

Another common source of errors when entering code from printed material is interchanging characters that appear similar, such as the number 0 and the letter O. Generally, the context provides good clues to figuring this out. For example, even if you don't know the function of the expression "value=0", the use of the word *value* gives you a good clue to type a number rather than a letter. Ultimately, the best way to avoid confusing these symbols is to analyze what the script is doing in the current line. Once you understand this, it should be obvious which character to type.

Others

Inevitably, various other sources of error will creep into your scripts. To help you deal with miscellaneous problems, as well as those detailed earlier, JavaScript-compatible browsers often display a JavaScript Error window, as shown in Figure H-4, when they can't interpret your code. Generally, the window describes the type of error the browser encountered and the error's location, referenced by its line number in the script. With this information, some investigation of your code, and a bit of thought, you can track down and fix most any bug that crops up.

Now that you understand the basics of working with scripts, you can begin to learn how to construct your own scripts.

▶ HTML H-6   **SCRIPTING FOR HTML**

FIGURE H-3: JavaScript containing common bugs

```
<HTML>

<HEAD>
<TITLE>Nomad Ltd online</TITLE>
<SCRIPT LANGUAGE="javascript">
<!--
function submit() {}

function verify() {
        if (document.info.elements[O].value == "" ||
        document.info.elements[1].value == "" ||
        Document.info.elements[2].value == "" ||
        document.info.elements[3].value == "" ||
        document. info.elements[4].value == "" ||
        document.info.elements[5].value == "" {
                alert("Please complete each field")
        }       else {
                submit()
        }
}
//-->
</SCRIPT>

</HEAD>

<BODY BACKGROUND="egg shell.jpg">
```

Letter instead of number

Unclosed parentheses

Incorrect capital

Extra space

FIGURE H-4: JavaScript Error window

Description of error

Erroneous code with error indicated

Location of error in code

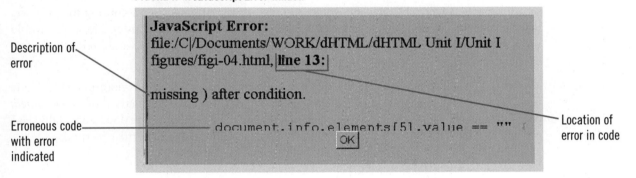

JavaScript Error:
file:/C|/Documents/WORK/dHTML/dHTML Unit I/Unit I figures/figi-04.html, line 13:

missing) after condition.

document.info.elements[5].value == "" {

[OK]

Commenting a script

While writing a script, it can be useful to include comments in ordinary language to explain what the script is doing at particular places. These notes can be helpful for you when editing or debugging your script or for someone else who wants to understand how the script works. To add a comment to the end of a line of the script, type // at the end of the line's script code, then type your comment. You also can mark several lines of text in a script as a comment by typing /* at the start of the block and */ at the end.

Understanding Objects

In order to organize and work with the various parts of the browser window, including the current Web page and each of its elements, JavaScript treats each element in the window as a unit called an **object**. JavaScript gives each object a default name and set of descriptive features based on its location and function. These features include **properties**, which are qualities such as size, location, and type. In a Web page containing a graphic, the IMG tag would be an object, and the WIDTH setting would be one of its properties. Each object also has associated **methods**, which are actions the object can carry out. For example, each frame in a browser window has an associated ALERT method, which allows you to create customized dialog boxes. JavaScript organizes objects in an **object hierarchy**, much like the system of folders used by Windows to keep track of disk contents. As Lydia researches the object hierarchy, she learns different ways to refer to the various elements in a document when writing a script.

 To specify an object on a Web page, you need to detail its position in the hierarchy, beginning on the document level and then separating each level name with a period. This method of referencing objects in the hierarchy is called **dot syntax**. For example, to specify an image on a Web page, the name would begin *document.images*. Because a document can contain more than one image, each image is assigned a number, based on the order in which it appears in the Web page code. Other elements such as anchors, hyperlinks, and forms also are assigned numbers. It is important to note, however, that in JavaScript, this numbering begins with 0. Thus, when writing a script that refers to the first image in your HTML code, you would use the name *document.images[0]*. The second image in your HTML code would be called *document.images[1]* according to the object hierarchy. To specify an element such as a button or a text field contained inside a form you would use a slightly longer address. For example *document.forms[0].elements[0]* would refer to the first element created in the first form in a Web document.

You also use dot syntax to refer to an object's methods. For example, the code *document.write("Copyright Course Technology, 1999.")* calls on the *write* method of the *document* object. This code causes the information in parenthesis to be written to the document. Table H-1 lists the default objects that are part of every browser window, along with their methods.

TABLE H-1: Default JavaScript objects and methods

object name	method name	description
window	alert(message)	Displays a dialog box with a message in the window
	close()	Closes the window
	prompt(message, default_text)	Displays a dialog box prompting the user for information
	scroll(x, y)	Scrolls to the x.y coordinate in the window
frame	alert(message)	Displays a dialog box with a message in the frame
	close()	Closes the frame
	prompt(message, default_text)	Displays a dialog box prompting the user for information
history	back()	Returns to the previous page in the history list
	forward()	Goes to the next page in the history list
location	reload()	Reloads the current page
document	write()	Writes text and HTML tags to the current document
	writeln()	Writes text and HTML tags to the current document on a new line
form	reset()	Resets the form
	submit()	Submits the form

CLUES TO USE

Naming an object

When you initially create a page element, you can assign it an ID using the ID property. Then, you can refer to the object by its name instead of using its index number. For example, the code <FORM ID="*input*"> assigns the ID *input* to the form. You can then use the form ID *input* rather than *forms[0]* to refer to the form or any elements within it.

You could now refer to this form as *document.input.elements[0]* rather than *document.forms[0].elements[0]*. By assigning a name to each element, such as check boxes or text boxes, you could eliminate the need for index numbers in the address as well.

HTML

Using JavaScript Event Handlers

In order for your Web pages to interact with users, your scripts must be able to recognize and respond to user actions. Each action by a user is known as an **event**. JavaScript can respond to a user's actions with **event handlers**, which are terms that specify possible user actions. By including an event handler along with a set of instructions, your script can respond to certain user actions when they happen. Table H-2 lists 12 event handlers and describes the event that each one names. ◆━━ Lydia has read about using event handlers. She wants the Nomad Ltd home page to display a message in the status bar window when a user moves the pointer over the e-mail address. She recognizes that this pointer positioning is an event, and that she can use a script containing an event handler to display the message.

Steps

1. Open HTML H-2.htm in your text editor and save it as a text document with the file-name **Event handler.htm**
   Lydia wants to insert her script code in the <A> code near the bottom of the page.

2. Scroll to the end of the document, select the text [**insert event handler here**] in the <A> tag, then press [**Delete**]

Trouble?

Be sure you use two apostrophes, rather than a quotation mark, following *onMouseOut="window. status=.*

3. Type the following all on the same line, without pressing [Enter]:
   onMouseOver="window.status='We will reply to your inquiry within 24 hours!';return true" onMouseOut="window.status='';return true"
   The completed script is shown in Figure H-5. Even without pressing Enter, your text editor may wrap the text onto multiple lines. This will not affect the accuracy of your code. The window.status object refers to the status bar. In this script, the onMouseOver event handler instructs the browser to display the text typed between the apostrophes in the status bar when the pointer is over the hypertext link. In this script, the onMouseOut event handler instructs the browser to clear the text—that is, to display nothing in the status bar—when the mouse pointer is moved off the hypertext link. The text is cleared as indicated by the apostrophes containing no text or spaces that follow the second window.status.

4. Check the document for errors, make changes as necessary, then save Event han-dler.htm as a text document

5. Open the file **Event handler.htm** in your Web browser, then scroll to the bottom of the page
   Notice that the status bar contains information about the loading status of the current Web page.

Trouble?

If your message does not appear correctly, check to be sure you have typed the script exactly as shown in Step 3.

6. Move the mouse pointer over the link **Tourdirector@nomadltd.com**, but do not click
   The scripted message appears in the status bar, as shown in Figure H-6.

7. Move the mouse pointer off the link
   The message no longer appears in the status bar.

```
<H2>Tell Us More About Yourself!</H2>
<FORM NAME="info">
First Name:<INPUT TYPE="TEXT" SIZE=20 NAME="firstname">
Last Name: <INPUT TYPE="TEXT" SIZE=20 NAME="lastname"><BR>
Street Address:<INPUT TYPE="TEXT" SIZE=50 NAME="address"><BR>
City: <INPUT TYPE="TEXT" SIZE=20 NAME="city">
State:<INPUT TYPE="TEXT" SIZE=6 NAME="state">
Zip Code:<INPUT TYPE="TEXT" SIZE=15 NAME="zipcode">
<BR>Click here to submit this information. <INPUT TYPE="BUTTON" VALUE="Send
now!" onClick="submitted()">
</FORM>

<H2>Contact Us Directly!</H2>

Find out more about what we have to offer. Contact the tour
office at <A HREF="MAILTO:Tourdirector@nomadltd.com"
onMouseOver="window.status='We will reply to your inquiry within 24
hours!';return true" onMouseOut="window.status='';return
true">Tourdirector@nomadltd.com</A>

</BODY>
</HTML>
```

Event handler code entered ⎯

FIGURE H-6: Browser displaying status bar message

Types Of Nomad Tours

- Athlete: For those who are sports participants.
- Arts: Dedicated to enjoying and appreciating the performing arts.
- Leisure: Designed to let you relax and rejuvenate.

Tell Us More About Yourself!

First Name: [ ]   Last Name: [ ]
Street Address: [ ]
City: [ ]   State: [ ]   Zip Code: [ ]
Click here to submit this information.   [Send now!]

Contact Us Directly!

Find out more about what we have to offer. Contact the tour office at
Tourdirector@nomadltd.com

We will reply to your inquiry within 24 hou   My Computer

Event handler activated by position of pointer

Message in status bar triggered by event handler

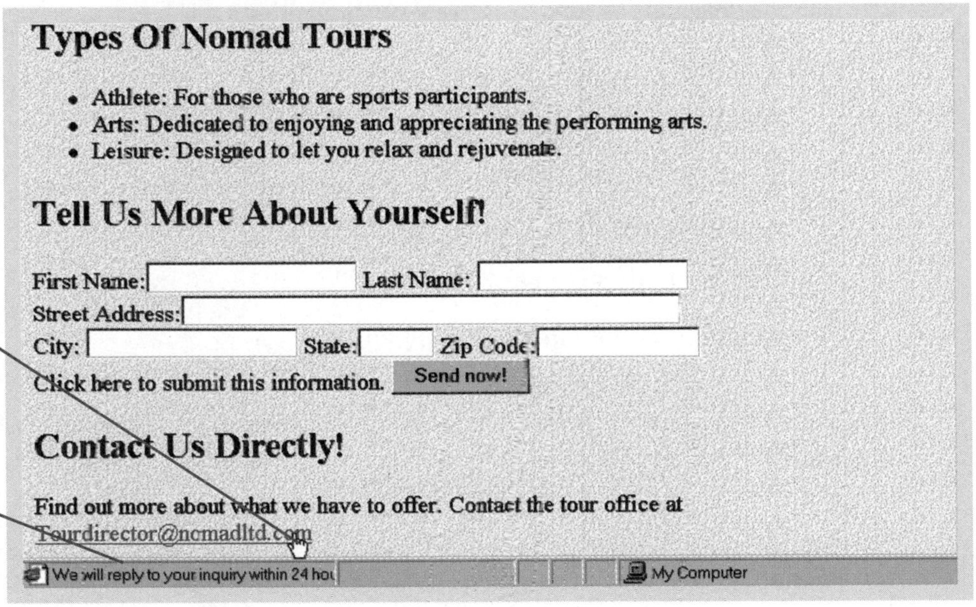

TABLE H-2: JavaScript event handlers

event handler	triggering action	event handler	triggering action
onAbort	Page loading halted	onLoad	Page or image opens
onBlur	Object not current or highlighted	onMouseOut	Mouse pointer not over link
onChange	Object value changed	onMouseOver	Mouse pointer over link
onClick	Hyperlink or button clicked	onSelect	Text selected
onError	Error executing script	onSubmit	Form submitted
onFocus	Object current or highlighted	onUnload	Different page opened

HTML

HTML

Creating a Function

As your scripts become more complex, you will begin to incorporate many lines of code in each one to store and process information. To help keep your scripts organized, JavaScript allows you to group and name sets of script code in units called **functions**. A function is a set of code that performs a specific task. When you group the lines of your scripts into functions, the code is logically broken down into functional units, which makes it easier to understand and to debug. You usually define functions in a page's head section, which allows any programmer to quickly scan a page's code. Additionally, because each function has a name, you can easily refer to it in several different parts of a Web page. This means you do not need to duplicate code each time you want your page to repeat a procedure. ✒ Lydia wants to add a button to the Web page that will clear the user's input in the form. She writes a function to perform this task.

Steps 1234

1. Open the file **HTML H-3.htm** in your text editor, then save it as a text document with the filename **Function.htm**

   Generally, it's best to define functions at the beginning of a Web page, to make sure they are available for all subsequent uses.

2. Select the text **[replace with clearUp function]** in the page's head section, then press **[Delete]**

3. Type the following, pressing **[Enter]** at the end of each line

   ```
   function clearUp() {

           document.info.elements[0].value=""

           document.info.elements[1].value=""

           document.info.elements[2].value=""

           document.info.elements[3].value=""

           document.info.elements[4].value=""

           document.info.elements[5].value=""
   ```

   These lines define a function that assigns the value **null**, or nothing, to each of the six text fields on the page. This null value is defined with the paired quotation marks that follow each equal sign and that contain nothing between them.

4. Type **}**

   Figure H-7 shows the completed function, including the opening and closing braces. The code for a function is always demarcated with braces {}.

5. Scroll to the end of the document, select the text **[replace with Clear button code]**, then press **[Delete]**

6. Type **<INPUT TYPE="BUTTON" value="Clear form" onClick = "clearUp()">**

   The button tag includes an event handler to trigger, or **call**, the function clearUp() when a user clicks the button. Figure H-8 shows the completed button tag in the document.

7. Check the document for errors, make changes as necessary, then save Function.htm as a text document

8. Open **Function.htm** in your Web browser, fill in the six input fields, then click the **Clear form button**

   The browser clears each of the text input fields.

FIGURE H-7: Document containing clearUp() function code

```
<HTML>

<HEAD>
<TITLE>Nomad Ltd online</TITLE>

<SCRIPT LANGUAGE="javascript">
<!--
function submitted() {
      alert("Information submitted!")
}

function clearUp() {
      document.info.elements[0].value=""
      document.info.elements[1].value=""
      document.info.elements[2].value=""
      document.info.elements[3].value=""
      document.info.elements[4].value=""
      document.info.elements[5].value=""
}


//-->
</SCRIPT>

</HEAD>
```

Code defining new function *(label pointing to the clearUp() function block)*

FIGURE H-8: Document containing clearUp() function reference

```
</UL>

<H2>Tell Us More About Yourself!</H2>
<FORM NAME="info">
First Name:<INPUT TYPE="TEXT" SIZE=20 ID="firstname">
Last Name: <INPUT TYPE="TEXT" SIZE=20 ID="lastname"><BR>
Street Address:<INPUT TYPE="TEXT" SIZE=50 ID="address"><BR>
City: <INPUT TYPE="TEXT" SIZE=20 ID="city">
State:<INPUT TYPE="TEXT" SIZE=6 ID="state">
Zip Code:<INPUT TYPE="TEXT" SIZE=15 ID="zipcode">
<BR>Click here to submit this information. <INPUT TYPE="BUTTON" VALUE="Send
now!" onClick="submitted()">
<BR>Click here to clear the form and start over.
<INPUT TYPE="BUTTON" VALUE="Clear form" onClick="clearUp()">
</FORM>

<H2>Contact Us Directly!</H2>

Find out more about what we have to offer. Contact the tour
office at <A HREF="MAILTO:Tourdirector@nomadltd.com"
onMouseOver="window.status='We will reply to your inquiry within 24
hours!';return true" onMouseOut="window.status='';return
true">Tourdirector@nomadltd.com</A>

</BODY>
</HTML>
```

Code referencing new function *(label pointing to the onClick="clearUp()" code)*

HTML

Assigning a Variable

In scripting, you often instruct JavaScript to perform functions on pieces of information that you specify, known as **values**. For example, the text *We will reply to your inquiry within 24 hours!*, which you used earlier in conjunction with an event handler, is a value. Values can also include "true" and "false" and information about the user's browser, such as the width of the window in pixels. JavaScript can add or manipulate any numeric value mathematically. When values are composed of many characters, such as the message text above, or when they change in different situations, such as browser window dimensions, they can be cumbersome if you need to enter them several times in your script. You can make this process easier and more efficient by assigning the value to a **variable**, which serves as a nickname. When you assign a value to a variable, you enter or look up the value only one time and then you use the variable to refer to the value. Using variables saves you time when writing scripts. Variables provide added flexibility by allowing you to modify the value in only one place and have the modifications reflected instantaneously throughout the document as indicated by the variable. ◄——— Lydia has modified the Nomad Ltd home page to personalize text by displaying the user's name. To finish her changes, she needs to define the variable she will use to represent the user's name, and then insert the variable name in the scripts.

Steps

1. Open the file **HTML H-4.htm** in your text editor, then save it as a text document with the filename **Variable.htm**

2. Select the text **[replace with variable definition]** near the top of the page, then press **[Delete]**

3. Type the following text on one line, without pressing [Enter]
   var name=prompt("For personal service, please type your first name and click OK.","")
   This line of script creates a dialog box that prompts the user to enter his or her first name and assigns the user's input to a variable named "name". Figure H-9 shows the document with this line of code inserted. The command "var" tells JavaScript that you are specifying a variable. The word following var—in this case, "name"—is the name of the variable you are creating. The value of the new variable follows the name after an equals sign. In this case, the value will be the result of user input in a dialog box created by the "prompt" method.

4. Scroll down to the beginning of the page's body section, select the text **[replace with heading script]**, then press **[Delete]**
   Notice that Lydia has already inserted the opening and closing script tags.

Trouble?

Be sure you type a space after the text **page**, and before the closing ".

5. Type the following text on one line, without pressing [Enter]
   document.write("<H1>Welcome to the Nomad Ltd home page, " + name + "!</H1>")
   This script writes a line of code to the Web page, containing H1 tags to format the text. Lydia uses the variable "name" to insert the user's name into the page heading.

6. Scroll down to the beginning of the form section, select the text **[replace with second heading script]**, then press **[Delete]**

7. Type the following all on one line, without pressing [Enter]
   document.write("<H2>Please tell us more about yourself, " + name + ".</H2>")
   This script places the user's name at a second location in the Web page.

8. Check the document for errors, make changes as necessary, then save Variable.htm as a text document

9. Open the file **Variable.htm** in your Web browser, type your first name in the prompt dialog box, then click **OK**
   The Nomad Ltd home page is now personalized. The name the user enters in the prompt dialog box is displayed. See Figure H-10.

FIGURE H-9: Script creating a variable

Variable inserted in script

```
<HTML>

<HEAD>
<TITLE>Nomad Ltd online</TITLE>

<SCRIPT LANGUAGE="javascript">
<!--
var name=prompt("For personal service, please type your first name and click
OK.","")

function submitted() {
       alert("Information submitted!")
}

function clearUp() {
       document.info.elements[0].value=""
       document.info.elements[1].value=""
       document.info.elements[2].value=""
       document.info.elements[3].value=""
       document.info.elements[4].value=""
       document.info.elements[5].value=""
}

//-->
</SCRIPT>
```

FIGURE H-10: Web page incorporating user information

Welcome to the Nomad Ltd home page, Lydia!

Nomad Ltd

Learn About Our Company's Philosophy

Nomad Ltd has been in business for over ten years. During that time, we have offered tours to exotic (and simple) lands and sold sporting equipment (for bicycling, hiking, and other activities). In all that time, we have always been aware that our employees are our corporate ambassadors, and our customers are our royalty. We know that any company can make a buck here and there, but we want to do more than that. We want you to enjoy shopping at our stores and contribute to making Nomad a fun and interesting place to shop. We also know that as a business, we are also community members. Nomad wants to contribute to community efforts and make each town we're in a better place to live and shop. How do we do that? By hiring from the community, offering educational and financial benefits to our employees, and becoming involved in various community efforts.

Types Of Nomad Tours

User name incorporated into Web page text generated by script

CLUES TO USE

Manipulating variables

In addition to simply using variable values that a user enters or that a script looks up, your scripts can process values using **arithmetic operators**, which allow you to manipulate variables mathematically to create new values. For example, to count page headings, you could create a script that reads through your Web page code, adding 1 to a variable value each time it encounters a heading tag. You also could combine several values that a user enters using a mathematical equation.

Creating a Conditional

Sometimes, you want a script to be able to create different results depending on different user actions or on the value of a certain browser attribute. JavaScript allows you to set up this situation by creating a **conditional** in your script. A conditional allows your script to choose one of two paths, depending on a condition that you specify. For example, you might want a graphic to display at a smaller size if a user's window is not maximized, to keep it fully in view. You could use a conditional to check the dimensions of the user's browser window and then set the graphic dimensions to one of two preset choices. Conditionals allow you to create flexible, interactive scripts whose output can change in different situations. Nomad Ltd has had a problem with users submitting forms missing the zip code information. Lydia wants her Web page to verify that the user has completed the zip code form field before it submits the data to the server. Using a conditional, her page can prompt the user to complete the field if it is left blank.

Steps

1. Open the file **HTML H-5.htm** in your text editor, then save it as a text document with the filename **Conditional.htm**

2. Select **[replace with verify function]** in the page's head section and press **[Delete]**

3. Type the following code, pressing **[Enter]** at the end of each line

```
function verify() {
        if (document.info.elements[5].value == "") {
                alert("Please complete each field.")
        }       else {
                submitted()
        }
}
```

Figure H-11 shows the document containing the verify function. The "if" statement code checks if the value of the zipcode field is null, indicating that the user has left it blank. When the "if" statement returns a value of "true," the function executes the code that immediately follows it. Here, the "true" result triggers the "alert" command to create a dialog box prompting the user to complete each field. When the "if" statement returns a value of "false," the function executes the code following the word *else*. In Lydia's script, the else command runs a function called "submitted()" that sends the user's information to the Web server.

4. Scroll to the bottom of the form section, select the text **[replace with event handler]** in the tag for the Send now! button, then press **[Delete]**

5. Type **onClick="verify()"**

6. Check scripts you added for errors, make changes as necessary, then save **Conditional.htm** as a text document

7. Open **Conditional.htm** in your Web browser, enter your name, scroll down to the form, then click the **Send now! button** without filling in any of the fields
The script runs and displays the dialog box shown in Figure H-12.

8. Click the **OK button**, then fill in each of the fields with sample information and click the **Send now! button**
The script you added verifies that the zip code field contains information and then allows the form submit function to execute.

FIGURE H-11: Web document containing completed script

Condition

Conditional terms

"false" result

"true" result

```
                    document.info.elements[5].value=""
}

function verify() {
    if (document.info.elements[5].value == "") {
        alert("Please complete each field.")
    } else {
        submitted()
    }
}

//-->
</SCRIPT>

</HEAD>

<BODY BACKGROUND="egg shell.jpg">

<IMG SRC="nomad.jpg" ALIGN="right" WIDTH=201 HEIGHT=63>

<SCRIPT LANGUAGE="javascript">
<!--
document.write("<H1>Welcome to the Nomad Ltd home page, " + name + "!</H1>")
//-->
</SCRIPT>
```

FIGURE H-12: Browser showing alert dialog box

- Athlete: For those who are sports participants.
- Arts: Dedicated to enjoying and appreciating the performing arts.
- Leisure: Designed to let you relax and rejuvenate.

Please tell us more about yourself, Lydia.

First Name:

Street Address:

City: State

Click here to submit this informat...

Click here to clear the form and start over.   Clear form

Microsoft Internet Explorer

⚠ Please complete each field.

OK

Contact Us Directly!

Find out more about what we have to offer. Contact the tour office at
Tourdirector@nomadltd.com

Testing multiple conditions

In addition to using a conditional to test a single condition, you test multiple conditions using logical comparison operators. JavaScript recognizes three logical comparison operators: && ("and"), || ("or"), and ! ("not"). A conditional using the && operator between two or more conditions returns "true" only if all conditions are true. Linking multiple conditions with the || operator, however, returns "true" if any one of the conditions is true. The ! operator returns true if its associated condition is not true.

Practice

► Concepts Review

Label each item shown in Figure H-13.

FIGURE H-13

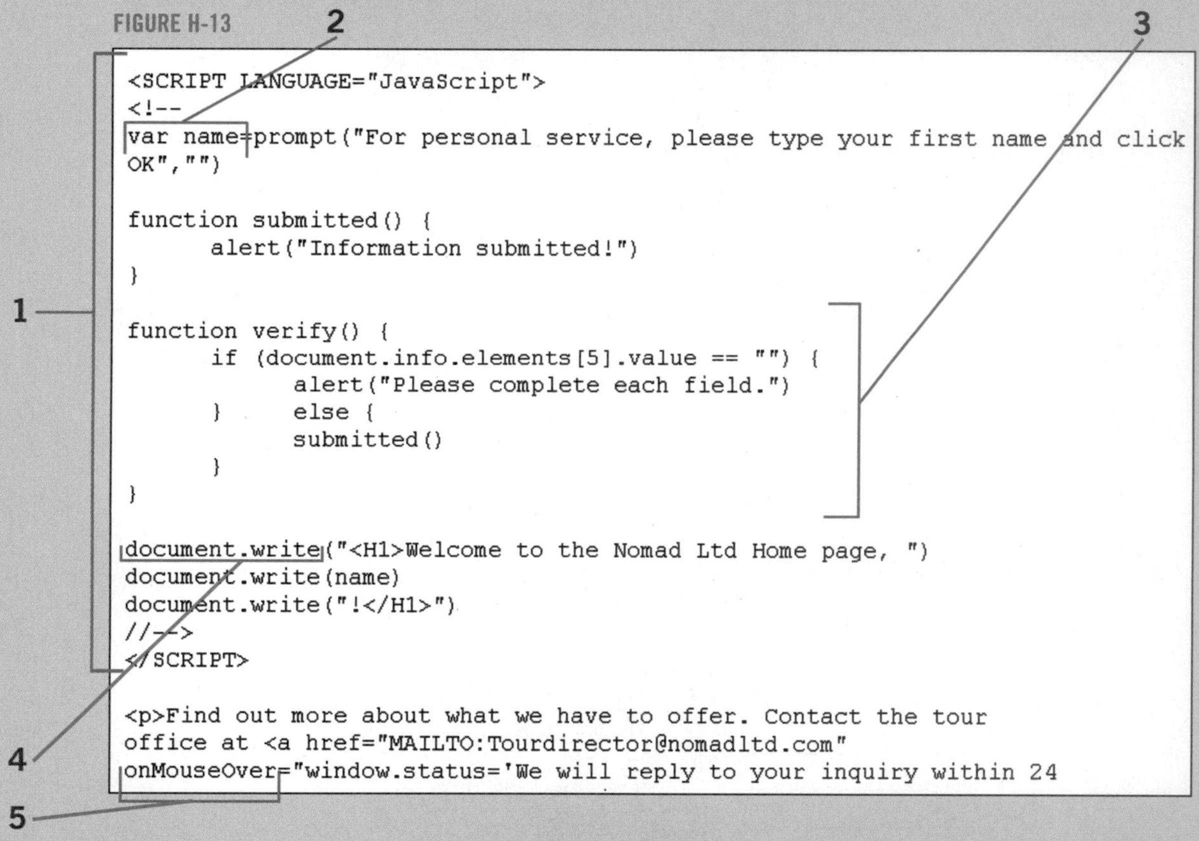

```
<SCRIPT LANGUAGE="JavaScript">
<!--
var name=prompt("For personal service, please type your first name and click
OK","")

function submitted() {
        alert("Information submitted!")
}

function verify() {
        if (document.info.elements[5].value == "") {
                alert("Please complete each field.")
        }       else {
                submitted()
        }
}

document.write("<H1>Welcome to the Nomad Ltd Home page, ")
document.write(name)
document.write("!</H1>")
//-->
</SCRIPT>

<p>Find out more about what we have to offer. Contact the tour
office at <a href="MAILTO:Tourdirector@nomadltd.com"
onMouseOver="window.status='We will reply to your inquiry within 24
```

1 2 3 4 5

Match each statement with the term it describes.

6. Object hierarchy
7. Event handler
8. Bug
9. Method
10. JavaScript

a. Term specifying a possible user action
b. An error in a script
c. A Web page scripting language
d. JavaScript's object organization
e. Any action an object can carry out

Select the best answer from the list of choices.

11. **What HTML tagset marks the beginning and end of a script?**
    a. <JS>..</JS>
    b. <JAVASCRIPT>..</JAVASCRIPT>
    c. <SCRIPT>..</SCRIPT>
    d. <JAVASCRIPT>..<JAVASCRIPT>

12. **Which scripting language is compatible with both Netscape Navigator 4 and Microsoft Internet Explorer 4?**
    a. JScript
    b. JavaScript
    c. HTML
    d. VBScript

13. **Which of the following typing mistakes would not result in an error in your script?**
    a. Substituting the letter l for the number 1
    b. Inserting an extra space
    c. Omitting a closing bracket
    d. All of the above could result in errors.

14. **What would be the proper form of address in the object hierarchy for the second element in a form called "info"?**
    a. document.info.elements[1]
    b. document.info.elements[2]
    c. document.forms.info.elements[2]
    d. info.elements[2]

15. **What is the function of the string <!-- in scripting?**
    a. It is the HTML code for the beginning of a script.
    b. It is the HTML code for the end of a script.
    c. It tells an incompatible browser to ignore the code that follows.
    d. It tells the browser to display the text "--"

16. **Which comparison operator returns true only if the values before and after are both true?**
    a. &&
    b. ||
    c. !
    d. ==

17. **A set of script code grouped logically and named is called a(n)**
    a. Object.
    b. Variable.
    c. Hierarchy.
    d. Function.

Skills Review

1. Create a script.

   a. Open the text editor, open the file HTML H-6.htm, then save it as a text document with the filename Script review.htm.

   b. Select the text [replace with script tags] in the page's head section, then press [Delete].

   c. Type <SCRIPT LANGUAGE="javascript"> and press [Enter].

   d. Type <!-- and press [Enter] twice.

   e. Type //--> and press [Enter], then type </SCRIPT>.

   f. Save Script review.htm as a text document.

   g. Open Script review.htm in your Web browser.

2. Debug a script.

   a. Open the file HTML H-7.htm in your browser, read the description of the error in the JavaScript Error dialog box, then click yes.

   b. Open the file HTML H-7.htm in your text editor, then save it as a text document with the filename Debug review.htm.

   c. Position the pointer in the third line of the clearUp() function, which begins document.info.elements[2].value, then insert a second quotation mark (") after the existing one at the end of the line.

   d. Save Debug review.htm as a text document, open Debug review.htm in your Web browser, enter information in the form, then click the Clear form button.

3. Use JavaScript event handlers.

   a. Open the file HTML H-8.htm in your text editor, then save it as a text document with the filename Event handler review.htm.

   b. Scroll to the bottom of the document, select the text "[replace with event handler]" in the first <A> tag, then press [Delete].

   c. Type the following without pressing [Enter]:
   onMouseOver="window.status='Guidelines on scheduling vacation time';return true"
   onMouseOut="window.status='';return true"

   d. Review your typing for errors, then save Event handler review.htm as a text document.

   e. Open Event handler review.htm in your Web browser, move the mouse pointer over the hypertext link "Additional vacation information" and verify that the message "Guidelines on scheduling vacation time" appears in the status bar.

   f. If necessary, fix any errors in your text editor, then save and preview the page.

4. Create a function.

   a. Open the file HTML H-9.htm in your text editor, then save it as a text document with the filename Function review.htm.

   b. Select the text "[replace with date function]" in the page's head section, then press [Delete].

   c. Type function writeDate() {

   d. Press [Enter], then type document.write(month + "/" + today.getDate() + "/" + today.getYear() + ".")

   e. Press [Enter], then type }

f. Select the text [replace with function call] near the bottom of the page, then type writeDate()

g. Save Function review.htm as a text document.

h. Open Function review.htm in your browser, verify that it displays the current date below the list of vacation dates, use your text editor to make changes if necessary, then save Function review.htm as a text document.

5. Assign a variable.

a. Open the file HTML H-10.htm in your text editor, then save it as a text document with the filename Variable review.htm.

b. Select the text [replace with variable code] in the page's head section, then type var name=prompt("Please type your first name and click OK","").

c. Select the text [replace with variable reference] at the top of the body section, then press [Delete].

d. Type document.write(name).

e. Save Variable review.htm as a text document, then open Variable review.htm in your browser.

f. Type your first name, then click OK.

g. Use your text editor to debug as needed.

6. Create a conditional.

a. Open the file HTML H-11.htm in your text editor, then save it as a text document with the filename Conditional review.htm.

b. Select the text [replace with conditional function] in the page's head section, then press [Delete].

c. Type the following code, pressing [Enter] at the end of each line:

```
function verify() {
        if (document.info.elements[0].value == "" ||
        document.info.elements[1].value == "" ||
        document.info.elements[2].value == "" ||
        document.info.elements[3].value == "" ||
        document.info.elements[4].value == "" ||
        document.info.elements[5].value == "") {
                alert("Please complete each field.")
        }       else {
                submitted()
        }
}
```

d. Review your code for typing errors, then save Conditional review.htm as a text document.

e. Open Conditional review.htm in your browser, fill in every field in the form except the last name field, click the "Submit now!" button, verify that your browser opens a dialog box asking you to complete all the fields, then click OK.

f. Close your text editor and browser.

► Independent Challenges

1. Green House, a local plant store, has hired you to add interactive features to their Web pages. You've decided to start by using an event handler to display link explanations in the status bar when users point to the page's links.

To complete this independent challenge:

a. Start your text editor program, open the file HTML H-12.htm, then save it as a text document with the filename Green House home.htm.

b. To define the text strings that will be displayed as variables, select the text [replace with variable script] at the top of the page, press [Delete], and insert the following script, pressing [Enter] at the end of each line:
```
<SCRIPT LANGUAGE="javascript">
<!--
var plants="An overview of our plant stock and sources"
var tips="Helpful growing hints on common houseplants"
var services="A guide to our professional plant care services"
//-->
</SCRIPT>
```

c. Select the text "[replace with first event handlers]" in the <A> tag for the first link at the bottom of the page, press [Delete], and type the following without pressing [Enter]:
onMouseOver="window.status=plants;return true"onMouseOut="window.status='';return true"

d. Repeat Step c to modify the second link with the following insertion:
onMouseOver="window.status=tips;return true" onMouseOut="window.status='';return true"

e. Repeat Step c to modify the third link with the following insertion:
onMouseOver="window.status=services;return true" onMouseOut="window.status='';return true"

f. Save Green House home.htm as a text document, then open the file Green House home.htm in your Web browser.

g. Use your text editor to make any changes necessary, always save the file as a text document, then close your text editor and browser.

2. You have designed a Web publication for Sandhills Regional Public Transit. You want to incorporate a function you've written to tell prospective riders which fare period is in effect. A sentence stating the fare period will display at the bottom of the Web page. This sentence will change depending on the time of day.

To complete this independent challenge:

a. Start your text editor program, open the file HTML H-13.htm, then save it as a text document with the filename SRPT home.htm.

b. Replace the text [replace with fare function] in the page's head section with the script located in the file HTML H-14.txt.

c. Scroll down immediately before the closing body section tag, delete the text [replace with function call script], enter the two opening script tags, type "schedTime()" (without the quotes) as the third line of the script, then enter the two closing script tags.

d. Save and preview your file in your Web browser program, debugging as necessary until you see no more JavaScript error messages.

3. You have been hired by Community Public School Volunteers to add advanced features to their Web publication using scripts. You have inserted a script into the home page they provided, but a JavaScript error dialog box opens when the page loads. To complete this independent challenge, preview the file HTML H-15.htm in your browser, noting the type of JavaScript error described and its location. Open the page in your text editor and save a copy as CPSV home.htm. Edit the script to fix the JavaScript error. Use the guidelines listed earlier in the unit to identify the types of errors that may be present. Continue to preview and edit the page until you no longer receive an error message, then save your work in your text editor as a text file.

WEB WORK

4. Scripts are used in many Web pages on the WWW today to add features, as well as to create interesting formatting that is not possible with standard HTML coding. To complete this independent challenge, find two pages on the Web that contain scripts. (*Hint:* after opening a page in your browser, choose the HTML or Page Source option in your browser's View menu to check the document code for <SCRIPT> tags.) Print their HTML source code, and circle all scripts you see on your printouts. Circle and label any variables, conditionals, and functions you see in the documents.

▶ Visual Workshop

Open your text editor program, open the file HTML H-16.htm, and save it as a text document named Touchstone.htm. Then open Touchstone.htm in your browser. Scroll down to see the Send now! button. Click the Send now! button on the form without entering information in any of the fields. Use the form-verification script located in the file HTML H-17.txt and your text editor to modify the document Touchstone.htm. Change the event handler for the Send now! button to run the verify() function. Save the changes as a text document with the filename Touchstone.htm. Click the browser program button on the taskbar, and refresh your screen. Click the Send now! button again. Your screen should look like Figure H-14. Debug as necessary. (*Hint:* Remember to insert the verification script in the document header section between the beginning and ending script tags.)

FIGURE H-14

Working
with Dynamic HTML (DHTML)

Objectives

- ► **Define Dynamic HTML**
- ► **Understand the building blocks of DHTML**
- ► **Tour DHTML pages**
- ► **Understand the DHTML Object Model**
- ► **Understand browser variability**
- ► **Design DHTML pages**
- ► **Research code architecture**
- ► **Keep up with DHTML changes**

Once you have an understanding of standard HTML and Web page design, you can create well-structured Web pages that use effective style combinations and that allow basic user input. However, recent innovations in Web page design and scripting, collectively known as **Dynamic HTML** (or **DHTML** for short), have revolutionized Web page design. DHTML has greatly increased the degree of interactivity possible in Web page design. With DHTML, your Web pages are enlivened as text and graphics change color, grow, shrink, and move on and off the page in response to user actions. ◄— Lydia Burgos, who works in the information systems department at Nomad Ltd, has read about Dynamic HTML and wants to explore using it in her company's Web pages. She starts with some research to learn about what DHTML is and how it works.

Unit I
HTML

Defining DHTML

During the early 1990's, all Web pages were simple documents that users downloaded and viewed on their local computers. Each Web page's interactivity was limited to hyperlinks, which opened other Web pages, opened new mail messages, or ran scripts on the server. Web pages that fit this description are known as **static HTML**. Today, however, many Web pages respond to and even interact with the user by changing their appearances based on user actions. Such pages use **dynamic HTML**, which describes a varied set of technologies that allow almost-immediate response to user actions in a Web page without accessing the Internet server. In her research, Lydia learns of several broad categories of design that DHTML allows.

Details

Dynamic style

When you create a page using standard HTML coding, you specify a style for each text element. These styles remain the same, regardless of user actions. The one exception to this is hyperlinks; their color may be changed by the browser if you have followed them recently. However, when you create a page using DHTML, you can incorporate styles—including font size, typeface, and color—that change immediately in response to user actions, such as moving the mouse pointer over a heading. This feature, known as **dynamic style**, allows your pages to emphasize an area when a user shows interest in it, without flooding the page with distracting large font sizes or bright colors. Figure I-1 provides an example of dynamic style. Notice on this DHTML page that the text color has changed, which is the result of DHTML. If the user selects this hyperlink, the color will change again to show that it has been viewed already.

Dynamic content

A DHTML Web page can display different content based on a user's activities, which is a feature known as **dynamic content**. Instead of taking the time to request, download, and display a new Web page (as standard HTML coding would do), DHTML utilities can simply hide or display blocks of text or other elements in the current page. This aspect of DHTML allows you to create a simple, well-organized, and visually appealing page that can instantly display extra information when the user is likely to be interested in it. Figure I-1 provides an example of dynamic content. Notice the message displayed in the status window, which is the result of DHTML.

Data-awareness

Standard HTML tools allow your Web pages to download chunks of information, such as database contents, from a Web server as a user requests access to them. With DHTML, this process is instantaneous for the user; for example, a DHTML Web page could be designed to download a complete database but then display only the information the user wants to view. A Web page equipped to work with data in this way is termed **data aware**, which means the user can work with information from a Web server without adding to Internet traffic by repeatedly requesting additional pieces of information. Also, data awareness can allow the user to manipulate and change the information right in the browser window.

Positioning

As with other formatting options, static HTML leaves many of the choices regarding the positioning of elements in a Web page to the browser's discretion. In addition to causing pages to display nonuniformly and unpredictably on different browsers, this aspect of HTML has prevented Web page design from rivaling the intricacy inherent in the best layouts of other media, such as magazines. DHTML represents an important step toward changing this by allowing Web page designers to specify precisely the location of all page elements, a feature known as **positioning**, which is unavailable in standard HTML. The Web page in Figure I-2, which is from an online tutorial on DHTML, uses DHTML to position text in combinations not possible with static HTML.

FIGURE I-1: Dynamic Web page

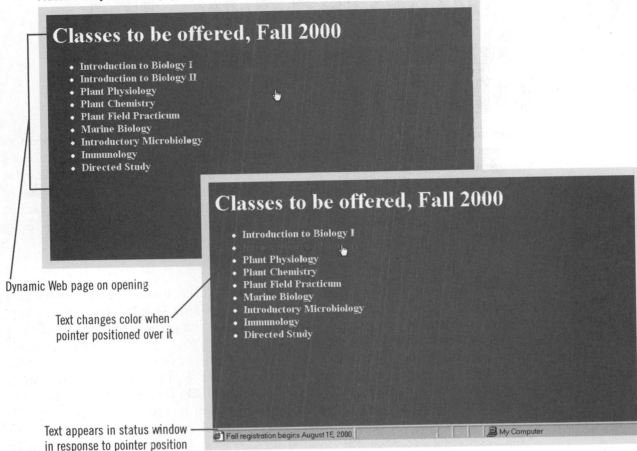

Dynamic Web page on opening

Text changes color when pointer positioned over it

Text appears in status window in response to pointer position

FIGURE I-2: Web page formatted with DHTML positioning

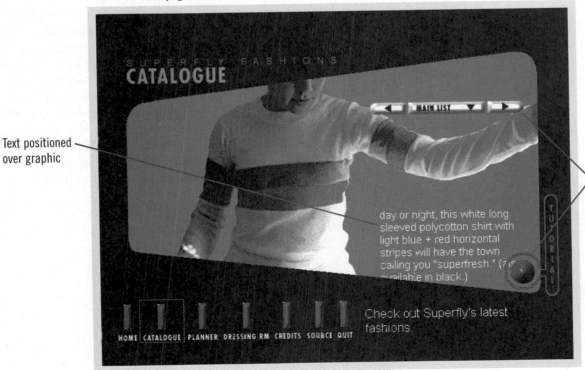

Text positioned over graphic

Graphics positioned over other graphic

Understanding the Building Blocks of DHTML

Details

The creation of simple Web pages, while drawing on organization, design, and content-production skills, uses only HTML for arrangement and display in a browser. By contrast, DHTML is not a language or even a single technology, but, rather, a collection of Web page tools that, when used in various combinations, let designers create the effects specified in the previous lesson. As she reads more about DHTML, Lydia learns that DHTML is comprised of two main tools that work in tandem with standard HTML. These DHTML tools are included in the Web page source code shown in Figure I-3.

Client-side scripts

Scripts are small programs that can be triggered by a user's action on a Web page. In the early days of the Web, browsers allowed only the use of **server-side scripts**, or scripts that were stored and run on the Web server. Using these server-side scripts was similar to triggering a hyperlink. Each time a server-side script was run, the Web page sent a message to the server instructing it to run the script. Users had to wait as the browser downloaded the results of the server-side script. The lag time involved in this setup made features such as dynamic content and dynamic style impractical. Recent versions of browsers have allowed Web page designers to create **client-side scripts**, or scripts that the browser itself interprets and runs. Client-side scripts are a key element in allowing DHTML to respond immediately to user actions. For example, the client-side script at the bottom of Figure I-3 changes the text color and adds text to the status window when the mouse pointer moves over certain text.

Cascading Style Sheets (CSS)

In standard HTML, you assign styles and properties to elements of your page—text blocks, images, and other objects—through HTML tags. This system means that each element has its own set of properties. Even if two elements share the same properties, you must assign them separately and make any subsequent changes to each element. Although you can assign similar properties to groups of elements using defined styles, such as <H1>, these styles are defined on each user's browser, and thus you cannot predict exactly how a viewer will see your page in the browser window. **Cascading Style Sheets (CSS)** is a tool that allows you to specify attributes such as color and font size for all page elements marked by a specific tag, name, or ID. CSS not only gives designers a more efficient way to specify style but also more control over an object's attributes as well as how each object should be displayed in certain situations. For example, the Cascading Style Sheet in Figure I-3 assigns attributes to various tags. All text marked with these tags, such as <LI> and <P>, will display the attributes defined for this tag in the style sheet.

FIGURE I-3: Code for Web page incorporating DHTML tools

Cascading
Style Sheet

```
<STYLE TYPE="text/css">
body {background:navy; color:white}
LI {list-style-image: none; list-style: none}
UL.toc {display:none}
UL.expanded {display:block}
A.select {color:white; background:blue}
.over {color:red}
P {margin-top:0; margin-bottom:0}
</STYLE>
```

Client-side
script

```
<SCRIPT LANGUAGE="JavaScript">
<!--
var curSelection = null;

function setStyle(src, toClass) {
        if (null != src)
        src.className = toClass;
}

function mouseEnters() {
        if ((curSelection != event.toElement) && ("A" ==
event.toElement.tagName)) {
                setStyle(event.toElement,"over");
                window.status="Fall registration begins August 15, 2000."
        }
}
```

CLUES TO USE

Proprietary features

Both Netscape and Microsoft have each introduced unique features, known as **proprietary features**, into their browsers. For example, Netscape Navigator 4 allows use of the <LAYER> tag to overlap screen elements easily. Microsoft Internet Explorer 4 supports the embedding of external tables in a Web page, as well as a set of features that affect element appearance in complex ways. Eventually, some of these technologies become part of new international Web page standards. When proprietary features become part of the industry standard, they eventually become supported by the major browsers and are then no longer considered proprietary features. However, proprietary features that are supported by only one of the two major browsers are most useful only in single-browser settings, such as intranets whose users all run the same browser.

Touring DHTML Pages

Although DHTML technology may sound intriguing, viewing and interacting with it is the only way to get a true sense of its impact and capabilities. Looking at existing pages, both successful and not, is also a useful way to begin planning the features you want to include in your own pages. ⬛⬛ Lydia has downloaded several sample Web pages that incorporate features she has researched. She opens and tests them as she begins collecting ideas for updating the Nomad Ltd Web site.

Trouble?

If you are using Navigator, some text on the page may be arranged differently from that shown in the figures. However, all of the features of the page should still work.

1. **Start your Web browser program, open the file HTML I-1.htm, then scroll down the page to view its layout**

   As Figure I-4 shows, this page contains several blocks of text positioned around the page; each of these is an example of DHTML positioning. The designer of this Web page created the sidebar along the right edge of the screen by using DHTML style specifications to position the text, specify its width, and specify a background color for the text block.

2. **Scroll down the page until the heading Blue Ray appears in your document window, then move your mouse pointer over the heading Blue Ray**

   If you are using Internet Explorer 4, notice that the text color changes from black to purple and that the text size increases—an example of **dynamic style**. Netscape Navigator 4 does not support most dynamic styles and shows no change when your mouse pointer is over this heading.

3. **Click the heading Blue Ray**

   A paragraph of detailed information appears beneath the heading, without the page reloading, as shown in Figure I-5. This is an example of **dynamic content** because user activity can affect the page content.

4. **Watch the text in the status window**

   A message continuously scrolls across the status window. This feature, created by a script, is another example of dynamic content.

5. **Scroll to the top of the page, and move your mouse pointer over one of the links under the heading "Learn more about Jim's!"**

   As the pointer moves over link text or an image, the link image changes. When the pointer moves off the link, the image returns to its original appearance, which is an instance of dynamic content. Rather than simply changing a graphic's display properties, the position of the pointer over the link triggers a script that changes the source of the image in the image tag. The pointer movement causes the image to toggle between two different source files.

QuickTip

Currently, data binding is a proprietary feature of Internet Explorer 4, but an extension is available from the Microsoft Web site that allows Netscape Navigator 4 to display this and other Internet Explorer 4 features.

6. **If you are using Internet Explorer, open the file HTML I-2.htm and scroll to the bottom of the page**

   As Figure I-6 shows, this page contains a data table. Unlike standard HTML tables, however, this table was generated from an external file as the Web page opened. Linking a Web page to an external data file is known as **data binding**. If you added or changed records in the external file, they would be reflected in the Web page the next time you opened it without requiring any changes in the Web page's code. A related feature, known as **data-awareness**, allows a Web page to load all the records from a database but display only some of them. Then, a user can access any record instantly without needing to download more information to the browser.

FIGURE I-4: Sample DHTML Web page

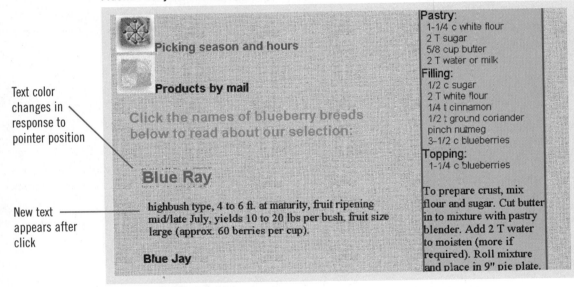

All-natural, quality berries and berry products

Jim's
Blueberry Farm

Positioned elements

Learn more about Jim's!

Tour the farm

Directions for visiting us

Here's another great blueberry idea from our kitchen!

Blueberry tart

Pastry:
1-1/4 c white flour
2 T sugar

FIGURE I-5: Dynamic content and style changes

Picking season and hours

Products by mail

Click the names of blueberry breeds below to read about our selection:

Text color changes in response to pointer position

Blue Ray

New text appears after click

highbush type, 4 to 6 ft. at maturity, fruit ripening mid/late July, yields 10 to 20 lbs per bush, fruit size large (approx. 60 berries per cup).

Blue Jay

Pastry:
1-1/4 c white flour
2 T sugar
5/8 cup butter
2 T water or milk
Filling:
1/2 c sugar
2 T white flour
1/4 t cinnamon
1/2 t ground coriander
pinch nutmeg
3-1/2 c blueberries
Topping:
1-1/4 c blueberries

To prepare crust, mix flour and sugar. Cut butter in to mixture with pastry blender. Add 2 T water to moisten (more if required). Roll mixture and place in 9" pie plate.

FIGURE I-6: Web page containing bound data

products

The following table summarizes the information on all our blueberry types. Click any table heading to sort the table by that column.

Table generated from linked external data source

Bush	Type	Height	Fruit maturity	Yield per bush	Berry size	Berries per cup
Blue Ray	high	4-6 ft.	mid/late July	10-20 lb.	large	60
Blue Jay	high	5-7 ft.	late July	7-10 lb.	small/medium	110
Jersey	high	5-7 ft.	late July	7-10 lb.	small/medium	110
Elliott	high	5-7 ft.	late Aug./early Sept.	10-20 lb	small/medium	75
Northland	medium	3-4 ft.	early July	15-20	small	135

Understanding the DHTML Object Model

Developers of early scripting languages created an **object hierarchy**, which is a system of organization that allows Web page developers to describe and work with the Web page elements in a browser window. This hierarchy, officially called the **Document Object Model (DOM)**, categorizes and groups Web page elements into a tree-like structure. Each part of this structure is referred to as an **object**. For example, in the basic JavaScript DOM, a page's images, forms, anchors, and links are all grouped beneath the document object. The document, its location, and its history are, in turn, grouped below the frame object. DOMs allow browsers to identify page elements and to make them available to scripts in Web pages that they display. Although the earliest DOMs were part of scripting languages, Navigator 4 and Internet Explorer 4 have increased the range and versatility of DHTML by including their own extended DOM versions in the browser code itself, which are sometimes referred to as **DHTML Object Models**. DHTML Object Models allow you to reference a particular object the same way in any scripting language on a particular browser. However, because Netscape and Microsoft have developed different DOMs, you must reference some objects differently in Navigator 4 than in Internet Explorer 4. Figure I-7 shows the basic structure of the DOM for Internet Explorer 4, which makes virtually all browser window elements available to scripts. In order to take full advantage of DHTML's capabilities, Lydia reviews the top level of object classes in the Microsoft DHTML Object Model.

Details

Location
The location object contains the URL of the current page.

Frames
The frames object contains a separate Window object for each frame in the current browser window. When the window is not divided into frames, this object is empty and the entire document contents are part of the document object The Microsoft DOM also contains a frames collection within the document object, to reference its <IFRAME> tag.

History
The history object allows access to the browser's list of previously visited URLs.

Navigator
The navigator object makes information about the browser available.

Event
The event object allows interaction with the event currently being processed by the browser, such as mouse movement or the press of a button.

Screen
The screen object makes information about the user's screen setup and display available.

Document
The document object represents the current Web page in the browser window. A document object contains many elements as listed in Figure I-7. These elements, including links, anchors, images, and so on, are what help to give each Web page its unique characteristics.

FIGURE I-7: Microsoft DHTML Object Model

window
- location
- frames
- history
- navigator
- event
- screen
- document
  - links
  - anchors
  - images
  - filters
  - forms
  - applets
  - embeds
  - plug-ins
  - frames
  - scripts
  - all
  - selection
  - stylesheets
  - body

Understanding Browser Variability

Although DHTML has few current standards, work is underway to change this situation. The **World Wide Web Consortium**, or the **W3C**—an international body whose mission is the creation of standards for WWW technologies—is creating official guidelines for DHTML. Although the W3C has created standards for the DOM and other DHTML technologies, these agreements have not yet resulted in a uniform interpretation of DHTML on the Web. The Microsoft and Netscape corporations, as the manufacturers of the vast majority of browsers in use today, have the greatest influence in DHTML implementation on the Web because the technology depends on each user's browser to interpret and run it. This difference in implementation means that code written for use on one browser may not work on the other, which requires writing two sets of code to incorporate some features into a page. As standards evolve and new browser versions are released, it will become easier to create today's features with a uniform code. However, both companies undoubtedly will continue to incorporate new, incompatible innovations into their browsers, which means that browser variability probably will always be a factor in creating DHTML pages. Lydia researches the implications of the different browsers available on the DHTML pages she is planning.

Details

 Some dynamic HTML code is compatible with the 3.x versions of Navigator and Internet Explorer, known as **third generation** browsers, but most features work only on the 4.x and later versions, the **fourth generation** browsers. Because many users have upgraded to fourth generation browsers already and many more will upgrade eventually, it is often easiest to create DHTML with these browsers in mind. Remember, however, that if you want your pages to reach the largest possible audience, they must still accommodate other browsers. By organizing your pages to display logically even without their DHTML features and adding a few extra tags to allow older browsers to process the code, your content can remain accessible by older browsers that can't interpret DHTML, by text-based browsers, and by Web interfaces for people with disabilities. Testing your pages on different browsers before publishing them is important because standard DHTML code could cause older browsers to stop functioning, or **hang**. Figure I-8 shows a DHTML page in a fourth-generation browser and in Lynx, a text-only browser. Notice that the text-only browser ignores all of the DHTML commands, such as those for positioning, while still displaying all the information logically.

 The differences in DHTML capabilities between fourth-generation browsers and earlier versions make writing interactive Web pages complicated because Internet Explorer 4 and Navigator 4 use and interpret DHTML differently. As you saw in the DHTML tour, therefore, they are not compatible when it comes to creating certain dynamic HTML features. Because DHTML components are still new technologies, many are not yet standardized in the software industry. For now, this incompatibility issue results in some features being available only in one browser and others being available only in the other. For some features to be available in either Web browser, DHTML Web page designers must write separate scripts to create similar features in the fourth-generation browsers.

Designing dynamic Web pages is easiest when they will reside on a network where all users run the same browser, such as a corporate intranet. When publishing to the WWW, the only way to make sure that most users can view your pages is to write **cross-platform code**, or DHTML code that works on both fourth generation browsers. This often requires two sets of code in your page, along with a script to recognize in which browser the Web page is opening. Using this technique allows you to make interesting and interactive pages without causing compatibility problems for potential users. Although cross-platform coding can be time-consuming, many Web sites freely distribute such code that they have developed for popular features, along with tutorials describing how the code works. Using existing code can save a lot of page-development time.

FIGURE I-8: One Web page as it displays in two different browsers

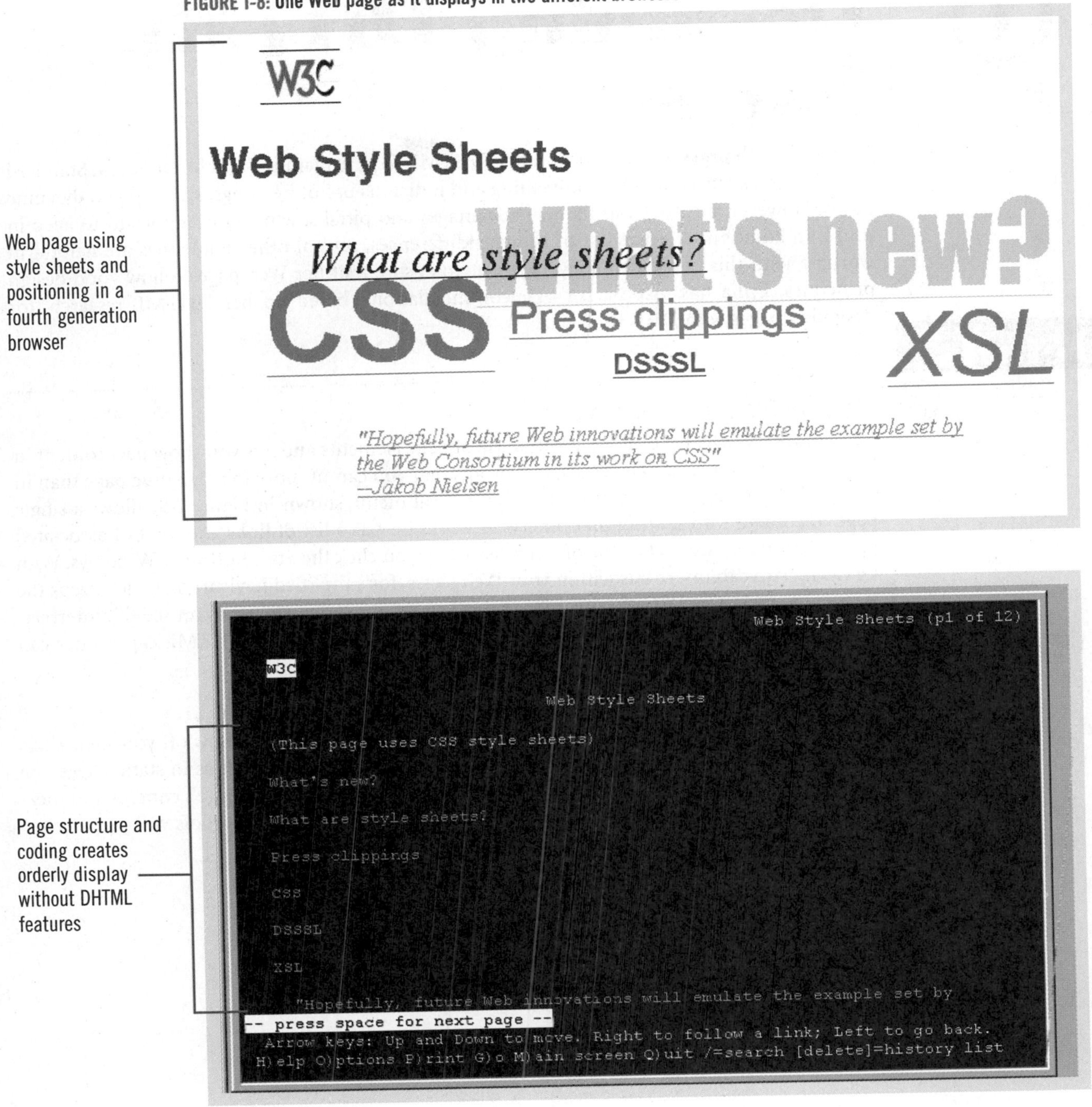

Web page using
style sheets and
positioning in a
fourth generation
browser

W3C

Web Style Sheets

What are style sheets?

What's new?

CSS Press clippings

DSSSL

XSL

"Hopefully, future Web innovations will emulate the example set by the Web Consortium in its work on CSS"
—Jakob Nielsen

Page structure and
coding creates
orderly display
without DHTML
features

```
                                                    Web Style Sheets (p1 of 12)

W3C
                              Web Style Sheets

(This page uses CSS style sheets)

What's new?

What are style sheets?

Press clippings

CSS

DSSSL

XSL

     "Hopefully, future Web innovations will emulate the example set by
-- press space for next page --
 Arrow keys: Up and Down to move. Right to follow a link; Left to go back.
 H)elp O)ptions P)rint G)o M)ain screen Q)uit /=search [delete]=history list
```

Designing DHTML Pages

Like static Web pages, those incorporating DHTML require planning and forethought. Standard HTML rules, such as careful proofreading and judicious use of headings, still apply to dynamic pages. However, DHTML has its own advantages and pitfalls, which are important to keep in mind. In addition to awareness of browser differences, several other guidelines are helpful in working with this new technology. To ensure that her Web pages follow good design principles, Lydia has made a list of recommendations, based on her DHTML research, for designing pages with DHTML.

Details

 Organize for dynamic content

Remember that DHTML allows positioning of page elements and lets you show new content in response to user actions. Generally, this means that you can fit more in a dynamic page than in a static HTML page. For example, the hierarchical menu, shown in Figure I-9, allows a single page to contain information that otherwise works best as a list of links and a set of associated pages. This menu works like the one you use when you click the Start button in Windows. With DHTML, you can insert this within your Web pages, for simplified navigation, which keeps the Web page uncluttered. It also organizes the information so that the user can see the interrelationships of choices. Organizing your Web site to take advantage of DHTML capabilities can make the site easier for users to navigate and for you to manage.

Use dynamic features purposefully

Dynamic HTML features appear impressive, and you may be eager to show off your new skills by incorporating many of them into the pages you create. However, just as in static pages, the best Web pages are focused and free of distracting elements. Your Web page's content and message, rather than newly available features, should dictate which dynamic tools you use.

FIGURE I-9: Web page containing a hierarchical menu

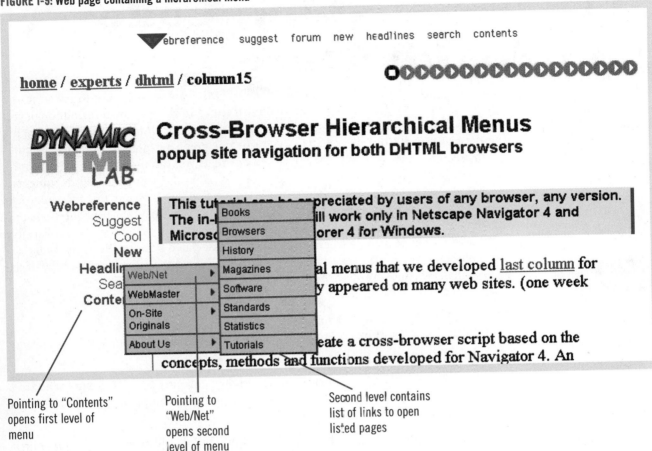

Pointing to "Contents" opens first level of menu

Pointing to "Web/Net" opens second level of menu

Second level contains list of links to open listed pages

Design resources

One advantage of the browser competition between Microsoft and Netscape is that both companies are eager to show off their browser's features. Both companies keep a list of links to well-designed pages (supporting their own proprietary features) on their corporate Web sites. Reviewing these pages can give you ideas for planning successful dynamic Web pages as well as introduce you to new features.

Researching Code Architecture

After you outline your Web page and identify the DHTML features you want to use in it, the next step is to sit down and write code to make these features work. In many cases, although you have seen a Web page incorporating a certain action, it can be difficult to determine exactly how to create the feature with scripts and style sheets. At this point, research on the Web is indispensable to creating a successful DHTML page. For example, you can use the Web to look at the page source of a Web page that uses a feature you like. You also can find well-documented sample code on Web sites, which often you are allowed to modify and use for your own purposes. Lydia has written the HTML for a new Web page that lists questions and answers. She wants to use DHTML to create a collapsible list on her Web page. In a collapsible list, explanatory text appears only when a user clicks its associated heading. Recently, Lydia saw the collapsible list feature on a page while browsing the Web, and she downloaded a copy of the Web page so that she could examine the code further.

Steps 1 2 3 4

1. Open the file **HTML I-3.htm** in your Web browser
   The page displays a list of blueberry breeds.

2. Click the phrase **Blue Jay**
   Associated text appears below the berry name, as shown in Figure I-10. Notice in the address bar that clicking the phrase did not open a new page; rather, it simply triggered a change in the appearance of the current Web page.

3. Start your text editor program, then open the file HTML I-3.htm to display the source code for the Web page
   Figure I-11 shows part of the script for creating the collapsible list.

4. Close the text editor without saving the document

5. Be sure your computer is connected to the Internet, then open a search engine of your choice

6. In the "Search" text box, type **DynamicHTML programming** and click the **Find button**, or its equivalent
   The browser returns a list of links to sites related to DHTML programming.

7. Review the links returned by the search engine, then follow one to a site that seems likely to contain tutorials or sample code
   Articles and sample scripts for dynamic HTML applications may be helpful in creating your own pages.

8. Scan the site's opening page for links to script libraries or articles about DHTML features, then follow the appropriate links

9. Locate sample code or a relevant article for an interesting DHTML feature, then download the page to your Project Disk with the name **Feature download.htm**
   This downloaded file can be a helpful reference when you plan your own DHTML applications.

FIGURE I-10: Web page containing collapsible list

Click the names of blueberry breeds
below to read about our selection:

Blue Ray

Blue Jay

New text
appears in
response to
mouse click

highbush type, 5 to 7 ft. at maturity, fruit ripening the first
to middle of July, yield is 10 to 20 lbs per bush, fruit
size medium/large (approx. 75 berries per cup).

Jersey

Elliott

Northland

2 t white flour
1/4 t cinnamon
1/2 t ground coriander
pinch nutmeg
3-1/2 c blueberries
Topping:
 1-1/4 c blueberries

To prepare crust, mix
flour and sugar. Cut butter
in to mixture with pastry
blender. Add 2 T water
to moisten (more if
required). Roll mixture
and place in 9" pie plate.

For the filling, mix sugar,
flour, cinnamon,
coriander, and nutmeg
thoroughly. Toss with 3-
1/2 c blueberries to coat

FIGURE I-11: Source code for expanding table of contents

Part of code
for expanding
elements in
Internet
Explorer

Part of code
for expanding
elements in
Navigator

```
function expandIE(el) {
        whichEl=eval(el + "Desc");
        if (whichEl.style.display == "none") {
                whichEl.style.display="block";
                whichEl.isExpanded=true;
        }
        else {
                whichEl.style.display="none";
                whichEl.isExpanded=false;
        }
}

function expandNav(el) {
        whichEl=eval("document." + el + "Desc");
        if (whichEl.visibility == "hide") {
                whichEl.visibility="show";
                whichEl.isExpanded=true;
        }
        else {
                whichEl.visibility="hide";
                whichEl.isExpanded=false;
        }
        arrange();
}
```

CLUES TO USE

Code-borrowing etiquette

When you find existing code on the Web that fits a project you are working on, it can save you time and frustration to use the existing code in your page instead of creating it from scratch. However, to be considerate to other designers, you should follow a few simple guidelines. First, be aware that some DHTML code is copyrighted and you cannot use it without permission from its author, which usually involves paying a fee as well. Some pages and sites offer code for free re-use. In this situation, it is still considered courteous to credit the source of the code in your Web page, usually with the creator's name and the source URL. If you find code you'd like to use and are unsure whether you are allowed to, it is best to contact the creator for permission. If you don't have permission to use someone else's code, you can still use its basic framework to help you plan the creation of your page and then augment the features with your own coding.

HTML

Keeping Up with DHTML Changes

Web and software designers have already developed many ideas and methods for using DHTML in Web pages. As with any new technology, this body of knowledge will continue to grow, and in the process, will provide new uses and workarounds for DHTML programming. In addition, browser creators update and expand the capabilities of their products, resulting in ever-expanding possibilities for new DHTML applications. As a consequence of all these factors, it's important to stay current with the latest new developments in DHTML if you want to take full advantage of its possibilities for your Web pages. Predictably, the Web is a rich source of information on DHTML. ▶ Lydia wants to see what new DHTML features are on the horizon.

Steps 1 2 3 4

1. Be sure you are connected to the Internet, open your browser, then use a search engine of your choice to search the Web for the keywords **DHTML news**
   The search engine returns descriptions and links to pages about DHTML.

2. Follow a link on the search results page to a site containing DHTML information

3. Scroll through and scan the opening page for tips on working with DHTML and for news about recent and upcoming developments
   Figure I-12 shows a Web page offering tips and articles on using DHTML.

4. Follow links to explanations of new DHTML features or to news about upcoming additions or changes, then read one of these articles

5. Close your Web browser

FIGURE I-12: **Web page containing DHTML tips**

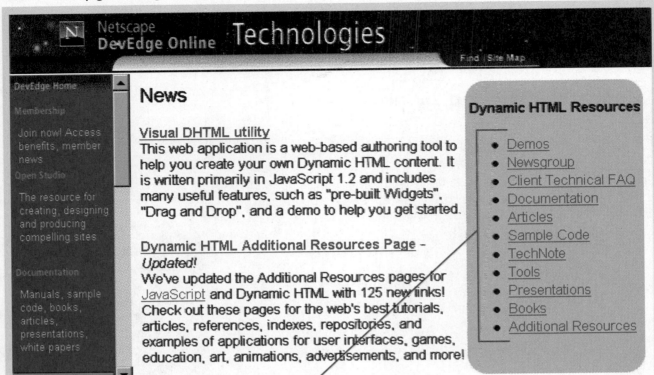

Resources available
on this site

► Concepts Review

Label each item in Figure I-13 with the DHTML category that best describes it.

FIGURE I-13

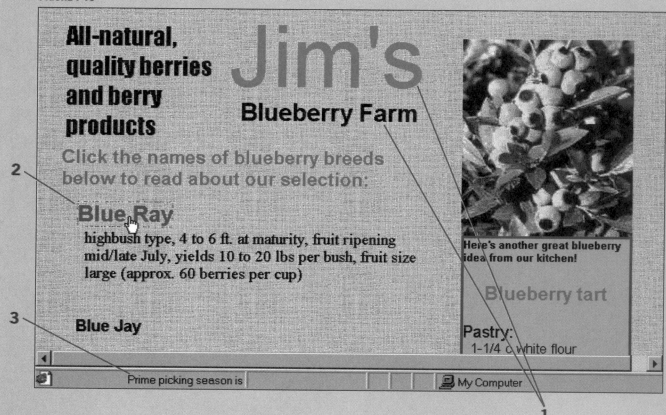

Match each term with its description.

4. **Dynamic style**

5. **Static HTML**

6. **Client-side scripts**

7. **Cascading Style Sheets (CSS)**

8. **DHTML Object Model**

9. **Cross-platform code**

10. **W3C**

11. **Positioning**

12. **Dynamic HTML**

a. Hierarchy organizing browser window elements

b. Collection of Web page technologies allowing quick response to user actions

c. Scripts that the browser itself interprets and runs

d. International body creating Web standards

e. Web page technologies allowing very limited interactivity

f. Ability to specify locations of all Web page elements

g. Component of DHTML allowing precise Web page style specification

h. Style that changes in response to user actions

i. Code that works on both fourth generation browsers

Select the best answer from the list of choices.

13. Which of the following is *not* a feature of DHTML?
    a. Dynamic style
    b. Dynamic content
    c. Server-side scripts
    d. Data awareness

14. Positioning allows Web page designers to
    a. Create interactive page formatting.
    b. Create predictable layouts.
    c. Download Web page data.
    d. Create interactive page content.

15. A collapsible list is a good example of
    a. Dynamic style.
    b. Dynamic content.
    c. Data awareness.
    d. Absolute positioning.

16. DHTML uses an object model called
    a. The World Wide Web Consortium.
    b. JavaScript.
    c. Cascading Style Sheets.
    d. The DHTML Object Model.

17. Fourth generation browsers include
    a. Internet Explorer 5.0.
    b. Navigator 4.0 and Internet Explorer 4.0.
    c. Navigator 3.0 and Internet Explorer 3.0.
    d. Lynx and other text-based browsers.

18. Creating DHTML pages for both fourth generation browsers requires
    a. Excluding CSS from your pages.
    b. Limiting the pages you write to working only on one browser.
    c. Eliminating all dynamic features from your pages.
    d. Using cross-platform code.

19. What should provide the underlying structure for your Web pages?
    a. The page's content and message
    b. The amount of information you want to include
    c. Other pages you see on the Web
    d. The dynamic features you want to include

Independent Challenges

1. The owners of the Green House plant store have asked you to add to their Web site a list of houseplant products they sell, along with a description of each. You think that a collapsible list would format and display this information easily and concisely. To begin, you design this Web page on paper.

To complete this independent challenge:

a. On a sheet of paper, write the text for one or more titles for the Web page.

b. Below the headings, copy the following list of products, along with description placeholder text:
Potting soil
[description]
Washed gravel
[description]
Peat moss
[description]
Houseplant fertilizer
[description]
Cactus soil mix
[description]

c. On your Web page outline, label each element to indicate what page elements will be part of the collapsible list and what page elements will be appear on the Web page at all times.

d. Indicate how you will format each text item.

e. Indicate next to each of the product names that it will be formatted with dynamic style and add a second style specification for how the text will display when a user interacts with it.

f. Indicate on your sketch any positioning you will use in your page.

g. Add any further text to your sketch, such as that for hypertext links, and label the text with its formatting specifications and any additional features.

2. Sandhills Regional Public Transit wants to discuss with you ways to make their Web pages more interactive. In preparation for meeting with your clients, you want to become more familiar with different DHTML formatting options.

To complete this independent challenge:

a. Log on to the Internet and open a search engine of your choice, then search on the phrase *DHTML formatting.*

b. Click one of the links provided by the search engine to open a Web site containing DHTML formatting resources.

c. Scan the opening page and navigate the site to locate articles or sample scripts for Web page features using DHTML.

d. Read and print the article or the explanatory text accompanying a script.

e. Write a paper detailing two DHTML formatting features you think would be useful in a home page that provides information to a wide range of people. Explain why you would include these features and how they would enhance the page.

3. Community Public School Volunteers has hired you to manage their Web site on an ongoing basis. To stay on top of the latest Web page design trends, you want to regularly research relevant news on the Web. Because you're preparing to create dynamic pages for CPSV, you want to research the state of W3C standards for DHTML.

To complete this independent challenge:

a. Log on to the Internet and search on the keywords *W3C DHTML standards.*

b. Investigate the sites listed on the search results page. Locate and print two articles regarding recommendations or standards released within the past six months.

c. For each article, use the Microsoft and Netscape Web sites to research whether the standard is supported in each company's fourth-generation browser or if the company has announced plans to comply with the standard in a future release.

d. Write a paragraph on each article, summarizing the area of DHTML it covers (for example, scripting or dynamic style), which browsers support it or will support it, and an overview of the article's content.

4. Explore sample DHTML pages on the Web, either at the Microsoft or Netscape Web sites, or by searching on the term *DHTML sample pages* in a search engine. Choose one Web page, print it out from your Web browser, and on the printout areas of the page that demonstrate DHTML features. On a separate sheet of paper, list these elements and, if applicable, describe briefly how they respond to user actions. Submit your printout and list to your instructor.

Specifying
Style Dynamically

► **Understand Cascading Style Sheets**
► **Create an embedded style sheet**
► **Create a class**
► **Detect browsers**
► **Show and hide page elements**
► **Change font size dynamically**
► **Control font color dynamically**
► **Use an external style sheet**

Cascading Style Sheets (CSS) and scripts form the foundation of DHTML. Whereas scripting allows the browser to alter the page, CSS lets you specify in detail how the page and its elements should appear. An understanding of CSS's simple syntax and organization opens the door to many new options for your Web pages' appearance. Lydia is looking forward to adding new effects to the Nomad Ltd Web pages. First, she will look at CSS a bit more in depth, then she will use CSS to create an interactive page for her department.

Unit J
HTML

Understanding Cascading Style Sheets

With CSS, you can organize and expand the style attributes available in a Web page. CSS allows a Web page designer to easily specify attributes such as color, font size, and even position on the page for single objects or groups of objects, including text blocks, images, and all other DOM objects. CSS offers three different ways to specify style, which simplifies creating and changing Web page code. As Lydia reviews how to implement CSS in her Web pages, she studies the three levels of style available.

Inline style

Use **inline style** to take advantage of CSS's extended formatting options for a small text block or other object a single time in your document. You use inline style—the most basic level of using CSS—to specify your selected attributes in the opening tag surrounding the text itself, as shown in Figure J-1. This method allows you to specify a format different from all others on the page. However, formatting all page objects using inline style is impractical, given the amount of typing required.

Embedded style

Use **embedded style** to simplify formatting multiple page elements. Figure J-2 shows the source for a page using embedded style. To create embedded styles, you associate style attributes with HTML tags between the HEAD tags at the top of your Web page, creating a set of HTML code known as an **embedded style sheet**. Then, any place in the Web page code where you use the tags specified in the embedded style sheet, the text or object is formatted automatically with that style. Embedded style rather than inline style is a more efficient way to format an entire Web page. However, you can specify inline styles in a page that uses embedded styles when you have single objects that need their own style or style adjustment. Each inline style supersedes the embedded style defined for the object where it is used.

External style

Use **external style** to apply the global formatting of embedded style to multiple pages. External style allows you to specify formats and apply them to multiple Web pages rather than just one. External style also is known as **linked style** because, instead of listing style specifications at the top of your Web page, you create a link to an external document that contains the style code, known as an **external style sheet**. This method allows you to format a set of Web pages, such as a Web publication, with a uniform style and allows you to change the style for all pages later simply by editing the external style sheet. External style can be used in a page together with both inline and embedded styles. Just as inline style takes precedence over embedded style wherever you use it, embedded styles and inline styles both take precedence over external style. This system of precedence is known as **cascading**, and it gives CSS its name. Cascading allows you to apply a general format for a page or group of pages as well as to make local exceptions to the global style.

FIGURE J-1: Web page containing inline style

```
<LINK REL="stylesheet" HREF="nomadltd.css" TYPE="text/css">

<SCRIPT LANGUAGE="JavaScript">
<!--
NS4 = (document.layers) ? 1:0;
IE4 = (document.all) ? 1:0;
//-->
</SCRIPT>

<STYLE TYPE="text/css">
<!--
H1 {font-family: arial, sans-serif; font-size: 20pt}
H2 {font-family: "times new roman", times, serif; font-size: 14pt; font-
style: italic}
.question {font-family: "times new roman", times, serif; font-size: 12pt;
font-weight: bold}
//-->
</STYLE>

</HEAD>

<BODY BACKGROUND="Egg shell.jpg">
<DIV STYLE="font-color: navy; text-decoration:underline" ALIGN="center">
<H2>Frequently Asked Questions about</H2>
<H1>Dynamic HTML (DHTML)</H1></DIV>
```

Inline style located in formatting tag

FIGURE J-2: Web page containing embedded style

```
<HTML>
<HEAD>
<TITLE>Nomad Ltd DHTML FAQ</TITLE>

<STYLE TYPE="text/css">
<!--
H1 {font-family: arial, sans-serif; font-size: 20pt; font-style: normal}
H2 {font-family: "times new roman", times, serif; font-size: 14pt; font-
style: italic}
//-->
</STYLE>

</HEAD>

<BODY BACKGROUND="Egg shell.jpg">
<DIV ALIGN="center"><IMG SRC="nomad.jpg" ALIGN="right">
<H2>Frequently Asked Questions about</H2>
<H1>Dynamic HTML (DHTML)</H1></DIV><BR>

<UL TYPE="disk">
<LI><DIV>What is Dynamic HTML?</DIV>

<DIV>Dynamic HTML (DHTML) describes a set of new technologies for designing
Web pages that allow new and more precise formatting features, along with
faster access for users.</DIV><BR>
```

Embedded style sheet

CLUES TO USE

<DIV> vs. <SPAN>

Although it's often useful to assign CSS styles to standard formatting tags such as <H1> or <LI>, HTML includes two specialized tags that are especially valuable for CSS. Both the <DIV> and <SPAN> tags can enclose an element or group of elements, which allows you to specify a style for everything they contain. The <DIV> tagset always includes a line break before and after the enclosed elements, which creates a unit divided from the surrounding page. The <SPAN> tagset does not include line breaks before or after, which causes its contents to flow with the objects surrounding them in the page. When formatting text, <DIV> is best for enclosing a paragraph or group of paragraphs, whereas <SPAN> allows you to create a special style for words or sentences within a paragraph.

Creating an Embedded Style Sheet

An embedded style sheet consists of one or more lines of HTML code specifying style attributes, surrounded by tags marking the section as CSS style specifications. You can associate style attributes with any HTML structuring or formatting tag and then apply them to Web page elements simply by inserting the tags. After completing her basic research, Lydia decides to create a **FAQ** (which is an acronym for Frequently Asked Questions, pronounced "fak") document about DHTML for her co-workers in Nomad Ltd's information systems department. Lydia wants to take advantage of CSS to specify exactly how the page will appear in a user's browser. Because she wants to create a uniform look for the page, she decides to create an embedded style sheet.

Steps

1. **Start your text editor, open the file HTML J-1.htm, then save it as a text document with the filename FAQ embedded style.htm**
   This file contains the text of the FAQ Lydia is creating, along with basic HTML structuring tags. Lydia has enclosed each unit of text in opening and closing DIV tags to make it easy for her to add style attributes later.

2. **Select the text [replace with embedded style sheet], press [Delete], type <STYLE TYPE="text/css"> and press [Enter], then type <!-- and press [Enter]**
   Embedded style sheets are placed in the Web page's head section, which allows the browser to incorporate the styles in the text it displays in the body section. A browser recognizes the code as an embedded style sheet from the beginning and ending <STYLE> tags. The TYPE property in the STYLE tag tells the browser the language and format of the style sheet it marks. In this case, the language is CSS, and the information is in text format. The <!-- tag tells browsers that are not compatible with embedded style sheets to ignore this section.

3. **Type H1 {font-family: arial, sans-serif; font-size: 20pt; font-style: normal} and press [Enter]**
   Lydia associates 20-point arial with the <H1> tag for use with the page's main heading. By putting it first in a list of two, Lydia specifies arial as her font preference. Her second choice, sans-serif, instructs the user's browser to use any sans-serif font if arial is not available.

QuickTip

Font names composed of multiple words, such as *times new roman*, must be listed within quotation marks for a browser to recognize them as single names.

4. **Type H2 {font-family: "times new roman", times, serif; font-size: 14pt; font-style: italic} and press [Enter]**
   Lydia has specified 14 point as the font size to associate with the <H2> tag, which is the subheading.

5. **Type //--> and press [Enter], then type </STYLE>**
   Figure J-3 shows the completed Web page source containing the style sheet.

6. **Check the document for errors, make changes as necessary, then save FAQ embedded style.htm as a text document**

7. **Start your browser program, cancel any dialup activities, then open the file FAQ embedded style.htm**
   The Web page appears as shown in Figure J-4.

FIGURE J-3: Completed embedded style sheet

Opening and closing embedded style sheet tags

Style specifications for heading tags

```
<HTML>
<HEAD>
<TITLE>Nomad Ltd DHTML FAQ</TITLE>

<STYLE TYPE="text/css">
<!--
H1 {font-family: arial, sans-serif; font-size: 20pt; font-style: normal}
H2 {font-family: "times new roman", times, serif; font-size: 14pt; font-
style: italic}
//-->
</STYLE>

</HEAD>

<BODY BACKGROUND="Egg shell.jpg">
<DIV ALIGN="center"><IMG SRC="nomad.jpg" ALIGN="right">
<H2>Frequently Asked Questions about</H2>
<H1>Dynamic HTML (DHTML)</H1></DIV><BR>

<UL TYPE="disk">
<LI><DIV>What is Dynamic HTML?</DIV>

<DIV>Dynamic HTML (DHTML) describes a set of new technologies for designing
Web pages that allow new and more precise formatting features, along with
faster access for users.</DIV><BR>
```

FIGURE J-4: Web page formatted with embedded style sheet

Text formatted with H2 style specified in embedded style sheet

Text formatted with H1 style specified in embedded style sheet

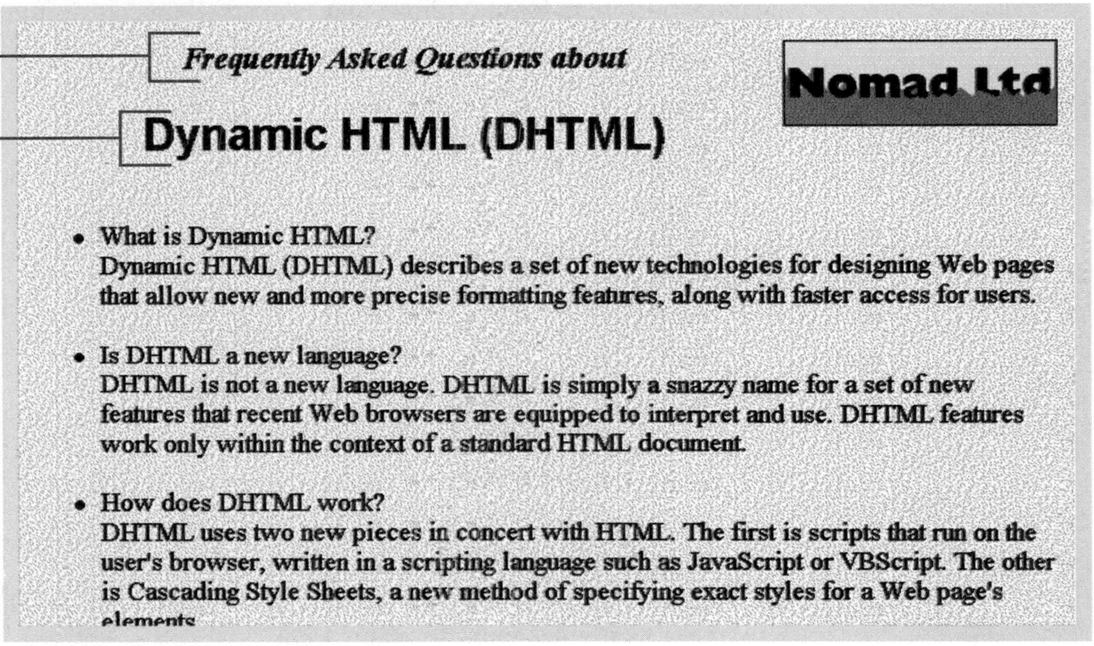

Frequently Asked Questions about

Nomad Ltd

Dynamic HTML (DHTML)

- **What is Dynamic HTML?**
  Dynamic HTML (DHTML) describes a set of new technologies for designing Web pages that allow new and more precise formatting features, along with faster access for users.

- **Is DHTML a new language?**
  DHTML is not a new language. DHTML is simply a snazzy name for a set of new features that recent Web browsers are equipped to interpret and use. DHTML features work only within the context of a standard HTML document.

- **How does DHTML work?**
  DHTML uses two new pieces in concert with HTML. The first is scripts that run on the user's browser, written in a scripting language such as JavaScript or VBScript. The other is Cascading Style Sheets, a new method of specifying exact styles for a Web page's elements.

Creating a Class

HTML

In addition to specifying style for all occurrences of a particular HTML tag, you also can name a set of style specifications and then associate, or **call**, this name in tags within your Web page. This named style, known as a **class**, allows you to format selected elements with an embedded style, without requiring that each element be enclosed in the same tag or that every occurrence of a certain tag display the same style. All class names begin with a period to mark them as classes. To apply a class to an element, you add the CLASS attribute to the element's opening HTML tag. ▰▰▰ Lydia's bulleted list is a series of questions and answers. Lydia wants to format the headings in her list, which are the questions, differently than the paragraph text, which are the answers. She creates a class that specifies the formatting for the questions and then calls the class within the opening <DIV> tag for each of the questions.

Steps

1. Open the file **HTML J-2.htm** in your text editor, then save it as a text document with the filename **FAQ class.htm**

2. Select the text **[replace with class style]** in the embedded style sheet, then press **[Delete]**

3. Type **.question {font-family: "times new roman", times, serif; font-size: 12pt; font-weight: bold}** and press **[Enter]**
   The dot preceding the style name "question" indicates that the style specification is for a class.

4. Select the text **[replace with class]** in the <DIV> tag for the first question, then press **[Delete]**

5. Type **CLASS="question"**
   The tag now reads <DIV CLASS="question">. This calls the class and applies the style associated with the class "question" to this text, which is the first question in the FAQ.

6. Repeat Steps 4 and 5 for the remaining six questions
   Figure J-5 shows a portion of the completed source for the bulleted list.

7. Check your document for errors, make changes as necessary, then save **FAQ class.htm** as a text document

8. Click the browser program button on the taskbar, then open the file **FAQ class.htm**
   The Web page appears as shown in Figure J-6.

FIGURE J-5: Web page source using a class

Class definition inserted in embedded style sheet

```
H2 {font-family: "times new roman", times, serif; font-size: 14pt; font-
style: italic}
.question {font-family: "times new roman", times, serif; font-size: 12pt;
font-weight: bold}
//-->
</STYLE>

</HEAD>

<BODY BACKGROUND="Egg shell.jpg">
<DIV ALIGN="center"><IMG SRC="nomad.jpg" ALIGN="right">
<H2>Frequently Asked Questions about</H2>
<H1>Dynamic HTML (DHTML)</H1></DIV><BR>

<UL TYPE="disk">
<LI><DIV CLASS="question">What is Dynamic HTML?</DIV>

<DIV>Dynamic HTML (DHTML) describes a set of new technologies for designing
Web pages that allow new and more precise formatting features, along with
faster access for users.</DIV><BR>

<LI><DIV CLASS="question">Is DHTML a new language?</DIV>

<DIV>DHTML is not a new language. DHTML is simply a snazzy name for a set of
new features that recent Web browsers are equipped to interpret and use.
DHTML features work only within the context of a standard HTML
```

Class question called in <DIV> tags

FIGURE J-6: Web page formatted with new class

Bold format added using class property

Frequently Asked Questions about

Nomad Ltd

Dynamic HTML (DHTML)

- **What is Dynamic HTML?**
  Dynamic HTML (DHTML) describes a set of new technologies for designing Web pages that allow new and more precise formatting features, along with faster access for users.

- **Is DHTML a new language?**
  DHTML is not a new language. DHTML is simply a snazzy name for a set of new features that recent Web browsers are equipped to interpret and use. DHTML features work only within the context of a standard HTML document.

- **How does DHTML work?**
  DHTML uses two new pieces in concert with HTML. The first is scripts that run on the user's browser, written in a scripting language such as JavaScript or VBScript. The other is Cascading Style Sheets, a new method of specifying exact styles for a Web page's

Creating an ID style

As well as assigning styles to tags and classes in your embedded style sheets, you can define styles for element IDs. Just as each class style name begins with a period, you preface each ID style name with a number sign (#). Because you can assign an ID to only one element, defining global ID styles is no more efficient than specifying the styles inline. However, ID styles allow you to group style information at the top of the document, rather than inline, which can help make your code less cluttered and easier to read and understand.

Detecting Browsers

The combination of scripts and CSS allows you to add lag-free interactivity to your Web pages. Although both fourth-generation browsers support DHTML, each does so in a different way. Whereas the methods for creating basic effects in Internet Explorer and Netscape Navigator are the same, the code for most advanced DHTML features is different for each browser. This means that creating code offering dynamic features in both browser platforms, known as **cross-browser code**, often requires writing and integrating two different sets of code into a single page. Additionally, a cross-browser DHTML page requires a **browser-detection script**, which determines the user's browser brand and generation. The browser then uses this information to determine which of the page's DHTML scripts are appropriate for a user's browser. Lydia wants to add interactive DHTML features to control her FAQ page's display. Before adding the coding to create these features, she inserts a browser-detection script into her page.

Steps

1. Open the file **HTML J-3.htm** in your text editor, then save it as a text document with the filename **FAQ browser detect.htm**
   This copy of the FAQ page contains the CSS features Lydia created in the last lesson.

2. Select the text **[replace with browser-detection script]**, then press **[Delete]**

3. Type the following script, pressing **[Enter]** at the end of each line:

   ```
   <SCRIPT LANGUAGE="javascript">

   <!--

   Nav4 = (document.layers) ? 1:0;

   IE4 = (document.all) ? 1:0;

   //-->

   </SCRIPT>
   ```

   Lydia's completed script, shown in Figure J-7, tells the browser to check for elements of the DOM, one of which is specific to Navigator 4 and the other of which is specific to Internet Explorer 4. The question mark in each line tells the browser to evaluate the preceding condition and to assign the variable the value 1, which equals "true" if the condition is true; otherwise, assign the variable the value 0, which is "false" if it is not true. This script determines if the browser is Netscape Navigator 4 or Internet Explorer 4. Based on the results of the conditional test, the browser reads the appropriate scripts, which create DHTML features in the user's browser.

4. Check the document for errors, then make changes as necessary

5. Save FAQ browser detect.htm as a text document

6. Open the file **FAQ browser detect.htm** in your browser to ensure it displays correctly, and debug the file as necessary until it displays as expected

QuickTip

Because all browsers have many unique properties, there are many different ways to detect which browser a user is running. You may see different browser-detection scripts in other Web pages.

FIGURE J-7: Web page containing browser-detection script

Browser-detection script ───

```
<HTML>
<HEAD>
<TITLE>Nomad Ltd DHTML FAQ</TITLE>

<SCRIPT LANGUAGE="javascript">
<!--
Nav4 = (document.layers) ? 1:0;
IE4 = (document.all) ? 1:0;
//-->
</SCRIPT>

<STYLE TYPE="text/css">
<!--
H1 {font-family: arial, sans-serif; font-size: 20pt}
H2 {font-family: "times new roman", times, serif; font-size: 14pt; font-
style: italic}
.question {font-family: "times new roman", times, serif; font-size: 12pt;
font-weight: bold}
//-->
</STYLE>

</HEAD>

<BODY BACKGROUND="Egg shell.jpg">
<DIV ALIGN="center"><IMG SRC="nomad.jpg" ALIGN="right">
<H2>Frequently Asked Questions about</H2>
```

CLUES TO USE

Future cross-browser coding

Much of the difference in browser support between Navigator 4 and Internet Explorer 4 stems from the lack of a DHTML standard. As the W3C organization refines and extends the industry standard, however, future browser releases should match more closely in how they support today's basic features. Although this may make future cross-browser coding as easy as writing for a single browser today, browser-detection routines will probably never become obsolete. As long as the browsers of multiple companies are popular, each company will continue to develop and add its own features, which will be standardized later. Additionally, some Web users will continue to use earlier-generation browsers. Because advanced scripts can hang older browsers, causing them to stop working and sometimes requiring the user to reboot, a browser-detection script can help you develop pages that identify and accommodate less-advanced browsers.

HTML

HTML

Showing and Hiding Page Elements

By working together with embedded scripts, CSS can specify how page elements should display in different situations and in response to user actions, which allows you to create the interactive features that are the hallmark of DHTML. ◀━━ Lydia wants her Web page to hide the paragraphs containing the answers and to display each answer only when the user clicks its corresponding question. Lydia can create this feature, known as an **expandable outline**, with a combination of style sheets and scripts. Lydia has already inserted the code to create this feature in Navigator 4. Now, she adds code that Internet Explorer 4 can interpret.

Steps

1. Open the file **HTML J-4.htm** in your text editor, then save it as a text document with the filename **FAQ show and hide.htm**

   Notice that this copy of the FAQ page already contains the browser detection script.

2. Scroll and select **[replace with expandIE function]**, then press **[Delete]**

Trouble?

"El" stands for element. Be sure to type *El* or *el* using the letter I and not the number 1.

3. Type the following code, pressing **[Enter]** at the end of each line

```
function expandIE(el) {
    theEl=eval(el + "Answer");
    if (theEl.style.display == "none") {
            theEl.style.display="block";
            theEl.expanded=true;
    }
    else {
            theEl.style.display="none";
            theEl.expanded=false;
    }
}
```

   Figure J-8 shows the new code.

4. Scroll down to the <DIV> tag for the first list item "What is Dynamic HTML?", select the text **[replace with opening A tag]** and the space following it, then press **[Delete]**

5. Type **<A HREF="#" onClick="expand('one'); return false">**

   Because Lydia uses an A tag with # as a dummy href, the mouse pointer becomes a hand when it moves over the question which indicates to the user that clicking the text triggers an action. The remaining code uses the onClick event handler to call the function expand and specifies the variable 'one' for the function to process. The function expand checks which browser the user is running and, in Internet Explorer 4, calls the expandIE function you entered earlier.

6. Replace the text **[replace with closing A tag]** in the next line with **</A>**

7. Repeat Steps 4 through 6 for the remaining six list items, substituting **'two'** for 'one' in item two, and so forth

   Figure J-9 shows a portion of the completed code for the expanding FAQ list.

8. Use Figures J-8 and J-9 to check the document for errors, make changes as necessary, then save FAQ show and hide.htm as a text document

Trouble?

In Navigator 4, all the text is visible briefly when the page opens.

9. Open **FAQ show and hide.htm** in your browser, then click the first question

   As Figure J-10 shows, the text for the first question is displayed.

FIGURE J-8: FAQ page with added script

```
function expand(el) {
        if (!ver4) return;
        if (IE4) {
                expandIE(el)
        }
        else {
                expandNav(el)
        }
}

function expandIE(el) {
        theEl=eval(el + "Answer");
        if (theEl.style.display == "none") {
                theEl.style.display="block";
                theEl.expanded=true;
        }
        else {
                theEl.style.display="none";
                theEl.expanded=false;
        }
}

function expandNav(el) {
        theEl=eval("document." + el + "Answer");
        if (theEl.visibility == "hide") {
```

Script to make outline expandable in IE4

Change value of display property for a clicked line

FIGURE J-9: <A> tags added to list items

```
<H3>Click any of the popular questions about DHTML below to see its
answer.</H3>

<DIV ID="oneQuestion" CLASS="question"><A HREF="#" onClick="expand('one');
return false"><P>What is Dynamic HTML?</P></A></DIV>

<DIV ID="oneAnswer" CLASS="answer"><P>Dynamic HTML (DHTML) describes a set
of new technologies for designing Web pages that allow new and more precise
formatting features, along with faster access for users.</P></DIV>

<DIV ID="twoQuestion" CLASS="question"><A HREF="#" onClick="expand('two');
return false"><P>Is DHTML a new language?</P></A></DIV>

<DIV ID="twoAnswer" CLASS="answer"><P>DHTML is not a new language. DHTML is
simply a snazzy name for a set of new features that recent Web browsers are
equipped to interpret and use. DHTML features work only within the context
of a standard HTML document.</P></DIV>

<DIV ID="threeQuestion" CLASS="question"><A HREF="#"
onClick="expand('three'); return false"><P>How does DHTML
work?</P></A></DIV>

<DIV ID="threeAnswer" CLASS="answer"><P>DHTML uses two new pieces in concert
with HTML. The first is scripts that run on the user's browser, written in a
scripting language such as JavaScript or VBScript. The other is Cascading
```

Opening <A> tag and event handler inserted

Closing </A> tag inserted

FIGURE J-10: Expanding FAQ list

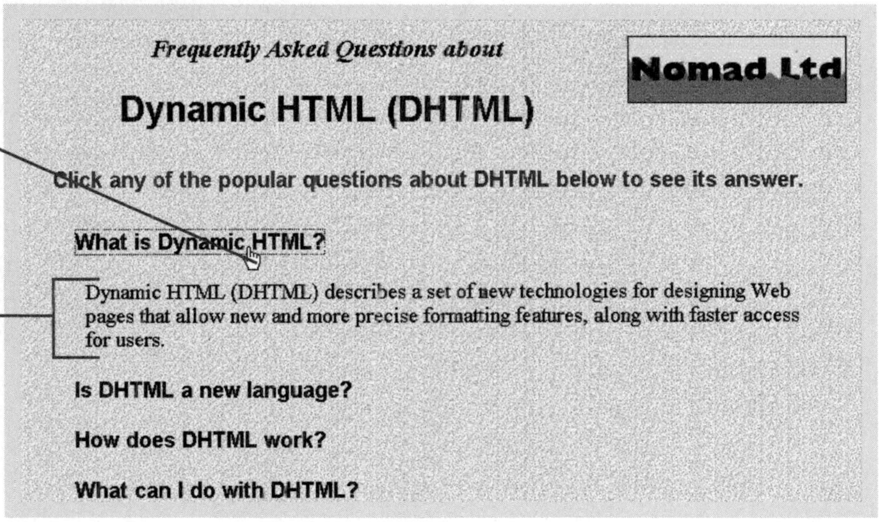

Mouse pointer becomes hand over question text

Clicking question displays answer text

Frequently Asked Questions about

Nomad Ltd

Dynamic HTML (DHTML)

Click any of the popular questions about DHTML below to see its answer.

What is Dynamic HTML?

Dynamic HTML (DHTML) describes a set of new technologies for designing Web pages that allow new and more precise formatting features, along with faster access for users.

Is DHTML a new language?

How does DHTML work?

What can I do with DHTML?

HTML

Changing Font Size Dynamically

In the last lesson, you used a script to modify the style of an element in response to a user action. Using this general formula, you can add dynamic formatting to most style aspects of any object on your Web pages. A popular application of this method has been to change the appearance of text when a user points at it, commonly referred to as a **rollover**. A rollover changes text attributes to make the text stand out. Lydia wants to change the text size of the FAQ questions when the user moves the pointer over them. Although adding this feature to graphics is straightforward in both browsers, Lydia finds that it is difficult to create for text blocks in Navigator. Because the feature is not crucial to the overall layout of her Web page, she decides to focus on creating the feature only in Internet Explorer.

Steps

1. Open the file **HTML J-5.htm** in your text editor, then save it as a text document with the filename **FAQ text size.htm**

2. Scroll down the document to the ending </SCRIPT> tag in the document's head section, select the text **[replace with text size functions]**, press **[Delete]**, then type the following functions, pressing **[Enter]** at the end of each line
```
function changeText(whichQuestion) {
    if (Nav4) {return}
    whichQuestion.style.fontSize="16pt";
}
function changeTextBack(whichQuestion) {
    if (Nav4) {return}
    whichQuestion.style.fontSize="12pt";
}
```
Figure J-11 shows the functions entered into the Web page source. The first function, changeText, changes the font size of the object from which it was called to 16 point. The second function, changeTextBack, changes the font size of the calling object back to 12 point.

3. Scroll down the page to the opening <A> tag for the first list item "What is Dynamic HTML?", select the text **[replace with event handlers]**, then press **[Delete]**

4. Type **onMouseOver="changeText(this)" onMouseOut="changeTextBack(this)"**
This code adds two new arguments to the heading. The first uses the onMouseOver event handler to call the changeText function you created earlier. The "this" is scripting shorthand to tell the function to make changes to the current object. The second argument calls the changeTextBack function for the current object in response to the mouse moving off the text.

5. Repeat Steps 3 and 4 for the remaining six list items
Figure J-12 shows source code containing the inline code for dynamically changing text size.

6. Use Figures J-11 and J-12 to check the document for errors, make changes as necessary, then save FAQ text size.htm as a text document

7. Open **FAQ text size.htm** in your browser, then move the pointer over a list item
Figure J-13 shows the result of this step in Internet Explorer 4. Notice that the text size of the heading increased. However, if you opened FAQ text size.htm in a different browser, such as Netscape Navigator 4, no change occurs.

8. Move the mouse pointer off the first heading
The first heading returns to its original size.

FIGURE J-11: Page containing new functions

Changes current
text to larger font
size

Changes larger text
back to smaller font
size

```
function changeText(whichQuestion) {
        if (Nav4) {return}
        whichQuestion.style.fontSize="16pt";
}
function changeTextBack(whichQuestion) {
        if (Nav4) {return}
        whichQuestion.style.fontSize="12pt";
}
//-->
</SCRIPT>
```

FIGURE J-12: Page containing code to change text size

Calls function to
increase text size

Calls function to
decrease text size

```
<H3>Click any of the popular questions about DHTML below to see its
answer.</H3>

<DIV ID="oneQuestion" CLASS="question" ><A HREF="#" onClick="expand('one');
return false" onMouseOver="changeText(this)"
onMouseOut="changeTextBack(this)"><P>What is Dynamic HTML?</P></A></DIV>

<DIV ID="oneAnswer" CLASS="answer"><P>Dynamic HTML (DHTML) describes a set
of new technologies for designing Web pages that allow new and more precise
formatting features, along with faster access for users.</P></DIV>

<DIV ID="twoQuestion" CLASS="question" ><A HREF="#" onClick="expand('two');
return false" onMouseOver="changeText(this)"
onMouseOut="changeTextBack(this)"><P>Is DHTML a new language?</P></A></DIV>

<DIV ID="twoAnswer" CLASS="answer"><P>DHTML is not a new language. DHTML is
simply a snazzy name for a set of new features that recent Web browsers are
equipped to interpret and use. DHTML features work only within the context
of a standard HTML document.</P></DIV>

<DIV ID="threeQuestion" CLASS="question"><A HREF="#"
onClick="expand('three'); return false" onMouseOver="changeText(this)"
onMouseOut="changeTextBack(this)"><P>How does DHTML work?</P></A></DIV>

<DIV ID="threeAnswer" CLASS="answer"><P>DHTML uses two new pieces in concert
```

FIGURE J-13: Changed text size in Internet Explorer 4

Question font size
increases in
response to pointer

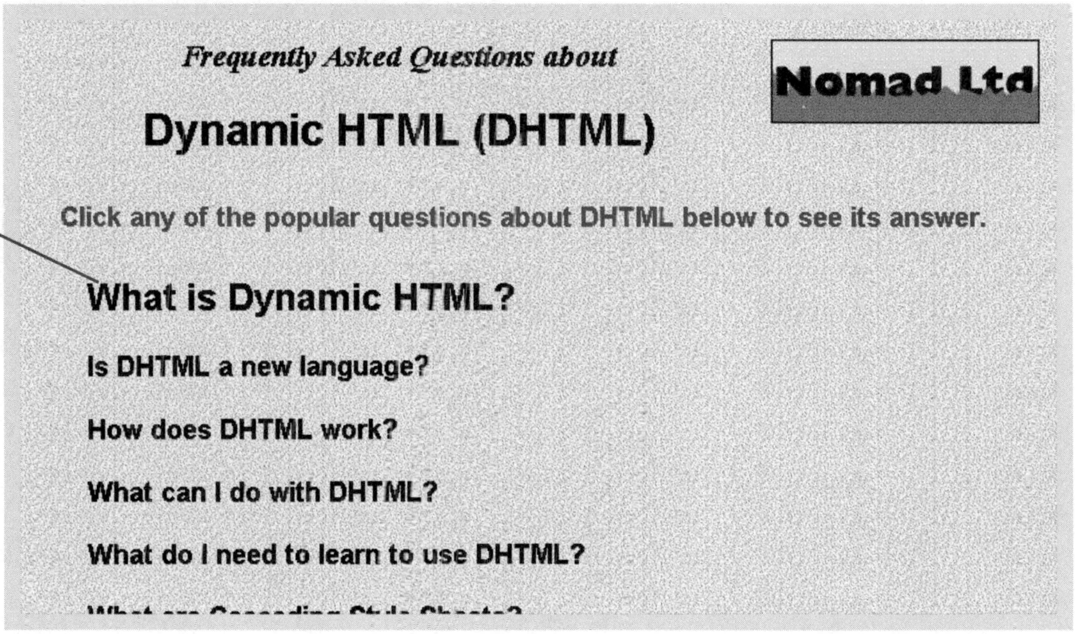

Frequently Asked Questions about

Nomad Ltd

Dynamic HTML (DHTML)

Click any of the popular questions about DHTML below to see its answer.

What is Dynamic HTML?

Is DHTML a new language?

How does DHTML work?

What can I do with DHTML?

What do I need to learn to use DHTML?

HTML

Changing Font Color Dynamically

Just as you can script a page to change text size in response to a user action, you can easily change or modify such scripts to change several other properties that control how text displays. ▬▬▬ In addition to the increase in text size, Lydia wants the heading font color to change in response to mouse pointing. She can modify the scripts she already created to alter font color at the same time they alter text size in Internet Explorer 4.

Steps

1. Open the file **HTML J-6.htm** in your text editor, then save it as a text document with the filename **FAQ text color.htm**

2. Scroll down the page to the changeText function in the page header, select the text **[replace with changeText color]**, then press **[Delete]**

3. Type **whichQuestion.style.color="#9400D3";**

4. Select the text **[replace with changeTextBack color]** in the changeTextBack function in the page header, then press **[Delete]**

5. Type **whichQuestion.style.color="#000000";**
   Figure J-14 shows the completed changes in the Web page source containing the color style. The changeText function increases the size of the text as well as changes the color for the selected object. The changeTextBack function returns the text to its original size and color.

6. Check the document for errors, make changes as necessary, then save FAQ text color.htm as a text document

7. Open the file **FAQ text color.htm** in your browser, then move the pointer over the first heading
   Figure J-15 shows the change, which again takes place only in Internet Explorer 4. In addition to the size increase, the text turns purple, making it stand out from the other questions on the page.

8. Move the mouse pointer off the first heading
   In Internet Explorer 4, the text size and color return to their default settings.

FIGURE J-14: Color change code inserted

New script lines to change text color

```
function changeText(whichQuestion) {
        if (Nav4) {return}
        whichQuestion.style.fontSize="16pt";
        whichQuestion.style.color="#94C0D3";
}
function changeTextBack(whichQuestion) {
        if (Nav4) {return}
        whichQuestion.style.fontSize="12pt";
        whichQuestion.style.color="#000000";
}
//-->
</SCRIPT>

<STYLE TYPE="text/css">
<!--
H1 {font-family: arial, sans-serif; font-size: 20pt; font-style: normal}
H2 {font-family: "times new roman", times, serif; font-size: 14pt; font-
style: italic}
H3 {font-family: arial; font-size: 12pt; color: #4619E1; position: relative;
left: 20px; top: -10px}
.question {font-family: "times new roman", times, serif; font-size: 12pt;
font-weight: bold}
.question A {font-family: arial; font-size: 12pt; font-weight: bold; text-
decoration: none; color: black}
.rest {position: absolute; left: 25px}
```

FIGURE J-15: Color change in browser

Frequently Asked Questions about

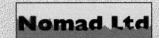

Dynamic HTML (DHTML)

Click any of the popular questions about DHTML below to see its answer.

Changed text color ——— What is Dynamic HTML?

Is DHTML a new language?

How does DHTML work?

What can I do with DHTML?

What do I need to learn to use DHTML?

Using an External Style Sheet

When you create or manage a group of related Web pages, it is often helpful to create an external style sheet. Just as you use hyperlinks to refer to external HTML documents, you can link each Web page to the style sheet with a simple line of code. Creating an external style sheet allows you to apply a standard style to a set of Web pages and to easily make changes that apply to all the pages. ◢──── Because Lydia plans to create other FAQ pages for her department, she has created an external style sheet to reflect the styles she wants all the FAQs to use. She also takes into account Nomad Ltd's standard Web page style. She replaces the existing embedded style sheet with a link to the external file. The rules of cascading precedence allow her to leave in place the inline styles that help individualize the Web page by creating her dynamic effects.

Steps

1. **Open the file HTML J-7.css, then save it as a text document with the filename nomadltd.css**
   This file contains the Nomad Ltd stylesheet. The document consists of text, just like an HTML document, and contains the opening and closing <STYLE> tags that tell browsers how to interpret the contents. A CSS document is formatted just like an embedded style sheet, except that it contains no HTML code outside of the <STYLE> tags. Lydia cut and pasted the styles from her FAQ page that she will apply to other pages she creates.

2. **Select the text #4619E1 in the color definition for the H3 heading, press [Delete], then type #238E68**
   This changes the color for the H3 style, which applies to the directions in Lydia's current page, from blue to green.

3. **Save nomadltd.css as a text document**

4. **Open the file HTML J-8.htm in your text editor, then save it as a text document with the filename FAQ external style.htm**
   Lydia has removed the heading definitions from the embedded style sheet for her FAQ page because the external style sheet contains these specifications.

5. **Scroll down and select [replace with external style sheet link] which is just above the embedded style sheet, then press [Delete]**

6. **Type <LINK REL="stylesheet" HREF="nomadltd.css" TYPE="text/css">**
   Figure J-16 shows the page source containing the insertion. The LINK tag contains information about a file related to the current document. The REL attribute identifies the file type of the related file. The value assigned to HREF is the name and address of the file, just as for a hyperlink. TYPE specifies the format of the associated file because you can code associated information including style sheets in different ways.

7. **Check the file for errors, make changes as necessary, then save FAQ external style.htm as a text document**

8. **Open the file FAQ external style.htm in your Web browser**
   The Web page appears as shown in Figure J-17. Because both Navigator 4 and Internet Explorer 4 support basic CSS, the standardized Nomad Ltd format appears in both browsers. The instruction text color displays in green, which confirms that the page is using the external styles you defined. When Lydia links other FAQ Web pages to this nomadltd.css file as she develops them, then all her FAQ Web pages will have the same style. This helps ensure consistency for all her FAQ Web pages.

FIGURE J-16: Web page code containing link to external style sheet

External style sheet link text

```
}
//-->
</SCRIPT>

<LINK REL="stylesheet" HREF="nomadltd.css" TYPE="text/css">

<STYLE TYPE="text/css">
<!--
.question {font-family: "times new roman", times, serif; font-size: 12pt;
font-weight: bold}
.question A {font-family: arial; font-size: 12pt; font-weight: bold; text-
decoration: none; color: black}
.rest {position: absolute; left: 25px}
//-->
</STYLE>

</HEAD>

<BODY BACKGROUND="Egg shell.jpg">

<DIV ALIGN="center"><IMG SRC="nomad.jpg" ALIGN="right">
<H2>Frequently Asked Questions about</H2>
<H1>Dynamic HTML (DHTML)</H1></DIV><BR>

<H3>Click any of the popular questions about DHTML below to see its
answer.</H3>
```

FIGURE J-17: Web page linked to external style sheet

Text color reflects change made to external style sheet

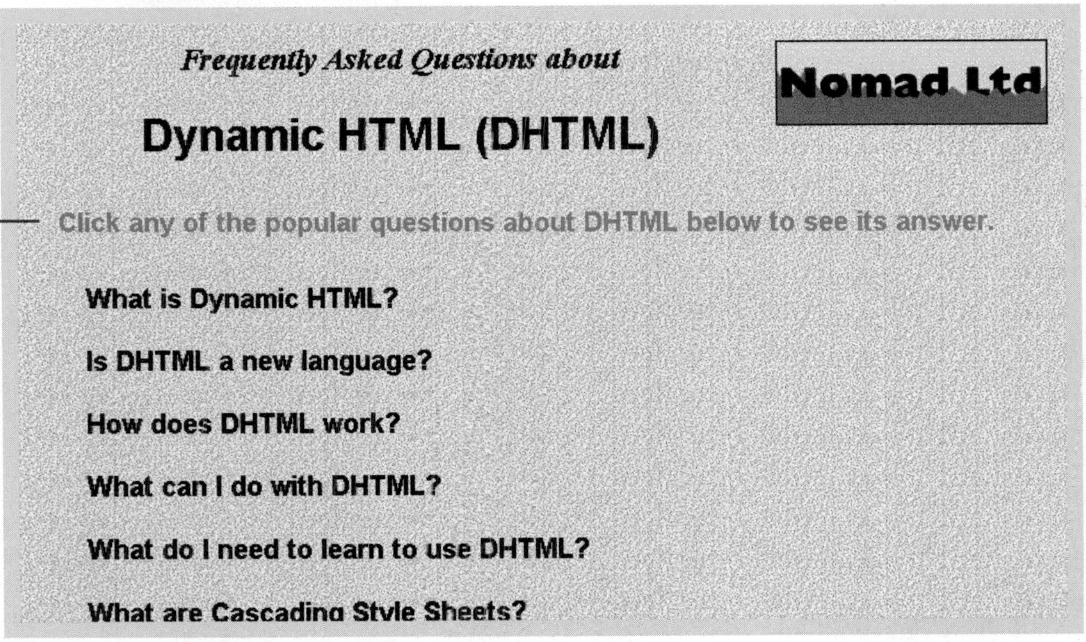

Frequently Asked Questions about

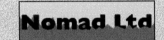

Dynamic HTML (DHTML)

Click any of the popular questions about DHTML below to see its answer.

What is Dynamic HTML?

Is DHTML a new language?

How does DHTML work?

What can I do with DHTML?

What do I need to learn to use DHTML?

What are Cascading Style Sheets?

Practice

► Concepts Review

Label each DHTML item marked in Figure J-18.

FIGURE J-18

```
1 ——— <LINK REL="stylesheet" HREF="nomadltd.css" TYPE="text/css">

      <SCRIPT LANGUAGE="JavaScript">
      <!--
2 ——— NS4 = (document.layers) ? 1:0;
      IE4 = (document.all) ? 1:0;
      //-->
      </SCRIPT>

3 ——— <STYLE TYPE="text/css">
      <!--
      H1 {font-family: arial, sans-serif; font-size: 20pt}
      H2 {font-family: "times new roman", times, serif; font-size: 14pt; font-
      style: italic}
4 ——— .question {font-family: "times new roman", times, serif; font-size: 12pt;
      font-weight: bold}
      //-->
      </STYLE>

      </HEAD>

5 ——— <BODY BACKGROUND="Egg shell.jpg">
      <DIV STYLE="font-color: navy; text-decoration:underline" ALIGN="center">
      <H2>Frequently Asked Questions about</H2>
      <H1>Dynamic HTML (DHTML)</H1></DIV>
```

Match each term with its description.

6. Inline style   a. System of precedence among style-sheet levels
7. Embedded style   b. Style associated with tags in Web page header
8. External style   c. Style specified in local occurrence of tag
9. Cascading   d. Named set of style specifications created as a tag attribute
10. Class   e. Style specified in separate linked document

Select the best answer from the list of choices.

11. The most efficient method for assigning style to several text blocks marked with the same tag on one Web page is
    a. Inline style.
    b. Embedded style.
    c. External style.
    d. Linked style.

12. Embedded style sheets begin and end with which tagset?
    a. <SCRIPT> .. </SCRIPT>
    b. <STYLE> .. </STYLE>
    c. <STYLESHEET> .. </STYLESHEET>
    d. <CSS> .. </CSS>

13. **A browser-detection script**
   a. Makes your page's DHTML features viewable with any browser.
   b. Tells the user's browser which version of HTML your page uses.
   c. Tells the user's browser which version of JavaScript your page uses.
   d. Determines and stores the user's browser brand and generation.

14. **Which HTML tags does an external style sheet contain?**
   a. An external style sheet contains no HTML tags.
   b. <SCRIPT> .. </SCRIPT>
   c. <STYLE> .. </STYLE>
   d. <SCRIPT> .. </SCRIPT> and <STYLE> .. </STYLE>

15. **Which HTML tag do you use to associate an external style sheet with a Web page?**
   a. <LINK>
   b. <A>
   c. <CSS>
   d. <STYLE>

▶ Skills Review

1. **Create an embedded style sheet.**
   a. Open the file HTML J-9.htm, then save it as a text document with the filename Tours FAQ embedded style.htm.
   b. Select the text [replace with embedded style sheet], press [Delete], type <STYLE TYPE="text/css">, press [Enter], then type <!-- and press [Enter].
   c. Type H1 {font-family: "comic sans ms", arial, sans-serif; font-size: 20pt} and press [Enter].
   d. Type H2 {font-family: "times new roman", times, bookman, serif; font-size: 16pt; font-style: italic} and press [Enter].
   e. Type //--> and press [Enter], then type </STYLE>.
   f. Check the document for errors, make changes as necessary, then save Tours FAQ embedded style.htm as a text document.
   g. Open your Web browser, then open Tours FAQ embedded style.htm to view the Web page.

2. **Create a class.**
   a. Open the file HTML J-10.htm in your text editor, then save it as a text document with the filename Tours FAQ class.htm.
   b. Select the text [replace with class style] in the embedded style sheet, then press [Delete].
   c. Type .title {font-family: garamond, arial, helvetica, sans-serif; font-size: 16pt; font-weight: bold}.
   d. Select the text [replace with class] in the <DIV> tag for the first bulleted list item, then press [Delete].
   e. Type CLASS="title".
   f. Repeat Steps d and e for the remaining two bulleted titles.
   g. Check the document for errors, make changes as necessary, then save Tours FAQ class.htm as a text document.
   h. Open Tours FAQ class.htm in your browser, then view the document.

3. **Detect browsers.**
   a. Open the file HTML J-11.htm in your text editor, then save it as a text document with the filename Tours FAQ browser detect.htm.
   b. Select the text [replace with browser detection script], then press [Delete].

c. Type the following script, pressing [Enter] at the end of each line:

```
<SCRIPT LANGUAGE="javascript">
<!--
NS4 = (document.layers) ? 1:0;
E4 = (document.all) ? 1:0;
//-->
</SCRIPT>
```

d. Check the document for errors, then make changes as necessary.

e. Save Tours FAQ browser detect.htm as a text document.

f. Open Tours FAQ browser detect.htm in your browser, then debug if necessary.

4. Show and hide page elements.

a. Open the file HTML J-12.htm in your text editor, then save it as a text document with the filename Tours FAQ show and hide.htm.

b. Scroll down and select the text [replace with expandIE function], then press [Delete].

c. Type the following code, pressing [Enter] at the end of each line

```
function expandIE(el) {
        theEl=eval(el + "Expl");
        if (theEl.style.display == "none") {
                theEl.style.display="block";
                theEl.expanded=true;
        }
        else {
                theEl.style.display="none";
                theEl.expanded=false;
        }
}
```

d. Scroll down to the <DIV> tag for the first list item "Athlete", select the text [replace with opening A tag] and the space following it, then press [Delete].

e. Type <A HREF="#" onClick="expand('one'); return false">

f. Replace the text [replace with closing A tag] on the next line with </A>.

g. Repeat Steps d through f for the remaining two tour titles, substituting 'two' for 'one' in item two, and so forth.

h. Check the document for errors, making changes as necessary, then save Tours FAQ show and hide.htm as a text document.

i. Open Tours FAQ show and hide.htm in your browser, then click the first title "Athlete".

5. Change font size dynamically.

a. Open the file HTML J-13.htm in your text editor, then save it as a text document with the filename Tours FAQ text size.htm.

b. Scroll down the page, select the text [replace with text size functions], press [Delete], then type the following functions, pressing [Enter] at the end of each line

```
function changeText(whichTitle) {
        if (Nav4) {return}
        whichTitle.style.fontSize="24pt";
}
function changeTextBack(whichTitle) {
        if (Nav4) {return}
```

```
        whichTitle.style.fontSize="12pt";
    }
```

c. Scroll down the page to select the text [replace with event handlers] in the opening <A> tag for the first tour title "Athlete", then press [Delete].

d. Type onMouseOver="changeText(this)" onMouseOut="changeTextBack(this)".

e. Repeat Steps c and d for the remaining two list items.

f. Check the document for errors, make changes as necessary, then save Tours FAQ text size.htm as a text document.

g. Open the file Tours FAQ text size.htm in your browser, then move the pointer over the first heading.

6. Control font color dynamically.

a. Open the file HTML J-14.htm in your text editor, then save it as a text document with the filename Tours FAQ text color.htm.

b. Select the text [replace with changeText color] in the changeText function in the page header, then press [Delete].

c. Type whichTitle.style.color="#236B8E";

d. Select the text [replace with changeTextBack color] in the changeTextBack function in the page header, then press [Delete].

e. Type whichTitle.style.color="#000000";

f. Check the document for errors, making changes as necessary, then save Tours FAQ text color.htm as a text document.

g. Open the file Tours FAQ text color.htm in your browser, then move the pointer over the first heading.

7. Use an external style sheet.

a. Open the file HTML J-15.htm, then save it as a text document with the filename Tours FAQ external style.htm.

b. Scroll down the page, select the text [replace with LINK tag] before the opening <STYLE> tag, then press [Delete].

c. Type <LINK REL="stylesheet" HREF="nomadltd.css" TYPE="text/css">.

d. Check the file for errors, make changes as necessary, then save Tours FAQ external style.htm as a text document.

e. Open the file FAQ external style.htm in your Web browser and notice the green color added to the instruction text.

▶ Independent Challenges

1. As you update and expand the Sandhills Regional Public Transit Web site, you decide to incorporate DHTML features into your pages. Currently, you are working to make a page on rider tips more interactive and easier to read. You decide to add dynamic size and color to the items on this page.

To complete this independent challenge:

a. Open the file HTML J-16.htm in your text editor, then save it as a text document with the filename SRPT rider tips.htm.

b. Select the text [replace with style sheet link] in the head section, press [Delete], then type <LINK REL=stylesheet HREF="HTML J-17.css" TYPE="text/css"> and save SRPT rider tips.htm as a text document.

c. Select the text [replace with script], press [Delete], and type the following script, pressing [Enter] at the end of each line.

```
<SCRIPT LANGUAGE="javascript">
<!--
Nav4 = (document.layers) ? 1:0;
IE4 = (document.all) ? 1:0;

function changeText(whichTitle) {
```

```
        if (Nav4) {return}
        whichTitle.style.fontSize="24pt";
        whichTitle.style.color="#FF6347"
    }

    function changeTextBack(whichTitle) {
        if (Nav4) {return}
        whichTitle.style.fontSize="16pt";
        whichTitle.style.color="#000000";
    }

    //-->
    </SCRIPT>
```

d. Select the text [replace with event handlers] in the opening <DIV> tag for each of the five tips, press [Delete], then type onMouseOver="changeText(this)" onMouseOut="changeTextBack(this)"

e. Save SRPT rider tips.htm as a text document.

f. Start your browser, cancel any dial-up activities, open SRPT rider tips.htm, then move the cursor over the tips to verify that they change color and increase in font size.

Note: This change will only be noticeable if you are using Internet Explorer 4.

g. If necessary, edit the code in your text editor until the DHTML features work in IE4, and save SRPT rider tips.htm as a text file.

2. While reorganizing the Community Public School Volunteers Web publication, you decide that the pages should have a uniform style. You think the easiest way to create and apply this style would be to make an external style sheet and link each page to it.

To complete this independent challenge:

a. Open the file HTML J-18.htm in your text editor, then save it as a text document with the filename CPSV home.htm.

b. Select the text of the embedded style sheet in the head section, including the opening and closing <STYLE> tags, then copy it to the Clipboard.

c. Open a new text file in your text editor, paste the style sheet from the Clipboard into it, then save this file as a text document with the name CPSV style.css.

d. Reopen CPSV home.htm in your text editor, delete the embedded style sheet from the head section, replace it with <LINK REL=stylesheet HREF="CPSV style.css" TYPE="text/css"> and save CPSV home.htm as a text document.

e. Open CPSV home.htm in your Web browser and notice the formatting created by the external style sheet.

f. If necessary, use your text editor to edit and save your document until it displays correctly.

3. The Green House plant store's most heavily viewed Web page lists popular items available at the store, along with descriptions and prices. The owners would like you to add DHTML features to this page. You decide to convert the list to an expanding outline.

To complete this independent challenge:

a. Open the file HTML J-19.htm in your text editor, then save it as a text document with the filename Green House supplies.htm.

b. Select the text [replace with LINK tag], press [Delete], then type <LINK REL="stylesheet" HREF="HTML J-20.css" TYPE="text/css"> and save Green House supplies.htm as a text document.

c. Select the text [replace with script], press [Delete], then type the following script, pressing [Enter] at the end of each line

```
Nav4 = (document.layers) ? 1:0;
IE4 = (document.all) ? 1:0;
```

```
ver4 =(Nav4 || IE4)?1:0;

function expandIE(el) {
        theEl=eval(el + "Desc");
        if (theEl.style.display == "none") {
                theEl.style.display="block";
                theEl.expanded=true;
        }
        else {
                theEl.style.display="none";
                theEl.expanded=false;
        }
}

function changeText(whichProduct) {
        if (Nav4) {return}
        whichProduct.style.fontSize="24pt";
        whichProduct.style.color="#215E21";
}

function changeTextBack(whichProduct) {
        if (Nav4) {return}
        whichProduct.style.fontSize="14pt";
        whichProduct.style.color="#000000";
}
```

d. In the <DIV> tag for the first product name, Potting soil, select the text [replace with opening A tag], press [Delete], then type <A HREF="#" onClick="expand('one'); return false"; onMouseOver="changeText(this)" onMouseOut="changeTextBack(this)">

e. Replace the text [replace with closing A tag] on the next line with </A>.

f. Repeat Steps d and e for the remaining four product names, replacing 'one' with 'two' for the second item, and so forth, then save Green House supplies.htm as a text document.

g. Open your browser, open Green House supplies.htm, then move the cursor over a heading and click it.
   Note: The text size and color events work only in Internet Explorer 4.

h. If necessary, edit the code in your text editor until the expanding outline works and the text size and color changes work in IE4, then save Green House supplies.htm as a text document.

WEB WORK

4. Even though it's complicated, many Web page designers have created cross-browser code to create text-rollover effects in both major fourth-generation browsers. To complete this independent challenge, open a search engine and search on one or more keywords, such as DHTML, cross-browser, or rollover. Using the results from the search engine, open and investigate Web sites that provide tutorials or articles on creating DHTML to find a sample of cross-browser text-rollover code. Print the code, along with any accompanying explanation. After reading the article and scanning the code, make a list on a separate sheet of paper of the compromises the designer found necessary when creating the code. Count the number of code lines necessary to create this feature and, if possible, total those used exclusively by each browser. Submit your printouts and your list to your instructor.

► **Visual Workshop**

Add the dynamic size and color features shown in Figure J-19 to each of the five bulleted items in the file HTML J-21.htm. Open HTML J-21 in your text editor, then save it as a text document with the filename Books.htm. Use the script listed in Independent Challenge 1, Step 3 in the page's head section. Use the code from Independent Challenge 1, Step C, in the opening <DIV> tags for the elements that will change color and size. Substitute the color #8E2323 (firebrick), or another color of your choice, to provide contrast to the background.

FIGURE J-19

Book ordering guidelines

In order to search for a book we don't have in stock, we need as much information as you have about it. At a minimum, we recommend one of the following:

- Author's name

- Full book title

Controlling
Content Dynamically

Objectives

- ► **Understand dynamic content**
- ► **Insert content dynamically**
- ► **Delete content dynamically**
- ► **Modify content dynamically**
- ► **Incorporate an advanced content function**
- ► **Replace graphics dynamically**
- ► **Bind data**
- ► **Manipulate bound data dynamically**

Just as dynamic HTML (DHTML) allows you to create pages whose style changes instantly based on user actions, it also provides tools that allow users to immediately modify a page's content. You can use this feature, known as **dynamic content**, to generate all or part of the page when it is opened, or even to alter the page's contents in response to user events. ◄━━ The manager of Nomad Ltd's retail division has heard about dynamic HTML and has asked Lydia to add dynamic content features to some of their Web pages to increase their interactivity. Lydia plans to use dynamic content features that will allow users to adapt the pages to their needs.

HTML

Understanding Dynamic Content

Dynamic HTML includes many tools for altering a Web page's appearance in response to user actions. Using scripts to change text attributes such as color and font size alter the style of elements, leaving the elements themselves, such as text or images, unchanged. Dynamic content tools, however, allow your Web page elements to move or change based on user input. These changes can include the elements themselves as well as the HTML tags associated with elements. Dynamic content can create an effect similar to an expanding outline. The outline actually uses a style attribute, "display" or "appearance," to simply show or hide text while the text remains part of the Web page. True dynamic content involves element reordering and replacing. ✏ As she learns about dynamic content, Lydia identifies several of its main uses and thinks about ways she can use it on the Nomad Ltd Web site.

Details

 ### Pointing

Dynamic content allows you to change an element in response to a user's mouse pointer movements. You already have learned about the formatting changes you can create using dynamic style. Now, using dynamic content, you can make your page's text and graphic contents available to user changes. Figure K-1 shows a Web page displaying an alternate graphic in response to user pointing.

 ### Run-time activities

Dynamic content tools can create portions of your Web pages for you at **run time**, the period when a browser first interprets and displays the Web page and runs scripts. A simple case would be a script that displays the text "Good Morning!" or "Good Evening!" based on the time of day according to your computer's clock. You also can program a page to generate a table of contents for the page at run time, which allows you to change the page's structure and contents without also revising the TOC each time you make a change.

 ### HTML tables

In addition to standard tools for working with Web page text, dynamic content includes special features for easily creating and working with tables. You can use dynamic content tools to associate an external database with a Web page, a process known as **data binding**. Data binding allows the user's browser to generate a Web page table from an external data file at run time. By adding some lines of script, you also can allow users to sort the table right on your Web page. Figure K-2 shows a dynamically generated table in a Web page that has been sorted by the Web page user.

FIGURE K-1: Dynamic content responding to user pointing

Color graphic replaces original line art in response to pointer

Line art of tent design

As you narrow your choices, click the Remove button for each tent that you're no longer considering, to remove it from the page.

Tent footprints and descriptions

XTC Starlite
One of the lightest, most compact three-season tents available. Featuring two-pole clip design with a built-in vestibule.

Remove Starlite

Amano Brevifolia
The simple, vaulted design characterized by two doors and two vestibules returns with the 2000 Brevifolia model. New features include: ground level, rainfly with vents, and vaulted sleeves for smoother pole feeding.

Remove Brevifolia

Amano Trifolia

FIGURE K-2: Table sorted by user

Bound data not sorted

Tent	Catalog number	Area (sq ft)	Vestibule (sq ft)	Description	Capacity	Weight	Price
XTC Starlite	BR-370	34	10	Staked	1 person	4 lbs. 3 oz.	$150
Amano Brevifolia	BT-356	38.5	19.6	Freestanding	2 people	5 lbs. 8 oz.	$215
Amano Trifolia	BT-358	49	25.7	Freestanding	2 people	7 lbs.	$250
Vista Hillside	BZ-339	32	15.3	Staked	1 person	4 lbs.	$120
Vista Hilltop	BZ-367	37.5	19.5			5 lbs. 3	
Vista Peak	BZ-323	42.5	24.4				
Vista Summit	BZ-334	51.5	28				

For more information on Nomad Ltd outdoor sup

Table sorted in response to click on column head

Tent	Catalog number	Area (sq ft)	Vestibule (sq ft)	Description	Capacity	Weight	Price
XTC Starlite	BR-370	34	10	Staked	1 person	4 lbs. 3 oz.	$150
Vista Hillside	BZ-339	32	15.3	Staked	1 person	4 lbs.	$120
Vista Hilltop	BZ-367	37.5	19.5	Staked	1 person	5 lbs. 3 oz.	$160
Amano Brevifolia	BT-356	38.5	19.6	Freestanding	2 people	5 lbs. 8 oz.	$215
Vista Peak	BZ-323	42.5	24.4	Freestanding	2 people	6 lbs. 3 oz.	$210
Amano Trifolia	BT-358	49	25.7	Freestanding	2 people	7 lbs.	$250
Vista Summit	BZ-334	51.5	28	Freestanding	2 people	7 lbs. 10 oz.	$275

For more information on Nomad Ltd outdoor supplies, please email our sales department

CLUES TO USE

Dynamic HTML features are not discrete

Although you can divide dynamic HTML effects into categories, such as dynamic style and dynamic content, the tools you use to create these effects often overlap. For example, to implement cross-browser dynamic style, you often need to identify the brand of the user's browser and then add lines to the embedded style sheet that are appropriate for the browser. Because you are adding code to the Web page at run time, this is a use of dynamic content to create dynamic style! As you learn more DHTML features and tools, their implementation will overlap increasingly.

Inserting Content Dynamically

Adding content at run time with scripts can allow you to create impressively customized and versatile Web pages. Because the DOM provides access to all the elements of a Web page, you can use scripts to alter any page elements based on conditions on the user's computer or on the page's current contents. ◀━━ Lydia's first project for the retail department is a Web page that compares the tents that Nomad Ltd sells. She wants to add a statement announcing the number of tent models that users can read about on the page. She can use a script to count the number of tent descriptions on the page and then insert the number dynamically in the page header statement that appears at the bottom of the page when the page loads. This means that the page header statement will still show the correct number even after the sales department adds to or removes tents and their descriptions from its tent selection.

Steps

1. Start your Web browser program and cancel any dial-up activities, then open the file **HTML K-1.htm**
   The page shows each tent's floor plan, or footprint, along with the tent's description.

2. Start your text editor program, open the file **HTML K-1.htm**, then save it as text document with the filename **Tent count.htm**
   Lydia has included a function in the page header that counts the number of tent-description headings in the page and assigns the number to the variable totalTents.

3. Scroll to the bottom of the page code, highlight the text **[replace with tent count code]**, then press **[Delete]**

QuickTip

Be sure to type a space after the word *describes* and a space before the word *tent*.

4. Type the following code, pressing **[Enter]** at the end of each line

```
<SCRIPT>
<!--
if (IE4) {
    countHeaders()
    document.write("<H1 ALIGN='center'>This page describes ")
    document.write(totalTents)
    document.write(" tent models.</H1>")
}
//-->
</SCRIPT>
```

   Figure K-3 shows the completed Web page code containing the script. The code formats the text "This page describes" and "tent models." as centered on the page with an H1 format. Between the two bits of text, the script uses the document.write method to insert the value counted by the countHeaders function, which is assigned to the variable "totalTents." Because the script that counts the headers works only in Internet Explorer 4, the script begins by checking the browser version.

5. Check your document for errors, make changes as necessary, then save Tent count.htm as a text document

6. Open **Tent count.htm** in your Web browser, then scroll to the bottom of the page
   Figure K-4 shows the Web page in Internet Explorer 4. The H1 text Lydia added appears near the bottom of the page. The statement includes the number of tents counted by the countHeaders function and inserted with a script.

FIGURE K-3: Completed Web page code

```
<DIV ID="tent7" name="tent">

<DIV CLASS="tenthead"><IMG SRC="summit.jpg" ALIGN="left">Vista Summit</DIV>

<DIV>Comfortable, rugged, 4-season tent. Quick setup, full rainfly, integral
vestibule, large door. Factory sealed, mesh window and door for
ventilation.</DIV><BR><BR>

<H2 ALIGN="center">Nomad Ltd has a tent that's right for you!</H2>

<SCRIPT>
<!--
if (IE4) {
        countHeaders()
        document.write("<H1 ALIGN='center'>This page describes ")
        document.write(totalTents)
        document.write(" tent models.</H1>")
}
//-->
</SCRIPT>

<DIV>For more information on Nomad Ltd outdoor supplies, please email our <A
HREF="MAILTO:sales@nomadltd.com">sales department</A></DIV>

</BODY>
</HTML>
```

Text and
script for
tent count
statement

FIGURE K-4: Web page displaying tent count

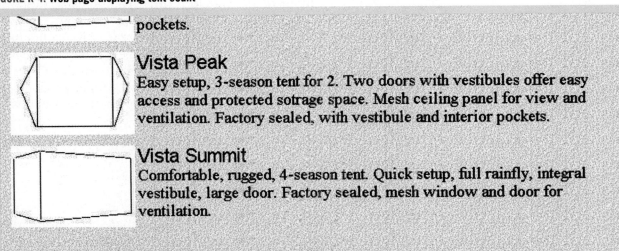

pockets.

Vista Peak
Easy setup, 3-season tent for 2. Two doors with vestibules offer easy access and protected sotrage space. Mesh ceiling panel for view and ventilation. Factory sealed, with vestibule and interior pockets.

Vista Summit
Comfortable, rugged, 4-season tent. Quick setup, full rainfly, integral vestibule, large door. Factory sealed, mesh window and door for ventilation.

Nomad Ltd has a tent that's right for you!

This page describes 7 tent models.

For more information on Nomad Ltd outdoor supplies, please email our sales department

Total calculated
by counting script

Deleting Content Dynamically

In addition to adding Web page elements dynamically at run time, you can script your Web page to allow users to tailor it to suit their needs. For example, some scripts can allow users to delete elements from a Web page, including text and graphics. This feature—especially useful in a content-laden page—allows the user to pare down the content in order to view only pertinent elements or sections. ▬▬▬ Because users of the tent comparison page will be trying to select a tent based on their needs, Lydia thinks it would be helpful to allow users to remove information they are not interested in from the page for tents.

Steps

1. Open the file **HTML K-2.htm** in your text editor, then save it as a text document with the filename **Tent delete.htm**

2. Scroll down the page to view the body text describing the first tent, the XTC Starlite, select the text **[insert button code for tent1]**, then press **[Delete]**

3. Type the following code, pressing **[Enter]** at the end of each line
   ```
   <SCRIPT LANGUAGE="javascript">
   <!--
   if (IE4) {
   ```

Trouble?
To specify the null value, be sure to type single quotes after HTML=.

4. Press **[Tab]**, then type **document.write("<BUTTON CLASS='button' onClick=tent1.outerHTML=''>Remove Starlite</BUTTON>")** and press **[Enter]**
   The <BUTTON> tag set creates a button with a customized function in Internet Explorer 4 only. The text between the tags is the label that appears on the button. Lydia has inserted a class definition called .button in the page's embedded style sheet. She uses the onClick event handler to change the **outerHTML** property of the object named tent1, which includes the description and graphic for the first tent. An element's outerHTML property includes the element contents and the tags surrounding it, so changing the property to a null value removes the element and its surrounding tags from the Web page.

5. Type **}** and press **[Enter]**, then type the following closing script tags, pressing **[Enter]** at the end of each line
   ```
   //-->
   </SCRIPT>
   ```

6. Repeat Steps 2 through 5 for the remaining six tent descriptions, substituting the button object names and tent names as listed in Table K-1
   Figure K-5 shows the Web page containing the button code for the first two tent descriptions.

7. Check the document for errors, make changes as necessary, then save Tent delete.htm as a text document

8. Open **Tent delete.htm** in your Web browser and scroll down the page until the Amano Brevifolia description appears in the document window
   Internet Explorer 4 displays the "Remove Brevifolia" button, but other browsers do not show the buttons. Even though the function for deleting content only works in Internet Explorer 4, your cross-browser Web page still displays the basic tent information in other browsers without causing JavaScript errors.

9. If you are using Internet Explorer, click the **Remove Brevifolia button**
   As Figure K-6 shows, the Web browser removes the tent's description and graphic. Next, Lydia will need to be sure the counter reflects this change by updating the number of tent descriptions displayed.

Code for first
delete button

Tent ID

Button text

Code for second
delete button

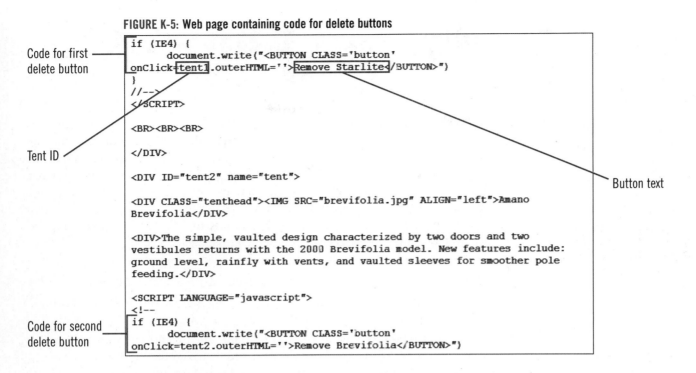

```
if (IE4) {
        document.write("<BUTTON CLASS='button'
onClick=tent1.outerHTML=''>Remove Starlite</BUTTON>")
}
//-->
</SCRIPT>

<BR><BR><BR>

</DIV>

<DIV ID="tent2" name="tent">

<DIV CLASS="tenthead"><IMG SRC="brevifolia.jpg" ALIGN="left">Amano
Brevifolia</DIV>

<DIV>The simple, vaulted design characterized by two doors and two
vestibules returns with the 2000 Brevifolia model. New features include:
ground level, rainfly with vents, and vaulted sleeves for smoother pole
feeding.</DIV>

<SCRIPT LANGUAGE="javascript">
<!--
if (IE4) {
        document.write("<BUTTON CLASS='button'
onClick=tent2.outerHTML=''>Remove Brevifolia</BUTTON>")
```

FIGURE K-6: Web page with Brevifolia removed

Brevifolia deleted
from position
between Starlite
and Trifolia

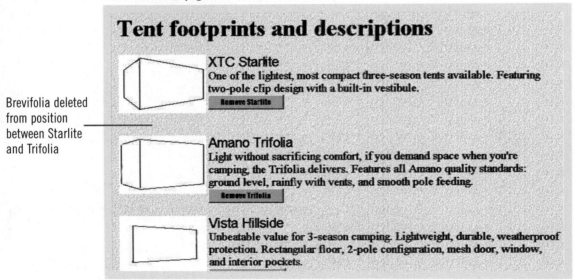

Tent footprints and descriptions

XTC Starlite
One of the lightest, most compact three-season tents available. Featuring
two-pole clip design with a built-in vestibule.
`Remove Starlite`

Amano Trifolia
Light without sacrificing comfort, if you demand space when you're
camping, the Trifolia delivers. Features all Amano quality standards:
ground level, rainfly with vents, and smooth pole feeding.
`Remove Trifolia`

Vista Hillside
Unbeatable value for 3-season camping. Lightweight, durable, weatherproof
protection. Rectangular floor, 2-pole configuration, mesh door, window,
and interior pockets.

TABLE K-1: Tent description IDs and button text

description number	substitute for "tent1"	substitute for "Starlite"
2	tent2	Brevifolia
3	tent3	Trifolia
4	tent4	Hillside
5	tent5	Hilltop
6	tent6	Peak
7	tent7	Summit

HTML

Modifying Content Dynamically

Dynamic content doesn't stop at adding or deleting static Web page content. Also, you can create pages that allow their contents to change in response to various events. You can use this feature to create a basic useful function, such as a DHTML clock, as part of a Web page. A DHTML clock function changes the contents of a text element displaying the time (for example, once per second) in response to the passing of time. You also can add interactivity by modifying page content in response to user actions. ◢◣ Because her page allows users to remove descriptions for tents that don't fit their needs, Lydia wants to ensure that the statement showing the number of tents available displays the correct number after user deletions.

Steps

1. Open the file **HTML K-3.htm** in your text editor, save it as a text document with the filename **Tent update.htm**, then scroll down the page until the function reCount appears in the document window
   Notice that Lydia has added the function named reCount. The function reCount subtracts 1 from the total count of tent descriptions on the page and then uses the **innerHTML** property to update the number that appears in the statement at the bottom of the page. InnerHTML replaces an element but leaves its enclosing HTML tags intact. Lydia uses innerHTML because she wants to replace only the number, which is within HTML tags, and not any of the surrounding text or HTML tags. Lydia has written the code so that each of the buttons that removes a tent description from the page triggers the reCount function.

2. Scroll down the page until the opening <BUTTON> tag for tent1 appears
   Notice that Lydia has added a reference to the reCount function in the onClick event handler. She has added this reference for each of the buttons.

3. Scroll to the bottom of the Web page code, select the text **[replace with code to write opening SPAN tag]**, then press **[Delete]**

4. Type **document.write("<SPAN ID='textnum'<>")**

5. Select the text **[replace with code to write closing SPAN tag]**, press **[Delete]**, then type **document.write("</SPAN>")**
   Figure K-7 shows the completed code containing the SPAN tags. By inserting the SPAN tags with an ID value, you create an inline object named "textnum" that you can manipulate with scripts. Lydia's reCount function changes textnum's innerHTML property each time the user clicks one of the delete buttons. This use of dynamic content keeps the contents of the Web page statement current with page changes produced by user actions.

6. Check your document for errors, make changes as necessary, then save **Tent update.htm** as a text document

7. Open **Tent update.htm** in your Web browser, then scroll to the bottom of the page
   In Internet Explorer 4, notice that the tent description total, which is currently 7, displays in the statement.

8. If you are using Internet Explorer, click the **Remove Summit button**
   The browser removes the description for the Vista Summit tent. Simultaneously, it updates the tent description total to 6, as Figure K-8 shows.

9. If you are using Internet Explorer, click the **Remove Hilltop button**
   The browser removes the Vista Hilltop description, and again changes the tent total to reflect the current number of descriptions on the page.

FIGURE K-7: Code containing SPAN tags

```
</SCRIPT>

<BR><BR>

</DIV>

<H2 ALIGN="center">Nomad Ltd has a tent that's right for you!</H2>

<SCRIPT>
<!--
if (IE4) {
       countHeaders()
       document.write("<H1 ALIGN='center'>This page describes ")
       document.write("<SPAN ID='textnum'>")
       document.write(totalTents)
       document.write("</SPAN>")
       document.write(" tent models.</H1>")
}
//-->
</SCRIPT>

<DIV>For more information on Nomad Ltd outdoor supplies, please email our <A
HREF="MAILTO:sales@nomadltd.com">sales department</A></DIV>

</BODY>
</HTML>
```

JavaScript to write opening and closing SPAN tags inserted

FIGURE K-8: Web page displaying updated total

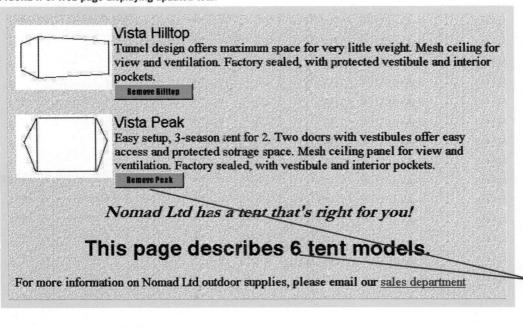

Vista Hilltop
Tunnel design offers maximum space for very little weight. Mesh ceiling for view and ventilation. Factory sealed, with protected vestibule and interior pockets.

`Remove Hilltop`

Vista Peak
Easy setup, 3-season tent for 2. Two doors with vestibules offer easy access and protected sotrage space. Mesh ceiling panel for view and ventilation. Factory sealed, with vestibule and interior pockets.

`Remove Peak`

Nomad Ltd has a tent that's right for you!

This page describes 6 tent models.

For more information on Nomad Ltd outdoor supplies, please email our sales department

Tent total updated to 6 because Summit tent description deleted

Tool Tips and other floating help

In both Internet Explorer and Netscape Navigator, you can create floating windows that display text relevant to an element when the user moves the cursor over it. This effect is similar to ToolTips in Microsoft applications. These windows are dynamic modifications of the page content in response to user actions. For images, you can use the ALT property to specify the text that displays in a floating window when the user holds the mouse pointer over the image. For other Web page elements, Netscape Navigator versions 3 and 4 require a script to add this effect. However, you can add this effect in Internet Explorer 4 by adding TITLE="text" to the opening tag for the element. Because these floating windows add and remove Web page text, they are part of your set of dynamic content tools.

Incorporating an Advanced Content Function

Combining different DHTML tools in your scripts allows for a great variety of possible new dynamic content effects, including different ways of presenting or changing your page elements. You can make your Web page unique as well as make it easier for users to read and navigate by incorporating special features into your Web page. These features also can increase your Web page readership. ◀▬▬ Lydia sees a page on the Web containing a script that cycles through different Web page elements in the same spot. This effect is like a slide show, with each new segment of text appearing after a short interval. She decides to use this feature on the tent page she is developing to display some additional information about Nomad Ltd's products.

Steps

1. Open the file **HTML K-4.htm** in your text editor, save it as a text document with the filename **Tent cycle.htm**, then scroll down the page until the code for the function cycle appears in the document window

   Notice that Lydia entered the function cycle in the page head script. This function replaces an object's contents at regular intervals by using the innerHTML property in conjunction with the script for counting time.

2. Scroll down the Web page code until the top of the body section appears in the document window, select the text **[replace with text cycle script]**, then press **[Delete]**

3. Type the following script, pressing **[Enter]** at the end of each line:

   ```
   <SCRIPT LANGUAGE="javascript">
   <!--
   function addCycle() {
   ```

4. Press **[Tab]**, the type **cycle(txt1, "Hiking,Bicycling,Camping,Kayaking,Climbing, find all your gear at,nomadltd.com", 30)** and press **[Enter]**

   This line defines the display parameters for the text you want to cycle as follows: txt1 indicates the name of the object whose value will be cycled; the text in quotes separated by commas specifies the different words and phrases that should cycle; and the number 30 tells how long one word or phrase should display before cycling to the next word or phrase.

5. Type the remaining code, pressing **[Enter]** at the end of each line

   ```
   }
   if (IE4) {window.onload = new Function("addCycle()")}
   //-->
   </SCRIPT>
   ```

   Figure K-9 shows the Web page source code containing the completed script. This script triggers the function cycle, which begins to cycle text after the page loads.

6. Check your document for errors, make changes as necessary, then save Tent cycle.htm as a text document and open it in your Web browser

   In Internet Explorer 4, the cycling text appears in the top right corner of the page, as shown in Figure K-10. The text cycles at a regular 3-second interval as specified by 30 in the script.

Script to invoke text cycling function

```
<IMG SRC="nomad.jpg" ALIGN="left">

<DIV ID="txt1" ALIGN="right" CLASS="tenthead" STYLE="font-size: 18pt"></DIV>

<SCRIPT LANGUAGE="javascript">
<!--
function addCycle() {
        cycle(txt1, "Hiking,Bicycling,Camping,Kayaking,Climbing,find all your
gear at,nomadltd.com", 30)
}

if(IE4) {window.onload = new Function("addCycle()")}
//-->
</SCRIPT>

<BR><BR><BR>
<DIV ALIGN="center" STYLE="font-size: 24pt; font-weight: bold; font-family:
arial; font-style: normal">Tents</DIV>
<H2 ALIGN="center">Selecting one that's right for you</H2>
<BR>

<DIV>Choosing a quality tent that meets your needs can be an intimidating
task. To help you out with this important decision, we've added features to
this page to make it easier to compare the characteristics of our tents.
<BR><BR>
As you narrow your choices, click the Remove button for each tent that
```

Text content changes every few seconds

FIGURE K-10: Web page displaying cycling text

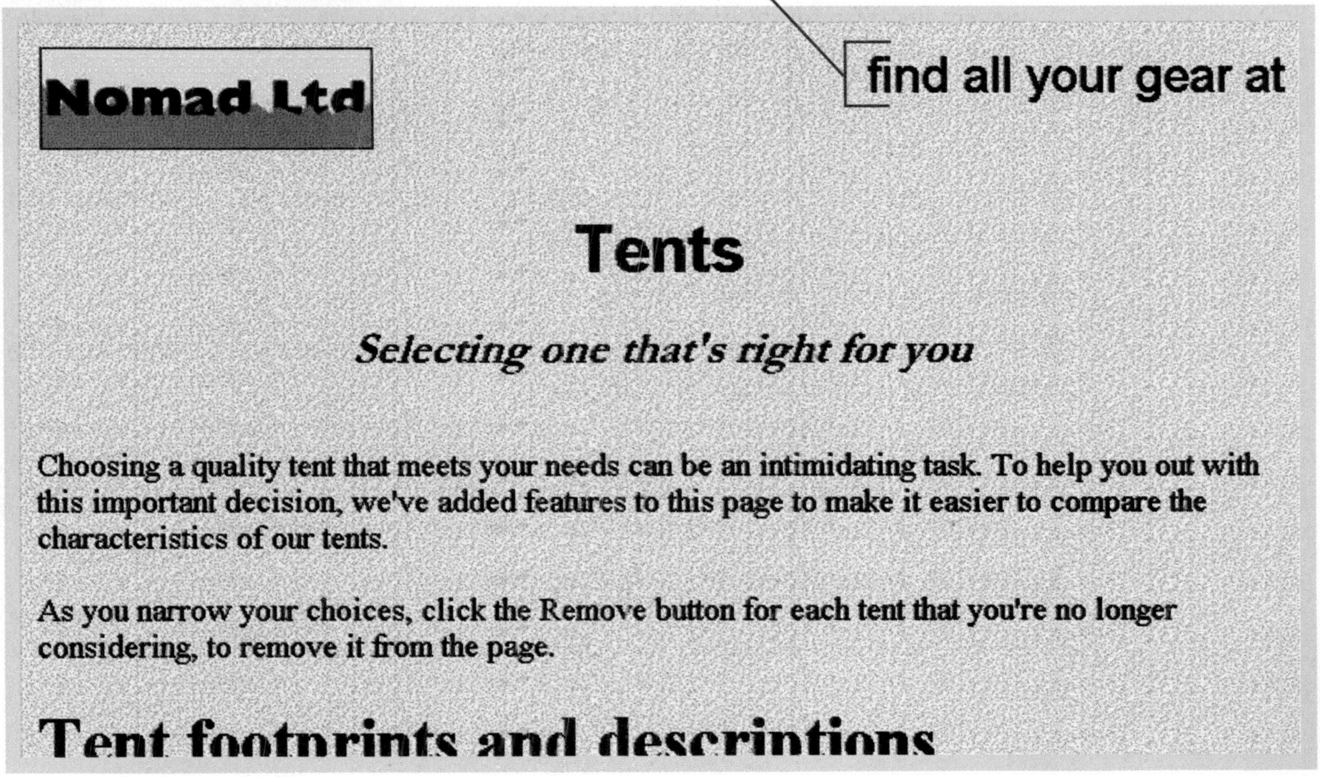

find all your gear at

Nomad Ltd

Tents

Selecting one that's right for you

Choosing a quality tent that meets your needs can be an intimidating task. To help you out with this important decision, we've added features to this page to make it easier to compare the characteristics of our tents.

As you narrow your choices, click the Remove button for each tent that you're no longer considering, to remove it from the page.

Tent footprints and descriptions

HTML

Replacing Graphics Dynamically

All the examples so far have used dynamic content tools to modify a Web page's text, but these features are equally valid for other page elements, including graphics. In a simple scenario, you can use dynamic content features to change the graphic displayed using the onMouseOver event handler. In a more complex scenario, you could gradually change a graphic's size to create the effect of animation. ◢▬▬ Lydia wants to use color to highlight the element that the user is currently pointing to. However, rather than using dynamic style, she creates colored versions of each of the tent footprint graphics. The color version of a text footprint graphic will appear in response to mouse movement over each graphic or its associated text.

Steps

1. Open the file **HTML K-5.htm** in your text editor, then save it as a text document with the filename **Tent color.htm**

2. Scroll down the Web page code until <DIV CLASS="tenthead"> appears in the document window, select the text [**replace with star event handlers**], then press [**Delete**]

3. Type **onMouseOver="star.src='starcolor.jpg'" onMouseOut="star.src='starlite.jpg'"**

4. Scroll down the Web page code, select the text [**replace with brev event handlers**], press [**Delete**], then type **onMouseOver="brev.src='brevcolor.jpg'" onMouseOut= "brev.src='brevifolia.jpg'"**
   Figure K-11 shows the completed code for the first two tent items. Notice that the IMG tag for each tent has a unique ID attribute. The onMouseOver event swaps a color graphic of the tent floorplan for the original image source. The onMouseOut event replaces the color image with the original black and white graphic.

5. Repeat Step 4 for the remaining five list items, using the IDs and graphic files listed in Table K-2

6. Check your document for errors, make changes as necessary, then save **Tent color.htm** as a text document

7. Open **Tent color.htm** in your browser

8. Scroll down to the list of tent descriptions, then move your mouse pointer over the heading or graphic for the XTC Starlite
   See Figure K-12. When you move the cursor over the black and white outline or its associated heading in Internet Explorer 4, the image is replaced with a color graphic. Even though you are simply swapping one graphic for another, this action creates the illusion of modifying the original graphic, much like changing text color using style sheets.

9. Move the mouse pointer off the first list item
   The graphic changes back to the black and white version. Notice that if you move the mouse pointer over other tent graphics, they change color in response to the mouse movement.

FIGURE K-11: Event handlers for first and second list items

Event handlers
for Starlite
inserted in
DIV tag

ID attribute

IMG source

```
<DIV ID="tent1" name="tent">

<DIV CLASS="tenthead" onMouseOver="star.src='starcolor.jpg'"
onMouseOut="star.src='starlite.jpg'"><IMG SRC="starlite.jpg" ALIGN="left"
ID="star">XTC Starlite</DIV>
<DIV>One of the lightest, most compact three-season tents available.
Featuring two-pole clip design with a built-in vestibule.</DIV>

<SCRIPT LANGUAGE="javascript">
<!--
if (IE4) {
        document.write("<BUTTON CLASS='button'
onClick=tent1.outerHTML='',reCount()>Remove Starlite</BUTTON>")
}
//-->
</SCRIPT>

<BR><BR><BR>

</DIV>

<DIV ID="tent2" name="tent">

<DIV CLASS="tenthead" onMouseOver="brev.src='brevcolor.jpg'"
onMouseOut="brev.src='brevifolia.jpg'"><IMG SRC="brevifolia.jpg"
ALIGN="left" ID="brev">Amano Brevifolia</DIV>
```

Event handlers
for Brevifolia
inserted in
DIV tag

FIGURE K-12: Web page showing substituted graphic

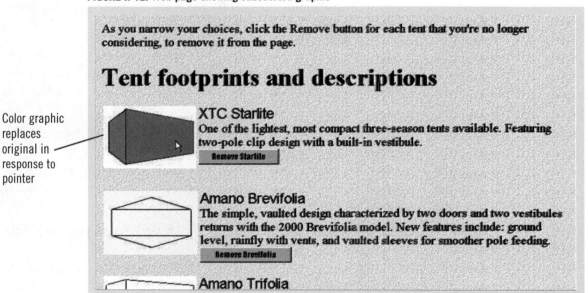

Color graphic
replaces
original in
response to
pointer

TABLE K-2: List item IDs and graphic filenames

list item	id	color graphic name (onMouseOver)	black and white graphic name (onMouseOut)
1	star	starcolor.jpg	starlite.jpg
2	brev	brevcolor.jpg	brevifolia.jpg
3	tri	trifolia.jpg	tricolor.jpg
4	hillside	hillsidecolor.jpg	hillside.jpg
5	hilltop	hilltopcolor.jpg	hilltop.jpg
6	peak	peakcolor.jpg	peak.jpg
7	summit	summitcolor.jpg	summit.jpg

Binding Data

DHTML's dynamic content tools offer specialized features for working with tables in your Web pages. One of the most powerful is dynamic table generation, first introduced in Internet Explorer 4. Instead of creating a table using a tag for each element, you can simply create the headers, then add code to reference data located in an external file. Linking an external database with a Web page is known as **data binding**. When the page loads, the browser creates the table at run time. Because the table is re-created each time a user opens the page, you can change the contents of the external data source without changing the Web page code. ➤ Because it's helpful for tent shoppers to be able to compare the details of different models, such as area and weight, Lydia decides to add a tent data table to the Web page. The sales department has provided a text file containing the appropriate information. Lydia binds the file to her Web page to create a dynamic table.

Steps

1. Open the file **HTML K-6.htm** in your text editor, then save it as a text document with the filename **Tent comparison table.htm**

2. Scroll to near the end of the code until the <OBJECT> tags and list of tent descriptions appears in the document window
   Figure K-13 shows the code including the OBJECT tags. These tags, which Lydia entered earlier, set up the external file containing the data for her table as a Web page object. The CLASSID attribute calls the Internet Explorer routine for dynamic table generation to format the linked data. The PARAM tags within the beginning and ending OBJECT tags denote parameters for this object. The DataURL parameter identifies the name of the external file to be bound, which is named tents.txt. The True value for the UseHeader attribute specifies that the data in the external file includes a row of information identifying the contents of each column.

3. Select the text **[replace with opening TABLE tag]**, press **[Delete]**, and type **<TABLE BORDER="1" ID="elemtbl" DATASRC="#tentlist">**
   The TABLE tag formats the code that follows as rows in a table. The DATASRC attribute refers to the preceding object, named "tentlist." The number sign indicates that the source is an object in the same Web page.

4. Scroll down, select the text **[replace with closing TABLE tag]**, press **[Delete]**, then type **</TABLE>**
   The rows within the TABLE tags contain row header display information and links to the columns in the external source. The DATAFLD attribute in each DIV tag names the column header in the external file that marks the column to be associated with the tag. Notice that below the closing TABLE tag, Lydia has inserted a script to display extra information for users not running IE4. Because these browsers will not display the bound data, Lydia provides another method for them to obtain the table information.

5. Check your document for errors, make changes as necessary, then save **Tent comparison table.htm** as a text document

6. Open **Tent comparison table.htm** in your browser, then scroll to the bottom of the page
   The tent comparison information from the bound data file appears in a table, as shown in Figure K-14. The sales department can add, remove, or edit lines from the external file, and the Web page table will automatically reflect the most current information each time the Web page is loaded.

FIGURE K-13: OBJECT tags in Web page source

Code to
format
imported
data

```
<OBJECT ID="tentlist" CLASSID="clsid:333C7BC4-460F-11D0-BC04-0080C7055A83">
      <PARAM NAME="DataURL" VALUE="tents.txt">
      <PARAM NAME="UseHeader" VALUE="True">
</OBJECT>

[replace with opening TABLE tag]

<THEAD>
<TR>
<TD><B><DIV ID=tent>Tent</DIV></B></TD>
<TD><B><DIV ID=catno>Catalog number</DIV></B></TD>
<TD><B><DIV ID=area>Area (sq ft)</DIV></B></TD>
<TD><B><DIV ID=vest>Vestibule (sq ft)</DIV></B></TD>
<TD><B><DIV ID=desc>Description</DIV></B></TD>
<TD><B><DIV ID=cap>Capacity</DIV></B></TD>
<TD><B><DIV ID=weight>Weight</DIV></B></TD>
<TD><B><DIV ID=price>Price</DIV></B></TD>
</TR>
</THEAD>
<TBODY>
<TR>
<TD><DIV DATAFLD="tent"></DIV></TD>
<TD><DIV DATAFLD="catno"></DIV></TD>
<TD><DIV DATAFLD="area"></DIV></TD>
```

FIGURE K-14: Tent comparison table

Browser-
generated
table based
on external
data source

Tent	Catalog number	Area (sq ft)	Vestibule (sq ft)	Description	Capacity	Weight	Price
XTC Starlite	BR-370	34	10	Staked	1 person	4 lbs. 3 oz.	$150
Amano Brevifolia	BT-356	38.5	19.6	Freestanding	2 people	5 lbs. 8 oz.	$215
Amano Trifolia	BT-358	49	25.7	Freestanding	2 people	7 lbs.	$250
Vista Hillside	BZ-339	32	15.3	Staked	1 person	4 lbs.	$120
Vista Hilltop	BZ-367	37.5	19.5	Staked	1 person	5 lbs. 3 oz.	$160
Vista Peak	BZ-323	42.5	24.4	Freestanding	2 people	6 lbs. 3 oz.	$210
Vista Summit	BZ-334	51.5	28	Freestanding	2 people	7 lbs. 10 oz.	$275

For more information on Nomad Ltd outdoor supplies, please email our sales department

HTML

Manipulating Bound Data Dynamically

In addition to dynamic table creation, Internet Explorer 4 introduced other cutting-edge tools for working with tables in Web pages. Perhaps one of the most useful is dynamic sorting, which enables users to sort the data in a table simply by clicking the relevant column heading. To allow users to compare tent statistics based on the most important categories, Lydia adds a script that sorts the tent information on a given column when a user clicks that column heading.

Steps

1. Open the file **HTML K-7.htm** in your text editor, then save it as a text document with the filename **Tent sortable comparison table.htm**

2. Scroll down to the script beneath the table code near the bottom of the page until function tentClick() { is visible
   Notice that Lydia has already entered scripts to sort the table. She created a separate script for each column. Each script sorts the table by the contents of that column using the tentlist.Sort= command, and then regenerates the table to show the sort, with tentlist.Reset(). Accompanying each script is a line of code triggering the script in response to the onclick event for the given column header.

3. Scroll to the bottom of the page, select the text **[replace with price script]**, then press **[Delete]**

4. Type the following script, pressing **[Enter]** at the end of each line:
   ```
   function priceClick() {
       tentlist.Sort="price";
       tentlist.Reset();
   }
   price.onclick=priceClick;
   ```
   Figure K-15 shows the completed Web page containing the script.

5. Check the script you entered for errors, then save **Tent sortable comparison table.htm** as a text document

6. Open **Tent sortable comparison table.htm** in your Web browser, then scroll to the bottom of the page
   The tent comparison table displays in its default order. Notice that the Vestibule (sq ft) column is not displayed in any particular order.

7. Click the **Vestibule (sq ft)** column heading, then scroll down to see the regenerated table
   The table disappears, then regenerates to show the records in ascending order by vestibule area, as shown in Figure K-16.

8. Click the **Price** column heading, then scroll down
   The table displays the records in order by price, using the script you entered.

9. Close the Web browser and text editor

```
              tentlist.Sort="weight";
              tentlist.Reset();
    }

    weight.onclick=weightClick;

    function priceClick() {
              tentlist.Sort="price";
              tentlist.Reset();
    }

    price.onclick=priceClick;

    if (!IE4) {
              document.write("If your browser does not display the above table,
    please email us at the address below for up-to-date tent details and
    prices.<BR><BR>")
    }
    //-->
    </SCRIPT>

    <DIV>For more information on Nomad Ltd outdoor supplies, please email our <A
    HREF="MAILTO:sales@nomadltd.com">sales department</A></DIV>

    </BODY>
    </HTML>
```

Script for sorting table on the price column

price Column ID for column to be sorted

Sorts column in ascending order by price

Regenerates the table to show the sort

FIGURE K-16: Table sorted on vestibule area column

Tent	Catalog number	Area (sq ft)	Vestibule (sq ft)	Description	Capacity	Weight	Price
XTC Starlite	BR-370	34	10	Staked	1 person	4 lbs. 3 oz.	$150
Vista Hillside	BZ-339	32	15.3	Staked	1 person	4 lbs.	$120
Vista Hilltop	BZ-367	37.5	19.5	Staked	1 person	5 lbs. 3 oz.	$160
Amano Brevifolia	BT-356	38.5	19.6	Freestanding	2 people	5 lbs. 8 oz.	$215
Vista Peak	BZ-323	42.5	24.4	Freestanding	2 people	6 lbs. 3 oz.	$210
Amano Trifolia	BT-358	49	25.7	Freestanding	2 people	7 lbs.	$250
Vista Summit	BZ-334	51.5	28	Freestanding	2 people	7 lbs. 10 oz.	$275

For more information on Nomad Ltd outdoor supplies, please email our sales department

Table sorted in response to click on column head

Suppressing errors

When creating cross-browser code, you may want to add features to your pages that generate error messages in some browsers. To allow your information to get out to everyone who wants to view it without alarming viewers, you can include a script that keeps error messages from appearing in incompatible browsers. By setting the value of the object window.onerror to "null", you prevent error windows from opening when scripts have problems completing. Take care not to add error suppression until you have completed and debugged your page because error suppression removes an important debugging aid.

HTML

Practice

▶ Concepts Review

Label the code segments marked in Figure K-17.

FIGURE K-17

```
<DIV ID="tent1" name="tent">

<DIV CLASS="tenthead" onMouseOver="star.src='starcolor.jpg'"
onMouseOut="star.src='starlite.jpg'"><IMG SRC="starlite.jpg" ALIGN="left"
ID="star">XTC Starlite</DIV>
<DIV>One of the lightest, most compact three-season tents available.
Featuring two-pole clip design with a built-in vestibule.</DIV>

<SCRIPT LANGUAGE="javascript">
<!--
if (IE4) {
        document.write("<BUTTON CLASS='button'
onClick=tent1.outerHTML='',reCount()>Remove Starlite</BUTTON>")
}
//-->
</SCRIPT>

<BR><BR><BR>

</DIV>

<DIV ID="tent2" name="tent">

<DIV CLASS="tenthead" onMouseOver="brev.src='brevcolor.jpg'"
onMouseOut="brev.src='brevifolia.jpg'"><IMG SRC="brevifolia.jpg"
ALIGN="left" ID="brev">Amano Brevifolia</DIV>
```

5 — onMouseOut="star.src='starlite.jpg'"
4 — onMouseOver="star.src='starcolor.jpg'"
2 — "star"
1 — starlite.jpg
3 — Remove Starlite

Match each statement with the term that it decribes.

6. DHTML features that make immediate modifications to a page's actual content
7. Period when a browser first interprets and displays a Web page
8. Associating an external database with a Web page
9. HTML property for replacing an element and the HTML tags enclosing it
10. HTML property for replacing an element but leaving its enclosing HTML tags

a. Data binding
b. InnerHTML
c. Run time
d. OuterHTML
e. Dynamic content

Select the best answer from the list of choices.

11. The outerHTML for the code <DIV>Welcome to the Nomad Ltd home page!</DIV> is
   a. <DIV>Welcome to the Nomad Ltd home page!</DIV>.
   b. <DIV>Welcome to the Nomad Ltd home page!
   c. Welcome to the Nomad Ltd home page!.
   d. Welcome to the Nomad Ltd home page!</DIV>.

12. **A DHTML clock would be an example of**
    a. Deleting content.
    b. Modifying content.
    c. Adding content.
    d. Dynamic table generation

13. **Which HTML tag set do you use to list the properties for a dynamically generated table?**
    a. <TBL>..</TBL>
    b. <TABLE>..</TABLE>
    c. <THEAD>..</THEAD>
    d. <OBJECT>..</OBJECT>

 # Skills Review

1. **Insert content dynamically.**
   a. Open the file HTML K-8.htm in your text editor, then save it as a text document with the filename Pack count.htm.
   b. Scroll to the bottom of the Web page code, highlight the text [replace with pack count code], then press [Delete].
   c. Type the following code, pressing [Enter] at the end of each line:
   ```
   <SCRIPT>
   <!--
   if (IE4) {
        countHeaders()
        document.write("<H1 ALIGN='center'>This page describes ")
        document.write(totalPacks)
        document.write(" pack models.</H1>")
   }
   //-->
   </SCRIPT>
   ```
   d. Check your document for errors, make changes as necessary, then save Pack count.htm as a text document.
   e. Open Pack count.htm in your Web browser, then scroll down to the bottom of the page.

2. **Delete content dynamically.**
   a. Open the file HTML K-9.htm, then save it as a text document with the filename Pack delete.htm.
   b. Scroll down below the body text describing the first pack, the Nomad Moonlight, select the text [replace with button code for pack1], then press [Delete].
   c. Type the following code, pressing [Enter] at the end of each line:
   ```
   <SCRIPT LANGUAGE="javascript">
   <!--
   if (IE4) {
   ```
   d. Press [Tab], then type document.write("<BUTTON CLASS='button' onClick=pack1.outerHTML="">Remove Moonlight</BUTTON>") and press [Enter].
   e. Type } and press [Enter], then enter the two closing SCRIPT tags.
   f. Repeat Steps b through e for the remaining six pack descriptions, substituting the object names and pack names, as listed in Table K-3.

TABLE K-3

description number	substitute for "pack1"	substitute for "Moonlight"
2	pack2	Blue Moon
3	pack3	Harvest Moon
4	pack4	New Moon
5	pack5	Full Moon
6	pack6	Trekker
7	pack7	Long Haul

g. Check the document for errors, make changes as necessary, then save Pack delete.htm as a text document.

h. Open Pack delete.htm in your Web browser, then scroll down the Web page until the Nomad Blue Moon pack description appears in the document window.

i. If you are using Internet Explorer, click the Remove Blue Moon button.

3. Modify content dynamically.

a. Open the file HTML K-10.htm in your text editor, then save it as a text document with the filename Pack update.htm.

b. Scroll to the bottom of the Web page code, select the text [replace with opening SPAN tag], then press [Delete].

c. Type document.write("<SPAN ID='textnum'>")

d. Select the text [replace with closing SPAN tag], press [Delete], type document.write("</SPAN>")

e. Check your document for errors, make changes as necessary, then save Pack update.htm as a text document.

f. Open Pack update.htm in your Web browser, then scroll to the bottom of the page.

g. If you are using Internet Explorer, click the Remove Long Haul button.

h. If you are using Internet Explorer, click the Remove Trekker button.

4. Incorporate an advanced function.

a. Open the file HTML K-11.htm in your text editor, then save it as a text document with the filename Pack scroll.htm.

b. Scroll down until the opening body tag appears in the document window, select the text [replace with text scroll script], then press [Delete].

c. Type onload="scrollit('Find all your outdoor supplies at nomadltd.com!');"

d. Check your document for errors, make changes as necessary, then save Pack scroll.htm as a text document.

e. Open Pack scroll.htm in your Web browser and watch the status bar to see the scrolling text that the new function creates. (*Note*: this feature functions in both Internet Explorer and Navigator.)

5. Replace graphics dynamically.

a. Open the file HTML K-12.htm in your text editor, then save it as a text document with the filename Pack color.htm.

b. Scroll down until the line <DIV CLASS="packhead" appears in the document window, select the text [replace with light event handlers], then press [Delete].

c. Type onMouseOver="light.src='lightcolor.jpg'" onMouseOut="light.src='moonlight.jpg'"

d. Scroll down and select the text [replace with blue event handlers], press [Delete], then type onMouseOver="blue.src='bluecolor.jpg'" onMouseOut="blue.src='bluemoon.jpg'"

e. Repeat Step d for the remaining five list items, using the IDs and graphic files listed in Table K-4.

TABLE K-4

list item	id	color graphic name (onMouseOver)	black and white graphic name (onMouseOut)
3	harvest	harvestcolor.jpg	harvest.jpg
4	newmoon	newcolor.jpg	newmoon.jpg
5	full	fullcolor.jpg	fullmoon.jpg
6	trek	trekcolor.jpg	trekker.jpg
7	long	longcolor.jpg	longhaul.jpg

   f. Check your document for errors, make necessary changes, then save Pack color.htm as a text document.

   g. Open Pack color.htm in your Web browser.

   h. If you are using Internet Explorer 4, scroll down to the list of pack descriptions, then move your mouse pointer over the heading or graphic for the Nomad Moonlight.

   i. Move your mouse pointer off the selected item.

6. Bind data.

   a. Open the file HTML K-13.htm in your text editor, then save it as a text document with the filename Pack comparison table.htm.

   b. Scroll to the end of the code for the list of pack descriptions until the <OBJECT> tags appear in the document window.

   c. Select the text [replace with opening TABLE tag], press [Delete], then type <TABLE BORDER="1" ID="elemtb" DATASRC="#packlist">

   d. Scroll down, select the text [replace with closing TABLE tag], press [Delete], then type </TABLE>

   e. Check your document for errors, make necessary changes, then save Pack comparison table.htm as a text document.

   f. Open Pack comparison table.htm in your browser, then scroll to the bottom of the page. (*Note*: remember that you will see the bound data only in IE 4.)

7. Manipulate bound data dynamically.

   a. Open the file HTML K-14.htm in your text editor, then save it as a text document with the filename Pack sortable comparison table.htm.

   b. Scroll to the bottom of the page, select the text [replace with price script], then press [Delete].

   c. Type the following script, pressing [Enter] at the end of each line:

```
function priceClick() {
    packlist.Sort="price";
    packlist.Reset();
}
price.onclick=priceClick;
```

   d. Check the script you entered for errors, make necessary changes, then save Pack sortable comparison table.htm as a text document.

   e. Open Pack sortable comparison table.htm in your Web browser, then scroll to the bottom of the page.

   f. If you are using Internet Explorer 4, click the Price column heading, then scroll down to see the regenerated table.

   g. Close the Web browser and text editor.

Independent Challenges

1. The owners of the Green House plant store want to allow online ordering on their Web page. On the page listing the Green House plant store's products, you have started adding a check box next to each item. Users can click on a check box next to each item they want to buy. Also, you have begun to add a line that reports the total number of items the user has marked for purchase.

To complete this independent challenge:

a. Open the file HTML K-15.htm in your text editor, then save it as a text document with the filename "Green House supply purchase.htm".

b. Scroll down to the end of the page's head section, select the text [replace with countChecks and reCount functions], then press [Delete].

c. Type the following lines of script, pressing [Enter] at the end of each line:

```
function countChecks() {
     items = 0;
     for (var i = 0; i < document.all.length; i++){
     var el = document.all[i];
     if (el.checked){
          items++;
          }
     }
}

function reCount() {
     countChecks()
     textnum.innerHTML=" " + items;
}
```

d. Check the script you entered for errors, make changes as necessary, then save Green House supply purchase.htm as a text document. *Hint*: To view a model of this script refer to the lesson "Modifying content dynamically" and the student files associated with that lesson.

e. Open "Green House supply purchase.htm" in your browser, then, if you are using Internet Explorer 4, click one of the check boxes and observe the value displayed for total number of items marked for purchase.

f. Check for errors, then use the text editor to make corrections as needed.

g. Close the browser and text editor.

2. You are creating a Web page containing route information for Sandhills Regional Public Transit. You want to allow riders to compare routes that different bus lines follow; and you want to ensure users can remove from the screen lines that do not apply to them.

To complete this independent challenge:

a. Open the file HTML K-16.htm in your text editor, then save it as a text document with the filename "SRPT route comparison.htm".

b. Scroll down to the first list item in the body section, delete the text "[replace with rt11 button code]", then type the following code, pressing [Enter] at the end of each line:

```
<SCRIPT LANGUAGE="javascript">
<!--
if (IE4) {
```

c. Press [Tab], type document.write("<BUTTON CLASS='button' onClick=rt11.outerHTML="">Remove Route 11</BUTTON>")

d. Press [Enter], type } and press [Enter], then add the two closing script tags.

e. Repeat Steps 2 through 4 for the remaining four buttons, replacing the text as indicated in Table K-5.

TABLE K-5

route	replace "rt11" with	replace "Route 11" with
12	rt12	Route 12
13	rt13	Route 13
14	rt14	Route 14
15	rt15	Route 15

f. Check your work, then save SRPT route comparison.htm as a text document.

g. Open "SRPT route comparison.htm" in the browser, and if you are using Internet Explorer, test the buttons to be sure they work.

h. Check for errors, use the text editor to make corrections as needed.

i. Close the browser and text editor.

3. The Community Public School Volunteers organization would like to add a page to their Web site listing schools that currently need volunteers. They also want to include contact information for each school so that potential volunteers can get started immediately. The organization maintains a database of the different schools' volunteer needs. They would like their Web page to reflect the current contents of the database.

To complete this independent challenge:

a. Open the file HTML K-17.htm in your text editor, then save it as a text document with the filename "CPSV volunteer opportunities.htm".

b. Select the text [replace with opening TABLE tag], press [Enter], then type the following code:
<TABLE BORDER="1" ID="elemtbl" DATASRC="#schools">

c. Add the following lines of script after the opening script tags and before the sorting function scripts:
if (!IE4) {
    document.write("If your browser does not display the above table, please contact us to find out about volunteer opportunities.")
}

d. Check your work, make changes as necessary, then save CPSV volunteer opportunities.htm as a text document.

e. Open CPSV volunteer opportunities.htm in the browser, and, if you are using Internet Explorer 4, test the table to verify that the table-generation and table-sorting functions work correctly.

f. Check for errors, use the text editor to make corrections as needed. *Hint:* To view model code, refer to the lessons "Generating a table dynamically" and "Manipulating table contents dynamically" as well as all student files associated with these files.

g. Close the browser and text editor.

4. By creating more complex scripts, you can adapt dynamic content features for a wide range of applications. To complete this independent challenge, connect to the Internet and find two Web pages that incorporate dynamic content in ways that are different than those you learned in this unit. Because you can write cross-browser code for some dynamic content features, you can complete this exercise using either Internet Explorer or Netscape Navigator. Print a copy of each page and circle the area of the page where the content changes dynamically. On another sheet of paper, briefly describe how the content changes, what triggers the change, and what qualifies the feature you circled as dynamic content.

▶ Visual Workshop

You have created a Web page for Touchstone Booksellers that makes their book-inventory database available online. They have provided you a preliminary text file that lists several books. Your task is to bind the text file to the Web page to create a dynamically generated table. The client has asked that you make the table sortable by users, as Figure K-18 illustrates. Open the file HTML K-18.htm, save it as a text document with the filename Touchstone sortable inventory.htm, then replace the text "[replace with sorting script]" with the necessary script to make the list sortable. You need to create a set of script code for each column in the database, as you did in the lesson "Manipulating table contents dynamically" in this unit. The script for the first column is:

```
function titleClick() {
        booklist.Sort="title";
        booklist.Reset();
}
title.onclick=titleClick;
```

Table K-6 shows the variables to substitute to create the remaining script segments. Remember to include the opening and closing SCRIPT tags.

TABLE K-6

column	replace all four occurrences of "title" with
2	alast
3	afirst
4	year
5	bind
6	copies

FIGURE K-18

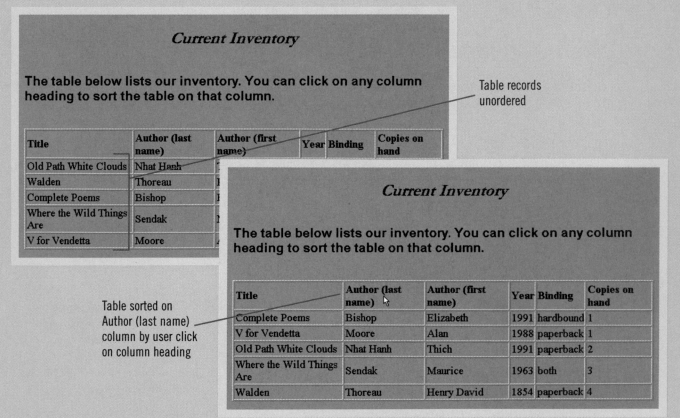

Table records unordered

Table sorted on Author (last name) column by user click on column heading

Positioning

with DHTML

Objectives

► Understand DHTML positioning
► Position an element absolutely
► Position an element relatively
► Size an element manually
► Stack screen elements
► Add a scroll bar
► Create a sidebar
► Incorporate an advanced positioning function

One of DHTML's greatest contributions to Web page design is a tool for **positioning**, or specifying the precise placement of elements within the page. Just like other DHTML components, DHTML positioning opens doors to many possibilities for new Web page features. Other DHTML features, such as scroll bars, complement positioning to help create effective page layouts. Lydia wants to enrich the Web page design for the Nomad Ltd Web publication. She will use positioning and other DHTML layout features to create a sophisticated, attractive style.

Understanding DHTML Positioning

A fundamental difference between document layouts in traditional media, such as posters and magazines, and document layouts in HTML is HTML's lack of tools for precise placement of page elements. DHTML allows precise positioning of page elements through an extension of cascading style sheets called **Cascading Style Sheets - Positioning (CSS-P)**. CSS-P allows you to position elements either **absolutely**, at fixed coordinates on a user's screen, or **relatively**, based on the position of other screen elements. To specify positioning, you use the **position** attribute, which is a style sheet property. Although some advanced page layout is possible with basic HTML, CSS-P makes the task much easier to code and offers features not possible with HTML alone. As Lydia researches CSS-P, she learns about several new features that she would like to include in her Web pages, including columns, overlap, and scripted effects.

Details

Columns

Many Web page designers have created advanced layout features using basic HTML formatting. For example, HTML-only pages can use tables to display text in columns, rather than in one single block. However, adding these features in HTML can be difficult and limiting because the tags were not designed originally to provide advanced formatting. CSS-P makes this type of formatting much simpler by allowing you to easily specify each element's width and location on a Web page. CSS-P also places elements more predictably in different screen resolutions. Lydia plans to use the CSS-P float feature to add a sidebar to the Nomad Ltd tents page, similar to the one shown in Figure L-1.

Overlap

A design feature not found in HTML but available in CSS-P, is the ability to overlap screen elements, which facilitates adding labels over graphics. Also, it allows you to create complex layouts such as ones that superimpose words in different colors or that overlap parts of images. The Web page in Figure L-2 uses CSS-P to overlap text and graphics. Lydia wants to use the overlap feature to create a distinctive design effect in her Web pages for Nomad Ltd. She plans to place the general category name for each Web page in large, light-colored text behind the page headings.

Scripted features

As with other DHTML tools, combining CSS-P with scripts allows you to create many new display features for your Web pages. For example, by changing a graphic's dimensions slightly at regular intervals, you can animate with DHTML. You also can use scripting to allow users to drag elements to new positions on the Web page. Lydia plans to add some draggable elements to her tents page to help users visualize the placement of sleeping bags in various tent designs.

FIGURE L-1: Web page containing sidebar

webmonkey/dynamic_html/

Resources

- - - - - - - - -

Inside DHTML

This site by Scott Isaacs, a member of the Internet Explorer design team, provides lots of juicy coverage of Dynamic HTML and excerpts his book - you guessed it, Inside Dynamic HTML.

Toolbox

- - - - - - - - -

Dreamweaver
Platform: Win 95, Power Mac
Cost: not yet set
Company: Macromedia

Taylor's Tutorial

- - - - - - - - -

Taylor's Dynamic HTML Tutorial - Day 1
Dynamic HTML is how Netscape's and Microsoft's 4.0 browsers are pushing the Web to new limits. In the first of five parts, Taylor looks at what dHTML is all about and what skills you need to code for it. *9 Mar 1998*

Taylor's Dynamic HTML Tutorial - Day 2
Taylor digs into dynamic HTML, showing you the basics of using CSS-P to lay out your pages. He even looks at the elusive z-index. *10 Mar 1998*

Taylor's Dynamic HTML Tutorial - Day 3
Today Taylor's series gets tricky: By the end of the day, he'll have you scripting dHTML and making monkeys run around

Sidebar created
using CSS-P

FIGURE L-2: Web page displaying element overlap

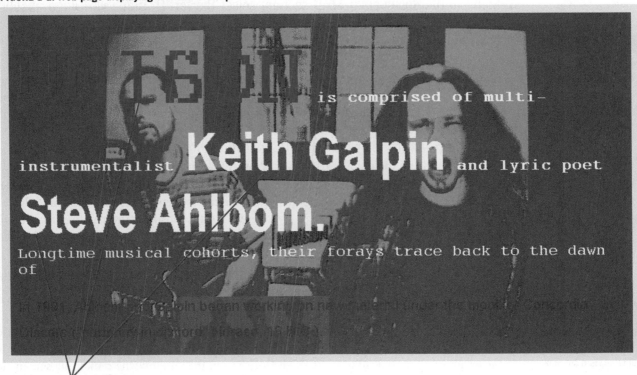

is comprised of multi-

instrumentalist Keith Galpin and lyric poet

Steve Ahlbom.

Longtime musical cohorts, their forays trace back to the dawn of

Text overlaps
graphic

Positioning an Element Absolutely

With CSS-P, you can specify an element's position in several different ways. The most straightforward way is to use **absolute positioning**, which lets you specify the left and top coordinates of an element on the Web page. You use the CSS-P **left** and **top** properties to specify an element's location relative to the top-left corner of its **parent**, or the object enclosing it. For example, a <SPAN> element nested within <DIV> tags would be positioned relative to the <DIV> element, its parent. In this case, the <SPAN> element is known as a **child** of the <DIV> element. Any element not enclosed by another element is a child of the browser window and is absolutely positioned with respect to the top-left corner of the window. You can specify left and top values in points (pt), pixels (px), inches (in), millimeters (mm), or centimeters (cm). If you don't specify units, the browser defaults to **pixels**, which are the tiny units of light that create the display on a monitor. The number of pixels visible on a user's screen varies depending on its resolution. However, even when using pixels, it is a good idea to specify units in order to make your code clearer when debugging it and when others read it. As she develops a Web page describing tents available from Nomad Ltd, Lydia wants to reposition the elements located at the top of the page to decrease the amount of blank space in her original design. She adds absolute position information to the elements to create a more compact layout.

Steps

1. Start your Web browser, cancel any dial-up activities, then open the file **HTML L-1.htm**
   Notice how the text flows around the image. In this version of the Web page, because Lydia was using only HTML, she made the text flow by grouping the image and the text together in a DIV tagset. However, text flow created in HTML can be unpredictable depending on the user's display font size and resolution settings.

2. Start your text editor program, open the file **HTML L-1.htm**, then save it as a text document with the filename **Tent absolute position.htm**

3. Scroll to the document's HEAD section, select the text **[replace with logo absolute position code]** in the embedded style sheet, then press **[Delete]**

4. Type **#logo {position: absolute; top: 30px; left: 30px}**
   The name #logo associates this style with the ID "logo". Figure L-3 shows the document containing the absolute position code. Lydia placed the logo so that it is 30 pixels from the top of the browser window and 30 pixels from the left edge of the browser window. By positioning the Nomad Ltd logo using absolute positioning, Lydia's headers can move up to fill in the empty area at the top of the page.

5. Scroll down until the opening DIV tag above the IMG tag for nomad.jpg appears in the document window, select the text **[replace with ID]**, then press **[Delete]**
   Lydia wants her layout to work on both fourth-generation browsers. Because Netscape Navigator does not recognize absolute positioning referenced in an IMG tag, she has enclosed the IMG tag in DIV tags. By referencing the position information in the DIV element, Lydia positions the graphic element.

6. Type **ID="logo"**

7. Check your document for errors, make any necessary changes, then save **Tent absolute position.htm** as a text document

8. Open **Tent absolute position.htm** in your Web browser
   As Figure L-4 shows, the Nomad Ltd logo appears in the top-left corner of the window, moved slightly down and to the right from its position in the file HTML L-1.htm. Because the graphic is placed absolutely at a fixed location in the window, the remaining screen elements flow beginning at the top of the window. The presence of the graphic to the left of the headings has no effect on their alignment or flow. As Figure L-4 shows, the result is overlap between the logo and the heading text. Next, Lydia will adjust the position of the heading text to keep it from overlapping the logo.

QuickTip

Determining the exact number of units for an element's position coordinates is a process of trial and error.

Trouble?

The text flow may appear differently on your screen, depending on its resolution.

FIGURE L-3: Web document containing absolute position code

```
<HTML>
<HEAD>

<TITLE>Nomad Ltd - Selecting a tent</TITLE>

<LINK REL=stylesheet HREF="nomadltd.css" TYPE="text/css">

<STYLE>
<!--
.tenthead {font-family: arial, sans-serif; font-size: 14pt}
.button {font-family: impact, arial; font-size: 8pt}
.norm {font-weight: normal}
.noital {font-style: normal}
#logo {position: absolute; top: 30px; left: 30px}
//-->
</STYLE>

<SCRIPT LANGUAGE="javascript">
<!--
Nav4 = (document.layers) ? 1:0;
IE4 = (document.all) ? 1:0;

if(!IE4) {window.onerror=null}

totalTents = 0;
function countHeaders() {
```

Code to position logo at top-left corner of page

Name associates style with ID "logo"

FIGURE L-4: Web page displaying absolutely positioned logo

Logo placed at precise coordinates

Tents
Selecting one that's right for you

Choosing a quality tent that meets your needs can be an intimidating task. To help you out with this important decision, we've added features to this page to make it easier to compare the characteristics of our tents.

As you narrow your choices, click the Remove button for each tent that you're no longer considering, to remove it from the page.

Tent footprints and descriptions

XTC Starlite
One of the lightest, most compact three-season tents available. Featuring two-pole clip design with a built-in vestibule.

Remove Starlite

Cross-browser positioning

Both fourth-generation browsers interpret and display CSS-P formatting, but as with the other parts of DHTML, each browser processes CSS-P differently. This disparity results in unique code to create features in each browser that you need to remember when creating cross-browser code. The main challenge is that Navigator 4 does not correctly interpret positioning information inserted directly in a tag. In fact, inline coding for position removes the style information from all elements in the page that follow the inline code. You can remedy this problem by defining all your positioning code in either embedded or external style sheets. Fortunately, grouping style information at the top or in a separate file brings other benefits because it organizes your code and makes it easier to read and understand.

Positioning an Element Relatively

In addition to placing elements at fixed screen coordinates, CSS-P allows you to simply offset elements from their default positions in the page flow. This format, called **relative positioning**, is useful when you want your document to always display an element before or after other elements, but at a specified horizontal or vertical offset. ◄───── Lydia wants to indent the page headings, while leaving them in the general page flow. She uses relative positioning to specify the new placement for the headings.

Steps

1. Open the file **HTML L-2.htm** in your text editor, then save it as a text document with the filename **Tent relative position.htm**

2. In the embedded style sheet, select the text **[replace with head relative position code]**, then press **[Delete]**

3. Type **#head {position: relative; left: 250px}**
   Figure L-5 shows the document containing the relative position code. Similar to the absolute position of the logo, the left property that Lydia used to position the text moves it left in relation to the parent element, which is the browser window. Absolute positioning removes an element from the flow of the document, which causes the elements below it to move up and to overlap its former position in the page flow. This caused the headings to move up in the last lesson. Relatively positioning leaves an element in the document flow. A relatively positioned element moves relative to its default location in the page, but the elements that follow a relatively positioned element do not move up to take that position. This is what Lydia wants to do in her document because she wants the headings indented from the left to appear next to the graphic, but she does not want the text that follows to overlap the headings and graphic.

4. Scroll until **<DIV ALIGN="center"** appears in the document window, select the text **[replace with ID]**, then press **[Delete]**

5. Select the adjacent text **ALIGN="center"** and press **[Delete]**

6. Type **ID="head"**
   Lydia references the position information in the DIV element to position the headings.

7. Check your document for errors, make any necessary changes, then save **Tent relative position.htm** as a text document

8. Open **Tent relative position.htm** in your Web browser
   As Figure L-6 shows, the main heading and the subheading are indented far enough from the left edge of the window to allow room for the logo. Because the indent was specified using relative positioning, the text after the headings does not move up into the positions previously held by the headings but, rather, continues to flow below them.

FIGURE L-5: Relative position code in Web document

Code to position heading within document flow

```
<HTML>
<HEAD>

<TITLE>Nomad Ltd - Selecting a tent</TITLE>

<LINK REL=stylesheet HREF="nomadltd.css" TYPE="text/css">

<STYLE>
<!--
.tenthead {font-family: arial, sans-serif; font-size: 14pt}
.button {font-family: impact, arial; font-size: 8pt}
.norm {font-weight: normal}
.noital {font-style: normal}
#logo {position: absolute; top: 30px; left: 30px}
#head {position: relative; left: 250px}
//-->
</STYLE>

<SCRIPT LANGUAGE="javascript">
<!--
Nav4 = (document.layers) ? 1:0;
IE4 = (document.all) ? 1:0;

if(!IE4) {window.onerror=null}

totalTents = 0;
```

FIGURE L-6: Web page displaying relatively positioned headings

Headings indented within main text flow

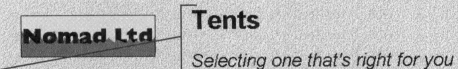

Tents

Selecting one that's right for you

Choosing a quality tent that meets your needs can be an intimidating task. To help you out with this important decision, we've added features to this page to make it easier to compare the characteristics of our tents.

As you narrow your choices, click the Remove button for each tent that you're no longer considering, to remove it from the page.

Tent footprints and descriptions

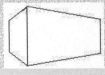

XTC Starlite
One of the lightest, most compact three-season tents available. Featuring two-pole clip design with a built-in vestibule.

Remove Starlite

Sizing an Element Manually

In addition to position on the page, DHTML style properties allow you to specify an element's dimensions using the **height** and **width** properties. You can specify the two dimensions separately by using the same units available for the positioning properties. Additionally, you can size the element relative to its parent by using percentages. If you choose not to specify the height or the width, the browser sizes the element automatically. Lydia wants to reformat the description text for each tent model, so it displays indented and in a narrower column. Because she is changing style information for several screen elements, she adds properties to the page's embedded style sheet.

Steps

1. Open the file **HTML L-3.htm** in your text editor, then save it as a text document with the filename **Tent element size.htm**

2. Select the text **[replace with tentbody class description]** in the embedded style sheet, then press **[Delete]**

3. Type **.tentbody {position: relative; left: 100px; width: 300px}**
   Figure L-7 shows the document code including the new width property.

4. Scroll down until the **<DIV ID="tent1" name="tent">** tag appears in the document window, then read through the code within this DIV element
   Notice that, in addition to the new style properties, Lydia has inserted CLASS="tentbody" in the DIV tag already, which applies the position information from the tenthead class description she created. She has added this information for each tent.

5. Check your document for errors, make any necessary changes, then save **Tent element size.htm** as a text document

6. Open **Tent element size.htm** in your Web browser, then scroll down until the tent descriptions appear in the document window
   As Figure L-8 shows, each description is indented from the left margin and the paragraph width is narrowed, which creates a column.

FIGURE L-7: Web document including width property code

```
<HTML>
<HEAD>

<TITLE>Nomad Ltd - Selecting a tent</TITLE>

<LINK REL=stylesheet HREF="nomadltd.css" TYPE="text/css">

<STYLE>
<!--
.tenthead {font-family: arial, sans-serif; font-size: 14pt; position:
relative; left: 100px}
.button {font-family: impact, arial; font-size: 8pt}
.norm {font-weight: normal}
.noital {font-style: normal}
#logo {position: absolute; top: 30px; left: 30px}
#head {position: relative; left: 250px}
.tentbody {position: relative; left: 100px; width: 300px}
//-->
</STYLE>

<SCRIPT LANGUAGE="javascript">
<!
Nav4 = (document.layers) ? 1:0;
IE4 = (document.all) ? 1:0;

if(!IE4) {window.onerror=null}
```

Width property for tentbody class

FIGURE L-8: Web page displaying adjusted width

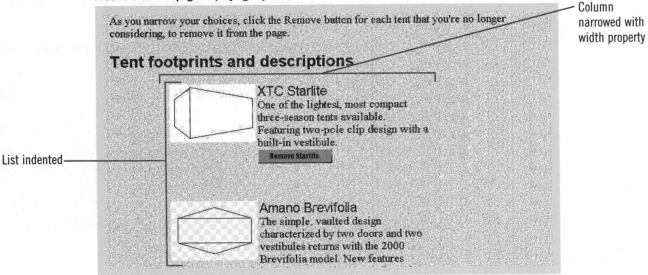

As you narrow your choices, click the Remove button for each tent that you're no longer considering, to remove it from the page.

Tent footprints and descriptions

XTC Starlite
One of the lightest, most compact three-season tents available. Featuring two-pole clip design with a built-in vestibule.

Remove Starlite

Amano Brevifolia
The simple, vaulted design characterized by two doors and two vestibules returns with the 2000 Brevifolia model. New features

List indented

Column narrowed with width property

Positioning and sizing using percentages

Although standard measurement units, such as pixels and points, are most familiar to Web page designers, the ability to use percentage as a positioning and sizing unit offers advantages for some screen elements. Because monitors of different screen resolutions display the document window with a larger or smaller area, a size in pixels or points appears at a different position on the screen at different resolutions. While a column of 150px may fit perfectly in an 800 x 600 display, that same column may be surrounded by space at 1024 x 768, reducing the effectiveness of your layout. Elements sized with percentages, however, automatically adjust to the size of their parent elements. Thus, if you size a graphic element that is a child of the document window at 35%, that graphic element will maintain the same size relative to the document window in different resolutions. You can use the same method to absolutely or relatively position an element as a percentage of its parent. For some applications, specifying an exact measurement is important, but percentage sizing and positioning are important tools in your Web page design toolbox.

Stacking Screen Elements

Because an absolutely positioned element can appear anywhere on a Web page, including the space occupied by other elements, the browser can't format pages containing these elements as it would standard HTML pages. Instead, each absolutely positioned element is considered to be on a separate **layer**, which is a transparent virtual page that determines overlap order. Web page layers are like sheets of clear plastic with writing or images on them in different areas. When the sheets are superimposed, as layers are in the browser window, all the contents of all sheets are visible; but some contents may block out others, depending on their order in the stack. Each layer's **z-index** property determines its position in the stack. Higher numbers are located closer to the top of the stack, and elements on these layers will block out elements in the same position on lower layers of the stack. An element that is positioned using absolute positioning is placed on a separate layer. An element positioned using relative positioning remains on the same layer as the rest of the standard page elements. Lydia plans to label each page in Nomad Ltd's Web publication based on its content category. She wants to place the category name at the top of the page so that it appears behind the headings. For the tent page, she wants to add the word *camping* to the heading background in large, light-colored type.

Steps

1. Open the file **HTML L-4.htm** in your text editor, then save it as a text document with the filename **Tent layers.htm**

2. In the embedded style sheet, select the text **[replace with backtext layer code]**, then press **[Delete]**

3. Type **#backtext {position: absolute; left: 250px; font-size: 64pt; font-family: arial; color: #7093DB; z-index: -1}**
   Figure L-9 shows the document code, including the new background text. The first element positioned in a Web page receives a z-index value of 0. Subsequently placed elements receive higher z-index values, resulting in later elements appearing on top of older elements by default. Because Lydia wants to make sure the word *CAMPING* appears behind the headings, she assigns it a z-index of -1, which is lower than all other default z-index values.

4. Scroll down and select the text **[replace with background text]**, then press **[Delete]**

5. Type **<DIV ID="backtext">** and press **[Enter]**

6. Type **CAMPING** and press **[Enter]**, then type **</DIV>**

7. Check your document for errors, make any necessary changes, then save **Tent layers.htm** as a text document

8. Open **Tent layers.htm** in your Web browser
   As Figure L-10 shows, the text *CAMPING* appears behind the headings in a large and light-colored font. This stacked layout allows Lydia to add extra information to the Web page without disrupting the flow of the page. It also adds an interesting, unusual visual effect.

FIGURE L-9: Web document including background text code

```
<HTML>
<HEAD>

<TITLE>Nomad Ltd - Selecting a tent</TITLE>

<LINK REL=stylesheet HREF="nomadltd.css" TYPE="text/css">

<STYLE>
<!--
.tenthead {font-family: arial, sans-serif; font-size: 14pt; position:
relative; left: 100px}
.button {font-family: impact, arial; font-size: 8pt}
.norm {font-weight: normal}
.noital {font-style: normal}
#logo {position: absolute; top: 30px; left: 30px}
#head {position: relative; left: 250px}
.tentbody {position: relative; left: 100px; width: 300px}
#backtext {position: absolute; left: 250px; font-size: 64pt; font-family:
arial; color: #7093DB; z-index: -1}
//-->
</STYLE>

<SCRIPT LANGUAGE="javascript">
<!--
Nav4 = (document.layers) ? 1:0;
IE4 = (document.all) ? 1:0;
```

z-index
property for
background
text

FIGURE L-10: Web page displaying background text

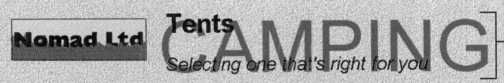

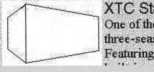

z-index
value places
background
text behind
headings

Choosing a quality tent that meets your needs can be an intimidating task. To help you out with this important decision, we've added features to this page to make it easier to compare the characteristics of our tents.

As you narrow your choices, click the Remove button for each tent that you're no longer considering, to remove it from the page.

Tent footprints and descriptions

XTC Starlite
One of the lightest, most compact
three-season tents available.
Featuring two-pole clip design with a

Adding a Scroll Bar

You can use CSS-P to associate a scroll bar with an element when the element is too large to fit its defined size. This effect, which you create using the **overflow** property, allows you to create the equivalent of an independent frame anywhere within your browser window. Of the fourth-generation browsers, only Internet Explorer accommodates the overflow property. To make the tent page layout more concise, Lydia formats the list of tent outlines and descriptions in a box with a scroll bar. This allows users to scroll from top to bottom in the page more quickly and still easily view the tent descriptions if they wish.

Steps

1. Open the file **HTML L-5.htm** in your text editor, then save it as a text document with the filename **Tent scroll.htm**

2. In the embedded style sheet, select the text **[replace with list scroll code]**, then press **[Delete]**

3. Type **#list {height: 300px; width: 600px; overflow: auto}**
   Figure L-11 shows the Web page code in the embedded style sheet. Because the list of tent descriptions is much longer than 300 pixels, the height specification creates a display area smaller than the object size. The "auto" value for the "overflow" property instructs the browser to display scroll bars only where necessary. Because the text in this case is longer than 300 pixels, the browser will create a vertical scroll bar for the object. The width of this DIV is not constrained by a style setting, so a horizontal scroll bar is not needed.

4. Scroll until the code for the heading Tent footprints and descriptions appears in the document window, select the text **[replace with opening DIV tag]**, then press **[Delete]**

5. Type **<DIV ID="list">**

Trouble?

The amount of text displayed in your scroll bar box will depend on the size of the font you are using and your screen resolution.

6. Scroll to the end of the tent description list which is after the description for tent 7, select the text **[replace with closing DIV tag]**, press **[Delete]**, then type **</DIV>**

7. Check your document for errors, make any necessary changes, then save **Tent scroll.htm** as a text document

8. Open **Tent scroll.htm** in your Web browser, then scroll down to view the list of tent outlines and descriptions
   As Figure L-12 shows, in IE 4 the tent-description list displays in a limited area with a vertical scroll bar on the right edge.

9. Use the scroll bar for the list to view all of the tent descriptions

FIGURE L-11: Web document including scroll bar code

```
<HTML>
<HEAD>

<TITLE>Nomad Ltd - Selecting a tent</TITLE>

<LINK REL=stylesheet HREF="nomadltd.css" TYPE="text/css">

<STYLE>
<!--
.tenthead {font-family: arial, sans-serif; font-size: 14pt; position:
relative; left: 100px}
.button {font-family: impact, arial; font-size: 8pt}
.norm {font-weight: normal}
.noital {font-style: normal}
#logo {position: absolute; top: 30px; left: 30px}
#head {position: relative; left: 250px}
.tentbody {position: relative; left: 100px; width: 300px}
#backtext {position: absolute; left: 250px; font-size: 64pt; font-family:
arial; color: #7093DB; z-index: -1}
#list {height: 300px; width: 600px; overflow: auto}
//-->
</STYLE>

<SCRIPT LANGUAGE="javascript">
<!--
Nav4 = (document.layers) ? 1:0;
```

overflow property
adds scroll bar

FIGURE L-12: List formatted with scroll bar

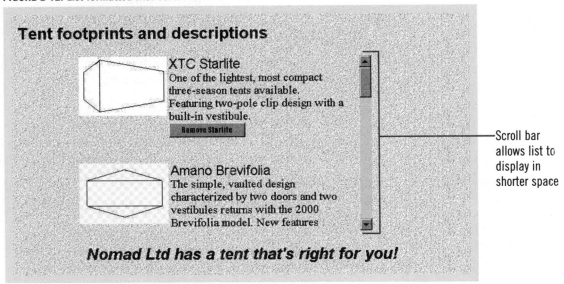

Scroll bar
allows list to
display in
shorter space

CLUES TO USE

Creating a clip region

Sometimes, you want to put a large element on your Web page but don't have room for the full element; other times, you only want to display a portion of a large element. CSS-P's **clip** property allows you to control how much of an element is visible on your Web page by acting as a layer above the element, covering all of it except for a hole you define, called a **clip region**. (Note that Netscape Navigator 4 does not support this property.) To create a clip region, you specify the coordinates of a rectangle, usually with an area smaller than the element, using the syntax **clip: rect(top right bottom left)**. The abbreviation "rect" stands for rectangle, which is the only shape currently supported by this property. Substitute each of the terms in parentheses with a coordinate value, or enter **auto** to leave the default. When the element appears in your Web page, the only portion of the element that will be visible is the section within the rectangle you specified.

Creating a Sidebar

Using CSS-P's placement and sizing properties, you can create and position text blocks independently of each other. You can use the **float** property to remove an element from the main text flow and display it to the side of the flow. The **left** and **right** values allow you to specify whether the element is positioned on the right or left side of the main document flow. The float feature allows you to create many text effects, including sidebars, which are difficult to create with HTML alone. ✎ Lydia wants to add scale outlines of backpacks and sleeping bags to the tents page to give users a better feel for the relative sizes of the tents. To make this area stand out from the page's main text, she creates a sidebar.

Steps

1. Open the file **HTML L-6.htm** in your text editor, then save it as a text document with the filename **Tent sidebar.htm**

2. In the embedded style sheet, select the text **[replace with sidebar code]**, then press **[Delete]**

3. Type **#sidebar {width: 350px; float: right; position: absolute; left: 400px; font-family: arial; font-size: 11pt; background: #8FBC8F}** and press **[Enter]**
   The "float" property removes the section from the document flow, and the "right" value specifies that it floats to the right of the flow. Lydia could specify the height, but the height property works in conjunction with the float property only in Internet Explorer. Navigator always adjusts the height of a sidebar to fit its contents, regardless of the height setting. By not assigning the height property, Lydia allows both browsers to automatically adjust the height to ensure uniform appearance.

4. Type **.expl {width: 375px}**
   To keep the paragraph to the left of the sidebar from overlapping it, Lydia associates it with a fixed width. Figure L-13 shows the Web page code containing the new style specifications.

5. Scroll until the DIV tag before the IMG tags appears in the document window, select the text **[replace with ALIGN and ID codes]**, then press **[Delete]**

6. Type **ALIGN="left" ID="sidebar"**
   Sidebars that float to the right of the main text also automatically align text along the right edge. You can override this setting using the HTML ALIGN property.

7. Check your document for errors, make any necessary changes, then save **Tent sidebar.htm** as a text document

8. Open **Tent sidebar.htm** in your Web browser
   As Figure L-14 shows, the text displays in a rectangle with a colored background to the right of the main text flow. Lydia specified absolute positioning settings for the graphics to position them just below the sidebar text.

Trouble?

If you are using Netscape Navigator 4 and the sidebar is slow to appear, simply scroll down the page and back to the top to see the scrollbar more quickly.

FIGURE L-13: Web document containing style specifications for sidebar

float property creates sidebar effect

Code added to adjust layout for new text

Absolute position code for pack and bag icons

```
.tentbody {position: relative; left: 100px; width: 300px}
#backtext {position: absolute; left: 250px; font-size: 64pt; font-family:
arial; color: #7093DB; z-index: -1}
#list {height: 300px; width: 600px; overflow: auto}
#sidebar {width: 350px; float: right; position: absolute; left: 400px; font-
family: arial; font-size: 11pt; background: #8F3C8F}
.expl {width: 375px}
#pack1 {position: absolute; left: 505px}
#pack2 {position: absolute; left: 535px}
#pack3 {position: absolute; left: 425px}
#pack4 {position: absolute; left: 460px}
#bag1 {position: absolute; left: 565px}
#bag2 {position: absolute; left: 670px}
//-->
</STYLE>

<SCRIPT LANGUAGE="javascript">
<!--
Nav4 = (document.layers) ? 1:0;
IE4 = (document.all) ? 1:0;

if(!IE4) {window.onerror=null}

totalTents = 0;
function countHeaders() {
    for (var i = 0; i < document.all.length; i++){
```

FIGURE L-14: Web page displaying sidebar

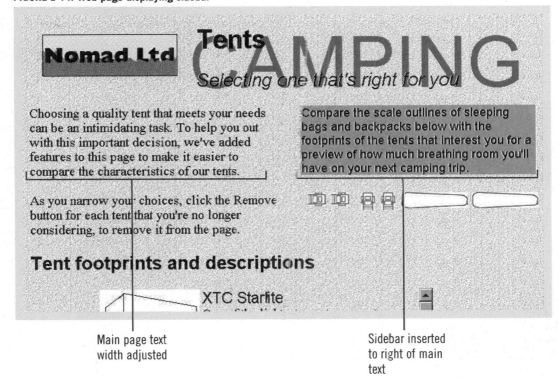

Main page text width adjusted

Sidebar inserted to right of main text

Incorporating an Advanced Positioning Function

By creating scripts to interact with position and layer information, you can add many advanced features to your Web pages. One exciting result of scripting position in Internet Explorer is dragging. A script enabling the drag feature can adjust the position of the selected element based on the coordinates of the pointer and then assign the element to its final position once the user releases the mouse button. This drag feature allows users to rearrange elements into an order that is more useful for them than the page's default organization or to interact with Web page models and games. Lydia wants to let Internet Explorer users drag the scale outlines of sleeping bags and backpacks over the tent outlines so they can explore how much each tent holds.

Steps

1. Open the file **HTML L-7.htm** in your text editor, then save it as a text document with the filename **Tent drag.htm**

   Notice that Lydia has created the class description .drag in the embedded style section for a draggable element.

2. Scroll down until the var elDrag=null code appears in the document window

   Notice that Lydia has created a script in the header section that handles dragging of absolute-positioned elements.

3. Scroll down until the IMG SRC code for the first draggable image appears in the document window, select the text **[replace with drag code]** in the opening DIV tag for the image tag, then press **[Delete]**

4. Type **CLASS="drag" canDrag**

   This code associates the image with the "drag" class that Lydia defined in the embedded style sheet, which specifies a z-index of 10. The script Lydia inserted earlier in the code identifies draggable images through the "canDrag" attribute.

5. Repeat Steps 2 and 3 for the remaining five IMG tags

   Figure L-15 shows the draggable image codes for this page.

6. Check your document for errors, make any necessary changes, then save **Tent drag.htm** as a text document

7. Open **Tent drag.htm** in your Web browser

8. If you are using IE4, drag some of the backpack and sleeping bag outlines onto a tent footprint

   Look at Figure L-16, and notice that the images move with the mouse pointer. The user can display the images on top of the tent outlines.

FIGURE L-15: Web document containing draggable image codes

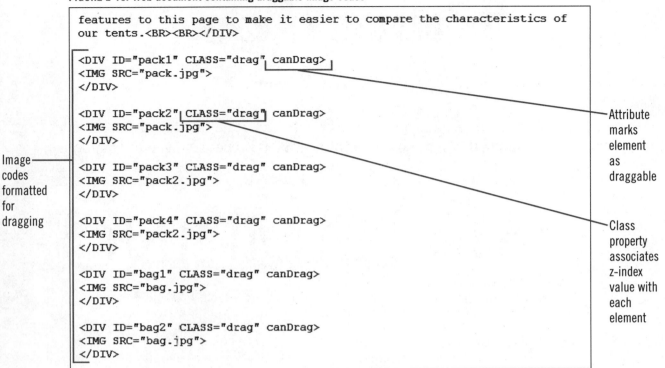

Image codes formatted for dragging

```
features to this page to make it easier to compare the characteristics of
our tents.<BR><BR></DIV>

<DIV ID="pack1" CLASS="drag" canDrag>
<IMG SRC="pack.jpg">
</DIV>

<DIV ID="pack2" CLASS="drag" canDrag>
<IMG SRC="pack.jpg">
</DIV>

<DIV ID="pack3" CLASS="drag" canDrag>
<IMG SRC="pack2.jpg">
</DIV>

<DIV ID="pack4" CLASS="drag" canDrag>
<IMG SRC="pack2.jpg">
</DIV>

<DIV ID="bag1" CLASS="drag" canDrag>
<IMG SRC="bag.jpg">
</DIV>

<DIV ID="bag2" CLASS="drag" canDrag>
<IMG SRC="bag.jpg">
</DIV>
```

Attribute marks element as draggable

Class property associates z-index value with each element

FIGURE L-16: Web page showing dragged images

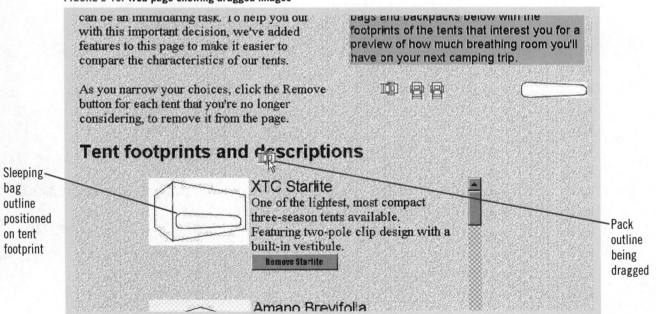

Sleeping bag outline positioned on tent footprint

Pack outline being dragged

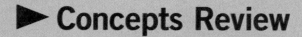
▶ Concepts Review

Label the elements marked in figure L-17 with the CSS-P properties used to create them.

FIGURE L-17

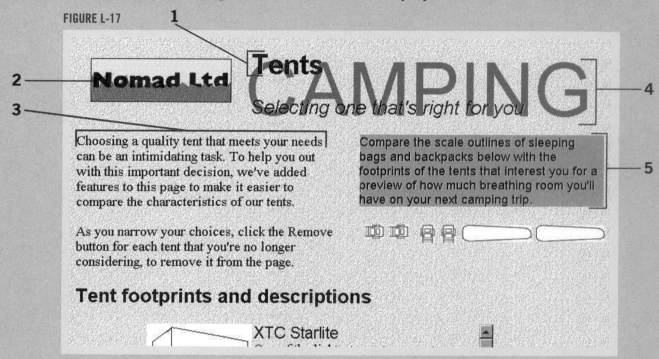

Match each term with its description.

6. **Absolute positioning**
7. **Relative positioning**
8. **Float**
9. **Height and width**
10. **Top and left**

a. Properties for specifying element dimensions
b. Places element at fixed coordinates outside page flow
c. Properties for specifying location
d. Property used to create sidebar
e. Places element relative to parent element's coordinates within page flow

Select the best answer from the list of choices.

11. An absolutely positioned element is located
    a. On a separate layer from the rest of the Web page, offset from the parent element.
    b. On a separate layer from the rest of the Web page, offset from the top-left corner of the browser window.
    c. On the same layer as the rest of the page, offset from the parent element.
    d. On the same layer as the rest of the page, offset from the top-left corner of the browser window.

12. DHTML allows precise positioning of page elements through an extension of Cascading Style Sheets called
    a. Absolute positioning.
    b. Cascading Style Sheets - Positioning.
    c. The "Position" style property.
    d. Tables.

13. The browser always places absolutely positioned text
    a. At the top-left corner of the browser window.
    b. At the specified coordinates relative to the top-left corner of the browser window.
    c. Behind the main page elements in z-index.
    d. At the specified coordinates relative to its parent element.

14. Which is not a valid measurement unit for specifying dimension and coordinate properties?
    a. Feet
    b. Inches
    c. Points
    d. Pixels

15. As you add new layers to a Web page, the elements on the most recent layers receive
    a. The same z-index value as earlier layers.
    b. Smaller z-index values than earlier layers.
    c. Larger z-index values than earlier layers.
    d. Negative z-index values.

16. Which property allows you to add scroll bars to specific elements?
    a. Scroll bar
    b. Float
    c. Layer
    d. Overflow

17. When adding a scroll bar to an element, assigning the value "auto" results in
    a. A scroll bar only when the element size requires it.
    b. Both horizontal and vertical scroll bars always appearing .
    c. No scroll bars.
    d. Addition of a vertical scroll bar only.

► Skills Review

1. **Position an element absolutely.**
   a. Open the file HTML L-8.htm in your Web browser.
   b. Open the file HTML L-8.htm in your text editor, then save it as a text document with the filename Pack absolute position.htm.
   c. Scroll to the top of the document's HEAD section, select the text [replace with logo absolute position code] in the embedded style sheet, then press [Delete].
   d. Type #logo {position: absolute; top: 30px; left: 30px}
   e. Scroll and select the text [replace with ID] in the opening DIV tag above the IMG tag for nomad.jpg, then press [Delete].
   f. Type ID="logo"
   g. Check your document for errors, make any necessary changes, then save Pack absolute position.htm as a text document.
   h. Open Pack absolute position.htm in your Web browser.

2. **Position an element relatively.**
   a. Open the file HTML L-9.htm in your text editor and save a copy as Pack relative position.htm.
   b. In the embedded style sheet, select the text [replace with head relative position code], then press [Delete].
   c. Type #head {position: relative; left: 275px}
   d. Scroll and select the text [replace with ID], then press [Delete].
   e. Select the adjacent text ALIGN="center" and press [Delete].
   f. Type ID="head"
   g. Check your document for errors, make any necessary changes, then save Pack relative position.htm as a text document.
   h. Open Pack relative position.htm in your Web browser.

3. **Size an element manually.**
   a. Open the file HTML L-10.htm in your text editor, and save it as a text document with the filename Pack element size.htm.
   b. Select the text [replace with packbody class description] in the embedded style sheet, then press [Delete].
   c. Type .packbody {position: relative; left: 100px; width: 300px}
   d. Check your document for errors, make any necessary changes, then save Pack element size.htm as a text document.
   e. Open Pack element size.htm in your Web browser and scroll down to the pack descriptions.

4. **Stack screen elements.**
   a. Open the file HTML L-11.htm in your text editor, then save it as a text document with the filename Pack layers.htm.
   b. In the embedded style sheet, select the text [replace with backtext layer code], then press [Delete].
   c. Type #backtext {position: absolute; left: 275px; font-size: 64pt; font-family: arial; color: #7093DB; z-index: -1}
   d. Scroll and select the text [replace with background text], then press [Delete].
   e. Type <DIV ID="backtext"> and press [Enter].
   f. Type HIKING and press [Enter], then type </DIV>
   g. Check your document for errors, make any necessary changes, then save Pack layers.htm as a text document.
   h. Open Pack layers.htm in your Web browser.

5. Add a scroll bar.

  a. Open the file HTML L-12.htm in your text editor, and save it as a text document with the filename Pack scroll.htm.

  b. In the embedded style sheet, select the text [replace with list scroll code], then press [Delete].

  c. Type #list {height: 300px; width: 600px; overflow: auto}

  d. Scroll and select the text [replace with opening DIV tag], then press [Delete].

  e. Type <DIV ID="list">

  f. Scroll, and select the text [replace with closing DIV tag], press [Delete], then type </DIV>

  g. Check your document for errors, make any necessary changes, then save Pack scroll.htm as a text document.

  h. Open Pack scroll.htm in your Web browser, and scroll down to view the list of pack outlines and descriptions.

  i. Use the scroll bar for the list to view all of the pack descriptions.

6. Create a sidebar.

  a. Open the file HTML L-13.htm in your text editor, then save it as a text document with the filename Pack sidebar.htm.

  b. In the embedded style sheet, select the text [replace with sidebar code], then press [Delete].

  c. Type #sidebar {width: 350; float: right; position: absolute; left: 400px; font-family: arial; font-size: 11pt; background: #8FBC8F}

  d. Scroll and select the text [replace with ID], then press [Delete].

  e. Type ALIGN="left" ID="sidebar"

  f. Check your document for errors, make any necessary changes, then save Pack sidebar.htm as a text document.

  g. Open Pack sidebar.htm in your Web browser.

7. Incorporate an advanced positioning function.

  a. Open the file HTML L-14.htm in your text editor, then save a copy as Pack drag.htm.

  b. Scroll and select the text [replace with drag code] in the first image tag, then press [Delete].

  c. Type CLASS="drag" canDrag

  d. Repeat Steps b and c for the remaining five IMG tags.

  e. Check your document for errors, make any necessary changes, then save Tent drag.htm as a text document.

  f. Open Tent drag.htm in your Web browser.

  g. If you are using Internet Explorer, drag some of the water bottle and tent outlines onto a backpack outline.

▶ Independent Challenges

1. You are revising the Popular supplies page for the Green House plant store. You have incorporated positioning using style sheets to improve the appearance of the Web page and to make sure it displays similarly in different screen resolutions. Also, you have removed some of the features you added earlier to keep the page from overwhelming users with features. The owners would like to add additional information to the page about how to use it. You think this would fit best in a sidebar next to the headings.

To complete this independent challenge:

a. Open the file HTML L-15.htm in your text editor, then save a copy as "Green House supplies with sidebar.htm".

b. In the embedded style sheet, select the text [replace with #sidebar definition], then press [Delete].

c. Type #sidebar {position: relative; width: 25%; float: right; font-family: arial; font-size: 11pt; background: #8FBC8F}

d. Scroll down to the opening DIV tag for the sidebar text, select the text [replace with ID], then press [Delete].

e. Type ALIGN="left" ID="sidebar"

f. Check your document for errors and make any necessary changes, save Green house supplies with sidebar.htm as a text document and close it, then open it in your Web browser. If necessary, edit your code until the page displays appropriately.

2. You are adding CSS positioning information to the rider tips page for Sandhills Regional Public Transit. To superimpose part of the heading text on the logo graphic, you would like to rearrange the heading section.

To complete this independent challenge:

a. Open the file HTML L-16.htm in your Web browser, then explore the page.

b. Open the file HTML L-16.htm in your text editor, then save a copy as "SRPT positioned rider tips.htm".

c. Create an embedded style sheet, define a style in the embedded style sheet named #logo specifying absolute position, top at 25px, left at 25px, and z-index of -1, then scroll down to the opening DIV tag above the IMG tag for bus.jpg and replace the text [replace with ID] with ID="logo".

d. Define a style in the embedded style sheet named #headtop specifying absolute position, left at 30px, and top at 25px, then scroll down to the opening DIV tag for the first line of the page heading and replace the text [replace with ID] with ID="headtop".

e. Define a style in the embedded style sheet named #headbtm specifying absolute position, left at 60 px, and top at 325px, then scroll down to the opening DIV tag for the second line of the page heading and replace the text [replace with ID] with ID="headbtm".

f. Define a style in the embedded style sheet named #sidetext specifying absolute position, text floating on the right, left at 400px, top at 25px, and width of 350px, then scroll down to the opening DIV tag for the instructions section and replace the text [replace with ID] with ALIGN="left" ID="sidetext".

g. Add style code to the UL tag for the bulleted list specifying relative position and top at 0px.

h. Check your document for errors and make any necessary changes, save and close it, then open it in your Web browser. If necessary, edit your code until the page displays appropriately.

3. You are updating Web pages for the Community Public School Volunteers organization by adding CSS positioning information. You want to improve the layout by placing the CPSV logo graphic behind the heading text.
  To complete this independent challenge:

a. Explore the file HTML L-17.htm in your Web browser, then explore the file.

b. Open HTML L-17 in your text editor, then save a copy as "CPSV positioned home.htm".

c. Create a style in the embedded style sheet to place the new, widened logo (which is the colored letters CPSV) behind the heading text at the top of the page with absolute positioning. Use the left and top properties to position it so that it appears centered behind the text. (*Hint*: The heading is positioned relatively to allow it to be displayed in front of the logo in Navigator. Be sure to set a z-index for the logo to place it behind the text.) Reference the style you created in the opening DIV tag for the logo graphic, which is named cpsvlog3.jpg.

d. Create a style in the embedded style sheet for the DIV tagset enclosing the H3 heading and the links to narrow the width of the text area to 50% of the page width, position the section relatively, 25% to the left, change the background color to white (#FFFFFF), and add a 1pt black solid border (the style code for this feature is border: 1pt black solid). Reference the style you created in the opening DIV before the <H3> heading.

e. Save your changes, preview the page in your Web browser, and make any changes necessary to improve the appearance of the Web page.

4. The World Wide Web Consortium (W3C) has included a new set of positioning specifications in its revised Cascading Style Sheet guidelines, known as CSS2. Many of the new features that the W3C has outlined are supported in Microsoft and Netscape fifth-generation browsers. To complete this independent challenge, log on to the Internet, open your Web browser, and use a search engine to locate and open the Web site for the W3C. Locate information about the CSS2 guidelines, then print details of two new positioning features in CSS2. Write a paragraph on each feature, including what it allows a Web programmer to do and suggested syntax for implementing it. Check the Microsoft and Netscape Web sites to find out if their fifth-generation browsers will support either of the features you selected and include this information in your paragraphs. Submit your printout and paragraphs to your instructor.

▶ Visual Workshop

You are improving the layout of the Web pages for Touchstone Booksellers using CSS positioning. Using the file HTML L-18.htm as a starting point, position the heading elements to create the layout in Figure L-18. (*Hint*: Think of the text blocks on the left and right sides of the graphic as two floating sidebars. You should add code only to the two sidebar text blocks.) Save your changes as a text document with the filename Touchstone positioned home.htm.

FIGURE L-18

Touchstone Booksellers

Specializing in nonfiction of all types  *a locally-owned, independent bookstore since 1948*

You can use our Web site to search our current stock, place an order, request a search for an out-of-print book, or find out about upcoming events at our store.

- Search our stock

- Place an order

Implementing
Advanced DHTML Features

Objectives

► **Understand advanced features**
► **Filter content**
► **Scale content**
► **Animate element position**
► **Create 3D animation**
► **Transition elements**
► **Create a slideshow**
► **Transition between pages**

Using tools such as CSS, dynamic style, dynamic content, and CSS positioning, you can create interactive Web pages with print-quality formatting and layout. By combining these tools and writing scripts to work with them, you can continually create new features. The companies making browsers also continue to simplify the process by adding browser-native features that require little code and no scripting. Lydia Burgos's supervisor has asked her to create a Web-based presentation about Nomad Ltd. In addition to incorporating CSS formatting and positioning to make the page attractive and easy to read, she plans to add advanced effects to keep her users' interest.

Understanding Advanced Features

In addition to the many effects that the basic DHTML tools offer, you can create complex-looking visual features through a combination of proprietary effects and simple scripts. Although overuse of any dynamic feature can overload users visually and slow down their computers, the limited and precise use of these advanced features can help users focus on the most important aspects of each page. Many proprietary advanced features work only on Internet Explorer 4. However, these innovations will likely be supported by both fifth-generation browsers. Learning these features now is a good way to stay current with trends in Web page design. As Lydia organizes her presentation, she notes different advanced features that she can use for different effects.

 ### Modifying an element's appearance

In addition to basic color and sizing formatting for text and graphics alike, Internet Explorer offers predefined element formats that affect appearance in complex ways. These formats, known as **filters**, allow you to create many effects, such as a shadow or glow, as shown in Figure M-1. Another way to affect element appearance is by combining a script with CSS position or size information to create the effect of movement, or **animation**. By slowly changing an element's placement or size with a script, you can create the effect of movement without requiring special software or extensive system resources. To help ensure your page layouts remain attractive at different screen resolutions and browser window sizes, you also can include simple scripts to resize elements, depending on each user's browser size.

Open and close effects

You can effectively draw attention to a particular page element by scripting its appearance when the page opens. Internet Explorer offers predefined effects called **transitions**, which cause elements to appear gradually and in specific patterns when the page opens or exits. You can apply these effects to selected elements or to the entire page, as shown in Figure M-2. By using an animation script with offscreen starting coordinates and a timer, you can create **presentation effects** in which elements appear on the screen gradually and in a specific order.

Glow filter adds
colored halo to text

Nomad Ltd

Nomad Ltd
Corporate goals

MISSION

Our mission

Nomad Ltd is a national sporting goods
retailer dedicated to delivering high-quality
sporting gear and adventure travel.

Achieving our mission

Nomad Ltd has been in business
for over ten years. During that
time, we have offered tours all
over the world and sold sporting

Tour types:
Art
Leisure
Athlete

Graphic appearing
gradually using
"blend" transition

Nomad Ltd

Nomad Ltd
Corporate goals

MISSION

Our mission

Nomad Ltd is a national sporting goods
retailer dedicated to delivering high-quality
sporting gear and adventure travel.

Achieving our mission

Nomad Ltd has been in business
for over ten years. During that
time, we have offered tours all

Tour types:
Art
Leisure
Athlete

Earth graphic as it
appears at start of
load

Filtering Content

DHTML includes several tools that let you change the basic appearance of text and graphics by varying the size, color, and other characteristics of selected elements. In addition, Internet Explorer supports an extended set of properties, known as **filters**, that allow you to modify element appearance in complex ways. Table M-1 lists and describes the filters available in Internet Explorer 4. Lydia wants to call attention to headings in her presentation page without adding more colored text to the page, so she decides to try filtering the headings instead.

Steps

1. Start your text-editor program, open **HTML M-1.htm**, then save it as a text document with the filename **Presentation filter.htm**

2. Select the text **[replace with misshead filter code]** in the embedded style sheet, then press **[Delete]**

3. Type **{height: 14pt; filter: glow(color=#B8860B)}**
   To apply a filter using a DIV or SPAN tag, the text must be absolutely positioned or have a defined height or width. In order to meet this requirement without affecting her layout, Lydia sets the height to 14pt, which is the same height as the heading text.

4. Select the text **[replace with second filter code]** in the #achieve style definition, then press **[Delete]**

5. Type **height: 12pt; filter: glow(color=#B8860B, strength=3)**
   Because the font size in the second heading is smaller than in the first, Lydia decides to lower the intensity of the glow by assigning a strength value. This keeps the glow effect proportional to the text dimensions. Figure M-3 shows the completed code for the glow filters in the embedded style sheet.

6. Scroll down until the <H2> heading "Our mission" appears in the document window
   Lydia wants to apply the filter to the text within the H2 tags. However, filters are incompatible with all heading tags, so she has to embed the H2 tags within DIV tags and then call the filter from the opening DIV tag instead.

7. Type **<DIV ID="misshead">** before <H2> Our mission </H2>, then position the insertion point after the closing H2 tag and type **</DIV>**

8. Check your document for errors, make changes as necessary, then save **Presentation filter.htm** as a text document

9. Open **Presentation filter.htm** in your Web browser
   See Figure M-4, which shows the presentation Web page containing the filtered text. If you are using Internet Explorer 4, the filter adds a halo of color around each letter.

Combining filters

In addition to the unique effect that each filter can create on a Web page, you can increase the possibilities by combining filters, a process known as **chaining**. You can add as many filters as you desire to an element by simply listing them in the element's tag or style sheet description. You must separate the code for each filter by a space. For example, you can chain a drop shadow and a glow to a graphic by calling both of these filters in the picture's style sheet description as follows: **#image: {position: absolute; top: 150px; filter: dropshadow(color=#483D8B, OffX=3, OffY=3) glow(color=#9933CC, strength=5)}**. This code would add both drop shadow and glow effects to the graphic.

FIGURE M-3: Web document containing filter code

```
#heading {position: relative; left: 250px}
#mission {width: 375px; font-family: arial}
#misshead {height: 14pt; filter: glow(color=#B8860B)}
#main {position: absolute; left: 60px; width: 275px}
#earth {float: right; position: relative; top: -20px}
.norm {font-weight: normal}
#head1 {font-style: italic; color: #8E236B}
#head2 {font-style: italic; color: #6B8E23}
#head3 {font-style: italic; color: #7093DB}
#head4 {font-style: italic; color: #9400D3}
#achieve {height: 12pt; filter: glow(color=#B8860B, strength=3)}
.font12 {font-size: 12pt}
.bot {color: #3232CD}
.space {line-height: 6pt; position: relative}
.item {position: relative; left: 10px; font-size: 10pt; font-weight: bold}
UL {position: relative; left: -20px; top: -20px; font-size: 10pt; font-
weight: bold}
.sidebar {float: right; position: absolute; left: 375px; font-family: arial;
width: 200px}
</STYLE>

</HEAD>

<BODY BACKGROUND="Egg shell.jpg">

<DIV ID="logo">
```

Style code to add filter effect to text

FIGURE M-4: Web page displaying filtered text

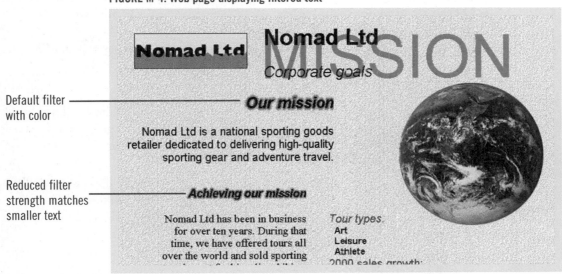

Default filter with color

Reduced filter strength matches smaller text

TABLE M-1: Internet Explorer 4 filter effects

filter effect	description	filter effect	description
Alpha	Sets a transparency level	Grayscale	Drops color information from the image
Blur	Creates the impression of moving at high speed	Invert	Reverses the hue, saturation, and brightness values
Chroma	Makes a specific color transparent	Light	Projects light sources onto an object
Drop Shadow	Creates an offset solid silhouette	Mask	Creates a transparent mask from an object
FlipH	Creates a horizontal mirror image	Shadow	Creates a solid silhouette of the object
FlipV	Creates a vertical mirror image	Wave	Creates a sine wave distortion along the x- and y-axes
Glow	Adds radiance around the outside edges of the object	XRay	Shows just the edges of the object

Scaling Content

One drawback of using basic DHTML positioning is a layout's reliance on a particular window size. For example, an image may fit well in a layout at a certain indentation in a maximized browser window on an SVGA screen. However, on a lower-resolution monitor or on a non-maximized browser window, the element may appear much closer to the right edge of the screen, thus changing the original layout design. Using basic scripts to complement CSS-P, however, you can automatically adjust the position of your Web page elements based on the browser window size. Because Navigator does not recognize changes in style properties (including element dimensions) after the page has loaded, this feature works only in Internet Explorer. Lydia has laid out her page in a maximized browser window set at a resolution of 800 × 600. However, she wants her layout to remain as consistent as possible in smaller windows and at lower resolutions.

Steps

1. Open **HTML M-2.htm** in your text editor, then save it as a text document with the file-name **Presentation scale.htm**

2. Scroll down to the script tags in the page's head section, select the text **[replace with scale script]**, then press **[Delete]**

   Lydia has already inserted a browser-detection script, along with a line of code to suppress errors in Navigator.

3. Type the following script, pressing **[Enter]** at the end of each line:

```
function change() {
        if (document.body.clientWidth < 640) {
                bgword.style.fontSize="48pt"
                earth.style.width="25%"
        }
        else {
                bgword.style.fontSize="64pt"
                earth.style.width="35%"
        }
}


window.onresize=change
window.onload=change
```

   Instead of trying to adjust every screen element to fit on a smaller screen, Lydia focuses on the elements along the right edge of the screen: the heading background text and the earth graphic. Her script adjusts both elements to a size that fits into a maximized browser window set at a 640 × 480 resolution. Figure M-5 shows the Web page document code containing the script.

4. Check your document for errors, make changes as necessary, then save **Presentation scale.htm** as a text document

5. Open **Presentation scale.htm** in your Web browser, then make sure your browser window is maximized

6. If you are using Internet Explorer and your display mode is 800 × 600 or greater, click the **Restore Window button** 🗗 at the top right of the browser window to decrease the size of the document window a fixed amount

   If your display is in 640 × 480 mode, note that the large background text and the earth graphic fit on the screen without requiring you to scroll right. Figure M-6 shows the presentation Web page in a reduced window. The scale script you inserted reduced the background text size and the graphic size to fit better in a limited display area.

FIGURE M-5: Web page document code containing scaling script

Script to resize elements based on window size

```
<SCRIPT LANGUAGE="javascript">
<!--
Nav4 = (document.layers) ? 1:0;
IE4 = (document.all) ? 1:0;

if(!IE4) {window.onerror=null}

function change() {
        if (document.body.clientWidth < 640) {
                bgword.style.fontSize="48pt"
                earth.style.width="25%"
        }
        else {
                bgword.style.fontSize="64pt"
                earth.style.width="35%"
        }
}

window.onresize=change
window.onload=change
//-->
</SCRIPT>

</HEAD>

<BODY BACKGROUND="Egg shell.jpg">
```

FIGURE M-6: Scaled objects in reduced browser window

Browser window size reduced from maximized view

Reduced text and graphic sizes fit in window

Scaling by percent

Specifying element dimensions in percentages, rather than pixels or points, has many applications in DHTML design. Usually, you can simply specify the height, width, or font size in percent. Because percentage measurements reflect a percentage of the parent element dimension, a percentage-sized element automatically resizes when the window size changes. To make sure the element remains proportionally scaled when specifying element dimensions, be sure to specify only height or width, but not both. Sometimes, screen elements need to change position depending on the screen size or when an element such as a graphic would look distorted if it became too big or too small. In these cases, you need a scaling script to resize your pages.

HTML

Animating Element Position

By creating simple scripts to interact with position and layer information, you can add impressive features to your Web pages without requiring extensive system resources on a user's computer. To create basic animation, for example, you can script an element's position coordinates to increase or decrease slowly when the user first opens the page, until the element reaches its final, absolute coordinates. ▰▰▰ Lydia decides to animate the Nomad Ltd logo to move into place when a user first opens the page.

Steps

1. Open the file **HTML M-3.htm** in your text editor, then save it as a text document with the filename **Presentation position animate.htm**

2. Scroll down to the **function slide()** in the head section and examine the script
   The function slide() positions the logo graphic out of screen range on the right side of the page and then incrementally reduces its left coordinate until it reaches the final position of 30. Lydia also has changed the left coordinate for the #logo style to -1000, a value that triggers the slide() function.

3. Scroll down to the opening BODY tag, select the text **[replace with event handler]**, then press **[Delete]**

4. Type **onLoad="slide()"**
   The onLoad event handler triggers the "slide" script every time the browser loads the BODY section. Figure M-7 shows the code for the event handler to call the slide() function.

5. Check your document for errors, make any necessary changes, then save **Presentation position animate.htm** as a text file

6. Open **Presentation position animate.htm** in your Web browser
   As Figure M-8 shows, the graphic slides into position from the right edge of the window after you open the page. Because Navigator can't change a page's style information after loading, it does not display the logo in its final location.

FIGURE M-7: Web document showing code to call slide() function

Slide function in page head

```
window.onresize=change
window.onload=change

function slide() {
      var pic = document.all.logo;
      if (-1000 == pic.style.pixelLeft) {
             pic.style.pixelLeft = document.body.offsetWidth +
document.body.scrollLeft;
      }
      if (50 <= pic.style.pixelLeft) {
             pic.style.pixelLeft -= 20;
             setTimeout("slide();", 50);
      }
      else {pic.style.pixelLeft =30;}
}
//-->
</SCRIPT>

</HEAD>

<BODY BACKGROUND="Egg shell.jpg" onLoad="slide()">

<DIV ID="logo">
<IMG SRC="nomad.jpg">
</DIV>
```

Event handler triggers slide script when page opens

FIGURE M-8: Nomad Ltd logo sliding into position

Nomad Ltd logo sliding right to left into final position

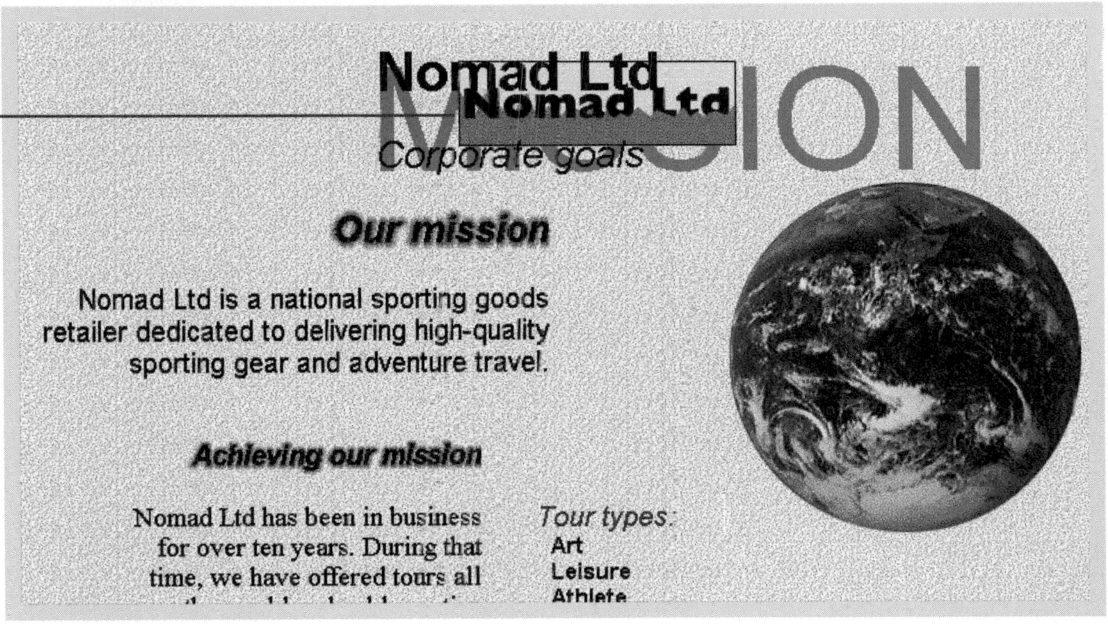

Creating 3D Animation

You can easily create simple animation on your Web pages with a script that slowly adjusts an element's top or left attribute over a period of time. By incorporating changes in element size, using the width and height properties, you also can create the illusion of 3D movement. Although animation in standard multimedia formats can require special software or browser extensions and significant computer memory, DHTML animation creates the effect of movement using just one image and a small script running on the user's browser. A lot of animation could distract users from the rest of your Web page, but a short animation, or animation of a small element, can make a page interesting and distinctive. ▰▰▰ Lydia decides that instead of having the Nomad Ltd logo graphic move into position sideways, she would like the earth graphic to appear to approach the user. She creates this effect with 3D animation.

Steps

1. Open the file **HTML M-4.htm** in your text editor, save it as a text document with the filename **Presentation 3D animate.htm**

QuickTip
You can use a semicolon to mark the end of a line of code in JavaScript. The semicolon is not required at the end of a line, and it is often used only after short commands in a script.

2. Scroll down and select the text **[replace with 3D animation script]** in the page's head section, press **[Delete]**, then type the following script, pressing **[Enter]** at the end of each line:

```
function grow() {
    if (earthpic.width<250) {
            x=window.setTimeout('grow()', 100)
            earthpic.width=earthpic.width + 10
    }
}

window.onload = grow;
```

Figure M-9 shows the Web page code containing the script. The script uses the graphic's HTML width property, rather than the CSS width, because HTML width is easier to work with in this situation. Lydia has deleted the logo animation script.

3. Scroll down to the IMG tag for the earth graphic, and replace the text **[replace with width property]** with **WIDTH=0**
The script you entered increases the width value by 10 pixels at a time and pauses for a fraction of a second between each increase, which creates the illusion of animation.

4. Check your document for errors, make any necessary changes, then save **Presentation 3D animate.htm** as a text document

5. Open **Presentation 3D animate.htm** in your Web browser
Figure M-10 shows the page as it is loading. As the page loads, the earth graphic appears and slowly grows as it seems to move toward you.

FIGURE M-9: Web document containing grow script

3D animation script
for earth graphic ⎯⎯

```
window.onload=change

function grow() {
        if (earthpic.width<250) {
                x=window.setTimeout('grow()', 100)
                earthpic.width=earthpic.width + 10
        }
}

window.onload = grow;
//-->
</SCRIPT>

</HEAD>

<BODY BACKGROUND="Egg shell.jpg">

<DIV ID="logo">
<IMG SRC="nomad.jpg">
</DIV>

<DIV ID="bgword">
MISSION
</DIV>

<DIV ID="heading">
```

FIGURE M-10: 3D animation of earth graphic

Gradual size
increase on load
creates illusion of
earth approaching

Animated GIFs

Another popular way to create animation in Web pages is to create **animated GIFs**. A GIF is a graphic file in a specific format. Although most GIFs are static, showing just one image, the GIF format also supports animation. To create an animated GIF, you use special software to combine two or more static graphics and to specify the delay between the display of each frame. You can create a movie-like movement effect with animated GIFs, but one of their most widespread uses on the Web today is in banner advertisements on Web pages. These static GIFs often alternate between two different frames of information, such as an advertising motto and the company logo. Although DHTML animation is easier and cheaper to create, animated GIFs are not limited to fourth-generation browsers and are thus accessible by a wider Web audience.

HTML

Transitioning Elements

Beyond simply hiding and showing an element, or applying filters to an element's display, you can affect the way an element becomes visible or hidden by using filter effects known as **transitions**. For example, one popular transition effect is to make an element appear or disappear gradually in a checkerboard pattern. Because Navigator does not recognize transitions, this feature works only with Internet Explorer. Internet Explorer 4 comes with two transition filters: **blend**, which creates a simple fade-in or fade-out effect, and **reveal**, which allows the more complex filtering effects. These effects, which can be applied to text as well as graphics, can keep a user's interest and distinguish your pages from others on the Web. ◄▬▬▬ Lydia decides to use the blend transition on the Nomad Ltd logo when the page opens.

Steps 1 2 3 4

1. Open the file **HTML M-5.htm** in your text editor, then save it as a text document with the filename **Presentation transition element.htm**

2. Select and replace the text **[replace with style information]** which is in the #logo style specification in the page's embedded style sheet with **visibility: hidden; filter: blendTrans(duration=7)**
   The blend transition can switch from hidden to visible or vice versa. Lydia specifies that she wants the graphic to start out hidden and then become visible using the blendTrans filter. The duration variable details the length of time in seconds of the transition from beginning to end.

3. Scroll down to the end of the page's head section, then replace the text **[replace with transition function]** with the following script, pressing **[Enter]** at the end of each line:
   ```
   function doTrans() {
        logo.filters.blendTrans.Apply();
        logo.style.visibility="visible";
        logo.filters.blendTrans.Play();
   }
   ```
   Unlike standard filters, transition filters require scripts to define what happens when they run. The first line of the doTrans() function calls the transition's Apply method, which creates the final state defined in the next line, which is "visible." Finally, the Play method starts the transition filter itself to create the smooth change from hidden to visible. Figure M-11 shows the Web document code containing the function.

4. Scroll to the bottom of the document just before the closing page tags, delete the text **[replace with function call]**, insert opening and closing script tags, and type **doTrans()** as the body of the script
   This script, shown in Figure M-12, calls the doTrans() function when the page finishes loading in the browser window.

5. Check your document for errors and make any necessary changes, then save **Presentation transition element.htm** as a text document

Trouble?

If the logo does not appear gradually, your video card or monitor is probably not compatible with transitions.

6. Open **Presentation transition element.htm** in your Web browser
   As Figure M-13 shows, the Nomad Ltd logo slowly fades into view as the page opens.

FIGURE M-11: Document code containing function

```
window.onload = grow;

function doTrans() {
      logo.filters.blendTrans.Apply();
      logo.style.visibility="visible";
      logo.filters.blendTrans.Play();
}
//-->
</SCRIPT>

</HEAD>
```

Function controlling transition effect

FIGURE M-12: Document code containing script to call function

```
<DIV>For more information on Nomad Ltd, please email our <A
HREF="MAILTO:relations@nomadltd.com">community relations
department</A>.</DIV>

</DIV>

<SCRIPT LANGUAGE="javascript">
<!--
doTrans()
//-->
</SCRIPT>

</BODY>
</HTML>
```

Script triggers doTrans() function after page loads

FIGURE M-13: Nomad Ltd logo showing blend transition

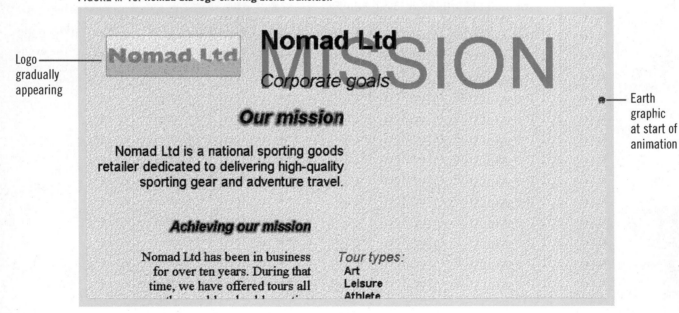

Logo gradually appearing

Earth graphic at start of animation

HTML

Creating a Slideshow

Presentation software, such as Microsoft PowerPoint, allows you to move through a related set of pages, or **slides**, by clicking a mouse button. It is easy to add this effect to Web pages with scripting. Although standard HTML hyperlinks can create a similar effect, DHTML features enable your users to advance by clicking anywhere on the page, rather than scrolling to locate and click a hyperlink. Also, by eliminating navigation-specific elements, you can keep your pages focused on the presentation topic and create a more unified design. Lydia has created the second page for her Web presentation. She wants to script the first page to open the second in response to a mouse click, which will allow Internet Explorer users to click anywhere on the Web page to advance to the second Web page.

Steps

1. Open the file **HTML M-6.htm** in your text editor, then save it as a text document with the filename **Presentation slideshow.htm**

2. Scroll down to the opening BODY tag, select and replace the text **[replace with event handler]** with **onClick="window.location.href='Presentation page 2.htm'"**
   This event handler changes the window's HREF, or page address, to "Presentation page 2.htm," the second page that Lydia prepared.

3. Scroll down below the text "Corporate goals," then select and replace the text **[replace with instruction text]** with the following script, pressing **[Enter]** at the end of each line:
   <DIV ID="instr">
   Click anywhere to advance to next slide.
   </DIV>
   This text tells users how to navigate through the presentation. Figure M-14 shows the Web page code containing the event handler and the instruction text. Lydia has already added an embedded style for the instructions and has edited the scaling code to reposition the text in smaller window sizes.

4. Check your document for errors, make any necessary changes, then save **Presentation slideshow.htm** as a text document

5. Open **Presentation slideshow.htm** in your Web browser, then click anywhere on the page
   The second presentation page opens, as shown in Figure M-15. By simply adding the event handler to all presentation pages except for the last one, Lydia can enable users to easily page through the presentation online.

Event handler
allows easy
navigation to
second page

Navigation
instructions

```
</HEAD>

<BODY BACKGROUND="Egg shell.jpg" onClick="window.location.href='Presentation
page 2.htm'">

<DIV ID="logo">
<IMG SRC="nomad.jpg">
</DIV>

<DIV ID="bgword">
MISSION
</DIV>

<DIV ID="heading">
<H1>Nomad Ltd</H1>
<H2 CLASS="norm">Corporate goals</H2>
</DIV>

<DIV ID="instr">
Click anywhere to advance to next slide.
</DIV>

<DIV ID="earth">
<IMG SRC="earth.jpg" ID="earthpic" WIDTH=0>
</DIV>
```

FIGURE M-15: Second presentation page

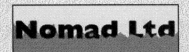

Nomad Ltd
Corporate beginnings

HISTORY

Where we came from

Jasper Barber started Nomad Ltd in 1987 as a single store in Boulder, Colorado, a popular area for many types of outdoor recreation. Jasper set out to create a store offering affordable, high-quality outdoor supplies. After opening two more stores in Colorado, Jasper began to expand Nomad Ltd nationally. In 1991 we introduced the Nomad line of outdoor equipment, and 1993 saw

HTML

Transitioning Between Pages

In addition to creating transition effects for specific elements on a Web page, you can apply transitions when opening or closing a page. In this situation, transitions can grab and hold a viewer's attention, and can help your page to stand out among pages a user has recently seen. Each Web page can trigger transitions upon opening and exiting, independent of the preceding or following page. ◄▬▬ As a final touch, Lydia decides she wants Internet Explorer 4 users to see a closing transition to each of the pages in her Web presentation. She starts by adding a closing transition that appears when the first page closes.

Steps 1 2 3 4

1. Open the file **HTML M-7.htm** in your text editor, then save it as a text document with the filename **Presentation page transition.htm**

2. Scroll down below the embedded style sheet in the page's head section and replace the text **[replace with META tag]** with **<META http-equiv="Page-Exit" CONTENT="RevealTrans(Duration=5,Transition=3)">**
   Figure M-16 shows the Web page code containing the META tag. Creating an interpage transition requires no scripting. Instead, you insert an HTML META tag in the page's head section, calling the transition and defining its properties. You can set the http-equiv property, which tells when the transition takes effect, to "Page-Enter" or "Page-Exit." You use the CONTENT property to specify the transition filter name and parameters, just as you do with the STYLE property for element transitions. Lydia uses the reveal transition's "Circle out" pattern, indicated by the Transition number 3. Table M-2 lists other reveal transitions and their number codes.

3. Check your document for errors, make any necessary changes, then save **Presentation page transition.htm** as a text document

Trouble?

Depending on your computer speed, you may see a small white circle in the center of the screen just before the transition starts.

4. Open **Presentation page transition.htm** in your Web browser, then click anywhere on the page
   The second presentation page opens in a circle spreading outward from the center of the browser window, as shown in Figure M-17. You can apply other transition patterns, as listed in Table M-2, to open or close pages.

5. Make and save changes in your text-editor program as needed, check changes in your Web browser program, close your Web browser program, then close your text editor program

FIGURE M-16: Web page code containing META tag

META tag inserted to control interpage transition

```
.sidebar {float: right; position: absolute; left: 375px; font-family: arial;
width: 200px}
</STYLE>

<META http-equiv="Page-Exit" CONTENT="RevealTrans(Duration=5,Transition=3)">

<SCRIPT LANGUAGE="javascript">
<!--
Nav4 = (document.layers) ? 1:0;
IE4 = (document.all) ? 1:0;

if(!IE4) {window.onerror=null}

function change() {
        if (document.body.clientWidth < 640) {
                bgword.style.fontSize="48pt"
                earth.style.width="25%"
        }
        else {
                bgword.style.fontSize="64pt"
                earth.style.width="35%"
        }
}

window.onresize=change
window.onload=change
```

FIGURE M-17: Web page closing with "Circle out" reveal transition

First presentation page

Second presentation page opening outward in circle

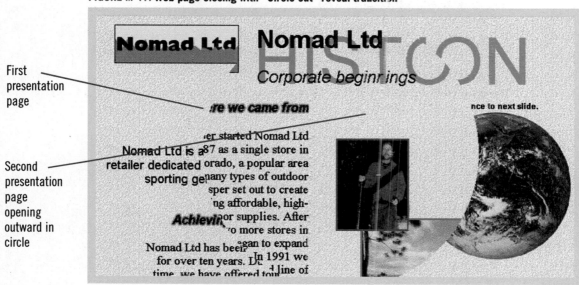

TABLE M-2: Reveal transition effects

reveal transition name	value	reveal transition name	value	reveal transition name	value
Box in	0	Vertical blinds	8	Split horizontal out	16
Box out	1	Horizontal blinds	9	Strips left down	17
Circle in	2	Checkerboard across	10	Strips left up	18
Circle out	3	Checkerboard down	11	Strips right down	19
Wipe up	4	Random dissolve	12	Strips right up	20
Wipe down	5	Split vertical in	13	Random bars horizontal	21
Wipe right	6	Split vertical out	14	Random bars vertical	22
Wipe left	7	Split horizontal in	15	Random	23

Practice

► Concepts Review

Label the advanced DHTML effects indicated on Lydia's Web page in Figure M-18.

FIGURE M-18

Match each term with its description.

4. Filter

5. Position animation

6. 3D animation

7. Transition

8. Scaling

a. Gradually changes element size, using the width and height properties

b. Gradually changes element appearance, becoming visible or hidden

c. Gradually changes element position, using top and left style properties

d. Fits page elements to lower screen resolution or smaller window size

e. Property that modifies element appearance in complex ways

Select the best answer from the list of choices.

9. You can continually create new advanced DHTML features by combining basic features with
   a. CSS.
   b. Dynamic style.
   c. Dynamic content.
   d. Scripts.

10. Which of the following is *not* a filter?
    a. Shadow
    b. Blur
    c. Animation
    d. Blend transition

11. What is the advantage of using DHTML animation rather than other animation methods on the Web?
    a. DHTML animation doesn't require scripts.
    b. DHTML animation uses few system resources.
    c. DHTML animation uses special software.
    d. DHTML animation uses no system resources.

12. Which method will *not* change an element's appearance over a period of time?
    a. Position animation
    b. 3D animation
    c. Glow filter
    d. Blend transition filter

13. Which HTML tag do you use to implement an interpage transition?
    a. <LINK>
    b. <META>
    c. <A>
    d. <SCRIPT>

14. Which is an advantage of using animated GIFs rather than DHTML animation?
    a. Animated GIFs use no system resources.
    b. Animated GIF display is not limited to fourth-generation browsers.
    c. Creating animated GIFs requires no special software.
    d. Animated GIFs can show 3D animation.

Skills Review

1. **Filter content.**
   a. Open HTML M-8.htm in your Web browser and explore the page.
   b. Open HTML M-8.htm in your text editor and save a copy as Tours filter.htm.
   c. In the embedded style sheet, select the text [replace with histhead filter code], then press [Delete].
   d. Type height: 14pt; filter: glow(color=#6B8E23)
   e. Select the text [replace with second filter code] in the #tourshead style definition, then press [Delete].
   f. Type height: 12pt; filter: glow(color=#6B8E23, strength=3)
   g. Check your document for errors, make changes as necessary, then save Tours filter.htm.
   h. Open Tours filter.htm in your Web browser.

2. **Scale content.**
   a. Open HTML M-9.htm in your text editor, then save a copy as Tours scale.htm.
   b. Select the text [replace with scale script], then press [Delete].
   c. Enter the opening tags for a JavaScript script, then type the following script, pressing [Enter] at the end of each line:

   ```
   function change() {
           if (document.body.clientWidth < 640) {
                   bgword.style.fontSize="48pt"
           }
           else {
                   bgword.style.fontSize="64pt"
           }
   }

   window.onresize=change
   window.onload=change
   ```
   d. Enter the closing script tags, check your document for errors, make changes as necessary, then save Tours scale.htm.
   e. Open Tours scale.htm in your Web browser, then click the Restore Window button to decrease the size of the document window a fixed amount and note the changes to the background text in the heading. If necessary, drag the right edge of the window to the left to decrease the screen width until the change takes place.
   f. Click the browser maximize button.

3. **Animate element position.**
   a. Open the file HTML M-10.htm in your text editor, then save it as a text document with the filename Tours position animate.htm.
   b. Scroll down to the opening BODY tag, select the text [replace with event handler], then press [Delete].
   c. Type onLoad="slide()"
   d. Check your document for errors, make any necessary changes, then save as Tours position animate.htm.
   e. Open Tours position animate.htm in your Web browser.

4. **Create 3D animation.**

   a. Open the file HTML M-11.htm in your text editor, then save it as a text document with the filename Tours 3D animate.htm.

   b. Select the text [replace with 3D animation script] in the page's head section, press [Delete], then type the following script, pressing [Enter] at the end of each line:

   ```
   function grow() {
           if (mtnpic.width<180) {
                   x=window.setTimeout('grow()', 100)
                   mtnpic.width=mtnpic.width + 10
           }
   }
   ```

   c. In the BODY tag, delete the text [replace with event handler], and type onLoad="grow()"

   d. Scroll down to the IMG tag for the mountain graphic and replace the text [replace with width setting] with WIDTH=0

   e. Check your document for errors, make any necessary changes, then save as Tours 3D animate.htm.

   f. Open Tours 3D animate.htm in your Web browser.

5. **Use transition elements.**

   a. Open the file HTML M-12.htm in your text editor, then save a copy as Tours transition element.htm.

   b. In the #logo style specification in the page's embedded style sheet, replace the text [replace with style information] with visibility: hidden; filter: revealTrans(Transition=12, Duration=5)

   c. Scroll down to the end of the page's head section and replace the text [replace with transition function] with the following, pressing [Enter] at the end of each line:

   ```
   function doTrans() {
           logo.filters.revealTrans.Apply();
           logo.style.visibility="visible";
           logo.filters.revealTrans.Play();
   }
   ```

   d. Scroll to the bottom of the document just before the closing page tags, delete the text [replace with function call], insert opening and closing script tags, and type doTrans() as the body of the script.

   e. Check your document for errors, make any necessary changes, then save as Tours transition element.htm.

   f. Open Tours transition element.htm in your Web browser.

6. **Create a slideshow.**

   a. Open the file HTML M-13.htm in your text editor, then save it as a text document with the filename Tours slideshow.htm.

   b. Scroll down to the opening BODY tag and replace the text [replace with event handler] with onClick="window.location.href='Tours page 2.htm'"

   c. Scroll down below the text "Tours division", select and replace the text [replace with instruction text] with the following script, pressing [Enter] at the end of each line:

   ```
   <DIV ID="instr">
   Click anywhere to advance to next slide.
   </DIV>
   ```

   d. Check your document for errors, make any necessary changes, then save Tours slideshow.htm.

   e. Open Tours slideshow.htm in your Web browser, then click anywhere on the page.

7. Transition between pages.

a. Open the file HTML M-14.htm in your text editor, then save a copy as Tours page transition.htm.

b. Scroll down below the embedded style sheet in the page's head section and replace the text [replace with META tag] with the following: <META http-equiv="Page-Exit" CONTENT="RevealTrans(Duration=5,Transition=10)">

c. Check your document for errors, make any necessary changes, then save as Tours page transition.htm.

d. Open Tours page transition.htm in your Web browser, then click anywhere on the page.

► Independent Challenges

1. The owners of the Green House plant store have seen transition filters in use on other Web pages and think this effect would make their pages more interesting. You decide to add the "random dissolve" reveal transition to the secondary heading on the "Popular supplies" page.

To complete this independent challenge:

a. Open the file HTML M-15.htm in your text editor, then save it as a text document with the filename Green House transition.htm.

b. Add the following style to the embedded style sheet in the page's head section:
#subhead {visibility: hidden; height: 16pt; filter: revealTrans(Transition=12, Duration=5)}.

c. Scroll down to the end of the page's head section and replace the text [replace with transition function] with the following script, pressing [Enter] at the end of each line. Be sure to include opening and closing script tags.
function doTrans() {
        subhead.filters.revealTrans.Apply();
        subhead.style.visibility="visible";
        subhead.filters.revealTrans.Play();
}

d. In the opening BODY tag, replace the text [replace with function call] with onLoad="doTrans()".

e. Check your document for errors, make any necessary changes, then save Green House transition.htm.

f. Open Green House transition.htm in your Web browser and verify that the subhead text appears slowly, in a random dissolve pattern.

2. You've long wanted to add an animated bus graphic to the home page you created for Sandhills Regional Public Transit (SRPT). Now that you know how to animate the position of Web page objects, you want to script this feature at the top of each SRPT Web page.

To complete this independent challenge:

a. Open the file HTML M-16.htm in your text editor, then save it as a text document with the filename SRPT animated.htm.

b. To create space at the top of the page and to avoid overlapping elements, change the "top" values in the embedded style sheet for the following styles to the values indicated:
#bus: 75px
#head1: 60px
#head2: 300px
#instr: 75px

c. Add the following entry to the embedded style sheet for the moving graphic:
#move {position: absolute; left: -1000px}

d. You have already inserted the slide() function for this task. Look at the script in the page's HEAD section, noting the differences from the one you used in this unit. Try to predict how this script will behave differently, if at all.

e. Add the following event handler to the opening BODY tag:
onLoad="slide()"

f. Add the following IMG tag for the moving bus graphic immediately after the page's opening BODY tag:
<IMG SRC="busmove.jpg" ID="move">

g. Check your document for errors, then save SRPT animated.htm.

h. Open SRPT animated.htm in your Web browser and verify that the new bus graphic moves across the page without overlapping other elements.

3. The public-relations coordinator of Community Public School Volunteers wants to make sure the organization's Web page has an appealing layout, regardless of the computer's screen resolution or window size. Rather than using a scaling script, however, you decide to specify element dimensions in percentages to ensure uniform appearance.
   To complete this independent challenge:

a. Open the file HTML M-17.htm in your text editor, then save it as a text document with the filename CPSV scale.htm.

b. In the #logo definition in the page's embedded style sheet, set the width value to 90%.

c. In the #box definition, change the width value to 75% and the left value to 12.5% (these settings ensure that the box is centered at any window size).

d. In the #instr definition, change the left value to 5% and the width value to 90% (these settings ensure that the text is centered in the box).

e. Check your changes, then save as CPSV scale.htm.

f. Preview CPSV scale.htm in your Web browser, then use your text editor to make any necessary changes, as well as any positioning and sizing changes that you think would improve the page's layout.

4. In addition to the filters and transitions that you've used in this unit, Internet Explorer 4 and 5 offer large selections of each of these features. To complete this independent challenge, connect to the Internet and locate a Web page that explains specific filters and transitions in detail. You can find this information on the Microsoft Web site, as well as on other DHTML sites. Find and print information on one standard filter and one Reveal transition filter that you have not used before. Make sure the information you print includes the name of the filter, the syntax for using it in your style specifications, and an explanation of any special parameters that it allows you to set. Then create a simple Web page named Unit M IC 4.htm, which contains one element. Apply the standard filter to the element and apply the Reveal transition filter to the page exit. Submit the printouts from your research and your file containing the filter and transition to your instructor.

► Visual Workshop

The owner of Touchstone Booksellers would like users to see an interesting effect when they first view his page. You decide to try an interpage transition that takes effect when the page opens. Save a copy of the file HTML M-18.htm as Touchstone transition.htm. Insert the necessary code to add the "Random bars vertical" transition, shown in Figure M-19. Use Table M-2 to look up the Transition value for this effect. The http-equiv value for this transition should be "Page-Enter" for the transition to occur as the page first loads. To test your changes, save your file, then open the file "Touchstone open.htm" in your Web browser, and click the link "Touchstone home page" to open the page you created.

FIGURE M-19

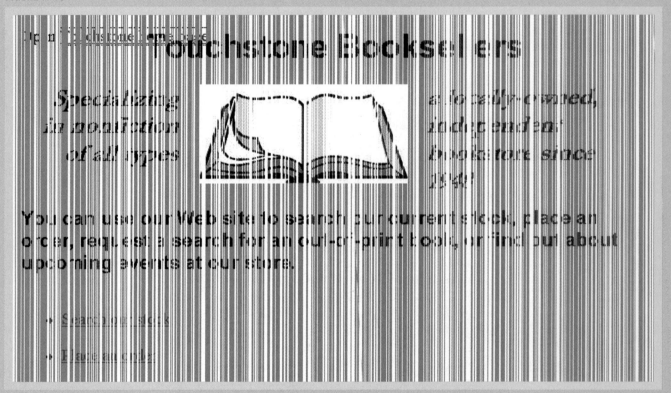

Structuring
Data with XML

Objectives

- ► **Understand eXtensible Markup Language (XML)**
- ► **Define XML elements and structure**
- ► **Enter XML data**
- ► **Bind XML data to HTML**
- ► **Format XML data with HTML**
- ► **Display XML data with HTML**
- ► **Modify an XML document**
- ► **Alter XML data view with HTML**

HTML has evolved from a way of structuring information into a language for controlling the format, or display, of Web content. With the vast growth of data on the Web, and the creation of many new applications, it has become critical to have a standard but expandable means to define, structure, and exchange the data on the Web. The **eXtensible Markup Language (XML)** is designed to ensure a **universal data structure** that can be read by any XML-compliant browser yet still allow Web designers the freedom to create **custom data definitions** for an endless variety of applications (e.g., a book or movie database). Lydia would like to create a "Recommended Backpacking Books" page for backpacking enthusiasts on the Nomad Web site. The HTML page will display book data she stores using XML and custom data definitions.

Understanding eXtensible Markup Language (XML)

XML (eXtensible Markup Language) is a text-based syntax especially designed to describe, deliver, and exchange structured data. XML documents use the file extension .xml and, like HTML files, can be created with a simple text editor. XML is not meant as a replacement for HTML but, rather, as a means to vastly extend its descriptive and structural power. XML uses a syntax that is similar to HTML, with four basic differences. These rules guarantee that a document is well-formed. A **well-formed** document requires that data be uniformly structured by tagsets so it can be read correctly by any XML-compliant program. Lydia is new to using XML, so she researches the language before starting to create the backpacking book list. To understand how the syntax of XML differs from HTML, Lydia examines each XML syntax rule carefully.

Details

 ### All elements must have start and end tags

An **element** consists of the start tag and corresponding end tag along with the content between the tagset. Unlike HTML, where you can mark up a document without using some closing tags (e.g., </P>), XML requires that both opening and closing tags be present. For example, the first line in Figure N-1 shows the correct way to code XML with both the start and end paragraph tags necessary to create a well-formed XML document. The same line in Figure N-2 lacks the required closing "</P>" tag, and thus violates the first rule of XML syntax.

 ### All elements must be nested correctly

Just as in HTML, when writing XML, you should close first whatever tagset you opened last. However, you cannot overlap elements in XML. The second line of code in Figure N-1 shows the heading tagset "<H2></H2>" correctly nested inside of the paragraph tagset "<P></P>." The same line in Figure N-2 breaks this rule by placing the closing "</H2>" tag after the end paragraph tag "</P>." Although this code would display properly in HTML, it is not well-formed and would not display in XML because of the inherent stricter rule enforcement.

 ### All attribute values must appear with quotation marks

HTML requires that only certain attribute values, such as URLs and strings, be in quotes. Values such as image and font size may be used without quotes. In XML, attributes must appear in quotes. The third line of code in Figure N-1 illustrates the proper way to code by quoting the font size attribute value "16," whereas the same line in Figure N-2 shows the font attribute value without quotes and, thus, wrongly marked up for XML.

 ### All empty elements must be self-identifying by ending with "/>"

An **empty element** is one that doesn't have a closing tag (e.g., <BR>, <HR>, and <IMG> in HTML). The last tag on the fourth line of code in Figure N-1 demonstrates the proper way to identify an empty element in XML by ending it with "/>." This forward slash at the end of the tag indicates that the element, or container, is not broken (i.e., missing a closing tag) but simply empty. The same tag in Figure N-2 does not contain the necessary ending slash and, hence, would prevent an XML document from being well-formed.

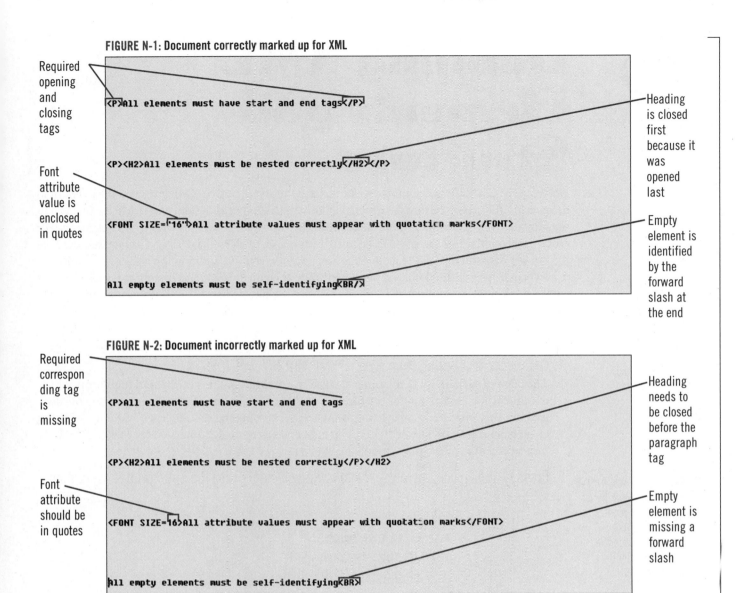

FIGURE N-1: Document correctly marked up for XML

Required opening and closing tags

`<P>All elements must have start and end tags</P>`

Heading is closed first because it was opened last

`<P><H2>All elements must be nested correctly</H2></P>`

Font attribute value is enclosed in quotes

`<FONT SIZE="16">All attribute values must appear with quotation marks</FONT>`

Empty element is identified by the forward slash at the end

`All empty elements must be self-identifying<BR/>`

FIGURE N-2: Document incorrectly marked up for XML

Required corresponding tag is missing

`<P>All elements must have start and end tags`

Heading needs to be closed before the paragraph tag

`<P><H2>All elements must be nested correctly</P></H2>`

Font attribute should be in quotes

`<FONT SIZE=16>All attribute values must appear with quotation marks</FONT>`

Empty element is missing a forward slash

`All empty elements must be self-identifying<BR>`

CLUES TO USE

Benefits of XML

With XML, it is possible to identify data in meaningful ways, much like a database lets you identify and organize data with unique fieldnames and records. XML allows custom "vocabularies," or element sets, to be defined for particular types of data, such as books, movies, auto parts, legal cases, and medical information. In other words, these custom vocabularies act like the fieldnames in a conventional database to clearly identify and segment data. If these highly descriptive elements come into widespread use on the Web, XML has the potential to organize the Web into a coherent body of knowledge. For instance, this new level of semantics should improve the ability of now-overburdened search engines to rapidly find relevant information—in the same way queries can quickly locate relevant data in a database. Additionally, XML offers the means to exchange and process data from otherwise-incompatible information repositories on the Internet. XML and DHTML also enable a significant portion of the processing load to be shifted from Web servers to Web browsers (clients). Consequently, applications that require high-level compatibility and performance, such as those in electronic commerce, will greatly benefit from the implementation of XML. Finally, intelligent Web applications that seek out choice bits of information on the Web to match the preferences of individual users also should realize equally significant gains in accuracy as a result of clearly labeled XML data.

HTML

Defining XML Elements and Structure

Unlike HTML, XML is not confined to a restricted library of tagsets. XML gives you the freedom to define a limitless set of custom elements to fit any application or situation. Also, XML enables you to organize data into a **tree-like hierarchical structure** by nesting elements within other elements. For example, Figure N-3 shows an XML document with a set of elements designed to precisely describe the type of data to be stored (e.g., Book, Name, Author, etc.). In addition, by nesting the **child** elements Name, Author, and Publisher within the **parent** element Book, and nesting the Book elements within BookList, you automatically establish a parent-child, or hierarchical, structure similar to the one illustrated in Figure N-4.  After completing her basic research on XML, Lydia decides to define the XML elements and structure necessary to store the data in the backpacking book list.

1. Open your text editor, then type <?XML VERSION='1.0'?>

The beginning of an XML document, called the **prolog**, contains the **XML declaration**, which is a processing instruction for the browser or other XML-compliant program reading the document. This processing instruction begins with the opening delimiter **<?** and ends with the closing delimiter **?>**. The instruction included between the delimiters, **XML VERSION='1.0'**, indicates that the document should be read as an XML file.

QuickTip

The indentation shown here is unnecessary for proper processing but helps to more clearly delineate the relationship between the document elements.

2. Press **[Enter]** twice, then type the following elements with the appropriate indentations:

```
<BookList>
        <Book>
                <Name></Name>
                <Author></Author>
                <Publisher></Publisher>
        </Book>
</BookList>
```

The elements in an XML document are **ranked** from the outermost set to the innermost elements. The highest ranked element forms the "root" of a tree-like structure, while the lower ranked elements make up the successive "branches" of the tree, as shown in Figure N-4. Thus, the rank of an element determines how much of the tree it controls.

3. To create two more instances of the Book elements, begin by selecting the highlighted area shown in Figure N-5

4. Press **[Ctrl][c]** to copy the highlighted area

QuickTip

The prefix "XML" is reserved for XML syntax, so you can't use it as a prefix for tag name (e.g., XMLbook).

5. Place the insertion point at the end of the Book element **</Book>**, then press **[Enter]** twice

6. Press **[Ctrl][v]** to paste a second Book record

A second instance of the Book elements appears in your document.

QuickTip

XML is case-sensitive. For example, the element <Author></Author> is not equivalent to the element <AUTHOR></AUTHOR>.

7. Press **[Enter]** once, paste another instance of the Book elements, then press **[Delete]**

Your document should now look like the one shown in Figure N-3.

8. Save the file as a text document with the filename **books.xml**

You are now ready to enter the data into your XML document.

FIGURE N-3: Elements and structure of book list XML document

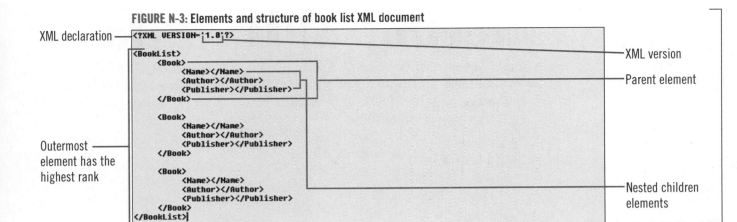

XML declaration

Outermost element has the highest rank

XML version

Parent element

Nested children elements

FIGURE N-4: Tree-like hierarchical structure of XML document

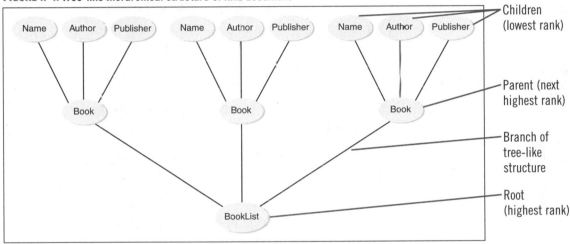

Children (lowest rank)

Parent (next highest rank)

Branch of tree-like structure

Root (highest rank)

FIGURE N-5: Highlighted book elements to copy

```
<?XML VERSION='1.0'?>

<BookList>
        <Book>
                <Name></Name>
                <Author></Author>
                <Publisher></Publisher>
        </Book>
</BookList>
```

Area to copy

 CLUES TO USE

Document Type Definition (DTD) and XML schemas

A **Document Type Definition (DTD)** is the formal specification of the rules of an XML document—namely, which elements are allowed and in what combinations. A Web page designer would create a DTD to ensure that any XML document using the DTD will be **valid** (i.e., comply with the formal specification). For example, a DTD could be set up to ensure that all XML files dealing with drug prescriptions include certain data elements (e.g., the prescribing doctor's name, expiration date, and refill information). Although a DTD can be called from an XML file, it uses a different syntax from XML. An **XML schema** combines the concepts of a DTD, relational databases, and object-oriented designs to create a richer and more powerful way to formally define the elements and structure of an XML document. In addition, XML schemas use the same syntax as XML, so they will be able to appear in the same document. However, support for XML schemas are not supported in Internet Explorer 4 and DTDs only enjoy limited support. To learn more about DTDs and XML schemas, visit http://www.microsoft.com/xml/, or search the http://www.microsoft.com for information on XML.

HTML

Entering XML Data

You enter data into an XML document the same way you do an HTML page—either manually with an editor or automated with a sophisticated HTML form. Lydia wants to enter data about three backpacking handbooks in the XML file to test her knowledge of how this new technology works. She decides to use a text editor to enter the data.

Steps

1. Make sure that **books.xml** is open in your text editor

2. Position the insertion point between the first set of **<Name></Name>** tagsets, as shown in Figure N-6

QuickTip
All the content of an XML element is treated as data, including white space. Make sure not to include unwanted blank space in between any opening and closing tagsets.

3. Type **The Backpacker's Field Manual**

4. Place the insertion point between the **<Author></Author>** tagset directly below, then type **Rick Curtis**

5. Move the insertion point between the **<Publisher></Publisher>** tagset directly below, then type **Crown Publishers Inc.**
   The text editor should match the contents of Figure N-7.

6. Type the following data in the appropriate tagsets for the next two instances of the Book elements:

   The Modern Backpacker's Handbook   **The Backpacker's Handbook**

   Glenn Randall   **Chris Townsend**

   Lyons and Burford Publishers   **Ragged Mountain Press**

   The text editor window should look like the one shown in Figure N-8.

7. Save, then close the file

FIGURE N-6: Insertion point position

```
<?XML VERSION='1.0'?>

<BookList>
    <Book>
        <Name>|</Name>
        <Author></Author>
        <Publisher></Publisher>
    </Book>

    <Book>
        <Name></Name>
        <Author></Author>
        <Publisher></Publisher>
    </Book>

    <Book>
        <Name></Name>
        <Author></Author>
        <Publisher></Publisher>
    </Book>
</BookList>
```

Correct insertion
point position

FIGURE N-7: XML document with first data record

```
<?XML VERSION='1.0'?>

<BookList>
    <Book>
        <Name>The Backpacker's Field Manual</Name>
        <Author>Rick Curtis</Author>
        <Publisher>Crown Publishers Inc.</Publisher>
    </Book>

    <Book>
        <Name></Name>
        <Author></Author>
        <Publisher></Publisher>
    </Book>

    <Book>
        <Name></Name>
        <Author></Author>
        <Publisher></Publisher>
    </Book>
</BookList>
```

Data record

FIGURE N-8: XML document with all data entered

```
<?XML VERSION='1.0'?>

<BookList>
    <Book>
        <Name>The Backpacker's Field Manual</Name>
        <Author>Rick Curtis</Author>
        <Publisher>Crown Publishers Inc.</Publisher>
    </Book>

    <Book>
        <Name>The Modern Backpacker's Handbook</Name>
        <Author>Glenn Randall</Author>
        <Publisher>Lyons and Burford Publishers</Publisher>
    </Book>

    <Book>
        <Name>The Backpacker's Handbook</Name>
        <Author>Chris Townsend</Author>
        <Publisher>Ragged Mountain Press</Publisher>
    </Book>
</BookList>
```

Data
record 1

Data
record 2

Data
record 3

Binding XML Data to HTML

XML-compliant browsers such as Internet Explorer 4 support XML by including an XML parser and an XML Data Source Object (XML DSO). An **XML parser** dissects and interprets XML elements, whereas the **XML DSO** enables binding of the XML data to the HTML document using the DHTMLObject Model. Thus, the parser and DSO cooperate to allow the display, or **rendering**, of XML data in HTML. Lydia wants to display the data in the books.xml file in an HTML document that will become part of Nomad Ltd's Web site. Before she can format the data, Lydia must first create the HTML document and bind the XML data to it.

Steps

1. Open your text editor, then type
```
<HTML>
<HEAD>
        <TITLE>Backpacking Book List</TITLE>
</HEAD>
<BODY>
<H2>Recommended Backpacking Books</H2>
```
The text editor screen now should look like the one shown in Figure N-9. Lydia is ready to enter the XML DSO Java applet necessary to bind the XML data you created in the last lesson. A **Java applet** is a small program written in the Java programming language that is summoned using the <applet></applet> tagset.

2. Press [Enter] twice, then type
```
<APPLET CODE="com.ms.xml.dso.XMLDSO.class" WIDTH="100%" HEIGHT="25" ID="xmldso" MAYSCRIPT="true">
    <PARAM NAME="url" VALUE="books.xml">
</APPLET>
```
The document should appear as shown in Figure N-10. Notice that the opening applet tag causes the browser to call the XML DSO Java applet. The parameter tag "<PARAM NAME="url" VALUE="books.xml">" specifies a URL with the name of the XML file to bind to this HTML document.

3. Press [Enter], then type:
```
</BODY>
</HTML>
```
With these closing HTML tags entered, the text editor screen should now match Figure N-11.

4. Save the file as a text document with the filename **books.htm**
Now Lydia has created an HTML document to which the XML data entered in the previous lesson is bound. The next step is to construct a table to format and display the bound data in your HTML document.

FIGURE N-9: Beginning HTML markup

```
<HTML>
<HEAD>
     <TITLE>Backpacking Book List</TITLE>
</HEAD>
<BODY>
<H2>Recommended Backpacking Books</H2>
```

FIGURE N-10: Applet to call the XML DSO

```
<HTML>
<HEAD>
     <TITLE>Backpacking Book List</TITLE>
</HEAD>
<BODY>
<H2>Recommended Backpacking Books</H2>

<APPLET CODE="com.ms.xml.dso.XMLDSO.class" WIDTH="100%"
HEIGHT="25" ID="xmldso" MAYSCRIPT="true">
     <PARAM NAME="url" VALUE="books.xml">
</APPLET>
```

Parameter name that specifies source as a URL

Value that specifies XML document filename

Applet to bind XML document to this HTML page

FIGURE N-11: HTML document with data-binding code

```
<HTML>
<HEAD>
     <TITLE>Backpacking Book List</TITLE>
</HEAD>
<BODY>
<H2>Recommended Backpacking Books</H2>

<APPLET CODE="com.ms.xml.dso.XMLDSO.class" WIDTH="100%"
HEIGHT="25" ID="xmldso" MAYSCRIPT="true">
     <PARAM NAME="url" VALUE="books.xml">
</APPLET>
</BODY>
</HTML>
```

Formatting XML Data with HTML

Once the data in an XML document has been bound to an HTML page, you can use all of the available formatting capabilities in HTML (plus CSS) to control its presentation in a browser. Because XML data often consists of a list, or database, the table feature in HTML is an ideal vehicle for displaying this tabular data. In addition to the conventional table attributes, several new HTML attributes enable Web page designers to control the binding of XML data to their documents. Table N-1 describes these new attributes. ◀━━━ Lydia decides to use a table to format and display her book-list data in the XML file.

Steps

1. Make sure the file **books.htm** is open in your text editor
2. Place the insertion point below the **</APPLET> tag**, then press **[Enter]**
   Lydia wants to use a table to display the data in the books.xml file.

QuickTip
You can use all the power and flexibility of DHTML to manipulate XML data once it appears in an HTML document.

3. Carefully type the following:

```
<TABLE ID="table" BORDER="2" WIDTH="100%" DATASRC="#xmldso"
CELLPADDING="5">
<THEAD>
<FONT FACE="Arial" SIZE="2">
    <TR>
        <TH>TITLE</TH>
        <TH>AUTHOR</TH>
        <TH>PUBLISHER</TH>
    </TR>
</FONT>
</THEAD>
<FONT FACE="Times New Roman" SIZE="2">
    <TR>
        <TD VALIGN="top"><DIV DATAFLD="NAME"
        DATAFORMATAS="HTML"></DIV></TD>
        <TD VALIGN="top"><DIV DATAFLD="AUTHOR"
        DATAFORMATAS="HTML"></DIV></TD>
        <TD VALIGN="top"><DIV DATAFLD="PUBLISHER"
        DATAFORMATAS="HTML"></DIV></TD>
    </TR>
</FONT>
</TABLE>
```

The text editor screen should match Figure N-12. This code creates a table that uses an Arial font style, with a size of 2, to display the headings TITLE, AUTHOR, and PUBLISHER across the top row. The DATAFLD attributes in this code specify the element from the XML document to be bound to each column. The DATAFORMATAS attributes indicate that the XML-based data should be displayed in HTML format. In other words, the DATAFORMATAS attributes tell your browser to interpret and format the imported XML data as HTML content. This code will create as many rows as necessary to display all the data (records) in your XML file.

4. Check your work to make sure your typing was completely accurate
5. Save, then close the file

```
<HTML>
<HEAD>
    <TITLE>Backpacking Book List</TITLE>
</HEAD>
<BODY>
<H2>Recommended Backpacking Books</H2>

<APPLET CODE="com.ms.xml.dso.XMLDSO.class" WIDTH="100%"
HEIGHT="25" ID="xmldso" MAYSCRIPT="true">
    <PARAM NAME="url" VALUE="books.xml">
</APPLET>

<TABLE ID="table" BORDER="2" WIDTH="100%"
DATASRC="#xmldso" CELLPADDING="5">
<THEAD>
<FONT FACE="Arial" SIZE="2">
    <TR>
        <TH>TITLE</TH>
        <TH>AUTHOR</TH>
        <TH>PUBLISHER</TH>
    </TR>
</FONT>
</THEAD>
<FONT FACE="Times New Roman" SIZE="2">
    <TR>
        <TD VALIGN="top"><DIV DATAFLD="NAME"
        DATAFORMATAS="HTML"></DIV></TD>
        <TD VALIGN="top"><DIV DATAFLD="AUTHOR"
        DATAFORMATAS="HTML"></DIV></TD>
        <TD VALIGN="top"><DIV DATAFLD="PUBLISHER"
        DATAFORMATAS="HTML"></DIV></TD>
    </TR>
</FONT>
</TABLE>
```

Font settings for table headings

Font settings for table rows

DATAFORMATAS attribute indicates the bound data should be displayed as HTML

DATAFLD attribute specifies the AUTHOR element be bound to this column

Table column heading for XML data

TABLE N-1: New table data-binding HTML attributes

attribute	description
DATASRC	Identifies the XML DSO applet used to bind the data.
DATAFLD	Specifies the particular column to bind the element to.
DATAFORMATAS	Indicates how the bound data should be rendered in the specified column (e.g., in HTML).
DATAPAGESIZE	Controls how many records are displayed in a table at once.

Formatting XML data with the Extensible Style Language (XSL)

In addition to formatting XML data with HTML and CSS, you also can use an XSL (Extensible Style Language) stylesheet. An **XSL stylesheet** is a set of programming rules that determine how XML data is displayed in an HTML document. Because XSL is designed to work with XML, it has the same flexibility and syntax as XML. However, native support for XSL is not built into Internet Explorer 4 or other browsers. To apply an XSL stylesheet to an XML document using Internet Explorer 4, first you must download and install the **Microsoft XSL ActiveX control**. This control is based on Microsoft's object-oriented ActiveX technology and is freely distributed. In fact, you can embed a script in your HTML document to automate the downloading and installation process. For more information on XSL and the XSL ActiveX control, see http://www.microsoft.com/xml/.

HTML

Displaying XML Data with HTML

Once you have created an HTML document to bind and format your XML-based data, you simply need to start your browser and open the HTML page to view the results. The XML document storing the data and the HTML page presenting it can reside on your local computer, network, or a remote Web server on the Internet. ◀━━━ Lydia wants to see the XML data displayed in her HTML document.

Steps

QuickTip

Use Internet Explorer 4 to display XML data with HTML. Netscape Navigator 4 doesn't support XML, Navigator 5 will.

1. Start your browser, then open the **books.htm** file

The document shown in Figure N-13 should appear, complete with the formatted data read from your books.xml file. Notice the colored line above the table indicating that the XML was successfully loaded: "file:/A:/books.xml." If the load was unsuccessful, this line indicates an error in parsing the XML file.

Trouble?

If no error appears, yet the table fails to display correctly, then your installation of Internet Explorer may be missing the Java VM (Virtual Machine). The Java VM is available from the Internet Explorer downloads section at the Microsoft Web site. See your instructor or technical support person for assistance.

2. If your HTML document displays an error when attempting to load the books.xml file like the one shown in Figure N-14, you need to edit your XML document, recheck your typing, and fix any syntax mistakes

Unlike HTML, an XML document won't load correctly unless you obey all the rules of a well-formed document.

3. After successfully viewing the book list in the HTML table, close your browser

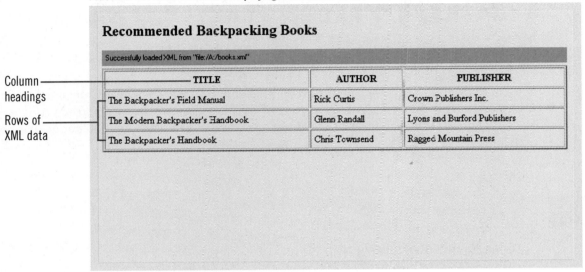

Column headings

Rows of XML data

Recommended Backpacking Books

Successfully loaded XML from "file:/A:/books.xml"

TITLE	AUTHOR	PUBLISHER
The Backpacker's Field Manual	Rick Curtis	Crown Publishers Inc.
The Modern Backpacker's Handbook	Glenn Randall	Lyons and Burford Publishers
The Backpacker's Handbook	Chris Townsend	Ragged Mountain Press

FIGURE N-14: HTML document displaying a parsing error

Highlighted line indicates nature of the problem

Recommended Backpacking Books

Error loading XML document 'books.xml'. com.ms.xml.parser.ParseException: Close tag BOOK does not match start tag PUBLISHER

TITLE	AUTHOR	PUBLISHER
The Backpacker's Field Manual	Rick Curts	Crown Publishers Inc.

CLUES TO USE

Multiple views of data

Once data has been moved into your browser, it can be displayed in many different ways. A Web page designer might build several different views of the same data depending on the audience. For example, in the case of a movie database, the average user might just want to see the title, actors, and general plot of films, whereas some devoted fans will want to view all the particulars like the date the movie was released, who directed it, and so forth. Because XML only describes data, not its appearance, a Web page designer is free to use HTML/CSS to create unique views of the data for different classes of users. In addition, with use of DHTML, the view of XML data can be manipulated easily by the end user to suit his or her needs and tastes.

HTML

Modifying an XML Document

You can change an XML document easily with your editor. Simply open the file and use the edit features to modify the elements and structure of the file. Lydia wants to add two new elements to her XML book file. She would like store the ISBN number and publication date of each book.

Steps

1. Open the file **books.xml** in your text editor

2. Position the insertion point at the end of the **first Publisher element,** as shown in Figure N-15

3. Press **[Enter]** to insert a blank line, use tabs to align the insertion point directly beneath the beginning of the tag above, then type

   <ISBN>0517887835</ISBN>

4. Press **[Enter]** again, align the insertion point, and type

   <Date>March 1998</Date>

   The text in the editor should now match Figure N-16. All that remains is to enter the new elements for the other two book records.

5. Insert the following elements in the two remaining book records:

   <ISBN>1558212485</ISBN>   <ISBN>0070653151</ISBN>

   <Date>February 1994</Date>   <Date>October 1996</Date>

   The XML document should now contain the text shown in Figure N-17.

6. Save, then close the file

FIGURE N-15: Correct position for insertion point

```
<?XML VERSION='1.0'?>

<BookList>
    <Book>
        <Name>The Backpacker's Field Manual</Name>
        <Author>Rick Curtis</Author>
        <Publisher>Crown Publishers Inc.</Publisher>|
    </Book>

    <Book>
        <Name>The Modern Backpacker's Handbook</Name>
        <Author>Glenn Randall</Author>
        <Publisher>Lyons and Burford Publishers</Publisher>
    </Book>

    <Book>
        <Name>The Backpacker's Handbook</Name>
        <Author>Chris Townsend</Author>
        <Publisher>Ragged Mountain Press</Publisher>
    </Book>
</BookList>
```

Insertion point at the end of the first Publisher element

FIGURE N-16: XML with two new elements

```
<?XML VERSION='1.0'?>

<BookList>
    <Book>
        <Name>The Backpacker's Field Manual</Name>
        <Author>Rick Curtis</Author>
        <Publisher>Crown Publishers Inc.</Publisher>
        <ISBN>0517887835</ISBN>
        <Date>March 1998</Date>
    </Book>

    <Book>
        <Name>The Modern Backpacker's Handbook</Name>
        <Author>Glenn Randall</Author>
        <Publisher>Lyons and Burford Publishers</Publisher>
    </Book>

    <Book>
        <Name>The Backpacker's Handbook</Name>
        <Author>Chris Townsend</Author>
        <Publisher>Ragged Mountain Press</Publisher>
    </Book>
</BookList>
```

ISBN element

Date element

FIGURE N-17: XML file modifications complete

```
<?XML VERSION='1.0'?>

<BookList>
    <Book>
        <Name>The Backpacker's Field Manual</Name>
        <Author>Rick Curtis</Author>
        <Publisher>Crown Publishers Inc.</Publisher>
        <ISBN>0517887835</ISBN>
        <Date>March 1998</Date>
    </Book>

    <Book>
        <Name>The Modern Backpacker's Handbook</Name>
        <Author>Glenn Randall</Author>
        <Publisher>Lyons and Burford Publishers</Publisher>
        <ISBN>1558212485</ISBN>
        <Date>February 1994</Date>
    </Book>

    <Book>
        <Name>The Backpacker's Handbook</Name>
        <Author>Chris Townsend</Author>
        <Publisher>Ragged Mountain Press</Publisher>
        <ISBN>0070653151</ISBN>
        <Date>October 1996</Date>
    </Book>
</BookList>
```

All records include new ISBN and Date elements

Altering XML Data View with HTML

When you add elements to an XML document, you must make corresponding changes to the HTML document you are using to view the data; otherwise, the new data will not be displayed. Fortunately, it is easy to bring the HTML document into alignment with the new XML elements. Simply insert the code necessary to display the new elements in the format you desire. Lydia decides to display the ISBN and publication date in the same table with the rest of her book-list data.

Steps

1. Open the file **books.htm** in your text editor

2. Change the font face for the Table header from **Arial** to **Arial Black** in the opening Table tag

3. Place the insertion point at the end of **<TH>PUBLISHER</TH>**

4. Press **[Enter]** to insert a blank line, tab over to align up directly beneath the tag above, then type **<TH>ISBN</TH>**

5. Press **[Enter]** to insert a blank line, align with the tag above, then type

   <TH>DATE</TH>

   These tags will create two new column headings—ISBN and DATE—for the data table.

6. Place the insertion point at the end of the **last row in the table**, as shown in Figure N-18

7. Press **[Enter]**, align the insertion point directly under the beginning of the first tag above, then type

   <TD VALIGN="top"><DIV DATAFLD="ISBN"
   DATAFORMATAS="HTML"></DIV></TD>

8. Press **[Enter]**, align the insertion point, then type

   <TD VALIGN="top"><DIV DATAFLD="DATE"
   DATAFORMATAS="HTML"></DIV></TD>

   The text in the editor should match Figure N-19. Check it carefully to make sure there are no typos.

9. Save the file, then close the document and text editor

Trouble?

If your HTML document displays a parsing error, use your text editor to find the syntax mistake in the books.xml file, then refresh your browser screen.

10. Start your browser, then open the **books.htm** file to view the changes made to the table

    The HTML document appears with the two new column headings and corresponding data, as shown in Figure N-20.

FIGURE N-18: Position insertion point to enter column data tags

```
<HTML>
<HEAD>
    <TITLE>Backpacking Book List</TITLE>
</HEAD>
<BODY>
<H2>Recommended Backpacking Books</H2>

<APPLET CODE="com.ms.xml.dso.XMLDSO.class" WIDTH="100%"
HEIGHT="25" ID="xmldso" MAYSCRIPT="true">
    <PARAM NAME="url" VALUE="books.xml">
</APPLET>

<TABLE ID="table" BORDER="2" WIDTH="100%"
DATASRC="#xmldso" CELLPADDING="5">
<THEAD>
<FONT FACE="Arial Black" SIZE="2">
    <TR>
        <TH>TITLE</TH>
        <TH>AUTHOR</TH>
        <TH>PUBLISHER</TH>
        <TH>ISBN</TH>
        <TH>DATE</TH>
    </TR>
</FONT>
</THEAD>
<FONT FACE="Times New Roman" SIZE="2">
    <TR>
        <TD VALIGN="top"><DIV DATAFLD="NAME"
        DATAFORMATAS="HTML"></DIV></TD>
        <TD VALIGN="top"><DIV DATAFLD="AUTHOR"
        DATAFORMATAS="HTML"></DIV></TD>
        <TD VALIGN="top"><DIV DATAFLD="PUBLISHER"
        DATAFORMATAS="HTML"></DIV></TD>|
    </TR>
```

— Insertion point at the end of the line

FIGURE N-19: HTML altered to display new XML data

```
<H2>Recommended Backpacking Books</H2>

<APPLET CODE="com.ms.xml.dso.XMLDSO.class" WIDTH="100%"
HEIGHT="25" ID="xmldso" MAYSCRIPT="true">
    <PARAM NAME="url" VALUE="books.xml">
</APPLET>

<TABLE ID="table" BORDER="2" WIDTH="100%"
DATASRC="#xmldso" CELLPADDING="5">
<THEAD>
<FONT FACE="Arial Black" SIZE="2">
    <TR>
        <TH>TITLE</TH>
        <TH>AUTHOR</TH>
        <TH>PUBLISHER</TH>
        <TH>ISBN</TH>
        <TH>DATE</TH>
    </TR>
</FONT>
</THEAD>
<FONT FACE="Times New Roman" SIZE="2">
    <TR>
        <TD VALIGN="top"><DIV DATAFLD="NAME"
        DATAFORMATAS="HTML"></DIV></TD>
        <TD VALIGN="top"><DIV DATAFLD="AUTHOR"
        DATAFORMATAS="HTML"></DIV></TD>
        <TD VALIGN="top"><DIV DATAFLD="PUBLISHER"
        DATAFORMATAS="HTML"></DIV></TD>
        <TD VALIGN="top"><DIV DATAFLD="ISBN"
        DATAFORMATAS="HTML"></DIV></TD>
        <TD VALIGN="top"><DIV DATAFLD="DATE"
        DATAFORMATAS="HTML"></DIV></TD>
    </TR>
</FONT>
```

Font face for table headings changed to Arial Black

Inserted column headings

New attributes to bind data to columns

FIGURE N-20: Five-column table with new data

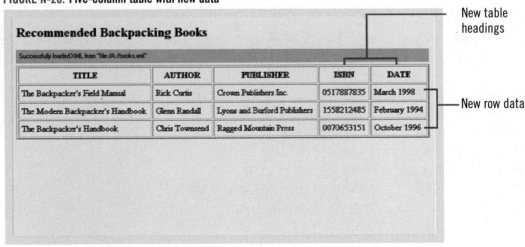

New table headings

New row data

STRUCTURING DATA WITH XML

HTML

Practice

▶ Concepts Review

Label each item marked in Figure N-21.

FIGURE N-21

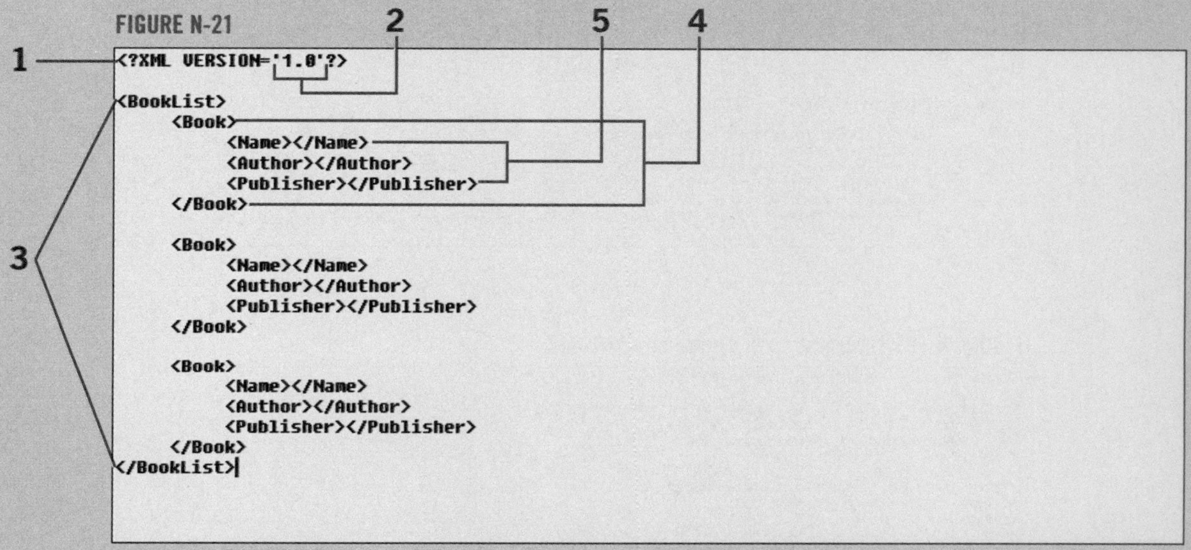

```
1 ── <?XML VERSION='1.0'?>

      <BookList>
          <Book>
              <Name></Name>
              <Author></Author>
              <Publisher></Publisher>
          </Book>

          <Book>
              <Name></Name>
              <Author></Author>
              <Publisher></Publisher>
          </Book>

          <Book>
              <Name></Name>
              <Author></Author>
              <Publisher></Publisher>
          </Book>
      </BookList>
```

Match each term with its description.

6. Element
7. Parser
8. XML
9. Correctly nested
10. Empty element

a. An element that doesn't have a closing tag
b. A text-based format that lets you describe, deliver, and exchange structured data
c. No overlapping elements
d. Dissects and interprets XML
e. The start and corresponding end tags, plus the contents in between the tagset

Select the best answer from the list of choices.

11. The XML declaration, in the prolog of an XML document, indicates that the document should be
    a. Encoded with XSL.
    b. Processed as an XML file.
    c. Rendered using HTML.
    d. Displayed as HTML.

12. Which is *not* an XML syntax rule?
    a. All elements must have start and end tags.
    b. All elements must be nested properly.
    c. All attribute values must appear within quotation marks.
    d. All empty elements must be terminated with "//>".

13. **Which statement is False?**
    a. Blank space appearing in the content of an element is read as data.
    b. XML is organized in a tree-like structure.
    c. The elements <Wine>red</Wine> and <wine>red</wine> are equivalent in XML.
    d. XML brings structure and customization to the Web.
14. **Which is *not* a new table data binding attribute for HTML?**
    a. DATASRC
    b. DATAFLD
    c. DATAFORMAT
    d. DATAPAGESIZE
15. **Which one of the following is *not* required to display XML data in a browser?**
    a. parser
    b. Cascading Style Sheet (CSS)
    c. data-binding applet
    d. data-binding attributes

 # Skills Review

1. **Define XML elements and structure.**
   a. Open your text editor, then type <?XML VERSION='1.0'?>
   b. Two lines down, enter the following elements, using the appropriate indentation to signify the structure of the document:
   ```
   <Catalog>
           <Product>
                   <Model></Model>
                   <Price></Price>
                   <Description></Description>
           </Product>

           <Product>
                   <Model></Model>
                   <Price></Price>
                   <Description></Description>
           </Product>

           <Product>
                   <Model></Model>
                   <Price></Price>
                   <Description></Description>
           </Product>
   </Catalog>
   ```
   c. Verify your typing and correct any typos.
   d. Save the file as a text document with the filename products.xml.

2. Enter XML data.

   a. Make sure products.xml is open in your text editor.

   b. Position the insertion point between the first instance of the <Model></Model> element and type "Cleaner 100".

   c. Type "$495" between the Price tags directly below the first Name element.

   d. Type "Domestic robot to vacuum and dust your home." between the Description tags.

   e. Enter the following content for the next two Product records:

     Whacker 300

     $1,195

     Yard robot that mows and trims the edges of your lawn.

     Nursemaid 400

     $4,995

     Personal robot to care for purchasers of Cleaner 100 and Whacker 200 robot models.

   f. Save and close the document.

3. Bind XML data to HTML.

   a. Start your text editor, then in a new document, type the following code with indicated alignments:

```
<HTML>
<HEAD>
<TITLE>Robot Product Catalog</TITLE>
</HEAD>
<BODY>
<H2>Robot Product Catalog</H2>
```

   b. Create two blank lines at the bottom the document, then bind the products.xml file to this HTML document by entering the following code:

```
<APPLET CODE="com.ms.xml.dso.XMLDSO.class" WIDTH="100%" HEIGHT="25"
ID="xmldso" MAYSCRIPT="true">
        <PARAM NAME="url" VALUE="products.xml">
</APPLET>
```

   c. Type the following HTML closing tags:

```
</BODY>
</HTML>
```

   d. Check the document for errors, making changes as necessary.

   e. Save the file as a text document with the filename products.htm.

4. Format XML data with HTML.

   a. Make sure products.htm is open in your text editor.

   b. To create a table to bind, format, and display the data in the products.xml file, type the following HTML code just below the closing applet tag:

```
<TABLE ID="table" BORDER="2" WIDTH="100%" DATASRC="#xmldso" CELLPADDING="5">
<THEAD>
<FONT FACE="Arial" SIZE="2">
<TR>
        <TH>MODEL</TH>
        <TH>PRICE</TH>
        <TH>DESCRIPTION</TH>
```

```
    </TR>
        </FONT>
    </THEAD>
    <FONT FACE="Times New Roman" SIZE="2">
        <TR>
                <TD VALIGN="top"><DIV DATAFLD="MODEL" DATAFORMATAS="HTML"></DIV></TD>
                <TD VALIGN="top"><DIV DATAFLD="PRICE" DATAFORMATAS="HTML"></DIV></TD>
                <TD VALIGN="top"><DIV DATAFLD="DESCRIPTION" DATAFORMATAS="HTML"></DIV></TD>
        </TR>
    </FONT>
    </TABLE>
```

  c. Check the document for errors, making changes as necessary, then save and close the file.

5. Display XML data with HTML.

  a. Start your browser, then open the file products.htm.

  b. If you receive a parsing error, use your text editor to find and fix typos in either the products.htm or products.xml documents, then open the products.htm file again with your browser.

  c. When you are done examining the table of data, print the page, then close your browser.

6. Modifying an XML document.

  a. Open the file products.xml in your text editor.

  b. In the first Product element, insert the following new elements just below the Description element:
    <Options>Turbo jet engine</Options>
    <Delivery>2-4 weeks</Delivery>

  c. Enter the following elements for the last two records in your XML file:
    <Options>Leaf collector</Options>
    <Delivery>2-4 weeks</Delivery>

    <Options>Medicine tray</Options>
    <Delivery>4-6 months</Delivery>

  d. Check the document for errors, making changes as necessary, then save the file.

7. Alter XML data view with HTML.

  a. Open the file products.htm in your text editor.

  b. Insert the following HTML aligned below <TH>DESCRIPTION</TH>:
    <TH>OPTIONS</TH>
    <TH>DELIVERY</TH>

  c. Type
    <TD VALIGN="top"><DIV DATAFLD="OPTIONS" DATAFORMATAS="HTML"></DIV></TD>
    <TD VALIGN="top"><DIV DATAFLD="DELIVERY" DATAFORMATAS="HTML"></DIV></TD>

  d. Check the file for errors, making changes as necessary, then save the file and close your text editor.

  e. Open the products.htm file in your browser, and view the newly expanded table.

  f. If you receive a parsing error, use your text editor to find and fix the typing mistakes in either the products.htm or products.xml documents, then open the products.htm file once more with your browser.

  g. Print the document, then close your browser.

▶ Independent Challenges

1. You have just started buying music CDs and you would like to keep a list of them on your computer as your collection grows. You decide to use an XML file to store the name, song titles, and type of music for each music CD. At this point, you just want to create the custom elements and hierarchical structure of the XML document.

To complete this independent challenge:

a. Open your text editor.

b. Enter the prolog for an XML document, use the [Enter] key to create a couple of blank lines in the document, then type "<CDlist>".

c. On the next line, press [Tab] once, then type "<CD>".

d. On the next line down, press [Tab] twice, then type "<Name></Name>".

e. On the next line down, press [Tab] three times, then type "<Song1></Song1>".

f. Repeat Step 5 until you have entered tagsets for 10 songs (i.e., <Song2></Song2>...<Song10><Song10>).

g. Below the last Song tagset, type "<Category></Category>".

k. On the next line, press [Tab] once, then type "</CD>".

i. Copy the <CD> element, and all its children elements, three times.

j. At the bottom of the document, at the beginning of a new line, type </CDlist>, then save the file as music list.xml.

k. Print a copy of the document, then close your text editor.

2. Your best friend collects and sells comic books for a living. She asks you to help her create a computerized list of her collection that she can display on her personal Web site. You decide to use XML and HTML as the means of storing and displaying information about her comics. You use five records to test the design.

To complete this independent challenge:

a. Open your text editor, then create an XML file with the root element <ComicList>.

b. Add the parent element <ComicBook> and the children elements <Name></Name>, <Issue></Issue>, <Publisher></Publisher>, and <Value></Value>.

c. Copy the ComicBook element and its children elements four times.

d. At the bottom of the document, on a blank line, type "</ComicList>".

e. Save the XML file as comics.xml.

f. Enter the data from the table below into each ComicBook element in your XML document:

g. Save the document, print it, then open a new document.

h. Create an HTML document to display your XML data. Use the following code to bind the XML data to a table in your HTML file:

```
<APPLET CODE="com.ms.xml.dso.XMLDSO.class"
WIDTH="100%"
HEIGHT="25" ID="xmldso" MAYSCRIPT="true">
<PARAM NAME="url" VALUE="comics.xml">
</APPLET>
<TABLE ID="table" BORDER="2" WIDTH="100%" DATASRC="#xmldso" CELLPADDING="5">
<THEAD>
   <TR>
      <TH>TITLE</TH>
```

name	issue	publisher	value
Bombastic Five	4	Cool Comics	$22,000
Radioactive Dog	12	Cool Comics	$640
Sludge Man	34	Night Owl	$26
Bombastic Five	7	Cool Comics	$18,500
Sludge Man	19	Night Owl	$35

```
        <TH>ISSUE #</TH>
        <TH>PUBLISHER</TH>
        <TH>VALUE</TH>
    </TR>
  </THEAD>
    <TR>
        <TD VALIGN="top"><DIV DATAFLD="NAME" DATAFORMATAS="HTML"></DIV></TD>
        <TD VALIGN="top"><DIV DATAFLD="ISSUE" DATAFORMATAS="HTML"></DIV></TD>
        <TD VALIGN="top"><DIV DATAFLD="PUBLISHER" DATAFORMATAS='HTML"></DIV></TD>
        <TD VALIGN="top"><DIV DATAFLD="VALUE"  DATAFORMATAS=""HTML"></DIV></TD>
    </TR>
  </FONT>
  </TABLE>
```

i. Format the table using the font style Arial with point size of 2.

j. Save the file as a text document called comics.htm, then close your text editor.

k. Open comics.htm in your browser to view your XML data. If the data fails to display, use your text editor to check your typing in comics.xml and comics.htm, and correct any typos.

l. Print a copy of comics.htm from your browser.

3. You have been asked to inventory all the computers in your building at work and make the results available for viewing on your company's Intranet. Management would like to know the make, model, year, and location of each machine.

To complete this independent challenge:

a. Create an XML file called computers.xml with the root element <Computers></Computers>.

b. Add the parent element <Make></Make>, with the children elements <Model></Model>, <Year></Year>, and <Location></Location>. Copy the <Make></Make> element and its children elements five times.

c. Populate the Model elements with data from the table below:

d. Create an HTML file called computers.htm that will display the XML data in a table; use Arial as the font face.

e. Open the HTML file in your browser.

f. Print a copy of the document from your browser.

make	model	year	location
Mega Bite	T-Rex	1998	Office 101
Mega Bite	T-Rex	1998	Office 102
Mega Bite	Raptor	1998	Office 103
Tera Gig	Condor	1997	Office 104
Mega Bite	Raptor	1998	Reception Area

4. You have decided to use XML and HTML to store and display a list of your favorite movies. Be sure to include custom elements (e.g., <MovieTitle></MovieTitle>) to store important information such as the name of the movie, your favorite actor, the plot, and other interesting data. Use the Internet to search for movie data if your information is not complete. In an XML file called movies.xml, structure the movie data so that each movie record is a child element of the parent element <MovieList></MovieList>. Display the data in a table with headings in an HTML file called movies.htm. Open the movies.htm file in your browser, then print the document.

Visual Workshop

Create a Web application using XML and HTML to display the table of formatted data shown in Figure N-22. Print the document from your browser.

FIGURE N-22

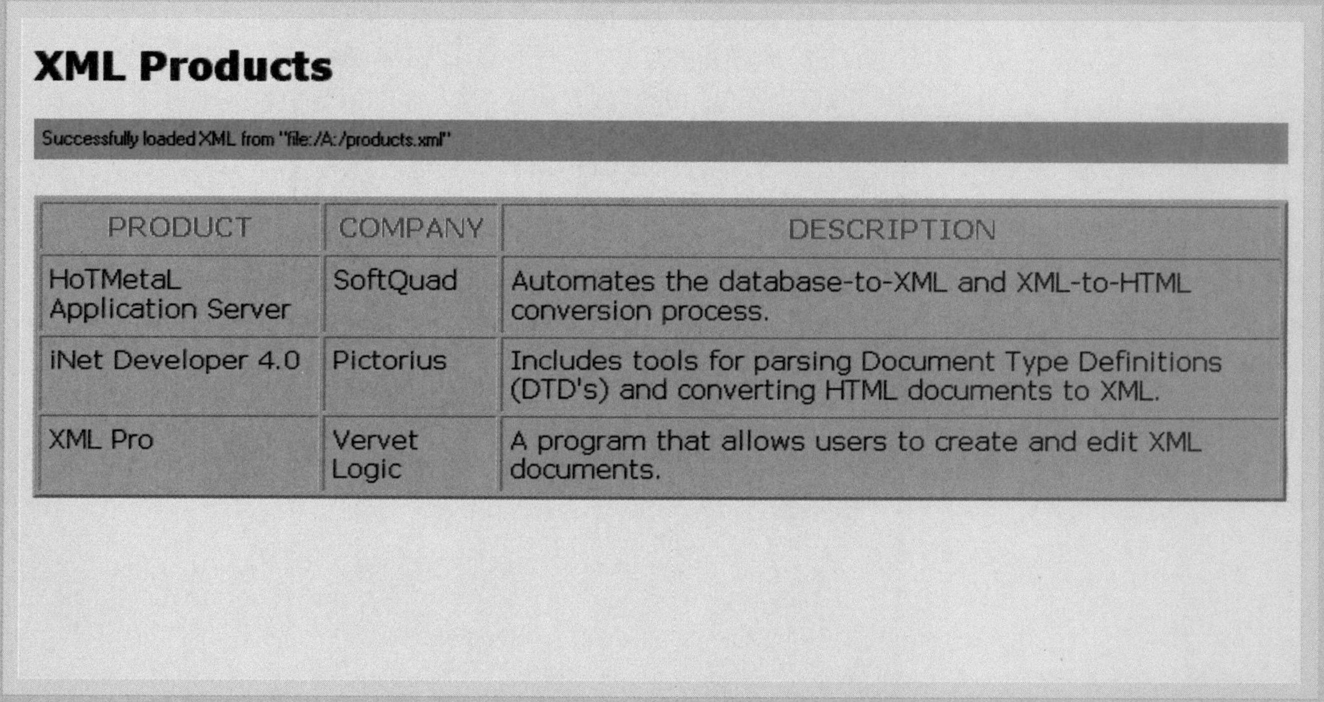

XML Products

Successfully loaded XML from "file:/A:/products.xml"

PRODUCT	COMPANY	DESCRIPTION
HoTMetaL Application Server	SoftQuad	Automates the database-to-XML and XML-to-HTML conversion process.
iNet Developer 4.0	Pictorius	Includes tools for parsing Document Type Definitions (DTD's) and converting HTML documents to XML.
XML Pro	Vervet Logic	A program that allows users to create and edit XML documents.

Appendix

Objectives

- ► **Put a document on the Web**
- ► **Increase Web Site traffic**
- ► **Review common tasks**
- ► **HTML tag reference**
- ► **HTML color names**
- ► **HTML special characters**
- ► **JavaScript object reference**
- ► **JavaScript operators**
- ► **Casading style sheet reference**
- ► **Filters and Transitions reference**

When you create HTML documents for use in a business setting, it is important not only to know how to construct Web pages, but also how to access and take advantage of resources on the Web. These resources include a variety of search engines and Web sites devoted to helping your business have a Web presence. You also should be aware of the variety of options to increase traffic to your Web site. This appendix provides useful HTML code and publishing references for you to use as you create and publish your Web pages.

Putting a Document on the Web

While creating Web pages is an important part of Web site creation, a crucial step in the process remains: making your HTML documents available to Web users. To make files available to the Web, they must be stored on a computer connected to the Web. Instead of dialing in over a phone line, such a computer—called a **Web server**—is usually connected to the Internet by means of lines reserved for that purpose. Because of this, the Web server is never, or only rarely, disconnected from the Web. Your school or Internet Service Provider (ISP)—the company that provides your Internet access—may have a Web server available for your use. Free Web space also is available on many Web sites. However, the sites usually require you to display an advertisement on your Web page in exchange for the free service. Figure AP-1 shows a Web page on one such site. Because each Web server might have a different procedure for storing Web pages, you should contact the provider of your Web space to find out how to copy your files to the server. Before you actually publish your files to the Web, to ensure that your Web site is ready for users at the time you publish it, you should complete the following steps

Details

QuickTip

The domain names ending in .com for almost all standard words have already been registered; many new companies are carefully choosing names for which the corresponding domain names are still available.

Establish your URL

When you place your Web site on a free or inexpensive Web server, the resulting URL is usually a subdirectory on the Web server's domain—for example, www.course.com/users/~torxdesign/. Such a URL is not easy for potential users to remember or to type. The alternative is to register your own domain name, such as www.thomson.com. Domain name registration involves payment of a yearly fee, in addition to paying a Web space provider to store your pages and domain name. In either case, the logistics of setting up your Web site location can take time, so begin making arrangements for a Web server well in advance of your target publishing date.

Submit your URL to search engines

While not required, submitting your URL for inclusion in search engine databases facilitates potential users locating your site. Each search engine has different policies regarding adding information about Web sites to its index. This process can take several months.

Test your Web pages

Extensively test your files under a variety of browsers and under different display conditions to weed out any errors and design problems before you publish.

Ensure Web server compatibility

Some Web servers require all Web pages to have the four-letter HTML extension, rather than the three-letter HTM extension. Check the requirements of your Web space provider and then review your filenames to be sure they are named accordingly.

Verify hyperlinks

Confirm that the hyperlinks in your documents point to the correct filenames. In particular, you should verify that the filenames are referenced in the correct letter-case, as some Web servers distinguish between uppercase and lowercase letters in filenames. This means, for example, that such a server would consider a file named "Image.jpg" to be a different file than one named "image.jpg." Also, be sure that hyperlinks between pages in your Web site use relative pathnames.

Learn the publishing procedure

Every Web server uses a unique system for adding new Web sites. Make sure you understand the procedure outlined by your Web space provider, and make sure you have the necessary software.

FIGURE AP-1: Web page located on a free Web server

Web page users
see banner
advertisement
when page opens

FIGURE AP-2: Software for uploading Web pages via FTP

Drag selected
files between
panes to
upload

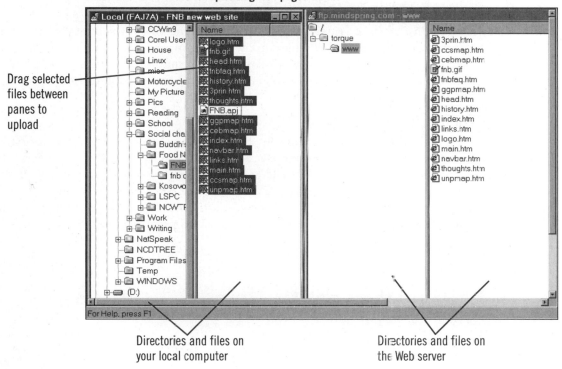

Directories and files on
your local computer

Directories and files on
the Web server

Increasing Web Site Traffic

Have you ever wondered why a Web site can be located by using one search engine, but not by another? How does a site get listed in an index? Some search engines conduct periodic—and laborious—searches of Web sites, and other search engines depend on site submissions to their indices. The key to a successful Web site is its accessibility to Web users. After all, if no users see your site, the caliber of its design is irrelevant. Make sure users can access your Web pages using search engines.

Details

Submit your URL to search engines

One of the simplest steps in getting your site listed by search engines is to provide them with your URL. Most search engine Web sites contain contact information for requesting your site to be added to their index. Figure AP-3 shows the submission form for Google. Because search engine databases have size limits and must continually purge outdated information, you should resubmit your URL on a regular basis to prevent your site's removal. To maximize the number of users sent to your site, target your requests to the search engines with the most visitors. Web traffic statistics are available on the Web from sites such as Media Metrix, shown in Figure AP-4.

Use keywords

When adding a Web page to its database, a search engine's goal is to locate terms in the page that identify the page's key concepts or focus. It adds these terms, known as **keywords**, to the index for its database. When a user conducts a search, the search engine uses these keywords to determine which URLs it provides as search results. For this reason, it is important to use relevant wording throughout your Web page.

Plan ahead

Some search engines can take as long as three months from the time you submit your URL until the time your site is included in their index. In the intervening period, your business may have minimal Web site traffic, which can be a serious problem. If your business plan relies heavily on Web traffic, you may need to schedule the rollout of your Web site to coincide with your appearance in search engine databases.

Make your page a high priority

Although a search may yield hundreds of sites, most people generally look at only the first few entries in search results. You can give your page a higher priority by skillfully implementing the <TITLE> and <META> tags in your Web site. Some search engines look only at the text marked by these tags when indexing, or give extra weight to this text when evaluating your page's relevance to particular topics. The <META> tag includes attributes that allow you to suggest to the search engines the most appropriate keywords for your Web page. Figure AP-5 shows the code for a Web page using <META> tags.

FIGURE AP-3: URL submission instructions on the Google search engine Web site

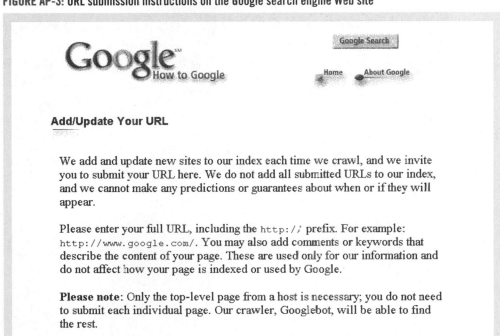

FIGURE AP-4: Media Metrix Web page listing the 50 most-visited Web sites

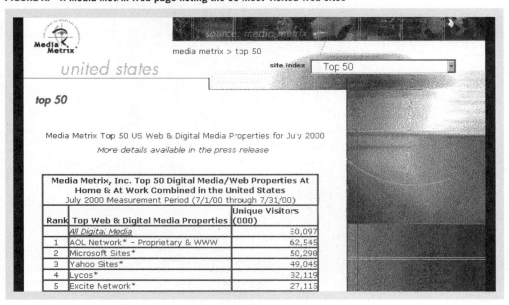

FIGURE AP-5: Web page incorporationg <META> tags

<META> tags in <HEAD> section keywords and description of page contents

```
<HTML>

<HEAD>
<TITLE>Nomad Ltd Checkout</TITLE>

<META NAME="keywords" CONTENT="outdoor, outdoors, travel, sporting goods">
<META NAME="description" CONTENT="Nomad Ltd sells outdoor gear and adventure
travel packages online and in stores worldwide.">
</HEAD>

<BODY BACKGROUND="images/eggshell.jpg">
<FONT FACE="arial, helvetica, sans serif">
```

HTML

Reviewing Common Tasks

There are some common tasks that you must do when creating Web pages. These tasks, while functionally similar across programs, are performed using different commands depending on the program you are using. Table AP-1 is provided to make you aware of some of these differences.

TABLE AP-1: Common HTML tasks

program	task	action
Microsoft FrontPage Express	View HTML source	Click View, then click HTML
Microsoft Internet Explorer	Exit the program	Click File, then click Close, or click the Close box
	View HTML source	Click View, then click Source
	Print the document	Click File, click Print, then click OK, or click the Print button
	View saved changes in open browser document	Click the Refresh button
Netscape Navigator	Exit the program	Click File, click Exit, or click the Close box
	View HTML source	Click View, then click Page Source
	Print the document	Click File, click Print, then click OK, or click the Print button
	View saved changes in open browser document	Click the Reload button
NotePad	Wrap text to ruler	Click Edit, then click Word Wrap
	Print	Click File, then click Print
	Select entire contents of file	Click Edit, then click Select All
	Exit	Click File, then click Exit
WordPad	Wrap text to ruler	Click View, click Options, click the Text tab, then click the Wrap to ruler checkbox
	Print	Click File, click Print, then click OK, or click the Print button
	Select entire contents of file	Click Edit, then click Select All
	Exit	Click File, then click Exit

HTML Tag Reference

The following are commonly supported HTML tags and properties. Opening and closing tags are both included where they are required; a single tag means that no closing tag is needed. You can view more detailed information about the latest HTML specifications at http://www.w3.org. Additional information about browser support for different HTML tags is available at http://www.htmlcompendium.org/. Because the World Wide Web constantly changes, you should check this information against the current browser versions.

Properties are of the following types:

- *Character*   A single text character
- *Color*   A recognized color name or color value
- *CGI Script*   The name of a CGI script on the Web server
- *Document*   The filename or URL of the file
- *List*   List of items separated by commas, usually enclosed in double quotation marks
- *Mime-Type*   A MIME data type, such as "text/css", "audio/wav", or "video/x-msvideo"
- *Options*   Limited to a specific set of values (values are shown below the property)
- *Text*   Any text string
- *URL*   The URL for a Web page or file
- *Value*   A number, usually an integer

TABLE AP-2: HTML tags

tags and properties	description
<!>	The <!> tag is used for comments in documenting the features of your HTML file; often divided into <!— at the start, and —> at the end of a comment
<A>..</A>	The <A> tag marks the beginning and end of a hypertext link
HREF=*URL*	Indicates the target, filename, or URL to which the hypertext points
NAME=*Text*	Specifies a name for the enclosed text, allowing it to be a target of a hyperlink
REL=*Text*	Specifies the relationship between the current page and the link specified by the HREF property
REV=*Text*	Specifies a reverse relationship between the current page and the link specified by the HREF property
TARGET=*Text*	Specifies the default target window or frame for the hyperlink.
TITLE=*Text*	Provides a title for the document whose address is given by the HREF property
<ADDRESS>..</ADDRESS>	The <ADDRESS> tag is used for information such as addresses, authorship, and so forth; the text is usually italicized and in some browsers it is indented
<AREA>	The <AREA> tag defines the type and coordinates of a hotspot within an image map
COORDS=*Value 1, value 2…*	The coordinates of the hotspot; coordinates depend on the shape of the hotspot: Rectangle: COORDS=x_left, y_upper, x_right, y_lower Circle: COORDS= x_center, y_center, radius Polygon: COORDS= x1, y1, x2, y2, x3, y3, …
HREF=*URL*	Indicates the target, filename, or URL to which the hotspot points
SHAPE=*Option* (RECT | CIRCLE | POLY)	The shape of the hotspot
TARGET=*Text*	Specifies the default target window or frame for the hotspot

HTML

tags and properties	description
<B>..</B>	The <B> tag displays the enclosed text in boldface
<BASE>	The <BASE> tag allows you to specify the URL for the HTML document; it is used by some browsers to interpret relative hyperlinks
HREF=*URL*	Specifies the URL from which all relative hyperlinks should be based
TARGET=*Text*	Specifies the default target window or frame for every hyperlink in the document
<BGSOUND>	The <BGSOUND> is used to play a background sound clip when the page is first opened
LOOP=*Value*	Specifies the number of times the sound clip should be played; LOOP can either be a digit or INFINITE
SRC=*Document*	The sound file used for the sound clip
<BIG>..</BIG>	The <BIG> tag increases the size of the enclosed text; the exact appearance of the text depends on the browser and the default font size
<BLOCKQUOTE>..</BLOCKQUOTE>	The <BLOCKQUOTE> tag is used to set off long quotes or citations, usually by indenting the enclosed text on both sides; some browsers italicize the text as well
<BODY>..</BODY>	The <BODY> tag encloses all text, images, and other elements that the user will see on the Web page
ALINK=*Color*	Color of activated hypertext links, which are links the user is currently clicking, but has not yet released
BACKGROUND=*Document*	The graphic image file used for the Web page background
BGCOLOR=*Color*	The color of the Web page background
BGPROPERTIES=FIXED	Keeps the background image fixed so that it does not scroll with the Web page
LEFTMARGIN=*Value*	Indents the left margin of the page by the number of pixels specified in value
LINK=*Color*	Color of all unvisited links
TEXT=*Color*	Color of all text in the document
TOPMARGIN=*Value*	Indents the top margin of the page by the number of pixels specified in value
VLINK=*Color*	Color of previously visited links
 The tag forces a line break in the text	
CLEAR=*Option* (LEFT | RIGHT | ALL | NONE)	Causes the next line to start at the spot where the specified margin is clear
<CAPTION>..</CAPTION>	The <CAPTION> tag encloses the table caption
ALIGN=Option (LEFT | RIGHT | CENTER | TOP | BOTTOM)	Specifies the alignment of the caption with respect to the table

tags and properties	description
<CENTER>.. </CENTER>	The <CENTER> tag horizontally centers the enclosed text or image
<CITE>..</CITE>	The <CITE> tag is used for citations and usually appears in italics
<CODE>..</CODE>	The <CODE> tag is used for text taken from the code for a computer program, and usually appears in a fixed width font
<DD>	The <DD> tag formats text to be used as relative definitions in a <DL> list
<DIR>..</DIR>	The <DIR> tag encloses an unordered list of <LI> items, formatted in narrow columns
TYPE=*Option* (CIRCLE I DISC I SQUARE)	Specifies the type of bullet used for displaying each <LI> item in the <DIR> list
<DFN>..</DFN>	The <DFN> tag is used for the defining instance of a term, that is, the first time the term is used; the enclosed text is usually italicized
<DIV>..</DIV>	The <DIV> tag is used to set the text alignment of blocks of text or images
<DL>..</DL>	The <DL> tag encloses a definition list in which the <DD> definition term is left-aligned, and the <DT> relative definition is indented
<DT>	The <DT> tag is used to format the definition term in a <DL> list
<EM>..</EM>	The <EM> tag is used to emphasize text; The enclosed text usually appears in italics
<FONT>..</FONT>	The <FONT> tag is used to control the appearance of the text it encloses
COLOR=*Color*	The color of the enclosed text
FACE=*List*	The font face of the text; multiple font faces can be specified, separated by commas; the browser will try to render the text in the order specified by the list
SIZE=*Value*	Size of the font on a seven-point scale (1 is smallest, 7 is largest); it can be absolute or relative. Specifying SIZE=5 sets the font size to size 5 on the scale; specifying SIZE=+5 sets the font size 5 points larger than default tag
<FORM>..</FORM>	The <FORM> tag marks the beginning and end of a Web page form
ACTION=*URL*	Specifies the URL to which the contents of the form are to be sent
ENCTYPE=*Text*	Specifies the encoding type used to submit the data to the server
METHOD=*Option* (POST I GET)	Specifies the method of accessing the URL indicated in the ACTION attribute
TARGET=*Text*	The frame or window that displays the form's results
<FRAME>	The <FRAME> tag defines a single frame within a set of frames
BORDERCOLOR=*Color*	Specifies the color of the frame border
FRAMEBORDER=*Option* (YES I NO)	Specifies whether the frame border is visible
FRAMESPACING=*Value*	Specifies the amount of space between frames, in pixels
MARGINHEIGHT=*Value*	Specifies the amount of space above and below the frame object and the frame borders
MARGINWIDTH=*Value*	Specifies the amount of space to the left and right of the frame object, in pixels
NAME=*Text*	Label assigned to the frame

HTML

tags and properties	description
NORESIZE	Prevents users from resizing the frame
SCROLLING=*Option* (YES I NO I AUTO)	Specifies whether scroll bars are visible AUTO (the default) displays scroll bars only as needed
SRC=*Document*	Specifies the document or URL of the object to be displayed in the frame
<FRAMESET>.. </FRAMESET>	The <FRAMESET> tag marks the beginning and the end of a set of frames
BORDER=*Value*	The size of the borders, in pixels
BORDERCOLOR	The color of the frame borders
COLS=*List*	The size of each column in a set of frames; columns can be specified either in pixels, as a percentage of the display area, or with an asterisk (*), indicating that any remaining space be allotted to that column (for example, COLS="40,25%,*")
ROWS=*List*	The size of each row in a set of frames; rows can be specified either in pixels, as a percentage of the display area, or with an asterisk (*), indicating that any remaining space be allotted to that column (for example, ROWS="40,25%,*")
<H1>..</H1><H4>..</H4> <H2>..</H2><H5>..</H5> <H3>..</H3><H6>..</H6>	The six levels of text headings ranging from the largest (<H1>) to the smallest (<H6>); text headings appear in a bold face font
ALIGN=*Option* (LEFT I RIGHT I CENTER)	The alignment of the heading
<HR>	The <HR> tag creates a horizontal line
ALIGN=*Option* (LEFT I CENTER I RIGHT)	Alignment of the horizontal line; the default is CENTER
COLOR=*Color*	Specifies a color for the line
NOSHADE	Removes 3-D shading from the line
SIZE=*Value*	The size (height) of the line in pixels
WIDTH=*Value*	The width (length) of the line either in pixels or as a percentage of the display area
<HEAD>..</HEAD>	The <HEAD> tag encloses code that provides information about the document
<HTML>..</HTML>	The <HTML> tag indicates the beginning and end of the HTML document
<I>..</I>	The <I> tag italicizes the enclosed text
<IMG>	The <IMG> tag is used to insert an inline image into the document
ALIGN=*Option* (LEFT I RIGHT I TOP I TEXTTOP I MIDDLE I ABSMIDDLE I BASELINE I BOTTOM I ABSBOTTOM)	Specifies the alignment of the image; specifying LEFT or RIGHT aligns the image with the left or right page margin; the other alignment options align the image with surrounding text

tags and properties	description
ALT=*Text*	Text to appear if the image cannot be displayed by the browser
BORDER=*Value*	The size of the border around the image, in pixels
CONTROLS	Display VCR-like controls under moving images; used in conjunction with the DYNSRC property
DYNSRC=*Document*	Specifies the file of a video, AVI clip, or VRML worlds displayed inside the page
HEIGHT=*Value*	The height of the image in pixels
HSPACE=*Value*	The amount of space to the left and right of the image, in pixels
ISMAP	Identifies the graphic as an image map; for use with server-side image maps
LOOP=*Value*	Specifies the number of times a moving image should be played; the value must be either a digit or INFINITE
LOWSRC=*Document*	A low-resolution version of the graphic that the browser should initially display before loading the high-resolution version
SRC=*Document*	The source file of the inline image
START=*Item* (FILEOPEN | MOUSEOVER)	Tells the browser when to start displaying a moving image file; FILEOPEN directs the browser to start when the file is open; MOUSEOVER directs the browser to start when the mouse moves over the image
USEMAP=*#Map_Name*	Identifies the graphic as an image map and specifies the name of image map definition to use with the graphic; for use with client-side image maps
VSPACE=*Value*	The amount of space above and below the image, in pixels
WIDTH=*Value*	The width of the image in pixels
<INPUT>..</INPUT>	The <INPUT> tag creates an input object for use in a Web page form
ALIGN=*Option* (LEFT | RIGHT | TOP | TEXTTOP | MIDDLE | ABSMIDDLE | BASELINE | BOTTOM | ABSBOTTOM)	Specifies the alignment of an input image Similar to the ALIGN attribute with the <IMG> tag
CHECKED	Specifies that an input checkbox or input radio button is selected
LOOP=*Value* INFINITE	Specifies the number of times a moving input image should be played; the value must be either a digit or
LOWSRC=*Document*	A low-resolution version of the input image that the browser should initially display before loading the high-resolution version
MAXLENGTH=*Value*	Specifies the maximum number of characters inserted into an input text box
NAME=*Text*	The label given to the input object
SIZE=*Value*	The visible size, in characters, of an input text box
SRC=*Document*	The source file of the graphic used for an input image object
START=*Option* (FILEOPEN | MOUSEOVER)	Tells the browser when to start displaying a moving image file. Similar to the START property for the <IMG> tag

HTML

tags and properties	description
TYPE=*Option* (CHECKBOX | HIDDEN | IMAGE | PASSWORD | RADIO | RESET | SUBMIT | TEXT | TEXTAREA)	Specifies the type of input object. CHECKBOX creates a checkbox. HIDDEN creates a hidden object. IMAGE creates an image object. PASSWORD creates a text box which hides the text as the user enters it. RADIO creates a radio button. RESET creates a button that resets the form's fields when pressed. SUBMIT creates a button that submits the form when pressed. TEXT creates a text box. TEXTAREA creates a text box with multiple line entry fields.
USEMAP=*#Map_Name*	Identifies the input image as an image map. similar to the USEMAP property used with the <IMG> tag
VALUE=*Value*	Specifies the information that is initially displayed in the input object
VSPACE=*Value*	The amount of space above and below the image, in pixels
WIDTH=*Value*	The width of the input image, in pixels
<KBD>..</KBD>	The <KBD> tag is used to make text look as if it came from a typewriter or keyboard, text is displayed with a fixed width font
<LI>	The <LI> tag identifies list items in a <DIR>, <MENU>, <OL>, or <UL> list
<LINK>	The <LINK> tag specifies the relationship between the document and other objects
HREF=*URL*	The URL of the <LINK> tag hotlinks the user to the specified document
ID=*Text*	The file, URL, or text that acts as a hypertext link to another document
REL=*URL*	Directs the browser to link forward to the next page in the document
REV=*URL*	Directs the browser to go back to the previous link in the document
TITLE=*Text*	The title of the document named in the link
<MAP>..</MAP>	The <MAP> tage specifies information about a client side image map (it must enclose <AREA> tags)
NAME=*Text*	The name of the image map
<MENU>..</MENU>	The <MENU> tag encloses an unordered list of items, similar to a <UL> or <DIR> list
<META>	The <META> tag is used to insert information about the document that is not defined by other HTML tags and properties; it can include special instructions for the Web server to perform
CONTENT=*Text*	Contains information associated with the NAME or HTTP-EQUIV attributes
HTTP-EQUIV=*Text*	Directs the browser to request the server to perform different HTTP operations
NAME=*Text*	The type of information specified in the CONTENT attribute
<NOBR>..</NOBR>	The <NOBR> tag prevents line breaks for the enclosed text
<NOFRAMES>.. </NOFRAMES>	Enclosing body tags to be used by browsers that do not support frames

tags and properties	description
<OL>..</OL>	The <OL> tag encloses an ordered list of <LI> items; typically, ordered lists are rendered as numbered lists
START=*Value*	The value of the starting number in the ordered list
TYPE=*Option* (A | a | I | i | 1)	Specifies how ordered items are to be marked A = uppercase letters. a = lowercase letters. I = uppercase Roman numerals. i = lowercase Roman numerals. 1 = Digits. The default is 1.
<OPTION>..</OPTION>	The <OPTION> tag is used for each item in a selection list; this tag must be placed within <SELECT> tags
SELECTED	The default or selected option in the selection list
VALUE=*Value*	The value returned to the server when the user selects this option
<P>..</P>	The <P> tag defines the beginning and ending of a paragraph of text
ALIGN=*Option* (LEFT | CENTER | RIGHT)	The alignment of the text in the paragraph
<PRE>..</PRE>	The <PRE> tag retains the preformatted appearance of the text in the HTML file, including any line breaks or spaces; text is usually displayed in a fixed width font
<SAMP>..</SAMP>	The <SAMP> tag displays text in a fixed width font
<SELECT>..</SELECT>	The <SELECT> tag encloses a set of <OPTION> tags for use in creating selection lists
MULTIPLE	Allows the user to select multiple options from the selection list
NAME=*Text*	The name assigned to the selection list
SIZE=*Value*	The number of visible items in the selection list
<SMALL>..</SMALL>	The <SMALL> tag decreases the size of the enclosed text; the exact appearance of the text depends on the browser and the default font size
<STRONG>..</STRONG>	The <STRONG> tag is used to strongly emphasize the enclosed text, usually in a bold font
<STYLE>..</STYLE>	Contains information that identifies the style sheet in use
_{..}	The <SUB> tag displays the enclosed text as a subscript
^{..}	The <SUP> tag displays the enclosed text as a superscript
<TEXTAREA>.. </TEXTAREA>	The <TEXTAREA> tag creates a text box
COLS=*Value*	The height of the text box in characters
NAME=*Text*	The name assigned to the text box
ROWS=*Value*	The width of the text box in characters

WRAP=*Option*
   (OFF | VIRTUAL
   | PHYSICAL)
	Specifies how text should be wrapped within the text box
	OFF turns off text wrapping. VIRTUAL wraps the text, but sends the text to the server as a single line. PHYSICAL wraps the text and sends the text to the server as it appears in the text box.

HTML

tags and properties	description
<TITLE>..</TITLE>	The <TITLE> tag is used to specify the text that appears in the Web browser's title bar
<TT>..</TT>	The <TT> tag displays text in a fixed width, teletype style font
<U>..</U>	The <U> tag underlines the enclosed text, should be avoided because it confuses users with hypertext, which is typically underlined
<UL>..</UL>	The <UL> tag encloses an unordered list of <LI> items; typically, unordered lists are rendered as bulleted lists
Type=*Option* (CIRCLE I DISK I SQUARE)	Specifies the type of bullet used for displaying each <LI> item in the <UL> list
<VAR>..</VAR>	The <VAR> tag is used for text that represents a variable, and usually appears in italics

HTML Color Names

The following is a list of extended color names and their corresponding hexadecimal triplets supported by most Web browsers. To view these colors, you must have a video card and monitor capable of displaying up to 256 colors. As with other aspects of Web page design, you should test these color names on a variety of browsers before committing to their use. Different browsers may render these colors differently, or not at all.

TABLE AP-3: HTML extended color names

color name	value	preview	color name	value	preview
ALICEBLUE	#F0F8FE		DARKPURPLE	#871F78	
ANTIQUEWHITE	#FAEBD7		DARKSALMON	#E9967A	
AQUA	#00FFFF		DARKSLATEBLUE	#6B238E	
AQUAMARINE	#70DB93		DARKSLATEGRAY	#2F4F4F	
AZURE	#F0FFFF		DARKTAN	#97694F	
BEIGE	#F5F5DC		DARKTURQUOISE	#7093DB	
BLACK	#000000		DARKVIOLET	#9400D3	
BLUE	#0000FF		DARKWOOD	#855E42	
BLUEVIOLET	#9F5F9F		DIMGRAY	#545454	
BRASS	#B5A642		DUSTYROSE	#856363	
BRIGHTGOLD	#D9D919		FELDSPAR	#D19275	
BRONZE	#8C7853		FIREBRICK	#8E2323	
BROWN	#A52A2A		FORESTGREEN	#238E23	
CADETBLUE	#5F9F9F		GOLD	#CD7F32	
CHOCOLATE	#D2691E		GOLDENROD	#DBDB70	
COOLCOPPER	#D98719		GRAY	#C0C0C0	
COPPER	#B87333		GREEN	#00FF00	
CORAL	#FF7F50		GREENCOPPER	#527F76	
CRIMSON	#DC143C		GREENYELLOW	#93DB70	
CYAN	#00FFFF		HOTPINK	#FF69B4	
DARKBLUE	#00008B		HUNTERGREEN	#215E21	
DARKBROWN	#5C4033		INDIANRED	#4E2F2F	
DARKCYAN	#008B8B		INDIGO	#4B0082	
DARKGOLDENROD	#B8860B		IVORY	#FFFFF0	
DARKGRAY	#A9A9A9		KHAKI	#9F9F5F	
DARKGREEN	#006400		LAVENDER	#E6E6FA	
DARKKHAKI	#BDB76B		LIGHTBLUE	#C0D9D9	
DARKMAGENTA	#8B008B		LIGHTCORAL	#F08080	
DARKOLIVEGREEN	#4F4F2F		LIGHTCYAN	#E0FFFF	
DARKORANGE	#FF8C00		LIGHTGRAY	#A8A8A8	
DARKORCHID	#9932CD		LIGHTGREEN	#90EE90	

HTML

color name	value	preview	color name	value	preview
LIGHTPINK	#FFB6C1		PINK	#BC8F8F	
LIGHTSTEELBLUE	#8F8FBD		PLUM	#EAADEA	
LIGHTWOOD	#E9C2A6		POWDERBLUE	#B0E0E6	
LIME	#00FF00		PURPLE	#800080	
LIMEGREEN	#32CD32		QUARTZ	#D9D9F3	
MAGENTA	#FF00FF		RED	#FF0000	
MANDARINORANGE	#E47833		RICHBLUE	#5959AB	
MAROON	#8E236B		ROYALBLUE	#4169E1	
MEDIUMAQUAMARINE	#32CD99		SADDLEBROWN	#8B4513	
MEDIUMBLUE	#3232CD		SALMON	#6F4242	
MEDIUMFORESTGREEN	#6B8E23		SANDYBROWN	#F4A460	
MEDIUMGOLDENROD	#EAEAAE		SCARLET	#8C1717	
MEDIUMORCHID	#9370DB		SEAGREEN	#238E68	
MEDIUMSEAGREEN	#426F42		SIENNA	#8E6B23	
MEDIUMSLATEBLUE	#7F00FF		SILVER	#E6E8FA	
MEDIUMSPRINGGREEN	#7FFF00		SKYBLUE	#3299CC	
MEDIUMTURQUOISE	#70DBDB		SLATEBLUE	#007FFF	
MEDIUMVIOLETRED	#DB7093		SNOW	#FFFAFA	
MEDIUMWOOD	#A68064		SPICYPINK	#FF1CAE	
MIDNIGHTBLUE	#2F2F4F		SPRINGGREEN	#00FF7F	
MINTCREAM	#F5FFFA		STEELBLUE	#236B8E	
MISTYROSE	#FFE4E1		SUMMERSKY	#38B0DE	
NAVYBLUE	#23238E		TAN	#DB9370	
NEONBLUE	#4D4DFF		TEAL	#008080	
NEONPINK	#FF6EC7		THISTLE	#D8BFD8	
NEWMIDNIGHTBLUE	#00009C		TOMATO	#FF6347	
NEWTAN	#EBC79E		TURQUOISE	#ADEAEA	
OLDGOLD	#CFB53B		VERYDARKBROWN	#5C4033	
OLIVE	#808000		VERYDARKGRAY	#CDCDCD	
ORANGE	#FF7F00		VIOLET	#4F2F4F	
ORANGERED	#FF2400		VIOLETRED	#CC3299	
ORCHID	#DB70DB		WHEAT	#D8D8BF	
PALEGOLDENROD	#EEE8AA		WHITE	#FFFFFF	
PALEGREEN	#8FBC8F		YELLOW	#FFFF00	
PALETURQUOISE	#AFEEEE		YELLOWGREEN	#99CC32	

HTML Special Characters

The following table lists a portion of the HTML extended character set , also known as the ISO Latin-1 Character set. Characters in this table can be entered either by code number or code name. For example, to insert the registered trademark symbol, ®, you would use either "&reg" or "&#174."

While code names can be easier to remember and type than code numbers, not all code names are recognized by all browsers. Some older browsers that support only the HTML 2.0 standard will not recognize the code name "&times," for instance. Code names that may not be recognized by older browsers are marked with an asterisk. If you are planning to use these symbols in your document, you may want to use the code number instead of the code name.

TABLE AP-4: HTML special characters

character	code	code name	description
	&#00 - &#08		Unused
	&#09		Tab
	&#10		Line feed
	&#11 - &#31		Unused
	&#32		Space
!	&#33		Exclamation point
"	&#34	&quot	Double quotation mark
#	&#35		Pound sign
$	&#36		Dollar sign
%	&#37		Percent sign
&	&#38	&amp	Ampersand
'	&#39		Apostrophe
(	&#40		Left parenthesis
)	&#41		Right parenthesis
*	&#42		Asterisk
+	&#43		Plus sign
,	&#44		Comma
-	&#45		Hyphen
.	&#46		Period
/	&#47		Forward slash
0–9	&#48 - &#57		Numbers 0–9
:	&#58		Colon
;	&#59		Semicolon
<	&#60	&lt	Less than sign
=	&#61		Equal sign

HTML

character	code	code name	description
>	&#62	&gt	Greater than sign
?	&#63		Question mark
@	&#64		Commercial at
A–Z	&#65 - &#90		Letters A–Z
[	&#91		Left square bracket
\	&#92		Back slash
]	&#93		Right square bracket
^	&#94		Caret
_	&#95		Horizontal bar
`	&#96		Grave accent
a–z	&#97 - &#122		Letters a–z
{	&#123		Left curly brace
|	&#124		Vertical bar
}	&#125		Right curly brace
~	&#126		Tilde
	&#127 - &#129		Unused
,	&#130		Low single comma quotation mark
ƒ	&#131		Function sign
„	&#132		Low double comma quotation mark
…	&#133		Ellipses
†	&#134		Dagger
‡	&#135		Double dagger
ˆ	&#136		Circumflex accent
‰	&#137		Per mile sign
Š	&#138		Capital S with hacek
‹	&#139		Left single angle quotation mark
Œ	&#140		Capital OE ligature
	&#141 - &#144		Unused
'	&#145		Single beginning quotation mark
'	&#146		Single ending quotation mark

character	code	code name	description
"	&#147		Double beginning quotation mark
"	&#148		Double ending quotation mark
•	&#149		Middle dot
–	&#150		En dash
—	&#151		Em dash
~	&#152		Tilde
™	&#153	&trade*	Trademark symbol
š	&#154		Small s with hacek
›	&#155		Right single angle quotation mark
œ	&#156		Small oe ligature
	&#157 – &#158		Unused
Ÿ	&#159		Capital Y with umlaut
		*	Nonbreaking space
¡	&#161	&iexcl*	Inverted exclamation point
¢	&#162	&cent*	Cent symbol
£	&#163	&pound*	Pound sterling
¤	&#164	&curren*	General currency symbol
¥	&#165	&yen*	Yen sign
¦	&#166	&brvbar*	Broken vertical bar
§	&#167	&sect*	Section sign
¨	&#168	&uml*	Umlaut
©	&#169	&copy*	Copyright symbol
ª	&#170	&ordf*	Feminine ordinal
«	&#171	&laquo*	Left angle quotation mark
¬	&#172	&not*	Not sign
	&#173	&shy*	Soft hyphen
®	&#174	&reg*	Registered trademark

HTML

character	code	code name	description
‾	&#175	&macr*	Macron
°	&#176	&deg*	Degree sign
±	&#177	&plusmn*	Plus/minus symbol
2	&#178	&sup2*	Superscript 2
3	&#179	&sup3*	Superscript 3
´	&#180	&acute*	Acute accent
μ	&#181	&micro*	Micro symbol
¶	&#182	&para*	Paragraph sign
·	&#183	&middot*	Middle dot
ç	&#184	&cedil*	Cedilla
1	&#185	&sup1*	Superscript 1
º	&#186	&ordm*	Masculine ordinal
»	&#187	&raquo*	Right angle quotation mark
¼	&#188	&frac14*	Fraction one-quarter
½	&#189	&frac12*	Fraction one-half
¾	&#190	&frac34*	Fraction three-quarters
¿	&#191	&iquest*	Inverted question mark

JavaScript Object Reference

The following are some of the more important JavaScript objects, properties, methods, and event handlers.

TABLE AP-5: JavaScript objects, properties, methods, and event handlers

JavaScript	descriptions and examples
button	A push button in an HTML form. Buttons can be referred to using their button names. For example, to emulate the action of clicking a button named "RUN," use the following expression: RUN.click();
Properties	
name	The name of the button element
value	The value of the button element
Methods	
click()	Emulates the action of clicking the button
Event Handlers	
onClick	Used to run JavaScript code when the button is clicked
checkbox	A check box in an HTML form. Check boxes can be referred to using their field names. For example, to emulate the action of clicking a check box named "SUBSCRIBE," use the following expression: SUBSCRIBE.click();
Properties	
checked	A Boolean value that indicates whether or not the check box is checked
defaultChecked	A Boolean value that indicates whether or not the check box is selected by default
name	The name of the check box element
value	The value of the check box element
Methods	
click()	Emulates the action of clicking the check box
Event Handlers	
onClick	Used to run JavaScript code when the check box is clicked
date	An object containing information about a specific date or the current date. You can assign a date object to a variable using standard date and time formatting, for example: SomeDay = new Date("June, 15, 2000, 14:35:00").You can also assign the values for each date and time component, such as day or seconds, individually; using this method, the same date object would read: SomeDay = new Date(2000, 5, 15, 14, 35, 0). The values in parentheses are year, month, day, hour, minute, second. You can create a variable containing the current date and time by removing the date and time values. For example: Today = new Date();
Methods	
getDate()	Returns the day of the month from 1 to 31
getDay()	Returns the day of the week from 0 to 6 (Sunday = 0, Monday = 1, ...)

HTML

JavaScript	descriptions and examples
getHours()	Returns the hour in military time from 0 to 23
getMinutes()	Returns the minute from 0 to 59
getMonth()	Returns the value of the month from 0 to 11 (January = 0, February = 1, …)
getSeconds()	Returns the seconds
getTime()	Returns the date as an integer representing the number of milliseconds since January 1st, 1970 at 00:00:00
getTimesoneOffset()	Returns the difference between the local time and Greenwich Mean Time in minutes
getYear()	Returns the number of years since 1900 (in other words, 1996 is represented by "96.") This value method is inconsistently applied past the year 1999.
setDate(*date*)	Sets the day of the month to the value specified in *date*
setHours(*hour*)	Sets the hour to the value specified in *hour*
setMinutes(*minutes*)	Sets the minute to the value specified in *minutes*
setMonth(*month*)	Sets the month to the value specified in *month*
setSeconds(*seconds*)	Sets the second to the value specified in *seconds*
setTime(*time*)	Sets the time using the value specified in *time*, where *time* is a variable containing the number of milliseconds since January 1st, 1970 at 00:00:00
setYear(*year*)	Sets the year to the value specified in *year*
toGMTString()	Converts the date to a text string in Greenwich Mean Time
toLocaleString()	Converts a date object's date to a text string, using the date format that the Web browser is set up to use
UTC()	Returns the date in the form of the number of milliseconds since January 1st, 1970, 00:00:00
document	**An HTML document**
Properties	
alinkColor	The color of active hyperlinks in the document
anchors	An array of anchors within the document. Use anchors[0] to refer to the first anchor, anchors[1] to refer to the second anchor, and so forth.
bgColor	The background color used in the document
cookie	A text string containing the document's cookie values
fgColor	The text color used in the document
form	A form within the document (the form itself is also an object)
forms	An array of forms within the document. Use forms[0] to refer to the first form, forms[1] to refer to the second form, and so forth.
lastModified	The date the document was last modified

JavaScript	descriptions and examples
linkColor	The color of hyperlinks in the document
links	An array of links within the document. Use links[0] to refer to the first hyperlink, links[1] to refer to the second hyperlink, and so forth.
location	The URL of the document
referrer	The URL of the document containing the link that the user accessed to get to the current document
title	The title of the document
vlinkColor	The color of followed hyperlinks
Methods	
clear()	Clears the contents of the document window
close()	Closes the document stream
open	Opens the document stream
write()	Writes to the document window
writeln()	Writes to the document window on a single line (used only with preformatted text)
elements	**Elements within an HTML form**
Properties	
length	The number of elements within the form
form	**An HTML form within a document. You can refer to a specific form using that form's name. For example, for a form named "REG," you can apply the submit method with the following expression: REG.submit();**
Properties	
action	The location of the CGI script that receives the form values
elements	An array of elements within the form (including input boxes, check boxes, buttons, and other fields). Use elements[0] to refer to the first element, elements[1] to refer to the second element, and so forth. Use the field name of the element to work with a specific element.
encoding	The type of encoding used in the form
method	The type of method used when submitting the form
target	The name of the window into which CGI output should be directed
Methods	
submit()	Submits the form to the CGI script
Event Handlers	
onSubmit	Used to run JavaScript code when the form is submitted by the browser
frame	**A frame window within the Web browser**
Properties	
frames	An array of frames within the frame window. Use frames[0] to refer to the first frame, frames[1] to refer to the second frame and so forth.

JavaScript	descriptions and examples
parent	The name of the window that contains the frame
self	The name of the current frame window
top	The name of the topmost window in the hierarchy of frame windows
window	The name of the current frame window
Methods	
alert(*message*)	Displays the text contained in *message* in a dialog box
clearTimeout(*name*)	Cancels the time out whose value is *name*
close()	Closes the window
confirm(*message*)	Displays the text contained in *message* in a dialog box along with OK and Cancel buttons
prompt(*message*, *default_text*)	Displays the text contained in *message* in a dialog box with a text entry box into which the user can enter a value or text string. The default value or text is specified by the value of *default_text*.
setTimeout(*expression, time*)	Evaluates the value of *expression* after the number of milliseconds specified in the value of *time* has passed
hidden	**A hidden field on an HTML form. Hidden fields can be referred to using their field names. For example, to change the value of the hidden field "PWORD" to "newpassword," use the expression: PWORD.value = "newpassword"**
Properties	
name	The name of the hidden field
value	The value of the hidden field
history	**An object containing information about the Web browser's history list**
Properties	
length	The number of items in the history list
Methods	
back()	Goes back to the previous item in the history list
forward()	Goes forward to the next item in the history list
go(*location*)	Goes to the item in the history list specified by the value of *location*. The *location* variable can be either an integer or the name of the Web page.
image	**An embedded image within the document (available only in Netscape Navigator 3.0 or higher)**
Properties	
border	The value of the BORDER property of the <IMG> tag
complete	A Boolean value that indicates whether or not the image has been completely loaded by the browser

JavaScript	descriptions and examples
height	The height of the image in pixels
hspace	The horizontal space around the image in pixels
lowsrc	The value of the LOWSRC property of the <IMG> tag
src	The source of the inline image
vspace	The vertical space around the image in pixels
width	The width of the image in pixels
link	**A link within an HTML document**
Properties	
target	The target window of the hyperlinks
location	**An object that contains information about the location of a Web document**
Properties	
hash	The location's anchor name
host	The location's hostname and port number
href	The location's URL
pathname	The path portion of the location's URL
port	The port number of the location's URL
protocol	The protocol used with the location's URL
math	**A JavaScript object used for advanced mathematical calculations. For example, to calculate the square root of 27 and store this value in the variable "SQ27," use the following JavaScript expression: var SQ27 = math.sqrt(27);**
Properties	
E	The value of the base of natural logarithms (2.7182...)
LN10	The value of the natural logarithm of 10
LN2	The value of the natural logarithm of 2
PI	The value of pi (3.1416...)
Methods	
abs(*number*)	Returns the absolute value of *number*
acos(*number*)	Returns the arc cosine of *number* in radians
asin(*number*)	Returns the arc sine of *number* in radians
atan(*number*)	Returns the arc tangent of *number* in radians
ceil(*number*)	Rounds *number* up to the next highest integer
cos(*number*)	Returns the cosine of *number*, where *number* is an angle expressed in radians
exp(*number*)	Raises the value of E (2.7182...) to the value of *number*
floor(*number*)	Rounds *number* down to the next lowest integer
log(*number*)	Returns the natural logarithm of *number*

HTML

HTML

JavaScript	descriptions and examples
max(*number1*, *number2*)	Returns the greater of *number1* and *number2*
min(*number1*, *number2*)	Returns the lesser of *number1* and *number2*
pow(*number1*, *number2*)	Returns the value of *number1* raised to the power of *number2*
random()	Returns a random number between 0 and 1
round(*number*)	Rounds *number* to the closest integer
sin(*number*)	Returns the sine of *number*, where *number* is an angle expressed in radians
tan(number)	Returns the tangent of *number*, where *number* is an angle expressed in radians
navigator	**An object representing the Web browser currently in use**
Properties	
appCodeName	The code name of the Web browser
appName	The name of the Web browser
appVersion	The version of the Web browser
userAgent	The user-agent text string sent from the client to the Web server
option	**An option from a selection list**
Properties	
defaultSelected	A Boolean value indicating whether or not the option is selected by default
index	The index value of the option
selected	A Boolean value indicating whether or not the option is currently selected
text	The text of the option as displayed on the Web page
value	The value of the option
password	**A password field in an HTML form. You can refer to a specific password field using the field name. For example, for a password field named "PWORD," you can apply the focus() method with the following expression: PWORD.submit();**
Properties	
defaultValue	The default value of the password
name	The name of the password field
value	The value of the password field
Methods	
blur()	Emulates the action of leaving the text area box
focus()	Emulates the action of moving into the text area box
select()	Emulates the action of selecting the text in a text area box

radio

An array of radio buttons on an HTML form . Use the name of the radio button set to refer to individual buttons. For example if the name of the radio button set is "Products," use Products[0] to refer to the first radio button, Products[1] to refer to the second radio button, and so forth.

Properties

checked	A Boolean value indicating whether or not a specific radio button has been checked
defaultChecked	A Boolean value indicating whether or not a specific radio button is checked by default
length	The number of radio buttons in the set
name	The name of a set of radio buttons
value	The value of a specific radio button

Methods

click()	Emulates the action of clicking the radio button

Event Handlers

onClick	Used to run JavaScript code when the radio button is clicked

reset

A Reset button in an HTML form. You can refer to a specific Reset button using the button's name. For a Reset button named "RELOAD," you can apply the click() method with the following expression: RELOAD.click();

Properties

name	The name of the Reset button
value	The value of the Reset button

Methods

click()	Emulates the action of clicking the Reset button

Event Handlers

onClick	Used to run JavaScript code when the Reset button is clicked

select

A selection list in an HTML form. You can refer to a specific selection list using the selection list's name. For example, to determine the number of options in a selection list named "PRODUCT," use the following expression: PRODUCT.length;

Properties

length	The number of options in the selection list
name	The name of the selection list
options	An array of options within the selection list. Use options[0] to refer to the first option, options[1] to refer to the second option, and so forth. See the options object for more information on working with individual selection list options.
selectedIndex	The index value of the selected option from the selection list

Event Handlers

onBlur	Used to run JavaScript code when the user leaves the selection list
onChange	Used to run JavaScript code when the user changes the selected option in the selection list
onFocus	Used to run JavaScript code when the user enters the selection list

HTML

JavaScript	descriptions and examples
string	An object representing a text string or string of characters. For example, to italicize the text string "Order Today!", use the following expression: "Order Today!".italics();
Properties	
length	The number of characters in the string
Methods	
anchor(*name*)	Turns the text string into a hyperlink anchor with a name value set to *name*
big()	Modifies the text string to display big characters (similar to the effect of applying the <BIG> tag)
blink()	Modifies the text string to display blinking characters (similar to the effect of applying the <BLINK> tag)
bold()	Modifies the text string to display characters in bold (similar to the effect of applying the <B> tag)
charAt(*index*)	Returns the character in the text string at the location specified by *index*
fixed()	Modifies the text string to display fixed-width characters (similar to the effect of applying the <FIXED> tag)
fontColor(*color*)	Modifies the text string to display text in a color specified by *color* (similar to applying the <FONT> tag to the text along with the COLOR property)
fontSize(*value*)	Modifies the text string to display text in the font size specified by the *value* parameter (similar to applying the <FONT> tag to the text along with the SIZE property)
indexOf(*string, start*)	Searches the text string and returns the index value of the first occurrence of the text string *string*. The search starts at the character indicated by the value of *start*.
italics()	Modifies the text string to display characters in italics (similar to the effect of applying the <I> tag)
lastIndexOf(*string, start*)	Searches the text string and locates the index value of the last occurrence of the text string *string*. The search starts at the character indicated by the value of *start*.
link(*href*)	Turns the text string into a hyperlink pointing to the URL contained in *href*
small()	Modifies the text string to display small characters (similar to the effect of applying the <SMALL> tag)
strike()	Applies the strikeout character to the text string (similar to the effect of applying the <STRIKE> tag)
sub()	Modifies the text string to display subscript characters (similar to the effect of applying the <SUB> tag)
substring(*first, last*)	Returns a substring of characters from the text string, starting with the character at the index number *first* and ending with the character at the index number *last*
sup()	Modifies the text string to display superscript characters (similar to the effect of applying the <SUP> tag)
toLowerCase()	Changes all of the characters in the text string to lowercase
toUpperCase()	Changes all of the characters in the text string to uppercase

JavaScript	descriptions and examples
submit	A Submit button in an HTML form. You can refer to a specific Submit button using the button's name. For a Submit button named "SAVE," you can apply the click() method with the following expression: SAVE.click();
Properties	
name	The name of the Submit button
value	The value of the Submit button
Methods	
click()	Emulates the action of clicking the Submit button
Event Handlers	
onClick	Used to run JavaScript code when the user clicks the Submit button
text	An input box from an HTML form. You can refer to an input box using the box's name. For example, to move the cursor to an input box named "ADDRESS," use the following expression: ADDRESS.focus();
Properties	
defaultValue	The default value of the input box
name	The name of the input box
value	The value of the input box
Methods	
blur()	Emulates the action of leaving the input box
focus()	Emulates the action of moving into the input box
select()	Emulates the action of selecting the text in an input box
Event Handlers	
onBlur	Used to run JavaScript code when the user leaves the input box
onChange	Used to run JavaScript code when the user changes the value of the input box
onFocus	Used to run JavaScript code when the user enters the input box
onSelect	Used to run JavaScript code when the user selects some or all of the text in the input box
textarea	A text area box in an HTML form. You can refer to a specific text area box using the box's name. For example, to move the cursor out of a text area box named "COMMENTS," use the expression: COMMENTS.blur();
Properties	
defaultValue	The default value of the text area box
name	The name of the text area box
value	The value of the text area box
Methods	
blur()	Emulates the action of leaving the text area box

HTML

JavaScript	descriptions and examples
focus()	Emulates the action of moving into the text area box
select()	Emulates the action of selecting the text in a text area box
Event Handlers	
onBlur	Used to run JavaScript code when the user leaves the text area box
onChange	Used to run JavaScript code when the user changes the value of the text area box
onFocus	Used to run JavaScript code when the user enters the text area box
onSelect	Used to run JavaScript code when the user selects some or all of the text in the text area box
window	**The document window contained within the Web browser**
Properties	
defaultStatus	The default text string displayed in the window's status bar
frames	An array of frames within the window. Use frames[0] to refer to the first frame, frames[1] to refer to the second frame, and so forth. See the frames object for properties and methods that can be applied to individual frames.
length	The number of frames in the parent window
name	The name of the window
parent	The name of the window containing this particular window
self	The name of the current window
status	The text string displayed in the window's status bar
top	The name of the topmost window in a hierarchy of windows
window	The name of the current window
Methods	
alert(*message*)	Displays the text contained in *message* in a dialog box
clearTimeout(*name*)	Cancels the time out whose value is *name*
close()	Closes the window
confirm(*message*)	Displays the text contained in *message* in a dialog box along with OK and Cancel buttons
prompt(*message*, *default_text*)	Displays the text contained in *message* in a dialog box with a text entry box into which the user can enter a value or text string. The default value or text is specified by the value of *default_text*.
setTimeout(*expression*, *time*)	Evaluates the value of *expression* after the number of milliseconds specified in the value of *time* has passed
Event Handlers	
onLoad	Used to run JavaScript code when the window or frame finishes loading
onUnload	Used to run JavaScript code when the window or frame finishes unloading

JavaScript Operators

The following are some operators used in JavaScript expressions.

TABLE AP-6: JavaScript operators

operators	description
Assignment	**Assignment operators are used to assign values to variables.**
=	Assigns the value of the variable on the right to the variable on the left (x=y)
+=	Adds the two variables and assigns the result to the variable on the left (x+=y is equivalent to x=x+y)
–=	Subtracts the variable on the right from the variable on the left and assigns the result to the variable on the left (x–=y is equivalent to x=x–y)
*=	Multiplies the two variables together and assigns the result to the left variable (x*=y is equivalent to x=x*y)
/=	Divides the variable on the left by the variable on the right and assigns the result to the variable on the left (x/=y is equivalent to x=x/y)
%=	Divides the variable on the left by the variable on the right and assigns the remainder to the variable on the left (x%=y is equivalent to x=x%y)
Arithmetic	**Arithmetic operators are used for arithmetic functions.**
+	Adds two variables together (x+y)
–	Subtracts the variable on the right from the variable on the left (x–y)
*	Multiplies two variables together (x*y)
/	Divides the variable on the left by the variable on the right (x/y)
%	Calculates the remainder after dividing the variable on the left by the variable on the right (x%y)
++	Increases the value of a variable by 1 (x++ is equivalent to x=x+1)
--	Decreases the value of a variable by 1 (x-- is equivalent to x=x–1)
–	Changes the sign of a variable (–x)
Logical	**Logical operators are used for evaluating true and false expressions.**
&&	Returns true only if both expressions are true (also known as an AND operator)
||	Returns true when either expression is true (also known as an OR operator)
!	Returns true if the expression is false, and false if the expression is true (also known as a *negation* operator)
Comparison	**Comparison operators are used for comparing expressions.**
==	Returns true when the two expressions are equal (x==y)
!=	Returns true when the two expressions are not equal (x!=y)
>	Returns true when the expression on the left is greater than the expression on the right (x > y)
<	Returns true when the expression on the left is less than the expression on the right (x < y)
>=	Returns true when the expression on the left is greater than or equal to the expression on the right (x >= y)
<=	Returns true when the expression on the left is less than or equal to the expression on the right (x <= y)
Conditional (shorthand)	**Conditional operators determine values based on conditions that are either true or false.**
(condition) ? value1 : value2	If *condition* is true, then this expression equals *value1*, otherwise it equals *value2*.

Cascading Style Sheets

The following are CSS1 fourth-generation browser supported styles.

TABLE AP-7: **CSS1 fourth-generation browser supported styles**

property	explanation/syntax	example
Font Properties		
font-style	• *normal* • *oblique* (similar to italic, but created manually rather than using italic typeface) • *italic*	{font-style: italic}
font-variant	• *normal* (default) • *small-caps*	{font-variant: small-caps}
font-weight	• *extra-light* • *demi-light* • *light* • *medium* • *bold* • *demi-bold* • *extra-bold*	{font-weight: extra-bold}
font-size	a number with a unit abbreviation • points (*pt*) • pixels (*px*) • inches (*in*) • centimeters (*cm*) • percentage of default point size (%) • multiple of width of "m" character in current font family (*em*)	{font-size: 16pt}
line-height	sets distance between baselines of two adjacent elements; specify multiplication factor for font size as a value (such as 1.2), percentage (120%), or measurement (1.2em)	{line-height: 1.2}
font-family	any combination of the following, in order of preference • specific typeface name (*times new roman*) • general type family (*times*) • font type (*sans-serif*)	{font-family: "times new roman", times, garamond, serif}
font	shorthand for setting all six font-related attributes at once; no commas, except between font-family settings; order: font-style, font-variant, font-weight, font-size, line-height, font-family	{font: italic small-caps extra-bold 16pt 0.75in "times new roman", times, garamond, serif}
text-decoration	• *none* • *underline* • *italic* • *line-through*	{text-decoration: italic}
Color and Background Properties		
color	hexadecimal or keyword color equivalent for element color	{color: #93DB70}
background-color	hexadecimal or keyword color equivalent for background color	{background-color: navy}

property	explanation/syntax	example
background-image	• *none* • *url*(url)	{background-image: url(me.jpg)}
background-repeat	specifies if and how background image is repeated • *repeat* (tiles over entire background) • *repeat-x* (repeats in single band horizontally) • *repeat-y* (repeats in single band vertically) • *no-repeat* (single image only)	{background-repeat: repeat-x}
background-attachment	• *scroll* (image scrolls with foreground) • *fixed* (image remains fixed as foreground scrolls)	{background-attachment: fixed}
background-position	specifies initial position of background image; coordinates (in percent) match point at those coordinates on image with those coordinates on background	{background-position: 100% 100%}
background	shorthand for setting all five background attributes at once; no commas; order: background-color, background-image, background-repeat, background-attachment, background-position	{background: navy url(me.jpg) repeat-x fixed 100% 100%

Text Properties

property	explanation/syntax	example
word-spacing	specifies additional width to insert between words (default=normal); may be negative	{word-spacing: 0.4em}
letter-spacing	specifies additional width to insert between words (default=normal); may be negative	{letter-spacing: 0.1em}
text-decoration	• *underline* • *overline* • *line-through* • *blink* • *none* (default)	{text-decoration: underline}
vertical-align	• *baseline* • *sub* • *super* • *top* • *text-top* • *middle* • *bottom* • *text-bottom* • percentage value, positive and negative numbers possible, specifies percentage of the element's line-height property in relation to the parent baseline	{vertical-align: super}
text-transform	• *capitalize* capitalizes first character of each word • *uppercase* capitalizes all letters • *lowercase* makes all letters lowercase • *none*	{text-transform: capitalize}

HTML

property	explanation/syntax	example
text-align	<ul><li>*left*</li><li>*right*</li><li>*center*</li><li>*justify*</li></ul>	{text-align: center}
text-indent	positive and negative numbers possible, specifies indentation of first line, in an exact measurement, or a percentage of parent element width	{text-indent: 3em}
line-height	sets distance between baselines of two adjacent elements; specify multiplication factor for font size, as a value (such as 1.2), percentage (120%), or measurement (1.2em)	{line-height: 1.2}
Box Properties		
margin-top	sets element's top margin as measurement or percentage of parent element width	{margin-top: 2%}
margin-right	sets element's right margin, as measurement or percentage of parent element width	{margin-right: 2em}
margin-bottom	sets element's bottom margin, as measurement or percentage of parent element width	{margin-bottom: 2%}
margin-left	sets element's left margin, as measurement or percentage of parent element width	{margin-right: 2em}
margin	shorthand property for specifying margin-top, margin-right, margin-bottom, and margin-left properties; order: top, right, bottom, left; if only one value given, applies to all four; if one or two values missing, missing value copied from opposite side	{margin 2% 2em}
padding-top	sets an element's top padding, as measurement or percentage of parent element width	{padding-top: 0.3em}
padding-right	sets an element's right padding, as measurement or percentage of parent element width	{padding-right: 20%}
padding-bottom	sets an element's bottom padding, as measurement or percentage of parent element width	{padding-bottom: 0.3em}
padding-left	sets an element's left padding, as measurement or percentage of parent element width	{padding-left: 20%}
padding	shorthand property for specifying padding-top, padding-right, padding-bottom, and padding-left properties; order: top, right, bottom, left; if only one value given, applies to all four; if one or two values missing, missing value copied from opposite side	{padding: 0.3em 20% 0.2em}

property	explanation/syntax	example
border-top-width; border-right-width; border-bottom-width; border-left-width;	• *thin* • *medium* • *thick* • measurement	{border-top-width: 2pt}
border-width	shorthand property for specifying all four border thicknesses; order: top, right, bottom, left; if only one value given, applies to all four; if one or two values missing, missing value copied from opposite side	{border-width: 3em}
border-style	can specify between one and four styles, with same organization as border-width above • *none* • *dotted* • *dashed* • *solid* • *double* • *groove* • *ridge* • *inset* • *outset*	{border-style: groove}
border-color	hexadecimal or keyword color equivalent for element color; can specify between one and four colors, with same organization as border-width above	{border-color: navy red red}
border-top border-right border-bottom border-left	shorthand properties for setting each border's width, style, and color	{border-bottom: thick solid red}
border	shorthand property for setting same width, color, and style on all four borders of an element	{border: thin inset green}
width	element width, as a length or percentage, negative values are allowed (default=auto)	{width: 200px}
height	element height, as a length or percentage, negative values are allowed (default=auto)	{height: 50%}
float	moves element to left or right, and wraps text on opposite side	{float: left}
clear	specifies if an element allows floating elements around it, or should be moved clear of them • *none* • *left* • *right* • *both*	{clear: both}

Classification Properties

property	explanation/syntax	example
display	• *block* • *inline* • *list-item* • *none*	{display: inline}
white-space	• *normal* white space collapsed • *pre* formatted like HTML PRE element • *nowrap* wrapping triggered only by elements	{white-space: nowrap}

HTML

property	explanation/syntax	example
list-style-type	specifies marker style for list items • *disc* • *circle* • *square* • *decimal* • *lower-roman* • *upper-roman* • *lower-alpha* • *upper-alpha* • *none*	{list-style-type: lower-alpha}
list-style-image	specifies an image to use as a list item marker	{list-style-image: url(reddot.jpg)}
list-style-position	• *inside* less space between marker and item • *outside* more space between marker and item (default)	{list-style-position: inside}
list-style	shorthand property for setting list-style-type, list-style-image, and list-style-position	{list-style: lower-alpha url(reddot.jpg) inside}

The following are CSS-P positioning properties.

TABLE AP-8: CSS-P positioning properties

property	value	description
position	static	normal position in page flow (default)
	absolute	outside normal page flow
	relative	relative to normal position in page flow
top, left	auto	(default)
	[length]	offset from default position in points, pixels, inches, or centimeters with respect to the element's top left corner
	[percent]	offset from default position in percentage of the parent element dimension
width, height	auto	(default)
	[length]	element dimension in points, pixels, inches, or centimeters
	[percent]	element dimension in percentage of parent element dimension
clip	auto	(default)
	rect(top right bottom left)	specifies rectangle coordinates that define document area available for displaying element
z-index	auto	(default)
	number	specifies element's position in the page's set of overlap layers; negative values possible
overflow	visible	entire contents displayed (default)
	hidden	contents that do not fit within the element are hidden
	auto	element contains scroll bar only when some contents do not fit within the element
	scroll	element always contains associated scroll bar
visibility	visible	element displays normally
	hidden	element takes up same space in page as it would normally, but is not visible

APP
HTML

Filters and Transitions

The following are options available when creating filters and transitions for Microsoft Internet Explorer 4.

For all true/false parameters, false is represented by 0, and true is represented by 1.

TABLE AP-9: Filters for Microsoft Internet Explorer 4

filter effect	description	parameters	syntax
Filters	Change object or page appearance in complex ways		
Alpha	Sets a transparency level	• *opacity* Ranges from 0 (fully transparent) to 100 (fully opaque) • *finishopacity* (optional) Same values as *opacity*; allows opacity to change across object • *style* Shape of opacity gradient; 0 (uniform), 1(linear), 2 (radial), or 3 (rectangular) • *startX* X coordinate for start of opacity gradient • *startY* Y coordinate for start of opacity gradient • *finishX* X coordinate for end of opacity gradient • *finishY* Y coordinate for end of opacity gradient	{filter: alpha(opacity=*opacity*, finishopacity=*finishopacity*, style=*style*, startX=*startX*, startY=*startY*, finishX=*finishX*, finishY=*finishY*)}
Blur	Creates the impression of moving at high speed	• *add* True/false variable specifying whether original image should be added to motion-blurred image (true; default) or not (false) • *direction* Blur direction, in degrees (0-360) clockwise from vertical, rounded to 45-degree increments; default is 270 (left) • *strength* Number of pixels that blur extends (default=5)	{filter: blur(add=*add*, direction=*direction*, strength=*strength*)}
Chroma	Makes a specific color transparent	• *color* Color subject to transparency, expressed in hexadecimal format (#RRGGBB)	{filter: chroma(color=*color*)}
Drop Shadow	Creates an offset solid silhouette	• *color* Color for drop shadow effect, in hexadecimal format • *offX* X-axis offset of drop shadow, in pixels • *offY* Y-axis offset of drop shadow, in pixels • *positive* drop shadow of any nontransparent pixel (true; default), or drop shadow of any transparent pixel (false)	{filter: dropshadow(color=*color*, offX=*offX*, offY=*offY*, positive=*positive*)}
FlipH	Creates a horizontal mirror image	NONE	{filter: fliph}
FlipV	Creates a vertical mirror image	NONE	{filter: flipv}
Glow	Adds radiance around the outside edges of the object	• *color* Color of radiance around object, in hexadecimal format • *strength* Glow intensity (1-255)	{filter: glow(color=*color*, strength=*strength*)}
Grayscale	Drops color information from the image	NONE	{filter: gray}
Invert	Reverses the hue, saturation, and brightness values	NONE	{filter: invert}

filter effect	description	parameters	syntax
Light	Projects light sources onto an object	Methods: • *AddAmbient* Adds ambient light source • *AddCone* Adds cone light source • *AddPoint* Adds point light source • *ChangeColor* Changes light color • *ChangeStrength* Changes light strength • *Clear* Clears all lights • *MoveLight* Moves light source	{filter: light}
Mask	Creates a transparent mask from an object	• *color* Color painted on transparent regions, in hexadecimal format	{filter: mask(color=*color*)}
Shadow	Creates a solid silhouette of the object	• *color* Color of shadow effect, in hexadecimal format • *direction* Shadow offset direction, in degrees (0-360) clockwise from vertical, rounded to 45-degree increments; default is 225 (bottom-left)	{filter: shadow(color=color, direction=direction)}
Wave	Creates a sine wave distortion along the x-axis and y-axis	• *add* Adds original image to waved image (true; default) or does not add original image (false) • *freq* Number of waves appearing in distortion • *light* Strength of light on wave effect in percent • *phase* Phase offset from start of sine wave effect, in percent (default=0) • *strength* Wave intensity	{filter: wave(add=*add*, freq=*freq*, lightstrength=*strength*, phase=*phase*, strength=*strength*)}
XRay	Shows just the edges of the object	NONE	{filter: xray}

TABLE AP-10: Transitions for Microsoft Internet Explorer 4

transition type	description	parameters	syntax
Transitions	Filters that vary over time		
blend	Creates simple fade-in or fade-out with specified duration	• *duration* Length of fade, in seconds	filter: blendTrans(duration=*duration*)
reveal	Allows choice of effects	• *duration* Length of effect, in seconds • *transition* Number corresponding to reveal transition effect, as listed in table that follows	filter: revealTrans(duration=*duration*, transition=*transition*)

TABLE AP-11: Reveal transition effects

reveal transition name	value	reveal transition name	value
Box in	0	Random dissolve	12
Box out	1	Split vertical in	13
Circle in	2	Split vertical out	14
Circle out	3	Split horizontal in	15
Wipe up	4	Split horizontal out	16
Wipe down	5	Strips left down	17
Wipe right	6	Strips left up	18
Wipe left	7	Strips right down	19
Vertical blinds	8	Strips right up	20
Horizontal blinds	9	Random bars horizontal	21
Checkerboard across	10	Random bars vertical	22
Checkerboard down	11	Random	23

TABLE AP-12: Transition applications

transition application	description
interpage transition	Transition plays when containing page opens or exits Created with the META tag in the page head section; uses *http-equiv* parameter, specifying whether transition should play when page opens ("Page-Enter") or closes ("Page-Exit"), or site opens ("Site-Enter") or closes ("Site-Exit"). For example, the code to create the circle in transition when a page closes could read `<META HTTP-EQUIV="Page-Exit" CONTENT="revealTrans(duration=7, transition=2)">`
object transition	Requires three components: 1. **Transition filter reference** in style description for object to be filtered; for example, to filter an image with the horizontal blinds transition, the code could read `<IMG ID="mypic" SRC="me.jpg" STYLE="filter: revealTrans(duration=5, transition=9)">` 2. **Script to manage filter** consisting of three lines at minimum: `mypic.filters.revealTrans.apply()` *creates the final transition state* `mypic.src= "me2.jpg"` *specifies new condition(s) of transitioned object* `mypic.filters.revealTrans.play()` *animates transition effect* 3. **Event handler** to trigger script

Project Files List

To complete many of the lessons and practice exercises in this book, students need to use a Project File that is supplied by Course Technology and stored on a Project Disk. Below is a list of the files that are supplied, and the unit or practice exercise to which the files correspond. For information on how to obtain Project Files, please see the inside cover of this book. The following list only includes Project Files that are supplied; it does not include the files students create from scratch or the files students create by revising the supplied files.

Unit	File Supplied on Project Disk	Location file is used in unit
A	construction.htm	Lessons, Skills Review, Independent Challenge 1, Independent Challenge 2
B	HTM B-1.htm	Lessons
B	HTM B-2.htm	Skills Review
B	HTM B-3.htm	Independent Challenge 1
B	HTM B-4.htm	Independent Challenge 2
B	construction.htm	Independent Challenge 3
B	HTM B-5.htm	Visual Workshop
C	apptrail.htm	Lessons
C	HTM C-1.htm	Lessons
C	HTM C-2.htm	Lessons
C	HTM C-3.txt	Lessons
C	sequoia.htm	Lessons
C	teton.htm	Lessons
C	images\bootbg.jpg	Lessons
C	images\ideas.gif	Lessons
C	images\nomad.gif	Lessons
C	images\tree.jpg	Lessons
C	construction.htm	Lessons, Skills Review 3
C	frames.htm	Skills Review
C	HTM C-4.htm	Skills Review 1
C	images\glasses.jpg	Skills Review 2
C	HTM C-5.htm	Skills Review 3
C	images\cco.gif	Skills Review 3
C	HTM C-6.txt	Skills Review 4
C	lenses.htm	Skills Review 4
C	images\eggshell.jpg	Skills Review 5, Visual Workshop
C	HTM C-9.htm	Visual Workshop

Unit	File Supplied on Project Disk	Location file is used in unit
C	images\book.gif	Visual Workshop
C	HTM C-7.htm	Independent Challenge 1
C	images\sds.jpg	Independent Challenge 1
C	HTM C-8.htm	Independent Challenge 2
C	images\mw.gif	Independent Challenge 2
C	images\waterbg.jpg	Independent Challenge 2
C	images\construction.jpg	Lessons, Skills Review 3, Independent Challenge 3
C	images\genres.jpg	Independent Challenge 3
D	HTM D-1.htm	Lessons
D	HTM D-2.htm	Skills Review
D	HTM D-3.htm	Independent Challenge 1
D	HTM D-4.htm	Independent Challenge 2
D	HTM D-5.htm	Visual Workshop
D	images/cftitle.gif	Lessons
D	images/eggshell.jpg	Lessons, Visual Workshop
D	images/mw.gif	Independent Challenge 2
D	images/nomad.gif	Lessons, Skills Review
D	images/oof.gif	Visual Workshop
D	images/pi.gif	Lessons
D	images/po.gif	Lessons
D	images/sds.jpg	Independent Challenge 1
D	images/search.gif	Skills Review
D	images/sm.gif	Lessons
D	images/sta.gif	Lessons
D	images/tsb.gif	Visual Workshop
D	images/waterbg.jpg	Independent Challenge 2
E	HTM E-1.txt	Lessons
E	HTM E-2.htm	Lessons
E	HTM E-3.htm	Skills Review
E	HTM E-4.htm	Independent Challenge 1
E	HTM E-5.htm	Independent Challenge 1
E	HTM E-6.htm	Visual Workshop
E	construction.htm	Lessons, Skills Review, Independent Challenge 1
E	images/arts.gif	Lessons

Unit	File Supplied on Project Disk	Location file is used in unit
E	images/athlete.gif	Lessons
E	images/book.gif	Visual Workshop
E	images/bootbg.jpg	Skills Review
E	images/construction.jpg	Lessons, Skills Review, Independent Challenge 1
E	images/fclogo.gif	Independent Challenge 3
E	images/leisure.gif	Lessons
E	images/mw.gif	Independent Challenge 2
E	images/nomad.gif	Lessons, Skills Review
E	images/sds.gif	Independent Challenge 1
E	images/tree.jpg	Skills Review
E	images/waterbg.jpg	Independent Challenge 2
F	HTM F-1.htm	Lessons
F	HTM F-2.htm	Lessons
F	HTM F-3.htm	Skills Review 1
F	HTM F-4.htm	Skills Review 2
F	HTM F-5.htm	Independent Challenge 1
F	HTM F-6.htm	Independent Challenge 1
F	HTM F-7.htm	Independent Challenge 2
F	HTM F-8.htm	Independent Challenge 2
F	construction.htm	Lessons, Skills Review 1, Independent Challenge 1
F	main.htm	Lessons
F	cco-main.htm	Skills Review 1
F	images/about.gif	Lessons
F	images/arts.gif	Lessons
F	images/athlete.gif	Lessons
F	images/book.gif	Visual Workshop
F	images/bookfair.gif	Visual Workshop
F	images/cco.gif	Skills Review 1
F	images/construction.jpg	Lessons, Skills Review 1, Independent Challenge 1
F	images/darwinad.jpg	Skills Review 5
F	images/eclectic.gif	Skills Review 5
F	images/eggshell.jpg	Lessons
F	images/fclogo.gif	Independent Challenge 3
F	images/gear.gif	Lessons

Unit	File Supplied on Project Disk	Location file is used in unit
F	images/globe.gif	Independent Challenge 1
F	images/go.gif	Lessons
F	images/gradient.jpg	Lessons
F	images/graybg.jpg	Skills Review 6
F	images/leisure.gif	Lessons
F	images/mw.gif	Independent Challenge 2
F	images/nomad.gif	Lessons
F	images/sds.jpg	Independent Challenge 1
F	images/sdsbg.jpg	Independent Challenge 1
F	images/skibar.jpg	Lessons
F	images/tablebg.jpg	Lessons
F	images/travel.gif	Lessons
F	images/tsbbg.jpg	Visual Workshop
F	images/water.gif	Independent Challenge 2
F	images/waterbg.jpg	Independent Challenge 2
F	images/web.jpg	Independent Challenge 1
F	images/welcome.jpg	Lessons
G	construction.htm	Lessons, Independent Challenge 1, Independent Challenge 2, Visual Workshop
G	HTM G-1.htm	Lessons
G	HTM G-2.htm	Independent Challenge 1
G	HTM G-3.htm	Independent Challenge 2
G	HTM G-4.htm	Visual Workshop
G	images/about.gif	Lessons
G	images/aboutic.gif	Lessons
G	images/book.gif	Visual Workshop
G	images/bookfair.gif	Visual Workshop
G	images/cco.gif	Independent Challenge 2
G	images/construction.jpg	Lessons, Independent Challenge 1, Independent Challenge 2, Visual Workshop
G	images/darwinad.jpg	Independent Challenge 2
G	images/eclectic.gif	Independent Challenge 2
G	images/gear.gif	Lessons
G	images/gearic.gif	Lessons
G	images/go.gif	Lessons
G	images/graybg.jpg	Independent Challenge 2

Unit	File Supplied on Project Disk	Location file is used in unit
G	images/helpic.gif	Lessons
G	images/homeic.gif	Lessons
G	images/nomad.gif	Lessons
G	images/sds.jpg	Independent Challenge 1
G	images/sdsbg.jpg	Independent Challenge 1
G	images/tablebg.jpg	Lessons
G	images/travel.gif	Lessons
G	images/travelic.gif	Lessons
G	images/tsbbg.jpg	Visual Workshop
H	HTML H-1.htm	Lessons
H	HTML H-2.htm	Lessons
H	HTML H-3.htm	Lessons
H	HTML H-4.htm	Lessons
H	HTML H-5.htm	Lessons
H	HTML H-6.htm	Lessons
H	HTML H-7.htm	Skills Review
H	HTML H-8.htm	Skills Review
H	HTML H-9.htm	Skills Review
H	HTML H-10.htm	Skills Review
H	HTML H-11.htm	Skills Review
H	HTML H-12.htm	Independent Challenge 1
H	HTML H-13.htm	Independent Challenge 2
H	HTML H-14.txt	Independent Challenge 2
H	HTML H-15.htm	Independent Challenge 3
H	HTML H-16.htm	Visual Workshop
I	berries.txt	Lessons
I	berrybush.jpg	Lessons
I	construction.jpg	Lessons
I	image1off.jpg	Lessons
I	image1on.jpg	Lessons
I	image2off.jpg	Lessons
I	image2on.jpg	Lessons
I	image3off.jpg	Lessons
I	image3on.jpg	Lessons

Unit	File Supplied on Project Disk	Location file is used in unit
I	image4off.jpg	Lessons
I	image4on.jpg	Lessons
I	mat.jpg	Lessons
I	Construction.htm	Lessons
I	HTML I-1.htm	Lessons
I	HTML I-2.htm	Lessons
I	HTML I-3.htm	Lessons
J	book2.jpg	Visual Workshop
J	bus.jpg	Independent Challenge 1
J	construction.jpg	Lessons, Skills Review, Independent Challenge 2
J	CPSVback.jpg	Independent Challenge 2
J	CPSVlog2.pg	Independent Challenge 2
J	egg shell.jpg	Lessons, Skills Review
J	house.jpg	Independent Challenge 3
J	ivy.jpg	Independent Challenge 3
J	nomad.jpg	Lessons, Skills Review
J	sand.gif	Independent Challenge 1
J	HTML J-1.htm	Lessons
J	HTML J-2.htm	Lessons
J	HTML J-3.htm	Lessons
J	HTML J-4.htm	Lessons
J	HTML J-5.htm	Lessons
J	HTML J-6.htm	Lessons
J	HTML J-7.css	Lessons
J	HTML J-8.htm	Lessons
J	HTML J-9.htm	Skills Review
J	HTML J-10.htm	Skills Review
J	HTML J-11.htm	Skills Review
J	HTML J-12.htm	Skills Review
J	HTML J-13.htm	Skills Review
J	HTML J-14.htm	Skills Review
J	HTML J-15.htm	Skills Review
J	HTML J-16.htm	Independent Challenge 1
J	HTML J-17.css	Independent Challenge 1

Unit	File Supplied on Project Disk	Location file is used in unit
J	HTML J-18.htm	Independent Challenge 2
J	HTML J-19.htm	Independent Challenge 3
J	HTML J-20.css	Independent Challenge 3
J	HTML J-21.htm	Visual Workshop
J	Construction.htm	Lessons, Skills Review, Independent Challenge 2
K	bluecolor.jpg	Skills Review
K	bluemoon.jpg	Skills Review
K	book1.jpg	Visual Workshop
K	books.txt	Visual Workshop
K	brevcolor.jpg	Lessons
K	brevifolia.jpg	Lessons
K	bus.jpg	Independent Challenge 2
K	CPSVback.jpg	Independent Challenge 3
K	CPSVlog2.jpg	Independent Challenge 3
K	egg shell.jpg	Lessons
K	fullcolor.jpg	Skills Review
K	fullmoon.jpg	Skills Review
K	green.css	Independent Challenge 1
K	harvest.jpg	Skills Review
K	harvestcolor.jpg	Skills Review
K	hillside.jpg	Lessons
K	hillsidecolor.jpg	Lessons
K	hilltop.jpg	Lessons
K	hilltopcolor.jpg	Lessons
K	house.jpg	Independent Challenge 1
K	ivy.jpg	Independent Challenge 1
K	lightcolor.jpg	Skills Review
K	longcolor.jpg	Skills Review
K	longhaul.jpg	Skills Review
K	moonlight.jpg	Skills Review
K	newcolor.jpg	Skills Review
K	newmoon.jpg	Skills Review
K	nomad.jpg	Lessons, Skills Review
K	nomadltd.css	Lessons, Skills Review

Unit	File Supplied on Project Disk	Location file is used in unit
K	packs.txt	Skills Review
K	peak.jpg	Lessons
K	peakcolor.jpg	Lessons
K	sand.jpg	Independent Challenge 2
K	schools.txt	Independent Challenge 3
K	starcolor.jpg	Lessons
K	starlite.jpg	Lessons
K	summit.jpg	Lessons
K	summitcolor.jpg	Lessons
K	tents.txt	Lessons
K	trekcolor.jpg	Skills Review
K	trekker.jpg	Skills Review
K	tricolor.jpg	Lessons
K	trifolia.jpg	Lessons
K	HTML K-1.htm	Lessons
K	HTML K-2.htm	Lessons
K	HTML K-3.htm	Lessons
K	HTML K-4.htm	Lessons
K	HTML K-5.htm	Lessons
K	HTML K-6.htm	Lessons
K	HTML K-7.htm	Lessons
K	HTML K-8.htm	Skills Review
K	HTML K-9.htm	Skills Review
K	HTML K-10.htm	Skills Review
K	HTML K-11.htm	Skills Review
K	HTML K-12.htm	Skills Review
K	HTML K-13.htm	Skills Review
K	HTML K-14.htm	Skills Review
K	HTML K-15.htm	Independent Challenge 1
K	HTML K-16.htm	Independent Challenge 2
K	HTML K-17.htm	Independent Challenge 3
K	HTML K-18.htm	Visual Workshop
L	bag.jpg	Lessons
L	bag2.jpg	Lessons

Unit	File Supplied on Project Disk	Location file is used in unit
L	bluecolor.jpg	Skills Review
L	bluemoon.jpg	Skills Review
L	book2.jpg	Visual Workshop
L	books.txt	Visual Workshop
L	brevcolor.jpg	Lessons
L	brevifolia.jpg	Lessons
L	bus.jpg	Independent Challenge 2
L	construction.jpg	
L	CPSVback.jpg	Independent Challenge 3
L	CPSVlog2.jpg	
L	CPSVlog3.jpg	Independent Challenge 3
L	egg shell.jpg	Lessons, Skills Review
L	fullcolor.jpg	Skills Review
L	fullmoon.jpg	Skills Review
L	green.css	Independent Challenge 1
L	harvest.jpg	Skills Review
L	harvestcolor.jpg	Skills Review
L	hillside.jpg	Lessons
L	hillsidecolor.jpg	Lessons
L	hilltop.jpg	Lessons
L	hilltopcolor.jpg	Lessons
L	house.jpg	Independent Challenge 1
L	ivy.jpg	Independent Challenge 1
L	lightcolor.jpg	Skills Review
L	longcolor.jpg	Skills Review
L	longhaul.jpg	Skills Review
L	moonlight.jpg	Skills Review
L	newcolor.jpg	Skills Review
L	newmoon.jpg	Skills Review
L	nomad.jpg	Lessons, Skills Review
L	nomadltd.css	Skills Review
L	packs.txt	Skills Review
L	pack.jpg	Lessons
L	pack2.jpg	Lessons

Unit	File Supplied on Project Disk	Location file is used in unit
L	peak.jpg	Lessons
L	peakcolor.jpg	Lessons
L	roll.jpg	Skills Review
L	sand.jpg	Independent Challenge 2
L	schools.txt	Independent Challenge 2
L	SRPT.css	Independent Challenge 2
L	starcolor.jpg	Lessons
L	starlite.jpg	Lessons
L	summit.jpg	Lessons
L	summitcolor.jpg	Lessons
L	tents.txt	Lessons
L	trekcolor.jpg	Skills Review
L	trekker.jpg	Skills Review
L	tricolor.jpg	Lessons
L	trifolia.jpg	Lessons
L	water.jpg	Skills Review
L	water2.jpg	Skills Review
L	HTML L-1.htm	Lessons
L	HTML L-2.htm	Lessons
L	HTML L-3.htm	Lessons
L	HTML L-4.htm	Lessons
L	HTML L-5.htm	Lessons
L	HTML L-6.htm	Lessons
L	HTML L-7.htm	Lessons
L	HTML L-8.htm	Skills Review
L	HTML L-9.htm	Skills Review
L	HTML L-10.htm	Skills Review
L	HTML L-11.htm	Skills Review
L	HTML L-12.htm	Skills Review
L	HTML L-13.htm	Skills Review
L	HTML L-14.htm	Skills Review
L	HTML L-15.htm	Independent Challenge 1
L	HTML L-16.htm	Independent Challenge 2
L	HTML L-17.htm	Independent Challenge 3

Unit	File Supplied on Project Disk	Location file is used in unit
L	HTML L-18.htm	Visual Workshop
M	book2.jpg	Visual Workshop
M	bus.jpg	Independent Challenge 2
M	busmove.jpg	Independent Challenge 2
M	construction.jpg	Independent Challenge 2
M	CPSVback.jpg	Independent Challenge 3
M	CPSVlog3.jpg	Independent Challenge 3
M	earth.jpg	Lessons
M	egg shell.jpg	Lessons, Skills Review
M	founder.jpg	Lessons
M	green.css	Independent Challenge 1
M	house.jpg	Independent Challenge 1
M	map.jpg	
M	mountain.jpg	Skills Review
M	nomad.jpg	Lessons, Skills Review
M	nomad.ltd.css	Lessons, Skills Review
M	sand.jpg	Independent Challenge 2
M	store.jpg	Lessons
M	ivy.jpg	Lessons
M	Construction.htm	Lessons
M	Presentation page 2.htm	Lessons
M	Touchstone open.htm	Visual Workshop
M	Tours page 2.htm	Skills Review
M	HTML M-1.htm	Lessons
M	HTML M-2.htm	Lessons
M	HTML M-3.htm	Lessons
M	HTML M-4.htm	Lessons
M	HTML M-5.htm	Lessons
M	HTML M-6.htm	Lessons
M	HTML M-7.htm	Lessons
M	HTML M-8.htm	Skills Review
M	HTML M-9.htm	Skills Review
M	HTML M-10.htm	Skills Review
M	HTML M-11.htm	Skills Review

Unit	File Supplied on Project Disk	Location file is used in unit
M	HTML M-12.htm	Skills Review
M	HTML M-13.htm	Skills Review
M	HTML M-14.htm	Skills Review
M	HTML M-15.htm	Independent Challenge 1
M	HTML M-16.htm	Independent Challenge 2
M	HTML M-17.htm	Independent Challenge 3
M	HTML M-18.htm	Visual Workshop
N	No Project Files	

HTML

Glossary

Absolute link A link that includes the target page's full Web site location and directory information (for example, <A HREF="http://www.course.com/sl/default.htm">); most useful to reference a specific page on a different Web site. See also *Relative link*

Active white space An empty zone deliberately placed between page elements, which reinforces their separateness and helps the user mentally group the page into sections. See also *Passive white space, White space*

Add-on A small program you can download from the Web for free that extends a browser's capabilities; required for viewing some multimedia formats, including Flash animation.

Animated GIF A GIF file that combines two or more images into a single file, and includes instructions on how the images presented.

Arithmetic operators Symbols that allow you to program scripts to manipulate variables mathematically.

Attributes Extra settings available in most HTML tags that allow you to add to or change a tag's default features.

Back end The part of a Web page made up of the programs that reside on an organization's computer system that are responsible for processing submitted data. See also *Front end*

Bandwidth The data transfer capacity of a Web user's Internet connection.

Broadband Internet connection technologies that allow faster downloads than traditional dial-in modems.

Call To trigger a function; usually accomplished using an event handler.

Cascading Style Sheets (CSS) An HTML extension designed to streamline Web page formatting and layout; allows you to specify settings as attributes for more than 50 properties of any page element, rather than requiring separate tags.

Case-sensitive Describes a language that treats capital and lower-case versions of the same letter as different characters.

Cell The intersection of a row and a column in a column; contains a single unit of table data. See also *Column, Row, Table*

CGI See *Common Gateway Interface*

Checkbox A form field with a predefined value that users select by clicking; checkboxes may appear independently, or in a set from which users can make multiple selections.

Column A single vertical line of data in a table. See also *Cell, Row, Table*

Common Gateway Interface (CGI) A standardized protocol used in communication between the Web server and the programs that process the information collected in a form. See also *Script*

Conditional A programming decision point that allows your script to choose one of two paths, depending on a condition that you specify.

CSS See *Cascading Style Sheets*

Debugging The process of systematically identifying and fixing a code or script's bugs.

Dot syntax A method of referencing objects in an object hierarchy; begins on the document level, with each level name separated by a period.

Download time The amount of time it takes for a Web page and its associated files to transfer from their location on the Web to a user's browser.

Drop-down list See *Pull-down menu*

E-commerce software Software used in conjunction with online ordering to communicate with other organizational software systems, such as billing and order fulfillment.

Event Each action by a user.

Event handlers Terms that specify possible user actions.

Extensible Hypertext Markup Language (XHTML) A revision of HTML that transforms the language into a rigorous system in line with related languages used for other applications.

Extensible Markup Language (XML) A sister language to HTML, used to deliver reusable data from many databases and multiple platforms in a clear format.

Field A form element such as a text box or a pull-down menu that allows user input.

Flash animation A highly compressed multimedia presentation created with proprietary technology from Macromedia Inc.

Form A set of fields that allow Web page users to enter information and submit it for processing.

Frames A web page layout tool that allows you to divide up the browser window into parts, each of which displays a separate HTML document. See also *Frameset*

Frameset A separate HTML document specifying the organization of frame components within the browser window; includes only the page's structural information. See also *Frames*

Front end The Web page that users see in their browsers. See also *Back end*

Function A named script that performs a certain task.

Gamma settings Properties of a digitized image file that specify the degree of contrast between mid-level gray values.

GIF (graphics interchange format) A popular Web page graphics format for line art and animations; the format is proprietary and requires licensing fees in some cases.

Grid A layout feature consisting of a set of columns and rows that positions and groups a page's elements.

Hand-coding Creating Web pages by entering the HTML tags yourself, rather than using software to automatically generate code based on a design.

Hexadecimal See *Hexadecimal equivalent*

Hexadecimal equivalent The six-digit numerical equivalent used to describe the color of a Web page element.

Hot spot A linked area within an image map. See also *Image map*

HTML document A text file made up of text and HTML instructions, which a browser displays as a Web page.

HTML file See *HTML document*

Hyperlink see *Link*

Hypertext Markup Language (HTML) The language in which all pages on the Web are written.

Image map A graphic that has different areas which are linked to different Web pages. See also *Hot spot*

JavaScript A scripting language adapted from Sun Microsystems' Java programming language; supported by common browsers. See also *JScript, VBScript*

JScript Microsoft's adaptation of Sun Microsystems' Java programming language for Web use. See also *JavaScript, VBScript*

JPG A popular Web page graphics format for photographs.

JPEG *see JPG*

Keywords Terms in a Web page that identify the page's key concepts or focus; a search engine must determine these when adding a Web page to its database.

Label Text adjacent to a form field, which explains what information is required by the field.

Linear Describes a web page format that limits you to stacking page elements above and below each other, and provides few options for horizontal placement.

Link A specially formatted Web page object that the user can click to open a different Web page.

Logical formatting Formatting that indicates that a page element fits a certain function or role. See also *Physical formatting*

Methods Actions that an object can carry out.

Multi-line text area A type of form field that accommodates multiple lines of typed input.

Multimedia The integration of sound and video with a Web page's text and graphics.

Navigation bar A set of links to the home page and main sections of a Web site, which appears on every page.

Nested table A table which itself comprises the cell contents of a larger table; often used within a structuring table. See also *Structuring table*

Null A value equal to zero or nothing.

Object An element in the browser window identified by JavaScript as a distinct unit; each object has a default name and set of descriptive features based on its location and function.

Object hierarchy JavaScript's organization of objects; much like the system of folders used by Windows to keep track of disk contents.

Ordered list A list in which each item is automatically numbered or lettered. See also *Unordered list*

Passive white space A large area of unused space that doesn't serve a purpose for a Web page design. See also *Active white space, White space*

Physical formatting Format whose sole function is to tell the Web browser to apply a specific visual format. See also *Logical formatting*

Pipe A character (|) often used as a unique dividing character between each adjacent set of link text in a text-based horizontal navigation bar.

Pixel One of the points of light that make up the display on a computer screen; short for "picture elements," and abbreviated "px."

Placeholder A simple document that serves as a link target for an unfinished Web page; it contains text explaining that the target page is incomplete.

Platform The unique characteristics of a Web user's computer system, including browser brand, browser version, operating system, and screen resolution.

PNG A recently-developed Web page graphics format for line art and photographs; browser support is not widespread.

Properties An object's qualities such as size, location, and type.

Pull-down menu A form field that displays possible values in a collapsible menu; the field appears on a Web page as a single-line text area with an arrow button, and clicking the button displays the menu.

Push button A labeled form field that a user can click to perform a task.

Radio button A form field with a predefined value that users select by clicking; multiple radio buttons are grouped in a set of related options, from which users can make only one choice.

Relative link A link that includes only information about the target page's location relative to the current Web page (for example, <A HREF="justice.htm">); most useful for referencing other pages in your Web site, without needing to type the entire path to each page. See also *Absolute link*

Reset button A push button that clears all the input in a form, allowing a user to start over.

Resolution A monitor's screen display dimensions (width by height), in pixels; for example, 800 x 600 is a common resolution.

Row A single horizontal line of data in a table. See also *Cell, Column, Table*

Sans serif font A font that does not have serifs, the small strokes at the ends of the characters; Arial is a sans serif font. See also *Serif font*

Script In form processing, a file containing a short set of instructions on how to process data after submission; in Web page scripting, a program in a Web page that runs on the viewer's browser. See also *Common Gateway Interface*

Scripting The process of writing scripts.

Scroll box A form field that displays possible values in a scrollable menu.

Serif font A font that has small strokes (called serifs) at the ends of the characters; Times New Roman and Palatino are serif fonts. See also *Sans serif font*

Single-line text box A type of form field that accommodates one line of typed input.

Source The text and HTML code that make up a Web document.

Spanning To mark a single table cell as part of multiple rows or columns.

Story boarding Planning Web page or Web site design by sketching the elements you want to include and how you want them arranged.

Submit button A push button that submits information for processing.

Table A format for presenting information in a grid. See also *Cell, Column, Row*

Tag Each HTML instruction in an HTML document.

Target The Web page that opens when a user clicks a link.

Template A document containing Web page code for the structure and common elements of all the pages in a Web site.

Text image A graphic showing text; best used sparingly to implement formats that HTML cannot reliably create.

Toggle An element with two possible values that that are selected alternately by clicking it (for example, clicking a checkbox adds a check; clicking it again removes the check).

Uniform Resource Locator (URL) Web site address.

Unordered list A list in which a bullet icon displays next to each item. See also *Ordered list*

URL See *Uniform Resource Locator*

VBScript Microsoft's adaptation of its Visual Basic programming language for Web use.

Values Pieces of information that you specify to JavaScript, often with instructions to perform functions on them.

Variable A nickname for a value, which makes repeated references easier and more efficient.

Web server A computer permanently connected to the Internet, usually by means of lines reserved for that purpose; stores published Web documents.

Web site A group of related Web pages.

Webcasting The use of multimedia technology by radio and television stations to make their normal programming available live on their Web sites.

White space Any empty area in a Web page layout. See also *Active white space, Passive white space*

XHTML See *Extensible Hypertext Markup Language*

XML See *Extensible Markup Language*

Index

Index

Index

Index